T0271252

Classics of Buddhism and Zen

The Collected Translations of
Thomas Cleary

CLASSICS OF BUDDHISM AND ZEN

CLASSICS OF BUDDHISM AND ZEN

SHAMBHALA
Boston & London
2001

Shambhala Publications, Inc.
Horticultural Hall
300 Massachusetts Avenue
Boston, Massachusetts 02115
www.shambhala.com

© 1989, 1994, 1995, 1997 by Thomas Cleary

Instant Zen is reprinted by special arrangement with North Atlantic Books.

Printed in the United States of America

♾ This edition is printed on acid-free paper that meets the American National Standards Institute z39.48 Standard.

♻ Shambhala Publications makes every effort to print on recycled paper. For more information please visit www.shambhala.com.

Distributed in the United States by Penguin Random House LLC and in Canada by Random House of Canada Ltd

Library of Congress Cataloging-in-Publication Data
Cleary, Thomas.
Classics of Buddhism and Zen: the collected translations of Thomas Cleary / Thomas Cleary.—1st ed.
p. cm.
ISBN 978-1-57062-831-3 (v. 1).—ISBN 978-1-57062-832-0 (v. 2).—
ISBN 978-1-57062-833-7 (v. 3).—ISBN 978-1-57062-834-4 (v. 4).—
ISBN 978-1-57062-838-2 (v. 5).—ISBN 978-1-59030-218-7 (v. 1 paperback).—
ISBN 978-1-59030-219-4 (v. 2 paperback).—ISBN 978-1-59030-220-0 (v. 3 paperback).—ISBN 978-1-59030-221-7 (v. 4 paperback).—ISBN 978-1-59030-222-4 (v. 5 paperback).
1. Zen Buddhism. 2. Buddhism. I. Title.
BQ9258 .C54 2001
294.3'927—dc21
2001034385

Contents

PUBLISHER'S NOTE

The works contained in The Collected Translations of Thomas Cleary were published over a period of more than twenty years and originated from several publishing houses. As a result, the capitalization and romanization of Chinese words, and the treatment of the word Hui-neng, vary occasionally from one text to another within the volumes, due to changes in stylistic preferences from year to year and from house to house. In all cases, terms are rendered consistently within each text.

ZEN LESSONS
The Art of Leadership

INTRODUCTION

Zen Lessons is a collection of political, social, and psychological teachings of Chinese Zen (Chan) adepts of the Song dynasty, from the tenth to the thirteenth centuries.

If the Tang dynasty, from the early seventh through the ninth centuries, may be called the classical period of Chinese Zen, the Song dynasty may be called its baroque period, characterized by complexity of form and ingenious imagery with multiple meaning.

In contrast to the relatively plain and straightforward Zen literature of the Tang dynasty, Song dynasty Zen literature is convoluted and artful. This is not regarded, in Zen terms, as a development in Zen, but as a response to a more complex and pressured society and individual. The Zen adepts of Song times did not regard the reality of Zen as any different in its essence from that of classical times, but considered the function of Zen to have become complicated by the complexity of the contemporary mind and the rampant spread of artificial Zen based on imitations of a few Zen practices.

The proliferation of false Zen was stimulated by the enormous impact of real Zen on Asian civilization. After the Tang dynasty, there is hardly anywhere one can turn in Chinese culture without seeing the influence of the Zen charisma.

The ill effects of the resulting influx of insincere followers into public Zen institutions are already noted in the works of great masters of the latter Tang dynasty, and these *Zen Lessons* contain top-level notices of an even greater decline in quality of Zen institutions and followers in the Song dynasty, in spite of Zen's unparalleled prestige in cultural terms.

There is even reason to believe that the creation of new Confucian and Taoist schools using Zen methods was especially encouraged by Zen adepts because of their awareness that the original Zen Buddhist order had become seriously enervated through the attachment of worldly feelings to its forms and personalities.

From the point of Buddhist historiography, this sort of involution is predictable: a period of true teaching is eventually obscured by imitations, and even these break down into remnants with time. The *Mahāparinirvānasūtra*, or "Scripture of the Great Decease," among the classical scriptures traditionally most studied by Zen adepts, outlines these phenomena very clearly.

The false ideas about Zen and Buddhism that scandals at Zen centers have both arisen from and in turn recreated in many minds within and without these centers are also predictable and have existed ever since "Zen" became consciously articulated. Almost the entire literature of Zen, in all of its astonishing variety of forms, deals with nothing but misconceptions about the reality of Zen, which is said to be extremely simple in essence though complex in function or manifestation. The apparent complexity of Zen teaching and function is due to the complexity of the human mentality, as Zen perforce acted in more intricate ways to unify the threads of the contemporary mind.

A synthetic recreation of the original mental science of Buddhism, Zen played a unique role in the history of East Asia through its creation of entire schools of religion, philosophy, literature, art, music, social studies, psychology, psychiatry, and physical education.[1]

The inner dimension of the outward history of Zen, during which it first breathed life into a new Buddhism and later revived other philosophies when that Buddhism grew aged and ill, is hardly observed by those who think in political terms, but nevertheless it is consistently emphasized by the Zen adepts themselves.

These *Zen Lessons* illustrate the art of combining ultimate and ordinary truths, using society and conduct as a way into Zen enlightenment, by the practice of constructive criticism and higher education. This was one of the original tools of Buddhism, but in many schools it had lost its edge through excessive formalization by the time the Zen Buddhists revived its original open flexibility.

Among these schools may be counted even the Complete Reality schools of Taoism and the Inner Design schools of Confucianism. The results of Zen methods applied to Taoist and Confucian classics, these schools had as profound an impact on Chinese culture as had the original Chan schools.

The classical period of Chinese Zen is usually said to have been the Tang dynasty, from the seventh through the ninth centuries. The first large Zen commune was established in the mid-seventh century under the fourth founding teacher of Zen, and countless people were said to have been awakened by the public talks of the sixth founding teacher who was founder of the so-called southern tradition. The fourth, fifth, and sixth founding teachers were all invited to be imperial teachers, and many of their spiritual descendants became teachers of leaders of Chinese society at all levels of organization, from local to imperial.

During the Tang period some of the most influential men and women on earth studied Zen on a par with some of the humblest and most obscure men and women on earth. Zen introduced a revolution in social practice that maintained its energy through centuries of opposition and corruption, and provided one of the only historical forums for unbiased social understanding as well as spiritual understanding. Zen also influenced painting and poetry, two of the most important of Chinese arts, traditionally used for emotional education and therefore of great social significance.

As noted earlier, the Song dynasty was characterized by complexity of form and multiplicity of function within its intricate, ingenious, and often ambiguous designs. Song Zen further extended its influence through the urban arts and soft sciences, but also maintained its contact with the huge countryside of China by means of the travels and retreats of Zen workers through the network of Tang dynasty relics.

Over the Tang dynasty, Buddhism, and Zen Buddhism in particular, grew to the point where there could have been no class of people or general geographical region untouched by its influence in the China of the Song dynasty. The problem was, as predicted in Buddhist scripture, that the very success of the work would eventually attract the wrong kind of people, or rather that too many people would come with the wrong aspirations. By the last century of the Tang dynasty there are already notices of Zen establishments losing their order due to the invasion of people with faulty aspirations, and by Song times the tone among the distinguished teachers is one of emergency.[2]

Put in elementary Buddhist terms, Zen establishments were originally set up to free people from the poisons of greed, aggression, and ignorance that ordinarily afflict individuals and societies to greater or lesser degrees and do not allow humankind to attain complete practical understanding of its real destiny.

According to Zen teaching, when people in positions of great responsibility in society trust Zen adepts, it may be because of the reputation Zen gained over the centuries in this enterprise, or it may be an unconscious response to the safety felt in the presence of a truly detoxified human being. In either case, the false appeared in such profusion precisely because the true was so effective.

A complication introduced by this situation was that followers of Zen, both inside and outside the Zen establishments, often had no objective means of judging the authenticity of Zen adepts. These *Zen Lessons* reflect some of the lengths to which Zen teachers and outside supporters went in order to maintain the existence of certain organizational and psychological ideas capable of stimulating accurate perception of Zen mastery under appropriate conditions.

An enormous proportion of the Zen canon uses techniques honed to perfection during the baroque period, and therefore consists in one sense largely of technical descriptions of misconceptions of Zen and human values, analyses of the major problems of human thought and behavior in individual and social life. These descriptions are like designs of the locks that bind the conditioned human mentality, and are used to unlock those locks. The results of this unlocking are popularly called enlightenment, regarded in Zen as the initiation into higher learning experiences available to humankind.

One of the major problems encountered in the dissemination of the liberative Zen arts was the usurpation of the teaching function by imitators without the genuine inner knowledge of human psychology and Zen enlightenment. The fetishism that came to surround tokens of initiation and adepthood in Zen orders was to the true Zen leaders simply a sign of trivialization, but it was enough to deceive many naive Confucian grandees who, in the words of a late Song Zen teacher, "only admired the flowers and did not take the fruit."

Traditionally, the relationship between teacher and apprentice in Zen was formalized only after a period of association in which a certain tacit recognition had taken place. When the would-be apprentice was a monk or nun, a homeless wayfarer and professional student, it was ordinarily the teacher who recognized the student; when the would-be apprentice had home, family, and social ties, the teacher awaited the student's recognition.

By the dawn of Song times, there was already a considerable degree of formalization of many aspects of Zen procedure, demanded by the large number of followers who flocked to the gates of the prestigious Zen institutions. There developed a system of public monasteries under government control, where known Zen masters were invited to teach large assemblies during summer and winter study periods.

In the original Zen communities, everyone had to work, and duties were assigned according to ability as perceived by the core of adepts guiding the community. The Tang dynasty literature has tales of certain adepts working as cooks or hospitalers for twenty years in the communities of their teachers, but in the Song dynasty there seems to have been more rotation of internal administrators of Zen establishments through the reservoir of adepts who served in the various monasteries.

Eventually the Chinese government took official control over the appointments to the higher echelons of administrative and leadership duties. Of course, it was customary for the emperor, governor, military route commander, local grandee, or whoever was legally in charge of approving appointments to monastic office to consult the communities and adepts, but there was still ample room for imposture.

Objective criticism, particularly self-criticism, is an ancient tradition in Buddhism. It would not be too much to say that critical insight was one of the mainstays of the original schools of Buddhism. One of the strengths of the authentic projection of Zen Buddhism was its impersonal pursuit of the liberating effects of this practice. Applied to social, political, psychological, and deep contemplative experiences over the centuries, this method endowed Buddhism with a profound understanding of human nature. *Zen Lessons* explores the social, political, and psychological dimensions of this understanding.

Much of the most famous Zen literature of the Song dynasty, which in fact became the classical literature of Zen, derives from the public lectures of the masters, and therefore is highly veiled due to the inherently secret nature of Zen experience. These *Zen Lessons*, in contrast, are largely derived from private teachings and therefore are mostly explicit.

Notes

1. There were over a dozen sects of Buddhism in East Asia directly originating from or strongly influenced by Zen, at least three schools of philosophy, several genres of literature (including vernacular literature in general), numerous brands of visual, decorative, and architectural art, music for certain instruments, and traditional and modern schools of psychology and psychiatry, including the eighteenth-century Japanese urban Mind Studies movement and the twentieth-century Japanese Morita Therapy movement. Certain forms of physical education like martial arts are also customarily associated with Zen, at least in terms of recognition of past influence, and are still used as tools for teaching in some Zen schools. Needless to say, every form of Zen activity has real, imitation, and relic forms. The great Japanese master Musō, who lived shortly after the time of these *Zen Lessons*, discusses this in his *Dream Dialogues.*

2. The sayings of Baizhang Huaihai, or Dazhi, the late eighth- and early ninth-century teacher associated with the organization of early Zen communities in China, already contain strongly worded statements about institutional decadence at the core of that deterioration represented in the *Zen Lessons*, and provide early guidelines on the distinction between spontaneous authority and authoritarianism, one of the major problems of latter-day Zen. The famous *Admonitions* of Baizhang's successor Guishan also contains unambiguous language on the decay of the Zen order in the ninth century, and attributes it largely to insincerity, lack of self-control, ignorance, and assumption of self-importance within cliques. The *Ten Guidelines for Zen Schools* composed a century later by Fayan, one of the last of the classical masters, identifies even more elements in the decay of Zen, including cultism, imposture, schizoid tendencies, sterile intellectualism, covert nihilism, literary decadence, and illiteracy. Historically speaking, the *Zen Lessons* take up after the *Ten Guidelines* and provide a greatly detailed analysis of human psychology in its reaction to objective knowledge. Other material chronicling the decadence of Zen in the Song dynasty and efforts to keep it alive can be found in J. C. Cleary's translations of Dahui/Miaoxi's letters in *Swampland Flowers*, our translation of Yuanwu's *Blue Cliff Record*, and my translation of Wansong's *Book of Serenity*. Further material on the same subject as viewed by a Japanese pilgrim to Song China can be found in my translations of Dogen's *Shobogenzo Zuimonki* and *Shobogenzo.*

NOTES ON SOURCES

In the original Chinese, *Zen Lessons* is entitled *Chanlin baoxun*, or *Chanmen baoxun*, "Precious Lessons from the Chan (Zen) Schools." It was originally compiled in the early twelfth century by two outstanding Chinese Zen masters, Miaoxi (better known as Dahui) and Zhu-an. In the late twelfth century it was further expanded by a Zen master named Jingshan, into the form in which the text exists today. Several commentaries on the text were written in China over the next five hundred years. It was first published in Japan in 1279, about one hundred years after its recompilation.

Zen Lessons draws on the personal teachings of great Zen masters of the early Song dynasty, many from unusual sources, difficult to obtain or no longer extant, often originally available only through direct contact with the network of Chinese Zen schools. Some selections are not attributed to any written source and may have been written by one or another of the compilers, based on material derived from current oral tradition. Affording rare glimpses of the personalities of distinguished masters, *Zen Lessons* preserves a large body of special Zen lore that would otherwise have been lost to posterity.

Zen Lessons is a unique part of the enormous body of Song dynasty Chan Buddhist lore that still exists in written form. This text makes it apparent that the literature of Chan Buddhism was considerably more extensive than the massive corpus of Chan writing that is known today.

Numerous anthologies are cited in *Zen Lessons*; with the notable exception of the massive *Tanqin Annals*, most of these collections no longer exist, and apparently all that is left of them is what is to be found in *Zen Lessons*. These sources are sometimes given abbreviated titles, sometimes referred to only by generic names. Other sources include diaries, inscriptions, and letters. They contain rare reports of famous teachers, especially selected by the original compilers for their lack of crypticism and their application to social concerns.

Zen Lessons

[1]

ENLIGHTENED VIRTUE

Mingjiao said:

Nothing is more honorable than enlightenment, nothing is more beautiful than virtue. Those who have enlightened virtue have it even though they be ordinary people, while those who lack enlightened virtue lack it even though they be kings.

There were some people who starved to death in ancient times but have been admired ever since for their virtue; there were others who were kings but have been despised ever since for their lack of virtue.

So learners worry about not being imbued with virtue, they do not worry about not being in positions of power and authority.

TANQIN ANNALS

[2]

STUDY AND LEARNING

Mingjiao said:

The study of saints and sages is certainly not fulfilled in one day. When there is not enough time during the day, continue into the night; accumulate it over the months and years, and it will naturally develop. Therefore it is said, "Accumulate learning by study, understand what you learn by questioning."

This means that study cannot bring discovery without discernment and questioning. Nowadays where students go there is hardly anyone who asks a question to discern people. I do not know what they will use to help their spiritual stage and achieve the benefit of daily renewal.

JIUFENG ANNALS

[3]

GREAT AND SMALL EVIL

Mingjiao said:

Of the evil that people do, there is that which has form and that which has no form. Formless evil injures people, evil with form kills people. The evil that harms people is relatively small, the evil that kills people is great.

That is why "there is poison in a party, there is spear and shield in talk and laughter, there are a tiger and a panther inside the chamber, there are savages in the next alley."

Unless you are yourself a sage and nip these in the bud, guarding against them with standards of propriety, the injury they do will be considerable.

WEST LAKE ANNALS

[4]

HONESTY

Mingjiao related the following story:

When Chan Master Dajiao was abbot of Ashoka monastery, it happened that two monks were arguing endlessly over alms. The director of monastery affairs could not stop them, so Dajiao called them to him and upbraided them in these terms:

"Once when Bao Gong was judge in Kaifeng, one of the people reported on his own initiative that someone who had entrusted a hundred ounces of white gold to him had died, and when he tried to return the money to the man's family, the son would not accept it. So he asked the judge to summon the son and return the money.

"Bao Gong thought this admirably extraordinary, and called the son to talk to him. The son declined the money, saying, 'When my late father was alive, he had no white gold to entrust privately to another house.'

"Since both men, the trustee and the son, continued to firmly refuse, Bao had no choice but to give it to a monastery in the city, for unseen blessings to propitiate the deceased.

"I saw this with my own eyes. Even people in the mundane world are still able to be so aloof of wealth and look for what is right, as this story illustrates. You are Buddhist disciples, yet you are so shameless."

Finally Dajiao cast them out, according to the rule of Chan communities.

WEST LAKE ANNALS

[5]

A VESSEL OF ENLIGHTENMENT

When Master Dajiao first went to Mount Lu, Chan Master Yuantong Na, seeing him once, treated him as a great vessel of enlightenment. Someone asked Yuantong how he recognized Dajiao.

Yuantong said, "This man is true to the middle way, not biased or dependent. Whether active or at rest, he is noble and dignified. Furthermore, in his study of the Way his actions are correct, and his words are simple yet logically complete. Whenever people have endowments like this, seldom do they fail to become vessels of enlightenment."

JIUFENG ANNALS

[6]

MODESTY

In 1134, Renzong, Emperor of China, sent a court messenger with a letter to Chan Master Yuantong Na, summoning him to become abbot at the great monastery Xiaozi. Yuantong claimed to be unwell and did not rise to the summons; he sent a message that Dajiao was worthy to respond to the imperial command.

Someone said to him, "The emperor shows reverence for enlightened virtue, and his benevolence covers the beautiful landscape. Why do you firmly refuse?"

Yuantong said, "I am unworthy of monkhood, and my seeing and hearing are not clear. I am lucky to rest in the forest, eating vegetables and drinking water. There was that which even the Buddhas did not do, to say nothing of others.

"An ancient philosopher had a saying, 'It is hard to live long with a great name.' I carry out the plan of contentment in everyday life, and do not trouble myself for fame or gain. If such concerns press on your mind, when would you ever be satisfied?

"Therefore the great poet Su Shi once said, 'If you know peace, then you thrive; if you know contentment, then you are rich.' "

Avoiding fame, perfecting modesty and integrity, good from beginning to end—this was realized in Yuantong Na.

—BIOGRAPHY

[7]

RULES

Yuantong Na said:

In ancient times the Chan commune was established, with rules and guidelines, to rescue those at the end of the era of imitation from the shrouds of error. The founder never knew that students in the last part of the imitation era would usurp the rules and ruin the commune.

In remote antiquity all regulated themselves, even though they lived in nests and caves; later on everyone became reckless, even though they lived in spacious buildings. Therefore it is said, "The question of safety or danger is a matter of virtue; the question of flourishing or perishing is a matter of the time."

If virtue can be applied, what is the necessity of a monastery? If the time could be relied on, what would be the use of rules?

RECORDS OF THE FIELDS

[8]

WORRY AND TROUBLE

Yuantong said to Dajiao:

The ancient saints governed their minds before sprouting, stopped feelings before confusion. In general, preparing beforehand means no trouble. Therefore "the alarm is beaten at the outer gate to deal with thugs," and preparations are made beforehand.

When the task is done beforehand, then it is easy. If you do it hurriedly and carelessly, it must be hard. The fact that the ancient sages had not a worry all their lives and not a day's trouble truly lies in this.

JIUFENG ANNALS

[9]

A SWIFT BIRD

Yunji Shun said to Fushan Yuan:

If you want to find out all you can about supreme enlightenment, you must be all the more firm when you become exhausted, you should be all the more vigorous as you grow old. Do not follow the vulgar to swipe fame and profit to the detriment of higher virtue.

In jade, a pure luster is esteemed, so neither red nor purple can change its character. Pine stands out in the coldest part of winter, so neither frost nor snow can wither it. Thus we know that as propriety and righteousness are what is great in the world, it is only important to be steadfast.

Should you not strengthen yourself? An ancient said, "A swift bird flies alone, a solitary mien has no companions." So it should be.

EXTENSIVE RECORD

[10]

WORK AND THE WAY

Fushan Yuan said:

The ancients associated with teachers and selected companions, never letting themselves slack off. They were never afraid to work hard, even down to husking grain and preparing food, immersed in common labor. During my own apprenticeship I experienced this fully.

But as soon as there is any consideration of whether you will get any profit or not, as soon as there is any comparison of gain and loss, then there will be no end of wavering and compromise.

And if one is not personally upright and true, how could one be able to study the Way of enlightenment?

TALKS OF AN ATTENDANT

[11]

HOT AND COLD

Fushan Yuan said:

There are certainly things in the world that grow easily, but we have never seen anything that could live given one day of warmth and ten days of cold.

The supreme Way is clearly there before the mind's eye, so it is not hard to see, but it is essential to be firm of will and powerful in practice.

This should be dealt with whatever you are doing. If you believe for one day and doubt for ten, if you are diligent in the mornings but put it off at night, not only will it be hard to see the Way right before your eyes, I fear you will be turning your back on it to the end of your life.

—LETTER TO A SENIOR STUDENT

[12]

SAFETY AND DANGER

Fushan Yuan said:

Nothing is more essential to leadership and teachership than carefully discerning what to take and what to leave aside. The consummation of taking or leaving is determined within; the beginnings of safety and danger are determined without.

Safety is not the safety of one day, nor is danger the danger of one day. Both safety and danger come from gradual development.

It is imperative to examine the matter of leadership. To uphold leadership by means of enlightened qualities accumulates enlightened qualities, to uphold leadership with courtesy and justice accumulates courtesy and justice. Exploitative leadership accumulates resentment and enmity.

When resentment and enmity build up, inside and outside are estranged and opposed. When courtesy and justice build up, inside and outside are harmonious and happy. When enlightened qualities accumulate, inside and outside are sensitive and compliant.

So where there is a plenitude of enlightened qualities, courtesy and justice, then inside and outside are happy. When exploitation and resentment are extreme, inside and outside are miserable. It is the feelings of misery and happiness to which calamity and blessing respond.

—LETTER TO MASTER JINGYIN TAI

[13]

THREE ESSENTIALS OF LEADERSHIP

Master Fushan Yuan said:

There are three essentials to leadership: humanity, clarity, and courage.

Humanely practicing the virtues of the Way promotes the influence of the teaching, pacifies those in both high and low positions, and delights those who pass by.

Someone with clarity follows proper behavior and just duty, recognizes what is safe and what is dangerous, examines people to see whether they are wise or foolish, and distinguishes right and wrong.

The courageous see things through to their conclusion, settling them without doubt. They get rid of whatever is wrong or false.

Humanity without clarity is like having a field but not plowing it. Clarity without courage is like having sprouts but not weeding. Courage without humanity is like knowing how to reap but not how to sow.

When all three of these are present, the community thrives. When one is lacking, the community deteriorates. When two are lacking the community is in peril, and when there is not one of the three, the way of leadership is in ruins.

—LETTER TO MASTER JINGYIN TAI

[14]

INCOMPATIBILITY

Fushan Yuan said:

Wise and foolish, virtuous and corrupt—they are like water and fire not being put in the same vessel, like cold and heat not being simultaneous. It is a matter of their natures.

The virtuous and wise are pure and refined, honest and considerate. They make their designs on the basis of enlightened virtues, humanity, and justice. When they speak out or do something, they only fear that they may not accord with people's states or not penetrate the underlying principles of things.

The corrupt are treacherous and deceitful, proud of themselves, flaunting their abilities, indulging in cravings, grabbing profit, totally heedless.

So when a spiritual community has wise and virtuous people, the virtues of the Way are practiced, comprehensive principles are established, and eventually it becomes a seat of true teaching. Let one bad one mix in among them, disturbing the group, and inside and outside will be uneasy—even if they had the original rules of Chan communes, what use would they be then?

The excellence and inferiority of the wise and foolish, the good and the bad, is such as this; how can we not choose between them?

—A LETTER OF MASTER HUILI FANG

[15]

LEADERSHIP AND THE COMMUNITY

Fushan Yuan said:

The leader, who is in a position overseeing others, should be humble and respectful in dealing with subordinates. Functionaries should work wholeheartedly for the leadership. When above and below are in harmony, then the path of leadership goes through.

If the leader is proud and haughty, and subordinates are lazy and personally careless, the minds of those above and below do not communicate. Then the path of leadership is blocked.

When ancient saints served as overt leaders, they would casually have discussions with students during leisure time, touching upon just about everything. From this, one word or half a phrase is recorded in the annals, which even now we extol. What could the reason be?

One is the desire to cause higher minds to be communicated to those below, so that the Way of enlightenment is not blocked or obscured.

Second is their prior knowledge of the capabilities of students, and whether they were suitable or not.

When the saints came forth and when they withdrew, it was all in accord with what was appropriate. There was a natural respect and harmony between those above and those below, so people from far and near came to join with respect.

The rise of the Chan communities came about in this way only.

—LETTER TO MASTER TOUZI YIQING

[16]

VERMILION OUTHOUSES

Fushan Yuan said to Daowu Zhen:

The case of those who, while their study has not yet arrived on the Way, still flash their learning and run off at the mouth with intellectual understanding, using eloquence and sharpness of tongue to gain victories, is like outhouses painted vermilion—it only increases the odor.

RECOLLECTIONS OF WEST LAKE

[17]

MASTERING MIND

Master Yuan said to Wuzu:

Mind is the master of one body, the basis of myriad activities; if the mind is not perfectly enlightened, then delusions naturally arise.

Once delusions are born, perception of truth is not clear. When perception of truth is not clear, right and wrong are confused.

Therefore, in mastering the mind, one must seek perfect enlightenment.

When enlightened, the spirit is harmonious, the breath is quiet, the countenance is dignified, and the body is firm. Errant conceptions and emotional thinking all melt in the real mind. When you govern the mind this way, the mind will naturally be radiantly immaculate.

After this, if you guide people who are lost and confused, who would not follow the teaching?

TRUE RECORD OF FUSHAN

[18]

MISTRUST

Wuzu Fayan said:

In the monastic communes of present times, when students of the Way do not become known and are not believed by people, it is usually because their conduct is not purely good and their efforts for people are not truly appropriate. They may suddenly grab fame and profit, then show off their embellishments all over. So they are criticized by those who know.

This obscures the essential wonder of truth. Even if such people have buddhistic virtues, when heard or seen they will be doubted and mistrusted. If you have a roof over your head someday, you should remember this to make yourself work.

—LETTER OF REPLY FROM FOJIAN TO TOUZI

[19]

THE HOUSE OF HOMELEAVERS

Wuzu said:

When my teacher's teacher was first living at Yangqi, whose name he later made famous, the old building had broken beams and was barely enough to give shelter from the wind and rain.

One night as winter was approaching, snow and sleet covered the benches, so that there was no place to sit. The monks earnestly asked him to let it be repaired, but the old master put them off, saying:

"Buddha said, 'In the time of the aeon of decline, even the high cliffs and deep valleys are changing and inconstant—how can you have it all completely as you wish, seeking satisfaction for yourself?' You have all left home and society to study the Way, but your way of acting is frivolous. You are already forty to fifty—how can you have leisure time to be concerned with a fine building?"

And after all he did not consent. The following day he got up in the hall and said,

"The walls of this room I lodge in have chinks, the benches are all strewn with pearls of snow. Drawing in my neck, I sigh in the dark and think back to the ancients living under trees."

EXTENSIVE RECORD

[20]

CHAN ADEPTS

Wuzu said:

Chan adepts guard the citadel of the mind and serve the rules of the precepts. They think of this and practice this day and night.

Their actions do not go beyond their considerations, and their considerations do not go beyond their actions; they have a beginning and accomplish its end.

Just like a plowman with field borders, rarely do they go over.

RECORDS OF EQUANIMITY

[21]

CHAN COMMUNITIES

Wuzu said:

The Chan community is a place for the molding of sages and ordinary people, and for nurturing and developing potential ability. It is a source of teaching. Even though many people are living together, gathering in kind, they are guided and made equal. Each has a transmission from the teacher.

Now in many places they do not strive to maintain the standards of the sages of the past. Biased feelings of like and dislike are many, with people bending others to what they personally think is right. How should later students take an example?

RECORDS OF EQUANIMITY

[22]

KNOWING PEOPLE

Wuzu said:

To help others and transmit enlightenment, it is important to find suitable people. The difficulty of knowing people is a problem for sages. You may listen to what people say, but that does not guarantee their actions. You may observe their actions, but you might miss their ability.

How can you know people unless you have been associating with them and have had a chance to examine them thoroughly from the basis to the details, searching into their resolve and practice, observing their capacity and ability, eventually to see if they can maintain the Way and conceal their function?

As for those who sell their names and adorn their appearances, they are imposters and should not be admitted. See to the depths, every hidden subtlety.

This principle of searching observation and careful listening is not something that can be done in a day and a night. That is why some of the greatest ancient adepts went through apprenticeships lasting ten or fifteen years. The cause of the transmission of the ancient sages was definitely not something that the shallow could presume to inherit and uphold. The universal guidance can be successfully continued only when there is complete mind to mind communication.

This principle of searching observation and careful listening has clear evidential proof in experience. It does not admit of clever words and commanding appearance, expedient partisanship and flattery, as satisfactory for selection.

—LETTER OF YUANWU

[23]

VIRTUE AND BENEVOLENCE

Wuzu said:

The power of an exemplary leader lies in the practice of benevolence and virtue—it will not do to neglect one of them. If you have benevolence without virtue, people will not respect you. If you have virtue without benevolence, the people will not approach you.

If one knows benevolence attracts, and goes on to help out with virtue as well, then the benevolence which is carried out will be sufficient to settle above and below and invite people from all quarters.

If one is guided by virtues worthy of respect and goes on to help with benevolence as well, then the virtue which is upheld will be sufficient to succeed to the enlightened ones of the past and guide the ignorant and deluded.

Therefore a good leader nourishes virtue, thereby to practice benevolence, and spreads benevolence, thereby to uphold virtue. When one has virtue and is able to nourish it, then one is never cramped; when one has benevolence and is able to practice it, then there is gratitude.

Thus do virtue and benevolence store each other, benevolence and virtue activate each other. Thus one will be spontaneously respected yet remain approachable. What seeker of the Way would not come to such a guide? It is necessary to understand these essentials to transmit the qualities of enlightenment and promote education.

—LETTER TO FOYAN

[24]

MASTERY IN BOTH WORLDS

When Wuzu Fayan moved from Haihui to Dongshan, Master Taiping Fojian and Master Longmen Foyan, both his former disciples, went there to pay him a visit.

Wuzu gathered the elders and advanced working monks for an evening chat.

Wuzu asked Fojian about the weather where he lived. Then he asked about the harvest from the monastery estates under Fojian's mission. As Fojian took some time to figure the yield, his old teacher Wuzu solemnly upbraided him for failing to live up to his responsibility, as evidenced by not being completely current on the status of the permanent endowment supporting the whole community.

In a letter to a younger adept of a later generation, the master Geng Longxue wrote of Wuzu, "In general, Wuzu was always stern and swift in discernment of states. Ever since Fojian had become a disciple of Wuzu, his replies were slow, even to the point of being like this. An ancient said, 'When the teacher is strict, the Way studied is honored.' Therefore the fact that many descendants of the East Mountain School of Chan, that is the school of Wuzu Fayan, were outstandingly wise and virtuous, is a true case of the proverb 'When the source is deep, the flow is long.' "

[25]

AN INSCRUTABLE BUDDHA

When Chan Master Wuzu Fayan saw monks of integrity who were worthy of promotion, in private meetings he sternly put them off and did not make any accommodations in words or attitude.

When he saw those who were prejudiced and deluded, flattering and deceitful, base in their actions, he would be extra kind and respectful to them. Nobody could fathom this.

In Wuzu's choices as to what to take and what to cast aside, there was always a reason.

—GENG LONGXUE'S POSTSCRIPT TO WUZU'S SERMONS

[26]

GREAT LIGHT

Wuzu said:

The ancients were glad to hear of their own errors, delighted in doing good, were great in magnanimity, generous in concealing others' wrongs, humble in association with companions, and diligent in helping and saving the people. They did not defile their minds, therefore their light was great, shining through present and past.

—LETTERS OF REPLY TO LINGYUN

[27]

ESSENTIALS OF LEADERSHIP

Wuzu said to Fojian:

As a leader it is essential to be generous with the community while being frugal with oneself. As for the rest, the petty matters, do not be concerned with them.

When you give people tasks, probe them deeply to see if they are sincere. When you choose your words, take the most serious. Leaders are naturally honored when their words are taken seriously; the community is naturally impressed when people are chosen for their sincerity.

When you are honorable, the community obeys even if you are not stern; when the community is impressed, things get done even if no orders are given. The wise and the stupid each naturally convey their minds, small and great each exert their effort.

This is more than ten thousand times better than those who hold on by authoritarian power and those who cannot help following them, oppressed by compulsion.

—LETTER TO FOJIAN, IN THE PERSONAL RECORD
OF AN ATTENDANT

[28]

WORRY

Wuzu said to Guo Gongfu:

The temper and feelings of people are certainly inconsistent. They shift daily, along with changes. Although Buddhism has flourished and declined repeatedly since ancient times, the reason for its thriving or degeneration has always come from the teaching activity.

In ancient times when the early Chan masters were helping people, they fanned with a clear wind, regulated with purity, covered with moral virtue, and taught propriety and right, causing students to control their seeing and hearing, to stop bad tendencies, to cut off indulgence in desire and to forget about gain and honor.

Thereby they moved daily toward goodness, put error at a distance, realized the Way and fulfilled its virtues, all without being self-consciously aware of it.

People of today are far from being like the ancients. If they want to investigate this path all the way, they must make their determination firm and unbending, until they reach enlightenment; afterward it is left to nature whether one may experience calamity or distress, gain or loss. People should not try unreasonably to escape them.

Why should anyone fail to do this because they are worried beforehand that they may not succeed? As soon as there is the slightest concern sprouting in your heart, not only will you fail to realize enlightenment in this life—you will never have a time of fulfillment.

ANNALS OF THE HOUSE OF EQUANIMITY

[29]

THE SELF-POINTER

Baiyun said to Gongfu:

In former times Cuiyan Zhen, "the Self-Pointer," deeply savored Chan contemplations, and being eloquent and sharp of tongue, he reviled everyone, no one ever meeting with his approval.

Yet in reality the great truth was not perfectly clear to him. One day a senior student from another cloister, seeing him, laughed and said, "Elder brother, although you have studied a lot of Chan, you are still not perfectly enlightened. This should be called ignorant Chan."

EVENING TALKS OF BAIYUN

[30]

DEFEATISM

Baiyun said:

How could the flourishing or decline of the Way be constant? It is just a matter of people spreading it. This is why it is said, "Putting it into practice means survival, giving it up means perishing."

So it is not that the Way is apart from people—people depart from the Way.

People of old stayed in mountains and forests, lived inconspicuously in cities and towns; they were not drawn by fame and profit, they were not deluded by sound and form. Eventually they were able to purify and order one time, and leave an excellent legacy to ten thousand generations.

Can what was possible in the past not be possible now? It is only because teaching is not complete and practice is not powerful. Some say the ancients were pure and simple, and therefore could be taught, while people of today are fickle and shallow, and therefore cannot be taught. These are actually words that foster delusion—truly they are not worthy of consideration.

—LETTER OF REPLY TO GUO GONGFU

[31]

SPEECH AND ACTION

Baiyun said to the layman Yang Wuwei:

What can be said but not practiced is better not said. What can be practiced but not spoken of is better not done.

When you utter words, you should always consider their end. When you establish a practice, you must always consider what it covers.

In this, ancient sages were careful about their words and chose their acts.

When they spoke they did not just demonstrate the principle of Chan, they used it to open the minds of students who were not yet enlightened.

When they established their practices, they did not just take care of themselves, they used them to educate students who were undeveloped.

Therefore, when they spoke their words had standards, and when they acted it was with proper manners. So ultimately they were able to speak without trouble and act without disgrace. Their words thus became scriptures, their acts became standards.

So it is said, "Speech and action are the pivot of ideal people, the basis of governing one's person." They can move heaven and earth, touch even ghosts and spirits, so they should be respected.

TRUE RECORD OF BAIYUN

[32]

SEEING THROUGH

Baiyun said to Wuzu:

Many Chan Buddhists with knowledge and ability see after something is already so, but cannot see before it is not yet so.

Cessation of conceptions, insight into objective reality, concentration, and knowledge guard beforehand. Doing, stopping, letting go, and extinction are noticed after they have already happened.

Therefore, what doing, stopping, letting go, and extinction use is easy to see, while what cessation and insight, concentration and knowledge do is hard to know.

But the determination of the ancients was on the Way. They cut off thoughts before they sprouted. Although they had cessation and insight, concentration and knowledge, doing, stopping, letting go, and extinction, all of it was a question of process.

Therefore it is said, "If there is any talk about beginning and end, it is all self-deception." This saying is that of an ancient master who saw all the way through and did not deceive himself.

TRUE RECORD OF BAIYUN

[33]

STUDY WITHOUT TURNING AWAY FROM PEOPLE

Baiyun said:

Many monks I have seen have never considered the long range. I fear that the monasteries will weaken from this. My late teacher Yangqi used to say that when those above and below try to take it easy, this is the greatest calamity for the teaching.

In the past when I was living in seclusion in the library at Guizong monastery and read through scriptures and histories, many hundreds of them crossed my eyes. The books were extremely worn and old, yet as I opened each volume I had a sense of new discovery.

As I think about the matter in these terms, study without turning away from people is like this.

TRUE RECORD OF BAIYUN

[34]

ACTING TOO EARLY

Zhantang related:

Baiyun first led the Chengtian public monastery in the Nine Rivers region, then moved to Yuantong monastery. He was very young for a Chan master.

At that time the great master Huitang was at Baofeng monastery. He said to Yue Gonghui, "The new abbot at Yuantong clearly sees through the fundamental, and does not disgrace Yangqi's succession. It is a pity, however, that he went into action too early—this is not fortunate for a monastery."

When Gonghui asked the reason, Huitang said, "Acknowledged accomplishment and excellent capacity are begrudged by Creation, and not given fully to humankind. What people strongly want, Heaven will surely take away."

When Baiyun died at Haihui, he was just fifty-six years old. This was an exceptionally early death for a Chan master. Those who know say that the great master Huitang was aware of subtle indications, a genuine man of wisdom.

RECORD OF THINGS HEARD BY ZHANTANG

[35]

CONTINUING EDUCATION

Master Huitang called on Yue Gonghui at Baofeng. Gonghui's clear understanding of the profound doctrines of the *Heroic March Scrip-*

ture was foremost in his time. Each phrase, each word that Huitang heard was like a precious jewel to him, and he was overcome with joy.

Among the monks in Huitang's community there were some who privately criticized their leader. When Huitang heard of it, he said, "I sound out his strengths and work on my shortcomings—what is there for me to be ashamed about?"

Ying Shaowu said, "Master Huitang's study of the Way is a model for Chan monks. Still he considers the inherent superiority of honorable virtue to be strength, and considers what he has not yet seen or heard to be a shame, causing those in the monasteries who inflate themselves and belittle others to have a standard of which to be mindful. This is of some help indeed."

LINGYUAN'S REMNANTS

[36]

DECISIONS

Huitang said:

It is essential to leadership that one should take the far-reaching and the great, and leave off the shortsighted and the petty. If a matter remains stubbornly unresolved, one should consult seasoned and mature people, and if there is still doubt one should question the knowledgeable. Then even if there is something unfinished, still it will not be too much.

If, on the other hand, leaders like to give free play to their own personal feelings and take or give solely by themselves, one day they will run afoul of the schemes of petty people. Whose fault is this?

So it is said, "Planning is with the many, decision is done alone." By planning with the group, one can examine the ultimate effect of benefit or harm; by deciding oneself, one can determine right and wrong for the community.

—LETTER TO CAOTANG

[37]

PERSONNEL PROBLEMS

One day Huitang saw the great master Huanglong with an appearance of unhappiness, and asked him about it. Huanglong said, "I haven't found anyone yet who can be the accountant for the monastery."

Huitang then recommended the assistant superintendent Gan.

Huanglong said, "Gan is still rough—I'm afraid that petty people might intrigue against him."

Huitang said, "Attendant Hua is rather honest and prudent."

Huanglong said, "Although Hua is honest and prudent, he is not as good as Xiu, the supervisor of the estate."

Lingyuan once asked Huitang, "When Huanglong needed an accountant, why did he give it so much thought?"

Huitang said, "Those with nations and those with families have always made this basic. Was it only Huanglong who was like this? The ancient sages also have enjoined this."

—RECORDED ON THE WALL AT TONGAN

[38]

GRADUATE STUDIES

Huitang said to Zhu Shiying:

When I first entered the Way, I relied on myself very readily. Then after I saw my late teacher Huanglong, I retreated and considered my daily activities. There was much in them that was contradictory to principle.

So finally I worked on this for three years. Even in extreme cold and humid heat my determination was unbending. Only after that did I finally manage to accord with principle in all events.

And now, every move I make is also the living meaning of Buddhism.

ZHANG RIVER RECORD

[39]

SAGES AND ORDINARY PEOPLE

Huitang said:

The Way of sages is like sky and earth raising myriad beings, nothing not provided by the Way.

The ways of ordinary people are like rivers, seas, mountains, streams, hills and valleys, plants, trees, and insects—each fulfills its own measure, and that is all. They do not know outside of that what is complete in everything.

But could the Way be two? Is it not that there turn out to be great and small only because of depth or shallowness of realization?

—LETTER OF REPLY TO THE LAYMAN ZHANG WUJIN

[40]

BEING IN THE WORLD WITHOUT MISERY

Huitang said:

What has been long neglected cannot be restored immediately.

Ills that have been accumulating for a long time cannot be cleared away immediately.

One cannot enjoy oneself forever.

Human emotions cannot be just right.

Calamity cannot be avoided by trying to run away from it.

Anyone working as a teacher who has realized these five things can be in the world without misery.

—LETTER TO MASTER XIANG

[41]

COMMUNICATION OF HEARTS

Huanglong said:

Essential to leadership is winning the community. Essential to winning the community is seeing into the hearts of the people. An ancient Buddha said, "Human hearts are fields of blessings for the world, since this is where the path of reason comes from."

Therefore, whether or not a time is safe or prohibitive, whether something is deleterious or beneficial, always depends on human hearts. What is in people's hearts may be communicated or blocked—thence do safety and prohibition arise. Things are done with more or less care—thence do harm and benefit come.

Only sages can communicate with the hearts of all under heaven. Therefore, in the hexagrams of *The Book of Changes,* when the sky trigram is below and the earth trigram is above, this hexagram is called safety. When sky is above and earth below, this hexagram is called prohibitive. Symbolically, decreasing above and increasing below is called prosperity, while decreasing below and increasing above is called decline.

Now if the sky is below and earth above, their positions are certainly contrary, yet it is called safety, because above and below are intermingling. If the host is above and the guest positioned below, their meanings are certainly in accord, yet that is called prohibitive, because above and below do not intermingle.

Therefore when heaven and earth do not intermingle, beings are not great. If human hearts do not communicate, things are not harmonious. The meaning of decline and prosperity, harm and benefit, also come from this.

Now if those who are above other people are able to control themselves and thereby be generous with those below, those below will gladly serve those above. Would this not be called prosperity? If those above slight those below and indulge themselves, those below will surely resent and oppose those above. Would this not be called decline?

Thus when those above and below intermingle, then there is safety and peace. When they do not intermingle, something is wrong. People who lessen themselves are a benefit to others; people who aggrandize themselves are harmful to others.

How could the winning or losing of hearts be easy? Ancient sages likened the human being to a boat, heart being the water—the water can carry the boat, and it can also overturn the boat. When the water goes with it, the boat floats, and when the water goes against it, the boat sinks.

Therefore, when a leader wins people's hearts there is flourishing, and a leader that loses people's hearts is abandoned. Winning them completely means complete flourishing, losing them completely means complete rejection.

So when both are good there are many blessings, and when both are bad the calamity is severe. Good and bad are of the same kind, just like pearls on a thread; flourishing and decline happen in this pattern, clear as the sun in the sky. This is a basic guide for generation after generation.

—LETTER TO HUANGLONG SHENG

[42]

MAKE THE WAY WIDE

Huanglong said to the great statesman Wang Anshi:*

Whatever you set your mind to do, you always should make the road before you wide open, so that all people may traverse it. This is the concern of a great man.

If the way is narrow and perilous, so that others cannot go on it, then you yourself will not have any place to set foot either.

ZHANG RIVER ANNALS

[43]

NO DECEPTION

Huanglong said:

If in your speech and silence, in what you do and what you do not do, you can say of yourself that you do not deceive heaven above, do not deceive people outwardly, and do not deceive your own mind within, this can truly be called achievement.

Yet remaining careful about the hidden and the subtle when alone, if you find that there is ultimately no deception going on at all, then this can be called achievement.

—LETTER OF REPLY TO WANG ANSHI

[44]

THE CHIEF ELDER

Huanglong said:

The position of the chief elder is to be a vessel of enlightened qualities. When ancient sages established communes, set forth organizing principles, and set up names and ranks, choosing a renunciant with enlightened qualities for the title of chief elder, it was so that the

---

*Also considered one of China's great poets, Wang Anshi was a Chan practitioner and an active statesman. At the peak of his career he was highly placed and tried to institute sweeping reforms in government. He met with great resistance from entrenched interests, and was eventually ousted.—Translator

elder would practice those enlightened qualities, not that anyone should have ambitions for this name.

My late teacher Ciming once said, "One who preserves the Way through old age to death in mountains and valleys is not as good as one who practices the Way leading a group of people in a commune."

Is it not the case that when one preserves the practice of the chief elder well, the virtues of the Way of the enlightened abide?

—LETTER TO CUIYAN ZHEN

[45]

PASSING THE TEST

In private teaching, Huanglong used to give three barrier sayings, but few comprehended this device. When someone occasionally made a reply, he would just close his eyes and sit still without any particular approval or disapproval.

The recluse Pan Yanzhi inquired further about this. Huanglong said, "One who has already passed the barrier goes on freely. The one who asks the gateman whether it is all right or not is one who has not yet gone through the pass."

BOOK OF THE FOREST

[46]

FARTHER AND FARTHER

Huanglong said:

The Way is like a mountain; the farther you climb, the higher it is. The Way is like the earth; the farther you go, the farther it extends. Shallow students use up their strength and stop. Only those who have will for enlightenment can reach its heights and depths. As for the others, who would have anything to do with them?

RECORD OF THINGS HEARD

[47]

WILL

Huanglong said to the layman Ying Shaowu:

The will should be made singleminded, unregressing, for a long time. Then someday you will surely know the ultimate goal of ineffable enlightenment.

If, on the other hand, the mind retains likes and dislikes, and your feelings indulge in prejudice, then even if you have a determined spirit like that of the ancients, I fear you will never see the Way.

—RECORDED ON A WALL

[48]

ADDING DIRT TO A MOUNTAIN

Master Baofeng Ying said:
The old abbots everywhere commenting on the sayings and teachings of the enlightened ones of old and criticizing them are adding dirt, as it were, to a mountain, pouring water into an ocean. How can they be made any higher or deeper than they are?

When you look into the intention of the commentators, you see that it is to add to the ancient teachings. But they do not realize themselves that they are not the ones who can do this.

EXTENSIVE RECORD

[49]

LOSS OF INTEGRITY

Ying Shaowu said to Huitang:
The whole matter of being known as a teacher and upholding the teaching in place of the Buddhas, causing mendicants to turn their minds to the Way, revising morals and changing customs, is not something that can be done by the shallow.

Monks of the last age do not cultivate virtues, and few have integrity. Time and again they bribe and curry favor, wagging their tails seeking sympathy, pursuing fame and fortune at the doors of temporal power.

One day their karma will be fulfilled and their luck will be dissipated—gods and humans will be sick of them. They will defile the true religion and be a burden to their teachers and companions. How can I not lament?

Huitang agreed.

LINGYUAN'S REMNANTS

[50]

MIND AND TRACES

Ying Shaowu said to Pan Yanzhi:
Those who studied in ancient times governed their minds, students nowadays deal with the traces. The difference between the mind and the traces is as that between sky and earth.

[51]

DON'T RUSH

Ying Shaowu said to Master Zhenjing Wen:
Whatever is rushed to maturity will surely break down early. Whatever is accomplished in a hurry will surely be easily destroyed. What is done without making consideration for the long run, and is hastily finished, is not of a far-reaching and great character.

Now sky and earth are most miraculous, but still it is only after three years and two intercalary months that they complete their accomplishment and fulfill their transformations. How much the more so for the miracle of the Great Way—how could it be easily mastered? It is essential to build up achievement and accumulate virtue. Therefore it is said, "When you want to be quick, you don't succeed; act carefully and you won't miss."

A beautiful accomplishment takes a long time, ultimately involving lifelong consideration. A sage said, "Keep it with faith, practice it with keenness, perfect it with faithfulness—then though the task be great, you will surely succeed."

LINGYUAN'S REMNANTS

[52]

THE CALL OF DUTY

When Zhenjing nominated Wayfarer Guang to be the leader of Wufeng monastery, the group protested that Guang was coarse and simple, lacking the talent to deal with people.

But when Guang held the leadership, he governed himself strictly and dealt with the community magnanimously. Before long a hundred ruins had been restored, and traveling monks all talked about it.

When Zhenjing heard of this, he said, "How can students criticize and praise so easily? I always see the critics saying, 'That leader practices the Way and takes care of the community; that leader doesn't exploit the communal endowment and suffers the same hardships as everyone.' But then for one who is known as a teacher and is leader of a community, it is a matter of course not to exploit the communal endowment and to suffer the same hardships as everyone else—how is it worthy of special mention?

"It is like when a grandee becomes a public official and takes care of the people for the nation, and says, 'I don't accept bribes, I don't harass the people.' But is the practice of not accepting bribes and not harassing the people anything beyond the call of duty?"

—INFORMAL TALKS OF SHANTANG

[53]

HYPOCRISY

Zhenjing said:

Few monks of the last age have integrity: whenever they see others' lofty conversation and broad discourse, they say to themselves that no one can equal themselves. But when they are given a meal, then they after all assist those with whom they had first differed, and praise those whom they had previously torn down.

It is hard to find anyone who will say that what is right is right and what is wrong is wrong, who is balanced, true, and upright, free from hypocrisy.

—RECORDED ON A WALL

[54]

GENUINE CARE

Zhenjing said:

The rule for Chan practitioners is that their lifestyle should not be luxurious and filling, for if it is there will be excess. Pleasing things should not be striven for much, because much striving ends in failure. When you try to succeed in something, something will surely be ruined.

I saw my late teacher Huanglong deal with the world for forty years, and in his speech and silence, action and inaction, he never tried to captivate students with expressions, manners, or literary skills. Only those who certainly had insight and were truly acting on reality, he would carefully develop in every way.

His care and respect were in the manner of the ancients. Rarely was there anyone in any of the Chan communities comparable to him. Therefore today, as I face the community I take him as an example in everything.

—DIARY

[55]

THE USE OF FINERY

When Zhenjing was abbot of Baoming monastery in Jiankang, the king of Shu sent him a present of plain silk. Zhenjing asked an attendant, "What's this stuff?"

The attendant said, "It's woven silk gauze."

Zhenjing said, "What's the use of it?"

The attendant replied, "It could be made into a vestment."

Zhenjing pointed to the muslin robe he wore and said, "I always wear this, and those who see do not object."

Then Zhenjing had the silk sent to the keeper of the storehouse to sell to feed the community.

—DIARY OF LI SHANGLAO

[56]

ADVICE TO A KING

Zhenjing said to the king of Shu:

In your daily activities, vigorously carry out whatever is right and put a firm stop to whatever is wrong. You should not change your will on account of difficulty or ease. If because of today's difficulty you shake your head and pay no heed, how can you know that another day it will not be as hard as today?

—DIARY OF LI SHANGLAO

[57]

THE JUST

Master Zhantang said:

Those with enlightened virtue please the people, those without enlightened virtue please themselves. Those who please the people grow, those who please themselves perish.

Nowadays many of those who are called leaders deal with the people on the basis of likes and dislikes. When we look for those who know what is bad about what they like and know what is good about what they dislike, we find that they are rare.

Therefore it is said, "Those who share the same grief and happiness as the people, the same good and bad, are the just." Who would not take refuge where there is justice?

LAIKE'S COLLECTION OF GROWTHS

[58]

ADAPTATION

Zhantang said:

For wayfarers of all times, the right strategy for skillfully spreading the Way essentially lies in adapting to communicate. Those who do not know how to adapt stick to the letter and cling to doctrines, get stuck on forms and mired in sentiments—none of them succeed in strategic adaptation.

An ancient sage said, "The hidden valley has no partiality—any call will be echoed. The huge bell, struck with the clapper, resounds every time."

So we know that advanced people who know how to get through counter the ordinary to merge with the Way. They do not fail to change responsively by sticking to one thing.

—LETTER TO LI SHANGLAO

[59]

SELECTING ASSOCIATES

Zhantang said:

When you seek an associate, it should be one who is worthy of being your teacher, one whom you will always honor and respect, and one you can take for an example in doing things, so there will be some benefit in your association.

You should still follow a teacher who is just a little better than you, to be alerted to what you have not yet reached. But if a teacher happens to be equal to you, it is better not to have such a teacher at all.

TRUE RECORD OF BAOFENG

[60]

KNOWING PEOPLE

Zhantang said:

Someone's conduct cannot be thoroughly known for sure from one reply or one question. In general, it seems that those who are eloquent and swift of tongue cannot always be believed in fact, and those whose words are clumsy and dumb may be inexhaustible in principle.

You may get to the bottom of people's words yet fail to get to the bottom of their reason. You may silence their tongues yet fail to conquer their minds.

The difficulty of knowing people is what ails sages. This is especially true as monks in recent times who are bright do not strive to communicate with the hearts of other beings. In what they see and hear they mostly look for faults and weaknesses. They go against the desires of the community and turn away from the Path. They deceive those who esteem them, and they seek the downfall of those who overshadow them. Thus they cause the Path of enlightened teaching that has continued since time immemorial to gradually deteriorate and weaken, almost to the point where it cannot be saved.

—LETTER TO A LAYMAN

[61]

INSECTS

Zhantang said to Miaoxi:

In the age of imitation, many outwardly follow along with things and inwardly fail to clarify their minds. Even if they do great works, they are not ultimate. In general, it is the baseness and vulgarity of the people with whom they associate that makes them that way.

It is like the case of insects: if they gather on an ox, they do not fly more than a few paces; but if they stick to a swift horse, they can chase the wind and pursue the sun, simply because of the superiority of what they cleave to.

So students should always choose carefully where they will stay, and always go with good people. Then eventually they can cut off error and bias, approach balance and right, and hear true words.

—DIARY

[62]

LOFTINESS OF SPIRIT

Zhantang said to Miaoxi:

When you study Chan, it is necessary that your consciousness and thought be lofty and far-reaching, that your determination and spirit be transcendent.

When speaking and acting, keep people's faith—do not follow devious expediency for power or gain. Then naturally you will not be defined by your company, who are uplifted and downcast by the changing times.

RECORD OF THINGS HEARD AT BAOFENG

[63]

SINCERE LIKING FOR LEARNING

Zhantang said:

Lingyuan liked to read through the classics and histories. When he read a classic or a history book, he would keep reading it until he had memorized it.

Huitang chided him about this, but Lingyuan said, "I have heard that one who uses much effort garners a far-reaching result."

Secretary of State Huang Luzhi, an advanced Chan student, said, "Lingyuan is as fond of learning as hungry and thirsty people are of food and drink, and he has no ambition for fame or profit. It seems to me that his sincere heart is natural and not forced."

LAIKE'S COLLECTION OF GROWTHS

[64]

TIMING

Lingyuan said to Changling Diao:

The activity of the Way certainly has its own timing. Long ago when Ciming was a vagabond he was slighted by everyone who saw him, but he just laughed. Asked why he laughed, Ciming said, "When a jewel and a pebble come in contact, you know the pebble cannot win."

Then after he saw the master Shending, Ciming's fame was heard throughout the Buddhist world. Eventually he revived the moribund Linji school of Chan Buddhism.

The Way and time—can they be forced?

—A SCROLL

[65]

TOO LATE

Lingyuan said to the astronomer Huang:

In ancient times someone said, "If there is fire at the bottom of a pile of brush on top of which you are reclining, as long as the fire has not reached you, you are sure it is safe."

This truly describes the workings of safety and danger, the principle of life and death. It is as clear as the sun in the sky, it does not admit of the slightest deviation.

People usually stay in their accustomed situations, rarely reflecting on the calamities of life and death. One day something will come up that they cannot fathom, and then they will sit down and beat their breasts, but all will be helpless to come to the rescue.

—A HANGING SCROLL

[66]

BACK TO BASICS

Lingyuan said to Fojian:

Anytime I have received a letter from your teacher Wuzu, he has never spoken of worldly matters. He sincerely forgets himself in spreading enlightenment, guiding and supporting those who come later.

Recently I received a letter that said, "The fields have been ruined by drought, but I am not worried. I am only worried by the fact that Chan students have no eyes. This summer there were over a hundred people, but not one of them understood the story about dogs having no enlightened nature. This is something one might worry about."

These words are sublime, are they not? If you compare him to those who worry that the temple will not be taken care of, who fear the censure of officials, who fret that their rank is not elevated, and who are afraid that they will not have many followers, he is as different from these as the sky is from earth.

—RECORD OF AN ATTENDANT

[67]

GRADUAL DEVELOPMENT

Lingyuan said:

When you cut and polish a stone, as you grind and rub you do not see it decreasing, yet with time it will be worn away. When you plant a tree and take care of it, you do not see it increase, but in time it gets big.

When you accumulate virtue with continued practice, you do not see the good of it, but in time it will function. If you abandon right and go against truth, you do not see the evil of it, but in time you will perish.

When students finally think this through and put it into practice, they will develop great capacity and emanate a fine reputation. This is the way that has not changed, now or ever.

—A SCROLL

[68]

NARROW-MINDEDNESS AND INDULGENCE

Lingyuan said to Master Huigu:

Calamity and fortune depend on each other, good and bad luck are in the same city. The fact is simply that it is people who call these on themselves.

So how can you not think?

Some only consider what delights or angers themselves, and are narrow-minded, or are lavishly wasteful in indulging themselves and go along with others' desires.

These are not what a leader should do—they are really a protraction of selfish indulgence, the source of the ills of excess.

—A SCROLL

[69]

GAIN AND LOSS

Lingyuan said to the Confucian sage Cheng Yi:

Calamity can produce fortune, fortune can produce calamity. This is because when one is in situations of disaster and danger, one is earnest in taking thought for safety, and when one is deeply immersed in seeking out order, one is capable of seriousness and discretion—therefore good fortune is born, and it is fitting.

When fortune produces calamity, it is because when living in tranquility people indulge their greed and laziness, and are mostly scornful and arrogant—therefore calamity is born.

A sage said, "Having many difficulties perfects the will; having no difficulties ruins the being."

Gain is the edge of loss, loss is the heart of gain. Therefore blessings cannot visit over and over again, one cannot always hope for gain. When you are in a fortunate situation and so consider calamity, then that fortune can be preserved; when you see gain and consider loss, then that gain will surely arrive.

Therefore a superior person is one who when safe does not forget danger, and who in times of order does not forget about disorder.

—A SCROLL

[70]

OVERREACHING ONESELF

Lingyuan said:

Those who overreach themselves in positions of leadership rarely finish anything successfully. It seems that their virtuous qualities are superficial and their measure is narrow, and their learning from experience is low. Also they cannot follow the good and strive for righteousness and use that to expand themselves and achieve realization.

—DAILY RECORD

[71]

BE CAREFUL

Lingyuan said:

Learners must be careful about what they take up and what they leave aside; they cannot be unthinking in what they say and do.

People of few words are not necessarily fools; glib people are not necessarily wise. Rustic, simple people are not necessarily unreasonable or rebellious; those who are servile and obedient are not necessarily loyal and true.

Therefore a teacher does not understand people's states on the basis of words, and does not select students on the basis of ideas.

Who among the mendicants in the world does not want to seek enlightenment? Yet those who are enlightened and see reality are hardly one out of a hundred or a thousand. Even those who are cultivating themselves and diligently practicing, storing learning and planting virtue, need thirty years to accomplish it. If there happens to be one thing wrong and the communities reject you, then you can never be established in all your life.

Even jewels that light the way for a chariot cannot be flawless, even a gem worth many cities cannot be free from defect. How can there be no faults in ordinary beings with feelings? Even Confucius, who was a sage, still said he studied *The Book of Changes* for fifty years before he became free from gross errors.

A scripture says, "Do not fear the arising of thoughts, just beware of being slow to become aware of it." How fitting this is—for who since the sages has ever been free from error?

It is a matter of one who really knows developing it completely—then the being is not wasted. So it is said, "Skillful carving is a function of following curves and angles; whether crooked or straight, there is no wasted material. Good riding is in the proper way of meeting situations of danger and ease; neither the slow nor the swift lose their nature."

Since things and animals are like this, so should people be. If you follow sentiments of like and dislike in your actions, leave those who are different from you and join those who are like you, this is due to laying out curves and lines without string and marker, or assessing weight without a balance. Although you may have a fine touch, you cannot be entirely free from error.

[72]

GOOD LEADERSHIP

Lingyuan said:

Good leaders make the mind of the community their mind, and never let their minds indulge in private prejudices. They make the eyes and ears of the community their eyes and ears, and never let their eyes and ears be partial.

Thus are they ultimately able to realize the will of the community and comprehend the feelings of the community.

When they make the mind of the community their own mind, good and bad are to the leaders what good and bad are to the community. Therefore the good is not wrongly so, and the bad is unmistakably so.

Then why resort to airing what is in your own mind, and accepting the flattery of others?

Once you use the community's ears and eyes for your ears and eyes, then the people's perceptivity is your own—thus it is so clear nothing is not seen, nothing not heard.

So then why add personal views and stubbornly invite hypocrisy and deception from others?

When they expressed their own hearts and added their own views, the accomplished sages were striving to find their own faults, to have the same wishes as the people of the community, and to be without bias.

Therefore it is said that for the wide spread of virtue, humanity, and justice, it is appropriate to be that way. Yet those with ignorant and impure minds strive to find others' faults, differing in their wishes from those of the community, sunk in personal prejudices. Therefore none of the people fail to become estranged from them. And therefore those whose bad name and perilous deeds are told far and near also must be like this.

By this we know that when leaders have the same desires as their communities, they are called wise sages. When their desires differ from those of their communities, they are called mediocre.

In general, there is a difference in the meanings of opening up and offering one's views—good and bad, success and failure, go in opposite ways like this. Can it not be the difference in the sentiments with which they seek fault, and the dissimilarity in the ways in which they entrust people?

[73]

TWO WINDS

Lingyuan said:

Those acting as chief elders in modern times are often seen to be unclear in their knowledge when involved in two conditions. Touched by two winds, they lose the substance of the teaching.

One of these conditions is adverse circumstances, in which most are touched by the wind of decline. The second condition is favorable circumstances, in which most are touched by the wind of gain.

Once you are touched by these two winds, the breaths of joy and anger mix in your heart, and looks of depression and moodiness show in your face. This brings disgrace on the teaching and vilifies the sages.

Only the wise can turn circumstances into methods of teaching, beautifully guiding the later generations. For example, when Master Langya went to Suzhou, he happened to receive donations amounting to over a thousand strings of cash. He sent people to count it secretly, had money sent anonymously to monks in the city monasteries, and the same day provided a feast for the community.

Langya himself, meanwhile, made his preparations and left before dawn the next day. At dawn, the community realized he was gone. Some followed him to Changzhou and got to see him, returning after obtaining the benefit of the teaching.

Seeing Langya made people develop faith and plant the seeds of the Way more deeply. This is what is called turning circumstances into a way of teaching. This is quite different from those who steal religious rank for their own personal profit.

—A LETTER

[74]

THE OBVIOUS AND THE UNKNOWN

Mr. Fan Wenzhang said to Chan Master Langya:

Last year when I came here I wanted to find someone from the Chan Buddhist community worth talking to. I asked an official whether there were any good monks in the mountains, and he praised two monks named Xi and Mao, who lived in a temple in the north.

I asked, "Are there no others beside these two among the meditators and disciplinarians?"

The officer said, "Confucians esteem the conduct of gentlemen, monks talk about virtuous action. As for these two men, Xi and Mao, they have not crossed the threshold of the temple for thirty years, they only wear plain muslin, and they are not concerned with becoming famous or getting anything for themselves. Therefore the local people esteem their practice and honor them as teachers. But whether they are of those who actually teach as the Buddha did with freedom of mind and masterful eloquence, to be known as true guides, this is not within my power to know."

When I had some free time I went to visit Xi and Mao, and saw that their conduct was just as the official had said. I retired and reflected how these regions have been praised for their good way of life since long ago. Now as I see that old official, even he could distinguish superior people from petty people—how much the more can those who really know!

Master Langya said, "What the official said was truly lofty—please record it to educate the unlearned."

SEPARATE RECORD OF LANGYA

[75]

BEYOND THE RANGE OF ARROWS

Lingyuan said:

Master Yuan of Zhongshan never associated with nobles all his life, and did not grasp fame or profit. He governed himself with humility, and enjoyed himself with the Way.

When grandees started urging him to become a public teacher, Yuan said, "If you have a good field, why worry that it will mature late? The only thing to fear is lack of ability and equipment."

A grandee who heard of this said, "Birds fly away on seeing men of foreboding countenance, and gather after flying beyond the range of arrows. So it is with Master Yuan."

LAIKE'S COLLECTION OF GROWTHS

[76]

COMMITMENT

Linyuan said:

An ancient teacher said, "In studying the Way, realizing it is hard; once you have realized it, preserving it is hard. When you can preserve it, putting it into practice is hard." When you are going to carry out the Way, this is even more difficult than realizing and preserving it.

Generally speaking, realization and preservation are a matter of diligent effort and firm perseverance, striving on your own alone; but practice necessitates an equanimous mind and a lifelong commitment to lose yourself and help others.

If the mind is not even and the commitment is not firm, then loss and benefit will be backward, and you will degenerate into a common mundane priest—this is something to beware of.

[77]

AN INIMITABLE TEACHER

Lingyuan said:

Wuzu Fayan was extraordinary by nature. He was balanced in speech and silence, and whenever he said anything his reasoning was naturally overwhelming. When others tried to imitate him, they were either weird and vulgar or wild and crude; ultimately no one could match him. One like him could not be found even among the ancients.

Nevertheless, he guided people with more humility than that of a hungry and thirsty man. He once said, "I have no teaching—how can I encourage disciples? I am a true criminal in this school."

[78]

SELF-EXAMINATION

Lingyuan's study of the Way and application of its principles was pure and sincere, rich in virtue. He had the air of the ancients. He was peaceful and serious, and spoke little. He was very much honored and respected by scholars and grandees. He once said,

"What the people take lightly and are careless of, the sage is careful with. In particular, to be the leader of a community and assist the process of enlightenment is impossible unless one's action and understanding are in mutual harmony.

"The essential thing is repeated self-examination and self-criticism, not letting thoughts of fame and profit sprout in the mind.

"If there is anything not believed in among the directives of the teachings, anything the students do not obey, then one should withdraw to consider and cultivate virtue, waiting until a way comes.

"I have never seen anyone who was personally upright whose community was not orderly. Truly in this lies the meaning of the saying

'Looking upon the countenance of a virtuous person clears people's minds.' "

RECORD OF THINGS HEARD

[79]

STORAGE AND DEVELOPMENT

Lingyuan said to Yuanwu:

If Chan practitioners who have the sustenance of seeing the Way nevertheless fail to store and develop it profoundly and richly, when they go into action it will inevitably be sharp and rough. This will not only fail to assist the teaching, it will also, I fear, incur trouble and disgrace.

[80]

SINCERITY AND TRUTHFULNESS

Chan Master Yuanwu said:

The study of the Way is in truthfulness, the establishment of truthfulness is in sincerity. Only after you can maintain inner sincerity can you free people from confusion; by maintaining truthfulness in yourself you can teach people to shed delusions. Only truthfulness and sincerity are helpful without drawbacks.

So we know that if sincerity is not whole, the mind cannot be safeguarded or trusted. If truthfulness is not whole, one's words cannot be acted upon. An ancient said, "Food and clothing can go, but truth must not be lost."

So a guide should teach people with sincerity and truthfulness. If one's heart is not sincere and one's acts are not truthful, how can one be called a guide?

The Book of Changes says, "Only when ultimate sincerity prevails in the world can nature be fulfilled." The ability to fulfill nature means to be able to fulfill human nature. If one cannot fulfill oneself and yet expects fulfillment of others, the people will surely be deceitful and uncooperative. If one is not sincere beforehand and yet speaks of sincerity afterward, the people will surely doubt and will not trust. This is the meaning of the saying "When you shave hair, you should get it down to the skin; when you cut nails, you should cut them down to the flesh."

Truly if sincerity is not complete, people are not moved by it. If there is no decrease, there will be no increase. All in all, it is quite clear that sincerity and truthfulness cannot be dispensed with for a moment.

—LETTER TO GOVERNMENT INSPECTOR WU

[81]

CORRECTING FAULTS

Yuanwu said:

Who has no faults? To err and yet be able to correct it is best of all. Since time immemorial, all have lauded the ability to correct faults as being wise, rather than considering having no faults to be beautiful. Thus human actions have many faults and errors—this is something that neither the wise nor the foolish can avoid—yet it is only the wise who can correct their faults and change to good, whereas the foolish mostly conceal their faults and cover up their wrongs.

When one changes to what is good, virtue is new every day. This is characteristic of what is called the ideal person. When one covers up one's faults, the evil is more and more manifest. This is characteristic of what is called the lesser person.

So it is that the ability to follow what is right when hearing of it is considered difficult from the standpoint of ordinary feelings. To gladly follow good when seeing it is what is esteemed by the wise and virtuous.

I hope you will forget about the outer expression of the words.

—LETTER TO WEN WANGBU

[82]

THE PHOENIX AND THE WOLF

Yuanwu said:

My late teacher said that among those who serve as chief elders there are those who move people by enlightened virtue and those who make people obedient by the power of authority. It is like the phoenix in flight, which all the animals like, or tigers and wolves stalking, which all the animals fear. As far as being moved and being obedient are concerned they are one, but the types are as different from each other as the sky is from the earth.

LAIKE'S COLLECTION OF GROWTHS

[83]

WINNING PEOPLE

Yuanwu said to Librarian Long:

If you want to order a community but do not work at winning people's hearts, the community cannot be ordered. If you work on winning people's hearts and do not take care to make contact with those in the lower echelons, people's hearts cannot be won. If you try to make contact with those in the lower echelons but do not distinguish the good from the bad, then those below cannot be contacted.

In trying to distinguish good people from bad, if you dislike it when they say you are wrong and like it when they follow you, then good and bad cannot be distinguished.

Only the wise adepts do not dislike to hear how they are wrong and do not delight in having others go along with them. Only the Way is to be followed, and this is how people's hearts are won and how communities are ordered.

EXTENSIVE RECORD

[84]

THE COMMUNITY MIND

Yuanwu said:

Leaders make the knowledge of the community their knowledge, they make the minds of the community their mind. They are always wary of failing to comprehend the feelings of even one person, or failing to apprehend the principle of even one thing.

Leaders should only seek what is good, diligently striving to seek and take advice. They should question right and wrong in principle regardless of whether the matter is great or small. If the principle is right, even though it involves great expense to carry it out, what is the harm? If the thing is wrong, even though it is a small measure to get rid of it, what is the loss?

The small is a step of the great, the subtle is the sprout of the obvious. This is why the wise are careful of the beginning, sages are mindful of warnings. Even dripping water, if it does not stop, can ultimately turn a mulberry orchard into a lake. A flame, if not removed, will ultimately burn a meadow.

When the water is streaming and the fire is raging, the disaster is already happening—even if you want to help, there is no way. Of old it has been said, "If you are not careful about minor actions, ultimately they will encumber great virtue." This is what is meant here.

—LETTER TO FOZHI

[85]

LEADERSHIP AND PRIDE

Yuanwu said to Yuan Budai:

In fulfilling the role of a leader assisting the spread of the Buddhist teaching, always be thinking of giving help and salvation, and practice this without pride. Then many will be those reached and many those saved.

However, if you have pride in yourself and an inclination to flaunt your abilities, then thoughts of ambition arise and an impure mind results.

—ENGRAVED IN STONE AT SHUANGLIN

[86]

BEGINNING AND END

Yuanwu said to Miaoxi:

In whatever you do, you should be careful about the ending and the beginning. What is done well inevitably turns out well, and what starts well finishes well. If you are as careful of the end as of the beginning, then there will be no failure.

As the ancient saying goes, "What a pity that the robe yet unfinished is turned into a shirt. The hundred-mile journey is still halfway at ninety." This expresses lament at having a beginning without an end. So it is said, "Anyone may begin something, but few can bring it to a conclusion."

In the old days my spiritual uncle Huitang said, "Master Huangbo Sheng was indeed an extraordinary monk, but he erred later in life. As he was when he began, could he not have been called wise?"

YUNMEN HERMITAGE COLLECTION

[87]

PRECEDENTS

Yuanwu said to Fojian:
Our spiritual grandfather Baiyun always considered the ancients in whatever he did. He once said, "If a matter is not referred to in ancient precedents, it is called unlawful. First being acquainted with many sayings and deeds of past sages, one can then accomplish one's will."

But it is not a matter of special liking for antiquity—it is simply that people of today are not sufficient as examples. My late teacher always used to say that his teacher held to the old and did not know the changes of the times, but the old teacher said, "Changing the old and the constant is the big trouble of people today, and I will never do it."

—DIARY OF MASTER CHAN

[88]

ELECTION

When Master Fojian moved from Taiping monastery to Zhihai monastery, the provincial governor Ceng Yuanli asked him who could succeed to the leadership of Taiping.

Fojian mentioned the assembly leader Ping. The governor wanted to see him, but Fojian said, "Ping is a strong and upright man, remote from mundane concerns and free from desires; even if you ask him to be abbot, still I think he may not go along. How could he agree to come on his own?"

The governor insisted on summoning him, but Ping said, "Then I would be a self-promoted leader," and finally ran away to Mount

Sikong. The governor said to Fojian, "No one knows a son like his father."

Then the governor bade all the major public monasteries to insist on the invitation to Ping to be the leader of the Taiping community, so he could not avoid it anymore and acceded to the order.

—DIARY OF ATTENDANT ZHAN

[89]

THE BEST PEOPLE

Fojian said to Shun Fodeng:

The most excellent people do not consider fame and position to be prosperity, and those who arrive at the truth are not troubled by oppression or devastation.

To exert one's strength when seeing there is favor to be gained, or to offer one's services when seeing there is profit in it, is the behavior of mediocre and lesser people.

—DIARY

[90]

MIND AND ENVIRONMENT

Fojian said to Assembly Leader Ping:

Anyone called a chief elder should not crave anything at all, for as soon as one craves anything one is plundered by outside objects. When you indulge in likes and desires, then an avaricious mind arises. When you like getting offerings, then thoughts of striving and contention arise. If you like obedient followers, then petty flatterers will join you. If you like to score victories, then there is a gigantic rift between yourself and others. If you like to exploit people, then voices of resentment will be heard.

When you get to the bottom of all this, it is not apart from one mind. If the mind is not aroused, myriad things spontaneously disappear. Nothing I have ever realized in my life goes beyond this. You should be diligent and set an example for future students.

—ENGRAVED ON STONE AT NANNING

[91]

FRUGALITY

Fojian said:

My late teacher Wuzu was frugal; he had one bowl pouch and one shoe bag, mended a hundred times, repaired a thousand times, yet he still could not bear to discard them.

He once said, "These two things accompanied me as I left my village hardly fifty years ago—how could I throw them away halfway along the road?"

A certain elder monk sent him a robe of rough cloth, which he said he had gotten from overseas and which was supposed to be warm in winter and cool in summer. My late teacher said, "When it is cold I have firewood for embers and paper for covering. When it is hot there is the breeze in the pines, there are water and stone. What should I keep this robe for?" And after all he refused it.

—DIARY

[92]

DEEP AND SHALLOW

Fojian said:

My late teacher Wuzu said that his teacher Baiyun was always open and clear, without any defensive facades. Whenever he would see some duty that should be done, he would jump up and lead the way. He liked to bring out the wise and able, and disliked those who joined and left people for opportunistic reasons. He sat upright all day in a single chair, untrammeled by anything.

He once said to an attendant, "To keep the Way, resting at ease in poverty, is the basic lot of the wearer of the patchwork robe. Those who change their devotion because of destitution or success, gain or loss, are simply not yet worthy of talking to about the Way."

—DIARY

[93]

LASTING PEACE

Fojian said:

If you do not trouble for the Way, then you cannot keep your mind steadfast for long; if you are always in a condition of ease, then your determination in action will not be great. The ancients experienced difficulty and hardship, and encountered perils and obstacles, and only after that did they obtain lasting peace.

It seems that when the task is difficult the will is sharp; hardship makes the thoughts deep. Eventually one can turn calamity into fortune, turn things into the Way.

I have seen many students who pursue things and forget the Way, who turn away from the light and plunge into darkness. Meanwhile they dress up their own inabilities and fool people who consider themselves wise. They emphasize the shortcomings of others to revile people and consider themselves above them. They deceive people in this way, but they do not know there are enlightened predecessors who cannot be deceived. They blind people in this way, but do not know there is a common sense that cannot be covered up.

Therefore those who consider themselves wise are considered fools by others; those who exalt themselves are demeaned by others.

Only sages are not like this. As it is said, 'Matters are diverse and inexhaustible; ability is bounded and has an end.' If you want to try to range over unlimited matters by means of limited knowledge, then your perception will have some bias and your spirit will have an exhaustion point; therefore you will surely have some lack in the Great Way.

—A LETTER

[94]

CONDUCT

Fojian said:

What is to be valued in a spiritual leader is purity of conduct, maintaining great faith whereby to deal with people who come to learn. If there is anything crude and undignified in oneself left unremedied, eventually it will be spied out by petty people, and then even though one may have enlightened powers comparable to those of the ancients, still students will doubt and mistrust.

—INFORMAL TALK OF SHANTANG

[95]

THE AIR OF THE ANCIENTS

Fojian said:

Of Foyan's disciples, only Gaoan is extraordinary, far beyond the state of ordinary people. He does not indulge in likes, he does things without partiality. He is pure and dignified, respectful and discreet. From start to finish he stands on his own with honor and morality. He has the air of the ancients; among the mendicants of recent times there are hardly any comparable to him.

—A LETTER

[96]

CONSIDERED ACTION

Master Foyan Yuan said:

One's demeanor when facing the community should be sobered while at leisure, one's words to guests should be made dignified when speaking to familiars.

When people in the Chan communities speak or act, whatever they say or do they should assess and consider first and then act on it, not being hasty or crude.

If you cannot decide for yourself beforehand, you should ask experienced elders about it. Ask widely of the wise ones of the older generation, in order to broaden your knowledge and amend your shortcomings, to shed light on what has not yet dawned on you.

How could you vainly make a show of authority, just indulge in self-esteem, showing your own ugliness? If you act mistakenly to begin with, even a hundred good things cannot cover it up in the end.

—A LETTER

[97]

CULTURE

Foyan said:

Human beings are born between heaven and earth, receiving the polar energies that form them. Unless they appear in the world in accord with reality, riding on the power of the vow of compassion, their desire for gain seems to be impossible to quickly eliminate.

Even sages know they cannot get rid of people's desire for gain, so they first rectify their minds by morality, and then civilize them with humanity, justice, culture, and knowledge, in order to guard against this. Over a period of time they cause people's desire for gain not to supersede their humanity, justice, culture, and knowledge, and thus complete their morality.

—A LETTER

[98]

RULES

Foyan said to Gaoan:

The overall design of the original rules for Chan communes was to show what is correct, to rein what is wrong, to provide a model and equalize the community, thus to govern the feelings of those of later generations, according to the times.

Human feelings are like water, guidelines and manners are like a dam. If the dam is not strong, the water will burst through. If human feelings are not governed, they will be self-indulgent and wild. So to get rid of feelings and end delusion, to prevent evil and stop wrong, we cannot forget guiding regulations for a moment.

But how can regulations and manners completely inhibit human feelings? They too are steps to assist entry into the Way. The establishment of guidelines is as clear as the sun and moon—those who look upon them do not get lost; it is as broad as the highway—those who travel on it do not get confused. The establishments of the sages of former times were different, but when you go back to the source you find there is no difference.

Among the Chan communities of recent times, there are those who vigorously employ regulations, there are those who stick to regulations to the death, there are those who slight regulations—all of them have turned away from the Path and have lost the principle. What brings this all about is indulging feelings and pursuing what is wrong. They never think of the ancient sages who rescued the final age from its decadence, preventing loose and indulgent states of mind, stopping cravings from the outset, cutting off the road of error and bias—that is the reason for the establishments.

EAST LAKE ANNALS

[99]

SLOGANS

Foyan said:

Students should not get bogged down in words and sayings. Generally speaking, relying on the words and sayings of others to formulate your understanding blocks the door of your own enlightenment, and you cannot get beyond verbal symbols.

In ancient times, when Da Guanpi first saw Master Shimen Cong in private interviews, he exercised his eloquence, but Shimen said to him, "What you say is words on paper—you have not seen into the essential pure subtlety of your mind. You should seek ineffable enlightenment; when enlightened, you stand out beyond, you do not ride on words or stick to phrases, you are like a lion roaring, so that all the beasts tremble with fear. Then when you look back on the study of words, it will be like comparing ten to a hundred, like comparing a thousand to a myriad."

RECORD OF THINGS HEARD AT LONGMEN

[100]

SEE YOURSELF

Foyan said to Gaoan:

One who can see the tip of a down hair cannot see his own eyebrow, one who can lift thirty thousand pounds cannot lift his own body. This is like the student who is bright when it comes to criticizing others but ignorant when it comes to self-knowledge.

COLLECTION OF THE REAL HERDSMAN

[101]

RECOGNIZING A TEACHER

Master Gaoan said:

When I first saw Master Fojian, I heard him speak in these terms at an informal gathering:

"Greed and hatred are worse than plunderers—oppose them with wisdom. Wisdom is like water—when unused it stagnates, when stagnant it does not circulate, and when it does not circulate, wisdom does not act. What can wisdom do about greed and hatred then?"

Although I was young at the time, in my heart I knew he was a true teacher, and so I finally asked to be allowed to stay there.

TRUE RECORD OF YUNJU

[102]

BALANCE

Gaoan said:

What students should keep in mind are balance and truthfulness; then even though thwarted in a hundred ways they will remain serene and untroubled.

But if they have any inclination or bias, and spend the days and nights in petty striving with gain as their aim, I fear their enormous bodies will not fit between heaven and earth.

COLLECTION OF THE TRUE HERDSMAN

[103]

HABIT

Gaoan said:

Virtue, humanity, and righteousness do not belong to the ancients alone; people of today have them too, but because their knowledge is not clear, their study is not broad, their faculties are not pure, and their wills are weak, they cannot carry them out with power, and eventually they are diverted by what they see and hear, which causes them to be unaware of their state. It is all due to delusive conceptions and emotional thinking, piling up into a deep accumulation of habit that cannot be eliminated all at once. This is the only reason that people today do not reach the ranks of the ancients.

—A LETTER

[104]

THE BEQUEST OF EXTRAVAGANCE

When Gaoan heard that life was extravagant at Jinshan while Cheng Gumu was leader there, he deeply lamented this, saying, "The norm of mendicants values unencumbered austerity—how could it be proper to act like that? How could anyone who for no reason conveys luxurious habits to the later generations, increasing insatiable demands, fail to be ashamed before the ancients?"

COLLECTION OF THE TRUE HERDSMAN

[105]

THE STATE OF THE COMMUNITY

Gaoan said:

The great body of the leader has the community for its house: distinctions are made appropriately, disbursal is suited to the vessel, action is concerned with the principles of peace and well-being, gain and loss are related to the source of the teaching. How could it be easy to be a model for people?

I have never seen a leader who was lax and easygoing win the obedience of mendicants, or one whose rules were neglected try to prevent the Chan communities from becoming barbaric and despised.

In olden times, Master Yuwang Shen sent his chief student away, Master Yangshan Wei expelled his attendant. These cases are listed in our classics, and are worthy of being taken as standards. Nowadays everyone follows personal desires, thus ruining the original guidelines for Chan communes to a great extent.

People nowadays are lazy about getting up, and many are deficient in manners when they congregate. Some indulge shamelessly in their appetite for food, some create disputes in their concern for getting support and honor.

It has gotten to the point where there is nowhere that the ugliness of opportunism does not exist. How can we ever have the flourishing of ways to truth and the full vigor of spiritual teaching that we look for?

LONGSHAN COLLECTION

[106]

WHAT ARE YOU DOING?

It is related that while Gaoan was leader of the community at Yunju, whenever he saw students who failed to comprehend his devices in private teaching, he would take them aside and upbraid them in a most serious manner, saying, "Your parents nourished your body, your teachers and companions formed your mind. You are not oppressed by hunger or cold, you do not have to toil on military campaigns. Under these conditions, if you do not make a dedicated effort to accomplish the practice of the Way, how can you face your parents, teachers, and companions?"

There were students who wept on hearing the words of the enlightened teacher. This is how correct and strict his order was.

ANECDOTES OF QIEAN

[107]

THE INFLUENCE OF CONDUCT

When Gaoan was leader of the community at Yunju, he would grieve and lament when he heard any of the students were ill and had been moved to the life-prolonging hall, as if it were he himself that were ill. Morning and night he would ask about their health, and he would personally heat medicine and boil gruel for them, not giving it to them until he had tested it himself. If the weather was chilly, he would rub their backs and say, "Do you have enough clothing on?" When it was hot, he would look into their faces and ask if they were too warm.

If unfortunately anyone were too ill to save, Gaoan would not ask what the student had or did not have, but would perform all funerary rites according to what was at hand in the treasury.

Once when one of the monastery officers refused to make such an expenditure, Gaoan upbraided him, saying, "In ancient times the founder of the Chan commune established the treasury for the sake of the aged and infirm. You are not sick and not dead."

People of discernment from all quarters esteemed Gaoan's personal conduct highly. When he retired from Yunju and went to Mount Tiantai, about fifty students followed him. Those who were unable to go wept as they parted with him. This is how much his virtue moved people.

—INFORMAL TALK OF SHANTANG

[108]

RETIREMENT HOME

When Gaoan retired from the leadership of Yunju, Master Yuanwu wanted to repair the Reclining Dragon Hermitage, which Foyan had built, to make a place for Gaoan to rest.

Gaoan said, "If a man of the forests has the delights of truth, the physical body can be ignored. I am seventy years old, and am now like the morning star or dawn moon—how much time can I have left? In the Lu hills of the western mountains, where the mountain forests and rocky springs adjoin, are all suitable places for me to retire in my old age—why should I necessarily have my own place before I can enjoy it?"

Before long he took his staff and went to holy Mount Tiantai, and later died on Flower Peak there.

COLLECTION OF THE TRUE HERDSMAN

[109]

EDUCATION

Gaoan said:

There are no wise or foolish students—it is just a matter of the teacher refining them to bring out virtuous actions in them, testing them to discover their potential abilities, bringing them out and encouraging them, to give weight to their words, taking care of them to make their practice complete. Over long months and years, the name and the reality will both grow rich.

All people have the spirit—it is just a matter of careful guidance. It is just like jade in the matrix—if you throw it away, it is a rock, but if you cut and polish it, it is a gem. It is also like water issuing from a spring; block it up and it makes a bog, open a deep channel for it and it becomes a river.

So we know that in the ages of imitation teachings and remnant teachings, it is not simply that intelligence is lost or unused—there is also something lacking in the way of education and upbringing.

When the Chan communities were fully flourishing, the people in them were the leftovers of the final age of Buddhism. Those who remained in decadence were fools, while those who took responsibility for their own development were wise. This is why I say that everyone has the spirit, only it takes careful guidance.

Therefore we know of the abilities of students and the ups and downs of the times, that they will peak if treated well, be exalted if encouraged, decline if oppressed, and die out if denied. This is the basis of the dissipation or development of the virtues and capabilities of students.

—LETTER TO COMMANDER LI

[110]

GREAT TEACHING

Gaoan said:

Nothing is more important for greatness of the teaching activity than virtue and propriety. If the leader honors virtue, the students will value reverence and respect. If the leader acts properly, the students will be ashamed to be greedy and competitive.

If the leader is at all lax and thereby loses face, then the students will become scornful and rowdy, an impediment to them. If the leader gets into a dispute and loses composure, then the students will be quarrelsome, a calamity for them.

The sages of old had prior knowledge, and eventually chose illumined knights of wisdom to be leaders of the Chan communities, to cause people who beheld them to be transformed without even being instructed.

That is why when the great ancient adepts' teaching of the Way was flourishing, outstanding people appeared. Their conduct was gentle and fine, harmonious, orderly, and peaceful. Thus should be those whose every word or indication could be guides for later generations.

—A LETTER

[111]

EXPECTATIONS

Gaoan said:

My late teacher once said, "When I set out on my pilgrimage, at many of the small temples I came to there were things that were not as I thought they should be. Then when I recalled that some of the greatest of the ancient masters met their teachers unexpectedly in the informal environment of a local temple, I no longer felt vexed."

RECORD OF THINGS HEARD

[112]

NOTHING TO BE ASHAMED OF

Gaoan was inwardly and outwardly upright and strong. His character was stern, and he was always proper in his manners. When he was a student, he was attacked and maligned time and again, but he never gave it a thought. All his life he bore himself with simplicity and modesty.

In private teaching he did not give careless approval. If there was any discord, he would deal with it soberly, in direct terms. All the students believed in him and accepted his teaching.

He once said, "My study of the Way is not greater than that of others. It is just that I have never done anything to be ashamed of in my heart."

[113]

BEYOND THE REACH OF MONKS

When Gaoan was abbot at Yunju monastery, when he saw a monk attacking another's hidden faults, he would casually admonish the attacker in these terms: "The fact is not like this. For people in a monastery, the Way alone is urgent business, along with self-cultivation. How can you arbitrarily indulge in likes and dislikes, slandering other people's actions?" This is how careful and thoughtful he was.

At first Master Gaoan had not accepted the abbacy at Yunju, but the elder master Foyan sent him a letter urging him to do so. The letter said:

"Yunju is a leading monastery in the area; there you may settle the community and carry on the Way. It seems you should not insist on refusing."

Gaoan said, "Ever since there have been monasteries, the students who have had their morality ruined by this kind of name have not been few."

The elder master Fojian, hearing of this, said, "Gaoan's conduct is beyond the reach of monks."

RECORD OF THINGS HEARD

[114]

SIGNS OF GOOD GOVERNMENT

When Master Xuetang was leading the community at Qianfu, one day he asked a recent arrival where he had come from. The student said he had come from Fujian. Xuetang said, "Did you see any good leaders along the way?"

The student said, "Recently I passed through such-and-such a province, and although I have never met him, I know Master Ben of Poshan there to be a good leader."

Xuetang said, "How do you know he is good?"

The monk said, "When you go into the monastery there, the paths are clear, the halls are in good repair, there are always incense and lamps burning in the shrines, morning and night the bell and drum are sounded precisely and clearly, the morning and noon gruel and rice are clean and wholesome, and the monks are polite when they see people as they go about their activities. This is how I know Ben is a good leader."

Xuetang smiled and said, "Ben is surely wise, and you have eyes, too." He then reported these words to the governor of the prefecture and added, "I am getting old, and I ask you to invite Ben to be leader here at Qianfu, in hopes of the prosperity of the work of the Chan community."

ANNALS OF EAST LAKE

[115]

INSIDIOUS DESTRUCTION

Xuetang said:

An iron dyke a thousand miles long leaks through anthills. The beauty of white jade is lost in a flaw. The supremely subtle Way is beyond iron dykes and white jade, yet greed and resentment are greater than anthills and flaws.

The essence of the matter lies in the will being true and sober, the practice being progressively refined, the perseverance being firm and sure, the cultivation being completely purified. After that it is possible to benefit oneself and benefit others.

ANNALS OF EAST LAKE

[116]

IRON FACE BING

Xuetang said:

When I was the leader of the community at Longmen, Iron Face Bing was leader of the community at Taiping. Someone told me that when Bing was first going on study travels, before he had been gone from his native place for long he suddenly took the notes of what he had heard from the teacher who had instructed him and burned them all to ashes one night. During that time, whenever he received a letter, he would throw it to the ground and say it was just uselessly disturbing people's minds.

ANNALS OF EAST LAKE

[117]

INNER MASTERY, OUTER RECTITUDE

Xuetang said to Master Huaian Guang:

When I was young I heard these words from my father: " 'Without inner mastery one cannot stand, without outward rectitude one cannot act.' This saying is worth practicing all your life; in it is summed up the work of sages and saints."

I remembered these words and cultivated myself while living at home. Even now, when I am leader of a group, these words are like the balance stone weighing heavy and light, the compass and rule determining square and round. Without this everything loses its order.

EXTENSIVE RECORD

[118]

SOMEONE OF PERCEPTION

Xuetang said:

When Gaoan addressed the assembly, he would always say, "In a group you must know when there is someone with perception." I asked him the reason for this, and Gaoan said, "Have you not read the words of Guishan, 'In your actions, take your examples from the superior, do not lazily follow the mediocre and the vulgar'? Those who while daily in the midst of the crowd do not sink into low folly all utter such words.

"In a multitude of people, the vulgar are many, the knowers are few. The vulgar are easy to get used to, the knowers are hard to get near to.

"If you can develop your will so that you are like one man facing a thousand enemies until the power of vulgar habits are ended, you will truly be transcendent, beyond measure."

EXTENSIVE RECORD

[119]

REFLECTION

Xuetang said to Master Qiean:

In managing affairs one must weigh the heavy and the light; when speaking out one must first think and reflect. Strive to accord with the middle way, do not allow bias.

Hasty and careless actions seldom bring success. Even if you can get done in this way, after all you cannot complete anything totally.

When I was in the community of students, I fully witnessed benefit and harm. Only those of virtue moved people by their magnanimity. I hope those in the future who have willpower will practice this carefully. Only this will be of sublime benefit.

Lingyuan used to say, "Usually when people always dwell in inner reflection, they are able to clearly understand much, but when they get involved in things, running outside, then they oppose integration and lose the body of reality."

If you really want to think of inheriting the responsibility of the enlightened teachers, I direct you future descendants to always examine and criticize yourselves.

EXTENSIVE RECORD

[120]

A WEARER OF THE PATCHWORK ROBE

It is related that when Master Yingan Hua was the exemplar of the community at Miaoguo monastery, the elder master Xuetang used to visit him every day.

Some were critical of Xuetang for this, but he said, "My spiritual nephew Hua does not delight in gain or strive for fame. He does not prefer praise to criticism, he does not act agreeable and conciliatory for gain, and he does not put on a false face or use clever words. Add to that the fact that he sees the Way perfectly clearly, and can go or stay at will—there you have a wearer of the patchwork robe such as is hard to find. Therefore I respect him."

ANECDOTES OF QIEAN

[121]

ENERGY AND WILL

Xuetang said:

When students' energy is greater than their will, they become small, petty people. When their will masters their energy, they become upright, true people. When their energy and their will are equal, they become enlightened sages.

Some people are stubbornly hostile and will not accept any guidance for admonition—it is their energy that makes them thus. Upright and true people, even if strongly compelled to do what is not good, will remain undivided and constant to the death—it is their will that makes them thus.

EXTENSIVE RECORD

[122]

PERSECUTION

Xuetang said:

When Lingyuan was the leader of the Chan community at Taiping, he was unjustly persecuted by a certain government official. Lingyuan wrote a letter to our late master Wuzu, saying, "It is getting to be impossible to carry out the Way straightforwardly, and it is not my wish to be a leader by being crooked. It is better for me to set my mind free among the thousand crags and myriad ravines, living each day on straw and millet, and thus pass my remaining life. Why bother anymore?"

Before ten days had passed, there was a petition for Lingyuan to become leader of the community at Huanglong. He took this opportunity and moved.

RECORD OF THINGS HEARD BY ASSEMBLY LEADER TING

[123]

HUMAN FIGURES

Xuetang said:

Lingyuan liked to categorize mendicants by comparisons. He quoted an old saying: "It is like making human figures of clay and of wood. When making a figure in wood, the nose and ears should at first be big, while the mouth and eyes should at first be small for the craftsman may get them wrong, and then the ears and nose, being big, can therefore be made smaller, while the mouth and eyes, being small, can therefore be made bigger.

"When making a human figure in clay, the ears and nose should at first be small, the mouth and eyes at first big. Then if the craftsman should go wrong, the ears and nose, being small, can be made bigger, while the mouth and eyes, being big, can be made smaller."

Lingyuan said, "Though this saying may seem trivial, it can be used as a similitude of the great. If students making choices in face of events do not tire of 'thinking it over thrice,' after that they can be called people rich in sincerity."

RECORD OF THINGS HEARD

[124]

A LIFE OF FREEDOM

Xuetang said:

Wanan accompanied Gaoan to holy Mount Tiantai. When they returned, Wanan told me that there was an elder Deguan there, who had been secluded in a crag for thirty years, during which his shadow had never left the mountain. Mr. Long Xuetan, the district magistrate and a practitioner of Chan Buddhism, offered a special welcome to Deguan to become abbot of Ruiyan monastery, but Deguan declined with a verse:

> For thirty years alone, I've closed the door;
> How can an ambassador's message reach the green mountain?
> Stop trying to use the trifling affairs of the human world
> To exchange for my life of freedom in the forest.

The invitation was sent again, but in the end Deguan never went to the monastery. Mr. Long admired him and likened him to a present-day Yinshan, one of the ancient eremitic masters.

Wanan also said there was an old-timer there who could remember Deguan's words: "Failing to comprehend the Way, getting excited on encountering objects, stirring thoughts along with feelings, having a wolfish heart and foxlike mind, flattering and deceiving people, cleaving to authorities, agreeing in order to flatter, pursuing fame and grabbing profit, turning away from the real, pursuing the false, turning back on enlightenment and joining the dusts—people of the Way in the forests do not do this."

ANECDOTES

[125]

RICH AND NOBLE

Xuetang was born in a rich and noble house, but he had no manner of hauteur or extravagance. He kept himself moderate and frugal, he was refined and unconcerned with material things.

Once someone presented Xuetang with an iron mirror, but Xuetang gave it away, saying, "The valley stream is clear enough to reflect even a hair or a whisker—what should I keep this mirror for?"

—BIOGRAPHY

[126]

LEARNERS AND DILETTANTES

Xuetang was humane and compassionate, sincere and sympathetic. He revered the wise and honored the able. Jokes and mundanities rarely issued from his mouth. He was not aloof or inaccessible, nor did he act in a harsh or angry manner. In his actions he was most steadfast and pure.

He once said, "When the ancients studied the Way, they were indifferent to outside things and did away with habitual cravings, until they thus got to the point where they forgot about authority and rank, and left the realm of sound and form. They seemed to have capabilities without study.

"Students now exert all their cleverness but in the end are helpless. Why is this? If the will is not firm and the task not unified, you will just be a dilettante."

—BIOGRAPHY

[127]

SELF AND OTHERS

Master Sixin related:

Yuantong Xiu once said, "If one cannot be upright oneself and yet wishes to make others so, that is called lapse of virtue. If one cannot be respectful oneself and yet wishes to make others so, that is called violation of propriety. If someone working as a teacher lapses from virtue and goes against propriety, what can be used to extend guide-lines for the future?"

LETTER TO LINGYUAN

[128]

NOT IN THE FOREFRONT

Sixin said to the lay student Chen Rongzhong:

If you want to seek the Great Way, first rectify the mind. If you have any anger you will not be able to rectify the mind, and if you have any craving you will not be able to rectify the mind.

However, who but saints and sages are able to be free from like and dislike, joy and anger? You just should not put these in the forefront, lest they harm rectitude—that is considered attainment.

EXTENSIVE RECORD

[129]

THE QUICKEST SHORTCUT

Sixin said:

The quickest shortcut to entry into the Way consists of modera-tion and relinquishment. I see many students with minds excited and mouths stammering, all eager to succeed to the Chan ancients, but I do not find one in ten thousand when I look for those with relinquish-ment and moderation. They are like sons of a family in society who are not willing to read books but want to be officials—even a little Confucian boy knows this is impossible.

EXTENSIVE RECORD

[130]

SINCERITY AND TRUSTWORTHINESS

Sixin said to Caotang:

For the task of leadership, sincerity and trustworthiness are essen-tial in speech and action. If your words are sincere and trustworthy, the impression they make will be deep. If your words are not sincere or trustworthy, the impression they make will be shallow.

Insincere words and untrustworthy deeds are intolerable even in ordinary life in the mundane world, lest one be slighted by the people—how much more so when acting as the leader of a community, expounding the teaching of the enlightened ones. If you lack sincerity and trustworthiness in what you say and do, who in the world would follow you?

True Record of Huanglong

[131]

Materialism and the Way

Sixin said:

Profit seeking has nothing to do with the Way, seeking the Way has nothing to do with profit. It is not that the ancients could not combine them, but that their forces do not accord.

If profit seeking and the Way went together, why would the ancients have given up their wealth and status, forgotten about achievement and fame, and mortified their bodies and minds in empty mountains and great swamps, drinking from streams and eating from trees all their lives?

If you must say profit making and the Way can both be carried out without mutual interference, that is like holding a leaking wine cup to pour on a burning pot—you cannot save it this way.

—A Letter

[132]

Impartiality

It is related that when Master Sixin was leader of the community at Cuiyan monastery, he heard that Master Jiaofan had been banished from the continent, and that he was passing through the region of Cuiyan on the way to his place of exile on the southern island of Hainan. Sixin sent a party to meet Jiaofan and bring him back to the monastery, where Sixin treated him cordially as a guest for several days and saw him off reluctantly.

Some people, noting that he had criticized Jiaofan in the past, said that Sixin was inconsistent. Sixin said, "Jiaofan is a virtuous wearer of the patchwork robe. In the past I used extreme words to remove the ostentation of his excellence. Now that he has run into foul play, this is his lot. I treat him according to the usual principles of the Chan communities."

Those who know say that Sixin acted in this manner because he had no partiality in regard to people.

RECORDS OF WEST MOUNTAIN

[133]

NATURE

Sixin said to Caotang:

My late teacher Huitang said, "Openness and affability in people are gotten from nature—if you try to force them, they will not last long. One who is forceful but not enduring will be treated with scorn and contempt by petty people.

"In the same way, false and true, good and evil, are also gotten from nature, and none of them can be changed. Only people with balanced nature, who can deal with the higher and the lower, are worth associating with and teaching."

TRUE RECORD

[134]

FEELINGS

Master Caotang Qing said:

The tire that burns a meadow starts from a little flame, the river that erodes a mountain starts drop by drop. A little bit of water can be blocked by a load of earth, but when there is a lot of water it can uproot trees, dislodge boulders, and wash away hills. A little bit of fire can be extinguished by a cup of water, but when there is a lot of fire it burns cities, towns, and mountain forests.

Is it ever different with the water of affection and attachment and the fire of malice and resentment?

When people of old governed their minds, they stopped their thoughts before they came up, stopped their sentiments before they arose. Therefore the energy they used was very little while the accomplishment they reaped was very great.

When feelings and nature are disturbing each other, and love and hatred mix and conflict, then in oneself it will harm one's life, and in relation to others it will harm their beings. How great is the peril, beyond salvation.

—A LETTER

[135]

DISCERNING FEELINGS

Caotang said:

There is essentially nothing to leadership but to carefully observe people's conditions and know them all, in both upper and lower echelons.

When people's inner conditions are thoroughly understood, then inside and outside are in harmony. When above and below communicate, all affairs are set in order. This is how leadership is made secure.

If the leader cannot minutely discern people's psychological conditions, and the feeling of those below is not communicated above, then above and below oppose each other and matters are disordered. This is how leadership goes to ruin.

It may happen that a leader will presume upon intellectual brilliance and often hold to biased views, failing to comprehend people's feelings, rejecting community counsel and giving importance to his own authority, neglecting public consideration and practicing private favoritism—all of this causes the road of advance in goodness to become narrower and narrower, and causes the path of responsibility for the community to become fainter and fainter.

Such leaders repudiate whatever they have never before seen or heard, and become set in their ways, to which they are habituated and by which they are veiled. To hope that the leadership of people like this would be great and far-reaching, is like walking backward trying to go forward.

—LETTER TO SHANTANG

[136]

NATURAL SELECTION

Caotang said to Master Ru:

My late teacher Huitang said, "In a large community, the virtuous and the corrupt are together, because of the greatness of the teaching; and so one cannot but draw near to some and avoid others. It is only a matter of a little more refined selection."

If there are people with ability and virtue who meet with the expectations of the community, you should not estrange them because of personal ire. And if there are people with ordinary perception whom the community dislikes, you should not be friendly with them because of personal liking. In this way the virtuous advance on their own, the corrupt regress on their own, and the community is at peace.

If the leader indulges in personal feelings and only goes by private liking or resentment in promoting or demoting people, then the virtuous will be restrained and silent, while the corrupt will struggle forward in competition. The constitution of the institution is disordered, and the community is ruined.

This selection is truly the great body of the living exemplar. If you can sincerely examine and practice this, then those near at hand will rejoice, and those far off will tell the story. Then why worry about the Way not being carried out or seekers not coming?

—CARVED ON STONE AT SUSHAN

[137]

CONTROLLING BIAS

Caotang said:

There is nothing special to leadership—essentially it is a matter of controlling the evils of biased information and autocracy. Do not just go by whatever is said to you first—then the obsequities of petty people seeking favor will not be able to confuse you.

After all, the feelings of a group of people are not one, and objective reason is hard to see. You should investigate something to see its benefit or harm, examine whether it is appropriate and suitable or not; then after that you may carry it out.

TRUE RECORD OF SUSHAN

[138]

OBJECTIVITY

Caotang said to Shantang:

In all things, if right and wrong are not clear, you must be careful. When right and wrong are clear, you should decide on the basis of reason, consider where the truth lies, and settle the issue without doubt. In this way, you cannot be confused by flattery and cannot be moved by powerful argument.

PURE SPRING ANNALS

[139]

HEART-TO-HEART COMMUNICATION

Shantang said:

Snakes and tigers are not enemies of buzzards and vultures—buzzards and vultures follow them and screech to them. Why? It is because they have vicious hearts. Cows and hogs are not driven by magpies and jackdaws—the magpies and jackdaws gather and ride on them. Why? Because they do not have vicious hearts.

Once when an ancient Chan master visited a hermit, he found the hermit setting out half-cooked rice. The master said, "Why do crows fly away when they see a man?" The hermit was at a loss; finally he put the same question back to the Chan master. The master said, "Because I still have a murderous heart."

So those who suspect others are suspected by others; those who forget about people are also forgotten by people. The ancients who were companions of serpents and tigers had realized this principle well. One ancient said, "An iron ox does not fear the roar of a lion—it is just like a wooden man seeing flowers and birds." These words take this principle to its consummation.

—LETTER TO A LAYMAN

[140]

GOVERNMENT

Shantang wrote to a high government official:

A rule for governing subordinates is that favor should not be excessive, for if it is excessive they will become haughty. And authority should not be too strict, for if it is too strict they will be resentful.

If you want favor without haughtiness and authority without resentment, then favor should be given to those with merit, and not given to people arbitrarily. Authority should be exercised where there is wrongdoing, and should not be wrongly brought to bear on those without offense.

In this way, though favor be rich, the people will not become haughty, and though authority be strict, the people will not become resentful.

If, on the other hand, you richly reward those whose merit is not worthy of elevation, and severely punish those whose offense is not worthy of blame, then eventually you will cause small people to give rise to hauteur and resentment.

—LETTER TO MINISTRY PRESIDENT ZHANG

[141]

THE MEAN

Shantang said:

The Way of the enlightened is not beyond finding the mean. Exceeding the mean is bias and error. Not everything in the world can fulfill your wishes, so trying to fulfill your wishes means trouble and confusion.

Many are the people of past and present who are immoderate and imprudent, in peril to the point of being in danger of destruction. So then who has no excesses? Only people of wisdom and attainment reform them unstintingly; this is extolled as excellence.

—LETTER TO A LAYMAN

[142]

PEACE AMID VIOLENCE

Chan Master Shantang fled to Yunmen hermitage along with Ministry President Han Zicang, Chan Master Wanan, and one or two other Chan adepts, to avoid the violence of a civil war in the early 1130s. Mr. Han asked Wanan, "Recently I heard you were captured by soldiers of the rebel leader Li Cheng. How did you contrive to escape?"

Wanan said, "I had been captured and bound, and starved and froze for days on end, until I thought to myself that I would surely die. Then it happened that there was a snowfall so heavy that it buried the building and caused the walls of the rooms where we were held to collapse. That night over a hundred people were lucky enough to escape."

Mr. Han said, "At the time you were captured, how did you handle it?"

Wanan did not reply. Mr. Han asked him again, pressing him for an answer.

Wanan said, "How is this even enough to talk about? People like us study the Way: we take right for sustenance and have only death. What is there to fear?"

Mr. Han nodded at this.

So we know that our predecessors had immutable will, even in the midst of mortal calamity and trouble in the world.

COLLECTION OF THE TRUE HERDSMAN

[143]

WHO TO ELECT

When Chan Master Shantang retired from leadership of the community at Baizhang, he said to the government officer Han Zicang:

Those who advanced in ancient times had virtue and responsibility. Therefore they would go only at the third invitation and leave with one farewell.

Of those who advance nowadays, only those with strength who know when to go forth and when to withdraw without losing the right way can be called wise masters.

RECORD OF THINGS HEARD

[144]

IMPARTIALITY

Shantang said to Yean:

The attitude of a leader must be impartial. In doing things, you should not necessarily consider what comes from yourself to be right while considering others wrong. Then like and dislike regarding difference and sameness do not arise in the mind. Then the breath of crass self-indulgence and misbegotten prejudice has no way to enter.

PHANTOM HERMITAGE COLLECTION

[145]

EXAMPLES

Miaoxi said:

The ancients would adopt what was good when they saw it, and if they made a mistake they would change it. Following virtue and cultivating accord, they wanted to escape without fault. They worried about nothing so much as not knowing their own bad points, and liked nothing so much as learning of their mistakes.

Were the ancients like this because of insufficiency of intelligence, or because their perception was not clear? In truth it was an admonition to those of later times who would try to aggrandize themselves and belittle others.

The expansion of a community, with people from all quarters, is not something that can be achieved by one person alone—it is necessary to be assisted by the ears, eyes, and thoughts of associates, in order to fully comprehend what is right and to know the people's feelings and conditions.

If one rests on high rank, taking oneself seriously, being fastidious about minor tasks but slighting the great body of the community as a whole, not knowing who the wise are, not perceiving who are no good, not changing what is wrong, not following what is right, acting arbitrarily as one pleases, without any deference, this is the foundation of calamity. How could one not beware?

Should it actually turn out that there are none among one's associates worth consulting, one should still take examples from sages of the past. If you shut everyone out, you cannot quite "let in the hundred rivers to become an ocean."

—LETTER TO MASTER BAO

[146]

NOMINEES

Miaoxi said:

In nominating leaders for public study communities, it is imperative to nominate those who preserve the Way and are peaceful and modest, who when nominated will grow stronger in will and integrity, who will not ruin the community finances wherever they go but will fully develop the community and also be master of the teaching, rescuing the present day from its decadence.

As for wily deceiving tricksters who have no sense of shame and, knowing how to flatter and wait on authority, cleave to powerful upper-class families, why should they be nominated?

—LETTER TO ZHU-AN

[147]

COMMON SENSE

Miaoxi said to the lay student Chaoran:

In all the world, common sense alone cannot be abandoned. Even if it is suppressed and not carried out, how can that affect common sense?

This is why when someone truly enlightened is elected to lead a spiritual community, all who see and hear are joyful and praise the election. If someone unsuitable is elected, the people sadly lament the election.

In reality it is nothing but a matter of whether common sense is carried out or not. By this you can figure out whether a Chan community will flourish or decline.

KE-AN'S COLLECTION

[148]

MISREPRESENTATION

Miaoxi said:

The ancients first chose those with enlightenment and virtue, then recommended those with ability and learning, to advance in their time.

If one who is not a good vessel is placed before others, most who see and hear will slight him, and due to this monks will think to themselves of polishing their reputation and merit to become established.

Recently we have seen the Chan communities decline as students are heedless of the virtues of the Way and lack integrity and humility. They slander the pure and plain as being crude simpletons and praise the noisy dilettantes as being smart.

Therefore the perceptions of newcomers are not clear. They go hunting and fishing to extract and copy in order to supply themselves with eloquent remarks and sayings, getting deeper into this as time goes on, until it has become a decadent trend. When you talk to them about the Way of the sages, they are as blind as if they had their faces to the wall. These people are just about impossible to help.

—LETTER TO ZICANG

[149]

A MEMORIAL

Miaoxi said:

In the old days Huitang wrote in a memorial of Huanglong: "Those engaged in this study in ancient times dwelt on cliffs and in caves, ate roots and fruits, wore hide and leaves. They did not concern their minds with fame or gain, and did not register their names in the government offices.

"Since the Wei, Jin, Qi, Liang, Sui, and Tang dynasties (third to ninth centuries C.E.), when sanctuaries were first built for assemblies of students from all quarters, the good have been chosen to regulate the corrupt, causing the wise to guide the foolish and deluded. Because of this, guest and host have been established, above and below have been distinguished.

"Now when people from all quarters are gathered in one sanctuary, it is truly difficult to bear the responsibility. It is essential to unify the great and discard the petty, to put the urgent first and the casual later, not to scheme for oneself but to concentrate on helping others. This is as different from selfish striving as the sky is from earth.

"Now the names of the successive generations of leaders at the Huanglong sanctuary are being inscribed on stone, to cause those who come later to see, look at them, and say who had virtue, who was benevolent and righteous, who was fair to the whole community, and who profited himself.

"Can we not beware?"

—STONE INSCRIPTION

[150]

THE QUALITY OF CANDIDATES

The government minister Zhang Zishao said to Miaoxi:

The position of assembly chief in a Chan community is a rank for which the virtuous and wise are to be chosen, but nowadays in many places there is no question as to whether the assembly chief is good or bad. All use this post as a steppingstone for their ambitions. This is also the fault of the teachers of the communities.

Now in the age of imitation, it is hard to find anyone suitable for this post. If you choose those whose practice is a bit better and whose virtue is a bit more complete, who are modest and upright, then that would be a bit better than choosing those who rush ahead precipitously.

KEAN'S COLLECTION

[151]

DIVISION OF RESPONSIBILITIES

Miaoxi said:

When the ancient worthies served as leaders of Chan communities, they did not manage the community property personally, but entrusted it to the direction of monastic officers. Chan abbots in recent times presume to extra ability and power, and refer all affairs great and small to the abbot, while the officers just have empty titles.

If you want to try to manage the affairs of a whole community by means of the capacities of just one person, keeping the people informed and keeping the general order undisturbed, would that not be hard?

—LETTER TO SHANTANG

[152]

EXILE OF A MASTER

Wanan said:

When our late teacher Miaoxi began teaching as the leader at Jingshan, in an evening gathering he discussed Chan teaching as it was carried out at various places throughout the land. When he came to the teachings of the moribund Cao-Dong school of Chan, he talked on and on.

The next day, Assembly Chief Yin, who was a master of the Cao-Dong school, said to the teacher, "Helping people is a serious matter. One must want to help activate spiritual teaching; one should save it from decadence, according to the times, not grasp immediate convenience. When you discussed various teachers in the past when you were a Chan follower, even then it could not have been arbitrary— how much less now that you are a public teacher."

The teacher said, "Last night's talk was just one occasion."

The assembly chief said, "The study of saints and sages is based on nature—how can you slight it?"

The teacher bowed his head and apologized, but the assembly chief kept talking endlessly about the matter.

Later, when our late teacher Miaoxi was banished, an attendant recorded the statement of his exile and posted it in front of the communal hall. The monks were weeping and sniveling like people who had lost their parents, lamenting sadly, unable to rest easy. Assembly Chief Yin went to the community quarters and said to them, "The calamities and stresses of human life are something that cannot be arbitrarily avoided. If we had Miaoxi be like a sissy all his life, submerged in the rank and file, keeping his mouth closed, not saying anything, surely this exile would not have happened. But do I need to say that what the sages of yore had to do did not stop at this? Why are you bothering to aggrieve yourselves? In olden times several sincere students banded together to see the great teacher Fenyang; they ran into military operations going on in the northwest at the time, so they changed their clothes and mixed in with the battalions to make their way up to Fenyang. Now the place of Miaoxi's exile is not so far from here, there are no gaps or obstacles in the road, the mountains and rivers are not steep or forbidding—if you want to see Miaoxi, what is so hard about that?"

From this the whole crowd became silent. The next day they left in a continuous stream.

LUSHAN COLLECTION OF THE FOREST OF WISDOM

[153]

CRITICISM

Wanan said:

When my late teacher Miaoxi was exiled, there were some among the students who made private criticisms. Assembly Chief Yin said, "In general, when criticizing and talking about people, you should seek to find where the faulty are faultless—how can you find the faultless faulty? If you do not look into people's hearts, and just doubt their actions, what help is that to the democracy of the community?

"Miaoxi's virtue and capacity come from nature. In bearing and conduct he only follows duty and right, in thought and judgment he definitely excels other people. Now that Creation is putting him down, there must be a reason; how can we know but that it will be a blessing for the teaching another day?"

Those who heard this did not criticize any longer.

FOREST OF WISDOM COLLECTION

[154]

SAFETY IN THE COMMUNITY

Assembly Chief Yin said to Wanan:

One who is known as a teacher should cleanse mind and heart, and receive people from all quarters with utmost impartiality and uprightness.

If there is one among them who embraces the Way and is virtuous, humane, and just, you should advance that person even if there is enmity between you.

And if there is anyone who is a crooked misanthrope, you must put that person at a distance even if you are privately indebted to the person.

This will cause everyone who comes there to know what to stand by, so all are of one mind, with the same virtue. Then the community is safe.

—LETTER TO MIAOXI

[155]

MAKING A COMMUNITY FLOURISH

Assembly Chief Yin said:

Few are the leaders who can succeed in making a community flourish. This is because most of them forget truth and virtue and give up benevolence and duty, abandoning the regulations of the Dharma and going by their personal feelings.

Sincerely considering the decline and disappearance of spiritual schools, one should make oneself true yet humble to others, pick out the wise and good for mutual assistance, honor those of long-standing virtue, be distant from petty people, cultivate oneself with moderation and frugality, and extend virtue to others.

After that, for those whom you employ as assistants, retain those who are more mature, and keep away the opportunistic flatterers. The value of this is that there will be no slander of corruption, and no disruption by factionalism.

FOREST OF WISDOM COLLECTION

[156]

TROUBLES

Assembly Chief Yin said:

The sages of ancient times were wary when they had no troubles, saying, "Could Heaven have abandoned the bad?"

A philosopher said, "Only a saint can be free from troubles inside and out. Unless one is a saint, when at peace one must be anxious within."

People of wisdom and understanding know that trouble cannot be escaped, so they are careful in the beginning to guard themselves against it.

So when human life has some worry and toil, it may turn into happiness for a whole lifetime. After all, calamity and trouble, slander and disgrace, could not be avoided even by ancient sage-kings, much less by others.

—LETTER TO MIAOXI

[157]

CHARADES

Wanan said:

Recently we see the Chan communities lacking mature people. Wherever you go there are hundreds of people, one acting as master, the group as associates. With one occupying the rank of spiritual monarch, taking up its regalia, they fool each other. Even though charlatans give speeches, they have no basis in scripture. That is the way it is—there are no mature people.

Unless one has clarified the mind and arrived at its basis, and acts in accordance with this understanding, how could one presume to teach in the Buddha's stead? It would be like someone falsely declared emperor—he brings about his own execution. Spiritual monarchy is even more serious than worldly monarchy—it cannot be taken arbitrarily.

The sages are ever more distant, while those convinced of their own school of thought are ever more ubiquitous, causing the teaching of the sages of yore to go into submergence day by day. As Confucius lamented, "I would like to say nothing, but can I?"

I set forth one or two items that have been most deleterious in crippling the Way and degrading the teaching. I have done this to circulate in the Chan communities, to let the younger generation know that their predecessors struggled hard and worked hard, with the bearing of the great teaching in their minds, like walking on ice, running on swords, not in a quest for honor or gain.

If those who understand me fault me for this, I have nothing to say about it.

FOREST OF WISDOM COLLECTION

[158]

GRANDEES AND CHAN TEACHERS

Wanan said:

Recently I have seen grandees, provincial inspectors and governors, enter the mountain cloisters, take care of official business, and then the next day have an attendant take word back to the chief elder of the Chan cloister, "Today you should give a lecture especially for such and such an official." This situation calls for reflection.

Although it is true that such instances have been recorded in books since ancient times, in every case it was the grandee who came seeking the teacher, while the Chan elder, on the occasion of the visit, would briefly mention the ideas of external protection of the teaching and glorification of nature.

Once grandees had become disciples, the Chan elders would tell a few light stories of the school to engender respect in them. There are well-known cases of distinguished Confucian grandees seeking out Chan masters for instruction—do you think this was particularly irrational behavior, bringing on laughter from the knowledgeable?

[159]

AUTHORITARIANISM

Wanan said:

When the ancients were going to hold private meetings, they would first hang out a sign to that effect, and each individual would come bounding forth because of the greatness of the matter of life and death, eager to settle doubts and determine what is so.

In recent times we often see community leaders making everybody come and submit to them respectfully in private interviews, without question of whether they are old or sick.

If there is musk, it is naturally fragrant—what need is there to publicize it? By this they wrongly create divisions, so guest and host are not at ease. Teachers should think about this.

[160]

CHAN HISTORY

Wanan said:

The Chan founder transmitted both the teaching and the robe of succession. After six generations, the robe stopped being transmitted. Those whose action and understanding corresponded were taken to continue the work of the school over the generations. The Chan path became ever more refulgent, with increasingly numerous descendants.

After the sixth patriarch of Chan, the great masters Shitou and Mazu were both true heirs. The profound words and marvelous sayings of these two great men circulated throughout the land, and from time to time there were those who personally realized their inner meaning.

Once there were many teachers' methods, students did not have one sole way open, as the original stream of Chan branched out into five, square or round according to the vessel, the essence of the water remaining the same. Each branch had an excellent reputation, and strived diligently to carry out its responsibilities. So Chan communities sprouted up all over, not without reason.

Henceforth the communities would respond and expound back and forth to each other, revealing the subtleties and opening up the mysteries, sometimes putting down, sometimes upholding, in this way and that assisting the process of the teaching. Their sayings were flavorless, like simmering board soup and cooking nail rice, served to those who came later, for them to chew on.

The practice that evolved from this is called bringing up the ancients. Verses on ancient stories began with Fenyang; then with Xuedou, shortly thereafter, the sound was widely broadcast, and he revealed its essential import, in its oceanic boundlessness.

Later authors ran after Xuedou and imitated him, not considering the issues of enlightenment and virtue, but striving for vividness and freshness of literary expression, thereby causing later students of subsequent generations to be unable to see the ancients' message in its pristine purity and wholeness.

I have traveled around to Chan communities, and I have seen those among my predecessors who do not read anything but the sayings of the ancients and do not practice anything but the original pure rules for Chan communes. Is it that they particularly like ancient things? No, it is simply that people of present times are not sufficient as models. I hope for people of comprehension and realization who will understand me beyond the words.

[161]

SOME BAD HABITS

Wanan said:

Recently we see students fondly clinging to prejudiced views, not comprehending people's conditions, shallow in faith, recalcitrant, liking people to flatter them, admiring those who follow them while estranging those who differ from them. Even if they have one bit of knowledge or half an understanding, yet it is covered by these kinds of bad habits. Many are those who grow old without attainment.

FOREST OF WISDOM COLLECTION

[162]

A FALSE TEACHING

Wanan said:

In the Chan communities wherever you go there is a false teaching rampant, saying that discipline, meditation, and knowledge are unnecessary, and that it is unnecessary to cultivate virtue or to get rid of craving. Talk like this is not only creating harm to the Chan communities in the present day, it is actually the bane of the teaching for ten thousand ages.

Ordinary people have cravings, they love and hate and desire, they are selfish and ignorant, their every thought is attached to things, like bubbles in one boiling pot. How can they be cleared and cooled? Much of what the ancient sages had to think about pertained to this. So it was that they set up the three studies of discipline, meditation, and knowledge, in order to control people so that they might be reformed and restored.

Nowadays younger students do not uphold the precepts, do not practice meditation, cultivate knowledge, and develop virtue. They just rely on wide learning and powerful intellect, acting in common, vulgar ways, so that they are impossible to reform. This is what I mean when I say that such talk is the bane of the Chan communities for ten thousand ages.

Only those lofty-minded people who travel on the correct basis, keeping sincere and faithful to understanding and clarifying the issue of life and death, will not be dragged in by this type. They say that such talk cannot be believed in and is like poisonous bird droppings, like water drunk and passed by a viper. It is not good even to read or hear of such talk, much less ingest it, for it will undoubtedly kill people. Those who know will naturally stay far away from it.

—LETTER TO CAOTANG

[163]

GIFTS OF TEACHING

It is related that the Chan master Wanan was frugal and austere, and used extemporaneous discussions and general talks for offerings. Among the monks of the community there were some who criticized him for this.

Hearing of this, Wanan said, "Dining on fine food in the morning and disliking coarse fare in the evening is ordinary human feeling. Since you people have your minds on the magnitude of the matter of life and death, and have sought out an island of peace and solitude, you should be thinking of how your practice of the Way is not yet accomplished and how far removed you are from the time of the sages. How can you be concerned with your covetous desires all the time?"

COLLECTION OF THE TRUE HERDSMAN

[164]

A CHAN MASTER

Wanan was humane and considerate, and he conducted himself with modesty and austerity. Whenever he spoke, his words were simple yet the meaning was profound. He studied widely and had a strong memory. He would pursue reason to its final conclusion, and did not stop on any account, or follow anything arbitrarily.

When he discussed a story, contemporary or ancient, it was like being there in person—to those who heard, it was as clear as seeing with their own eyes. Students used to say that a year of meditation was not as good as a day of listening to the master's talk.

RECORD OF THINGS HEARD

[165]

BUDDHAHOOD IN THIS LIFE

Wanan said to the community assembly chief Bian:

My spiritual grandfather Yuanwu said, "Among the Chan folk of present times, few have fidelity and integrity, and none have humility. Many of the Confucians therefore slight them.

"Someday you might not avoid acting like this, so always act within the basis of the rules, do not run after power and gain or curry favor with people.

"Life, death, calamity, or trouble—let them all be, and you enter the realm of buddhahood without leaving the realm of demons."

SERMONS

[166]

CASUAL ATTIRE

Assembly Chief Bian became leader and teacher of the community at a certain monastery on the holy Mount Lu. He always carried a bamboo staff and wore straw sandals. When he went to another monastery, the abbot, a monk named Hunrong, scolded him for his appearance, saying, "A teacher is a model and a guide for others; how can you avoid demeaning yourself when you behave like this?"

Bian laughed and said, "In human life it is considered pleasant to do as one wishes. What blame is on me in this regard?" He took up a brush, wrote a verse, and left.

That verse said:

Don't say I am destitute;
When the body is destitute, the Way is not.
These straw sandals are fierce as tigers,
This staff is lively as a dragon.

When thirsty, I drink the water of Chan,
When hungry, I eat chestnut thorn balls.
Folks with bronze skulls and iron foreheads
Are all on my mountain.

When that abbot read this he was ashamed.

MOON CAVE COLLECTION

[167]

SHOWBOATS

Master Bian said to Hunrong:

Statues of dragons cannot make rain; how can paintings of cakes satisfy hunger? Monks who have no real virtue within but outwardly rely on flowerly cleverness are like leaky boats brightly painted—if you put manikins in them and set them on dry ground they look fine, but once they go into the rivers and lakes, into the wind and waves, are they not in danger?

MOON CAVE COLLECTION

[168]

PERSONAL RESPONSIBILITY

Master Bian said:

The so-called chief elder teaches in the place of the Buddha. Essential to this is purification of oneself in dealing with the community, utmost honesty and sincerity in executing affairs, and care not to divide one's mind by choosing between gain and loss.

It is up to the individual to do this, so one should definitely act in this way. As for the matter of succeeding or otherwise, even the sages of old could not be sure—how can we force the issue?

MOON CAVE COLLECTION

[169]

UNIFORMS

Master Bian said:

When Fozhi was abbot at Xichan monastery, the monks strove for uniformity. Shuian alone, by nature empty and peaceful, took care of his body with utmost simplicity. He stood out in the crowd because of his appearance, yet he never gave it the slightest thought.

Fozhi scolded him, saying, "How can you be so offbeat?"

Shuian said, "It is not that I would not like to have a uniform, it is just that I am poor and do not have the wherewithal to make it. Had I the money, I too would like to make one or two suits of fine raiment and join the club. But since I am poor I cannot do anything about it."

Fozhi laughed at this. He knew Shuian could not be forced, so he let the matter drop.

MOON CAVE COLLECTION

[170]

THE DISCIPLINE OF AWARENESS

Master Fozhi said:

A swift horse can run fast, but does not dare to gallop freely because of the bit and halter. When petty people, while obstinate and belligerent, do not indulge their feelings, it is because of punishments and laws. When the flow of consciousness does not dare to cling to objects, this is the power of awareness.

If students have no awareness and are unreflective, they are like fast horses with no bit and bridle, like petty people without law. With what can they put an end to greed and craving and quell errant thoughts?

—INSTRUCTIONS TO A LAYMAN

[171]

FOUR LIMBS OF LEADERSHIP

Fozhi said to Shuian:

The body of leadership has four limbs: enlightenment and virtue, speech and action, humaneness and justice, etiquette and law. Enlightenment and virtue are the root of the teaching; humaneness and justice are the branches of the teaching. With no root, it is impossible to stand; with no branches it is impossible to be complete.

The ancient sages saw that students could not govern themselves, so they set up communities to settle them, and established leadership to direct them. Therefore the honor of the community is not for the leader, the plenitude of the necessities of life is not for the students—all of it is for the Way of enlightenment.

Therefore a good leader should honor first enlightenment and virtue, and be careful in speech and action. To be able to be a student, one should think first of goodness and right, and follow etiquette and law.

Thus the leadership could not stand but for the students, and the students cannot develop without the leadership. The leadership and the students are like the body and the arms, like the head and the feet. When great and small accord without opposition, they go by means of each other.

Therefore it is said, "Students keep the communities, the communities keep virtue." If the leadership has no virtue, then that community is on the verge of decline.

TRUE RECORD

[172]

THINKING OF TROUBLE

Master Shuian said:

The Book of Changes says, "An ideal person thinks of trouble and prevents it." Therefore people of ancient times thought of the great trouble of birth and death, and prevented it with the Way, until eventually the Way waxed great and was transmitted for a long time.

People nowadays think that the vast distances of the search for the Way do not compare to the urgent immediacy of material interests. Because of this they vie in their habits of useless extravagance, calculating down to a hair tip, keeping an eye on everything that passes in front of them, with opportunistic plans in their hearts.

Therefore one can serve as guides for the whole year round, much less for considerations of life and death. This is why students are getting worse day by day, the communities are degenerating day by day, their unifying principles decline day by day, until they have reached a state of prostration from which they can hardly be saved. We must be aware.

TRUE RECORD OF TWIN FORESTS

[173]

A DIRECT SHORTCUT

Shuian said:

In the old days when I was traveling in search of the Way, I saw Gaoan at an evening assembly. He said, "The ultimate Way is a direct shortcut not akin to human sentiments. Essentially you must make your heart sincere and your mind true. Do not be a servant of ostentation or partiality. Ostentation is near to deception, and when you are partial you are imbalanced—neither of these is meet for the ultimate Way."

I reflected on these words to myself, approached their reason, and then made up my mind to put them into practice. Then when I saw Fozhi, who was to become my teacher, for the first time my mind was opened up by great insight. Only then was I able to live up to the aspiration of my life pilgrimage.

—LETTER TO YUETANG

[174]

NIPPING IN THE BUD

Shuian said:

Wherever Yuetang was leader of a Chan community, he made the practice of the Way his own responsibility. He did not send out fundraisers, nor did he go visiting grandees. For the year's food he would just use what was obtained from the monastery property. He refused many monks who wished to go preach for alms.

Some said, "The Buddha instructed the mendicants to take their bowls and beg to support physical life—how can you stop them and not permit it?"

Yuetang said, "In the Buddha's day it was all right, but I am afraid if we do it today there will be those who are fond of gain, to the point where they will wind up selling themselves."

So I think that Yuetang's nipping in the bud was profoundly cutting and brilliantly clear. His realistic words are still in my ears. As I look upon the present day in this way, has it not gone even further than people selling themselves?

SERMONS

[175]

A THOUSAND DAYS OF EFFORT

Shuian said:

When the ancient worthies held leadership, they included themselves in carrying out the Way, never for a moment remiss or self-indulgent. In olden times the great Chan master Fenyang used to lament how deficient the imitation age was, and how students were difficult to teach, but his distinguished disciple Ciming said, "It is very easy—the trouble is that the teaching masters cannot guide well, that is all."

Fenyang said, "The ancients were pure and sincere, yet it was twenty or thirty years before they were successful in their accomplishment."

Ciming said, "This is not the talk of a sage philosopher. For someone who proceeds along the Path well, it is a matter of a thousand days of effort."

Some did not listen, saying that Ciming was talking nonsense.

Now the region where he worked was extremely cold, so Fenyang stopped the customary evening gathering. A foreign monk said to Fenyang (one version of the story has it that an Indian monk said this to him in a dream), "There are six great heroes in this assembly—why do you not teach?"

Before three years had passed, there were actually six people in Fenyang's group who realized enlightenment.

WEST LAKE ANNALS

[176]

TRADING OFF

Shuian said:

Recently we see leaders in various places with mind tricks to control their followers, while their followers serve the leaders with ulterior motives of influence, power, and profit. The leaders and followers trade off, above and below fooling each other. How can education prosper and communities flourish?

—A LETTER

[177]

MOVING PEOPLE

Shuian advised a disciple invited to speak at court:

To move people with words it is essential to be true and cutting. If your words are not true and to the point, the reaction they evoke will be shallow—who would take them to heart?

In olden times our spiritual ancestor Baiyun, sending his disciple Wuzu, our spiritual great-grandfather, to a teaching assignment, carefully admonished him in these terms:

"The Chan Way is in decline, and is in danger, like eggs piled up. Do not indulge in negligence and irresponsibility. That uselessly kills time and also undermines ultimate virtue. You should be easygoing and broad-minded, assess proper measures. Help people, thinking of the whole community. Bring out the truth to pay back your debt to the enlightened ones and spiritual forebears."

Who would not have been moved on hearing this?

You have recently been summoned to speak before the imperial court. This is truly auspicious for the teaching. You must humble yourself in honor of the Way, make help and salvation your heart. Do not cut yourself down by pride.

Since antiquity the sages have been modest and gentle, respectful and circumspect. They preserved themselves with complete virtue and did not consider authority or rank to be glorious. In this way they were able to purify a time, their fame resounding beautifully for ten thousand generations.

I think my days are not long, and we will not meet in person ever again. That is the reason for this urgent admonition.

—LETTER TO TOUZI

[178]

A RETIREMENT

Shuian was extraordinary from youth, and had great determination. He valued character and integrity, he did not go in for foolish waste, he did not pursue petty criticism. He was broad-minded and open-hearted. He put principles into practice in his actual behavior. Even when calamity and trouble were happening at once, he was never seen to be downcast.

Shuian was abbot at eight public monasteries in four cities. Wherever he went he toiled and labored with the establishment of practice of the Way at heart.

In 1178 he retired from Pure Kindness monastery on West Lake. He wrote:

> Six years of sprinkling and sweeping temples in the imperial
> capital;
> Tiles and pebbles turn into celestial chambers.
> Today the palace is done, and I return;
> A pure wind rises on all sides from the staff.

The gentry and commonfolk tried to get him to stay there, but he would not. He sailed a small boat up to Heavenly Brightness monastery in Longwater prefecture. Before long he appeared to be ill, took leave of the assembly, and announced his end.

—BIOGRAPHY

[179]

THE DERELICT AGE

Yuetang said:

In ancient times Baizhang, Chan Master of Great Wisdom, concerned about the haughtiness and laziness of monks of the age of dereliction, drew up special rules and guidelines to prevent this. According to capacity and potential, each was given a responsibility.

The leader lived in a ten-foot-square room, and the community lived in a common hall, arrayed in a strict order, with ten assembly chiefs. It was ordered like the civil government: the leaders brought up the essentials of the teaching, the subordinates took care of the many aspects of it, causing above and below to understand one another, like the body using the arms, the arms using the fingers— everyone followed.

Therefore those of our predecessors who followed this tradition and received its help and worked carefully to carry it out could do so because the remaining influence of the sages of old had not died out.

Recently we see the Chan communities declining and changing.

The students value talent and demean perseverance in practice, they like the ephemeral and the ostentatious and slight the true and the simple. Over the days and months they get into a decadent trend.

At first it is just taking things easy for a time, but after long indulgence and habituation people think it is natural to be this way, and do not consider it wrong or contrary to principle.

Now the leader timidly fears the subordinates, while the subordinates keep a watchful eye on the superior. When the leader is relaxed the subordinates speak sweetly and grovel for favor, but when they find an opening they scheme treacherously to encompass his downfall. Those who win are considered wise and those who lose are considered foolish—they no longer question the order of nobility and meanness, or the principles of right and wrong. What one has done, another will imitate; what is said below is followed above, what is done before is continued after.

Unless teachers of great sagacity mount the power of will and pile up a hundred years of effective work, this decadence and stagnation cannot be reformed.

—LETTER TO MASTER SHUN

[180]

WATERING MELONS AT MIDDAY

Yuetang held leadership longest at Pure Kindness monastery. Someone said to him, "You have been practicing the Way here for years, but I have never heard that you have had any successors among your disciples. Are you not letting your teacher down?"

Yuetang did not reply.

Another day that person repeated the question, and Yuetang said, "Have you not heard of the story of the man in ancient times who planted melons? He liked melons very much, and he watered them at midday in midsummer. As a result, the melons rotted where they lay.

"What does this mean? It is not that his liking for the melons was not earnest, but that his watering was not timely, and by that he ruined them.

"Old teachers in various places support monks without observing whether their work on the Way is fulfilled within them, or if their capacity is broad and far-reaching. They just want to speed up their careers, but when you carefully examine their morals, they are corrupt, and when you look into their words and actions, they are contradictory. What they call impartial and correct is biased and prejudicial.

"Is this not a matter of liking that goes beyond measure? This is just like watering melons at midday. I am deeply afraid the knowing would laugh, so I do not do it."

NORTH MOUNTAIN ANNALS

[181]

A TESTIMONIAL

Xuetang said:

Astronomer Huang Luzhi once said, "Chan Master Huanglong Huinan was profound in mind and generous in consideration, and he was not influenced by any thing or being. In all his life he never had any pretentions. Among his disciples there were those who had never seen him joyful or angry in his life. He treated everyone with equal sincerity, even servants and workers. Therefore he was able to cause the way of Ciming to flourish without raising his voice or changing his expression. This was not without reason."

—ENGRAVED ON A STONE AT HUANGLONG

[182]

A DEMONSTRATION

Yuetang said:

In 1129, when Zhong Xiang rebelled in Liyang, Chan Master Wenshu Dao was in danger. When the power of the rebels had grown to full force, his disciples fled, but the master said, "Can calamity be avoided?" Thus remaining resolutely in his room, the master was eventually killed by plunderers.

The lay disciple Wugou wrote an afterword to the collection of the master's sayings:

"Liking life and disliking death is the ordinary feeling for human beings. Only the complete human beings realize they are originally unborn, and while alive have no attachment, and comprehend that they never perish, so though they die they have no fear. Therefore they can face the times of tribulation of death and birth without wavering in their determination.

"The master was one such person. Because the master's enlightened virtue and fidelity to truth were worthy to teach the communities and set an example for later generations, therefore he was entitled Zhengdao, True Guide. He was a successor of Chan Master Fojian."

RECORDS OF GREAT MASTER HUI OF LUSHAN

[183]

A DIAGNOSIS

Master Xinwen Fen said:

Many are the monks who develop sickness because of Chan. Those whose sickness is in their eyes and ears think staring and glaring, inclining the ear and nodding, are Chan. Those whose sickness is in the mouth and tongue think crazy talk and wild shouting are Chan. Those whose sickness is in their hands and feet think walking back and forth and pointing east and west are Chan. Those whose sickness is in their hearts and guts think that investigating the mystery, studying the marvel, transcending feelings, and detaching from views are Chan.

Speaking from the standpoint of reality, all of these are sicknesses. Only a true teacher can clearly discern the subtle indications, knowing at a glance if people understand or not, discerning whether they have arrived or not, the moment they enter the door.

After that, using awl and needle, the teacher frees them from subtle entrapments, bears down on their sticking points, tests whether they are true or false, and determines if they are bogus or genuine, all this without sticking to one method or being unaware of when to change and pass on, to cause them eventually to walk in the realm of peace, happiness, and freedom from care, before the teacher finally rests.

TRUE RECORD

[184]

THE BLUE CLIFF RECORD

Xinwen said:

The Way that is specially transmitted outside of doctrine is utterly simple and quintessential. From the beginning there is no other discussion; our predecessors carried it out without doubt and kept it without deviation.

During the Tianxi era of the Song dynasty (1012–1022), the Chan master Xuedou, using his talents of eloquence and erudition, with beautiful ideas in kaleidoscopic display, seeking freshness and polishing skill, followed the example of Fenyang in making verses on ancient stories, to catch and control the students of the time. The manner of Chan went through a change from this point on.

Then during the Xuanho era (1119–1125) Yuanwu also set forth his own ideas on the stories and verses from Xuedou, and from then on the collection was known as *The Blue Cliff Record.* At that time, the perfectly complete masters of the age, like Wayfarer Ning, Huanglong Sixin, Lingyuan, and Fojian, could not contradict what he said, so new students of later generations prized his words and would recite them by day and memorize them by night, calling this the highest study. None realized this was wrong, and unfortunately students' meditational skills deteriorated.

In the beginning of the Shaoxing era (1131–1163), Yuanwu's enlightened successor Miaoxi went into eastern China and saw that the Chan students there were recalcitrant, pursuing the study of this book to such an extent that their involvement became an evil. So he broke up the woodblocks of *The Blue Cliff Record* and analyzed its explanations, thus to get rid of illusions and rescue those who were floundering, stripping away excess and setting aside exaggeration, demolishing the false and revealing the true, dealing with the text in a special way. Students gradually began to realize their error, and did not idolize it anymore.

So if not for Miaoxi's high illumination and far sight, riding on the power of the vow of compassion to save an age of dereliction from its ills, the Chan communities would be in peril.

—LETTER TO ZHANG ZISHAO

[185]

NO FIXED CLASSES

Chan Master Choan said to Prime Minister Yu Yunwen:

The Great Way is clear and open—no one is originally either foolish or wise on the Way. It is like the case of certain ancients who started out plowing and fishing but became advisors to emperors— how could this be tried with fixed classes of intelligence?

However, it requires a certain personal power to participate.

EXTENSIVE RECORD

[186]

LEADERSHIP TRAINING

Choan said:

To train yourself to deal with the assembly, it is necessary to use wisdom. To dispel delusion and remove sentiments, you must first be aware. If you turn away from awareness and mix with the dusts, then your mind will be enshrouded. When wisdom and folly are not distinguished, matters get tangled up.

—LETTER TO A MONASTERY SUPERINTENDENT

[187]

PENETRATING OBSTRUCTION BY REASON

Choan said:

When Fojian was the leader of the Great Peace community, Gaoan was in charge of taking care of guests. Gaoan was young and high-spirited, and he looked down on everyone else, there being few who met with his approval.

One day at the time of the noon meal, as Gaoan sounded the call he saw a worker placing food before Fojian in a special vessel. Gaoan left the hall, announcing in a loud voice, "If the teacher of five hundred monks acts like this, how can he be an example for later students?"

Fojian pretended not to see or hear this.

Then when Fojian left the hall, Gaoan looked and found that the special vessel contained pickled vegetables, for it turned out that Fojian had a chronic stomach ailment and did not partake of oil, which was ordinarily used in the monastic food for nutrition.

Gaoan was ashamed, and went to the leader's room to announce his resignation.

Fojian said, "What you said was quite right. But it just happens that I am sick, that is all. I have heard that a sage said, "Penetrate all obstructions by reason." Because what I eat is not better, I am not doubted by the community. Your will and temper are clear and far-reaching; someday you will be a cornerstone of the source teaching. Don't let this stick in your mind."

When Fojian moved, Gaoan went elsewhere, and later became a successor of Foyan.

[188]

TEACHING GOVERNMENT OFFICIALS

Choan said:

When discoursing on the Way to government officials, in dialogue you must strip away their intellectual understanding and not let them settle into clichés. It is just essential to purely clarify the one experience of transcendence.

The late teacher Miaoxi once said, "When you meet grandees, answer if they ask questions, otherwise refrain." And one must be such a person too, to be of assistance to the times on hearing such words, so as not to injure the body of living Buddhism.

—LETTER TO A CHAN ABBOT

[189]

THE PERIL OF LEADERSHIP

Choan said:

Fine land nurtures beings well, a benevolent ruler nurtures people well. Nowadays many who are known as leaders do not take the people to heart, instead giving precedence to their own desires. They do not like hearing good words, and do like to cover up their faults, indulging in improper practices and vainly pleasing themselves for a time. When petty people take to the likes and dislikes of the leaders, is the path of leadership not in peril?

—LETTER TO A CHAN ELDER

[190]

KILLED BUT NOT SHAMED

Choan said to Yean:

The Lay Master of the Purple Cliff said, "My former teacher Mi-aoxi makes virtue, integrity, and courage his priorities in everyday life. He can be befriended but not estranged, approached but not pressed, killed but not shamed. His abode is not extravagant, his food is not rich. He faces the troubles and problems of life and death as if they were nothing. He is truly an example of what is meant by the saying, 'The sword of the great smith is hard to clash with.' The only worry is unforeseen injury."

Ultimately it turned out as the lay master said.

ANNALS OF PHANTOM HERMITAGE

[191]

CHOOSING ASSISTANTS

Choan said:

As a leader, Ye-an comprehends the processes of the human mind and is aware of the great body of the community. He once said to me, "To be the host in a place you must choose people of determination and action for assistants. They are like a comb for hair, a mirror for a face—then what is beneficial and what is deleterious, what is fine and what is unseemly, cannot be hidden."

ANNALS OF PHANTOM HERMITAGE

[192]

SUPERFICIALITY AND DEPTH

Choan said:

Latter-day students are superficial, uselessly valuing their ears while slighting their eyes—ultimately none of them can fathom the profound mystery.

Therefore it is said, "No matter how high the mountain, on it are tiers of crags and clusters of bamboo; no matter how deep the ocean, in it are fonds and currents."

If you want to study the Great Way, the essence is in investigating its heights and depths. After that you can illumine the obscure subtleties, and adapt responsively with no limit.

—LETTER TO A CHAN ELDER

[193]
THE MIND OF SAINTS AND SAGES

Choan said to Cabinet Minister Yu:

The mind of saints and sages is tolerant and easygoing, still their reason is clear. They are serene and aloof, yet their deeds are evident.

Whatever they do, they do not expect hasty completion, and are willing to persevere long. They do not agree to insistence on advancement, but they approve of striving to approach the Way. Those who infer the will of saints and sages from this and then maintain it over a thousand generations will be thus.

ANNALS OF PHANTOM HERMITAGE

[194]
HISTORY REVIEW

Cabinet Minister Yu said:

Before Bodhidharma, the founder of Chan, there was no such thing as the Chan abbacy, the institutionalization of the living exemplar of Buddhism. Bodhidharma's descendants, carrying out the Way in response to the world, were pressed and could not avoid this development, but still they lived in simple huts, enough for shelter from wind and rain, and took food enough to appease hunger. Suffering bitter hardships, they were haggard and emaciated; there were those who couldn't stand their misery, and kings and important men wanted to see them but could not. Therefore, all that they set up was free and unfettered, startling the heavens and shaking the earth.

In later generations they weren't like that. In high buildings, with spacious rooms, fine raiment and rich food, they got whatever they wanted. At this, the cohorts of the evil one began to greatly affect their minds; they lingered at the gates of temporal power, wagging their tails begging for pity, in extreme cases taking by trickery and usurping by status, like stealing gold in broad daylight, not knowing there is such a thing as cause and effect in the world.

The letters of Chan Master Miaoxi bring out everyone's current mental habits, not leaving so much as a wisp, like the legendary pond water that enables one to see the internal organs clearly. If you can receive them with faith and put them into practice, what's the need to specially seek Buddhism besides?

—SEEN ON A STONE ENGRAVING

[195]

THE REVIVAL OF THE LINJI SCHOOL OF CHAN

Cabinet Minister Yu said to Choan:

In the old days Miaoxi revived the Way of Linji in the autumn of its withering and decline; but by nature he esteemed humility and emptiness. He never flaunted or advertised his insight and reason, and never in his life did he run to people of authority and power, and he did not grab profit and support.

Miaoxi once said, "Myriad affairs cannot be accomplished by taking it easy, nor can they be maintained with a haughty attitude. It seems that there is that which is beneficial to the times and helpful to the people, and that which is in error and has no merit. If you indulge the latter and haughtily take it easy, then you will fail." I have taken these words to heart, and they have become a lesson for my whole life.

—RECORDS OF AN ATTENDANT

[196]

CUSTOM

Chan Master Mian said:

The rise and decline of Chan communities is in their conduct and principles; the refinement or badness of students is in their customs and habits. Even if the ancients lived in nests and caves, drinking from streams and eating from the trees, to practice this in the present would not be suitable. Even if people of the present dress and eat richly, to practice this in ancient times would not have been suitable. Is it anything else but a matter of habituation?

What people see day and night as the ordinary, they inevitably think everything in the world should properly be that way. One day when they are driven to give this up and go to something else, they not only doubt and disbelieve, they probably will not go along.

When things are considered in this light, it is clear that people feel secure in what they are used to, and are startled by what they have never witnessed. This is their ordinary condition, so why wonder about it?

—LETTER TO COUNCILLOR SHI

[197]

THE GOOD AND THE CORRUPT

Mian said:

My late teacher Yingan used to say, "The good and the corrupt are opposite—we cannot but distinguish them. The good maintain truth, virtue, benevolence, and justice to take their stand. The corrupt are devoted to power and profit, and do things by flattery and deception.

"The good accomplish their will and always put into practice what they learn. The corrupt, occupying rank, mostly indulge their selfishness, jealous of the intelligent and envious of the able; they indulge their cravings and grasp for material possessions, and there is no telling how far they will go.

"Therefore, when there are good people there, a community flourishes; and when corrupt people are employed, then the community declines. If there is even one corrupt person present, it is surely impossible for there to be peace and tranquility."

—LETTER TO A TEACHER

[198]

THREE DON'TS

Mian said:

In leadership there are three don'ts: when there is much to do, don't be afraid; when there is nothing to do, don't be hasty; and don't talk about opinions of right and wrong.

A leader who succeeds in these three things won't be confused or deluded by external objects.

—AN ATTENDANT'S RECORD

[199]

WOLVES IN SHEEP'S CLOTHING

Mian said:

When mendicants whose conduct in everyday life is bad and who have a history of being no good are known as such in the community, this is not worrisome; but when those who are inwardly not good are called sages by the people, that is truly worrisome.

—A LETTER

[200]

THE REVEALING MIRROR OF TRUTH

Mian said to Shuian:

When people revile you, you should accept it docilely. One should not lightly hear the words of others and then arbitrarily set forth narrow views. For the most part, opportunistic flatterers have cliques, perverted cleverness has many methods: those with prejudice in their hearts like to publicize their private wishes, and those who create jealousy and envy unilaterally negate common discussion and consensus.

On the whole, the aims of these people are narrow and restricted, their vision is dim and short, they think those with individualistic differences must be extraordinary and consider those who undermine open discussion to be outstanding.

However, as long as you know that what you are doing is right after all, and the vilification itself is in them, then over a long time it will become clear of itself; you don't have to specially say it, and you don't have to insist on your rightness and offend people.

—A LETTER

[201]

MAKING CHOICES

Master Zide Hui said:

In general, when people are sincere and headed in the right direction, they can still be employed even if they are dull. If they are flatterers with ulterior motives, they are ultimately harmful even if they are smart.

On the whole, if their psychological orientation is not correct, people are unworthy of establishment in positions of service and leadership even if they have talent and ability.

—LETTER TO MASTER JIANTANG

[202]

LOSS OF ORDER

Zide said:

The Chan Master of Great Wisdom Baizhang Huaihai, (720–814, one of the founders of the Chan commune system) specially established pure rules to help save mendicants in the age of spiritual dereliction from the corruption into which they had fallen. Thenceforth the sages of the past followed and applied them, carrying them out seriously in practice. There was teaching, there was order, there was consistency.

At the end of the Shaoxing era (ca. 1160), there were still mature people in the communities who could keep the traditional laws and didn't presume to depart from them for a minute. In recent years they have lost the order of the school, and the fabric of the order is dissolute or incoherent.

Therefore it is said, "Lift up one net and a multitude of eyes open; neglect one opportunity and myriad affairs collapse." It has just about gotten to where the order is no longer working and the communities are no longer flourishing.

But the ancients embodied the fundamental, whereby they made the outgrowths straight. They just worried that the measures of the teaching were not strictly kept rather than worrying that students wouldn't reach where they were.

What they considered right was right in its impartiality, but leaders in various places nowadays mix partiality in with impartiality, using the outgrowths to direct the root. Those above like wealth without practicing the Way, while those below covet wealth without practicing duty. When above and below are confused and disordered, guest and host are mixed up, how can we have the wearers of the patched garment turn toward truth and have the communities flourish?

—LETTER TO MINISTER YU

[203]

MAKING DISTINCTIONS

Zide said:

Before a fine jade is cut, it is the same as tile or stone; before a good steed is raced, it is mixed in with nags. When cut and polished, raced and tested, then jade and stone, charger and nag are distinguished.

Now mendicants with sagacity and virtue have not yet been employed, they are mixed in with the crowd. Ultimately how can they be distinguished?

It is essential that highly perceptive people be elected by public consensus, entrusted with the affairs of office, tested for talent and ability, judged by accomplishment of tasks. Thus they will prove to be far different from the mediocre.

—LETTER TO HUOAN

[204]

SELECTING BUDDHAS

Master Huoan Ti first studied with Si-an Yuan Budai at Huguo monastery on the famous and holy Mount Tiantai. In an address in the teaching hall, Si-an quoted Layman Pang's verse on "Selection of Buddhas." When he came to the line "This is the place for selecting buddhas," Si-an shouted. At that moment Huoan was greatly enlightened.

He composed a verse on his realization:

Where the assessment culminates, you see the subject;
At the end of the road, you enter the examination place.

Pick up a hairtip—wind and rain are swift.
No graduation party this time.

After this he secluded himself on Mount Tiantai. The deputy premier, Mr. Qian, admired his character, and insisted that he respond to the needs of the world by becoming a public teacher at a certain monastery. When Huoan heard of this, he said, "I can't hang out mutton and sell dog flesh," and disappeared in the night.

[205]

RECOGNITION

In the beginning of the Jiandao era (1165–1174), Xiatang was resident master at a public monastery when he saw Huoan's eulogy on a portrait of Yuantong:

> Not resting on the fundamental, he disturbs sentient beings
> Looking up at him, gazing on him, with eyes as if blind.
> The scenery of the Capital City extends through all time—
> Who walks groping along a wall?

Xiatang was startled and delighted. He said, "I didn't think Si-an had such successors." Then Xiatang looked for Huoan all over and finally found him in Jiangxin. He invited him from among the crowd to fill the position of the first in the assembly.

RUSTIC ANNALS OF TIANTAI

[206]

FULFILLMENT OF CONDITIONS

In the beginning of the Jiandao era, Huoan drifted over to see Xiatang at Tiger Hill, where the monastics and lay folk of the metropolitan area heard of his lofty manner, prompting them to go to the prefectural capital to nominate him to be resident teacher at Jiaobao temple in the city.

When Huoan heard of this, he said, "My late teacher Si-an instructed me, 'Another day, meeting old age, stay.' Now it seems that this has been fulfilled." So he gladly answered the request to stay there. It turned out that the old name of Jiaobao temple was Lao-shouan, Old Age Hermitage.

TIGER HILL ANNALS

[207]

AN IMPROMPTU TALK

After Huoan had entered Jiaobao temple, a patron requested him to give an impromptu talk.

He said, "The Way is constant and unchanging; things deteriorate and must change. In ancient times the great Chan masters took lessons from the study of antiquity, considering what was appropriate or not, holding by the middle way, working to unify people's minds, with enlightenment as the guide. That is why their simple manner, cool as ice, has not disappeared to this very day.

"In terms of the Chan school, even getting understanding before anything is said still cramps the manner of our religion, and even discerning clearly on hearing a phrase buries the enlightened ones.

"Even though it is so, 'Going, I reach the water's end; sitting, I watch when the clouds rise.' "

Thenceforth monks, nuns, and lay folk rejoiced in what they had never heard before, and a veritable city of people took refuge with him.

[208]

GOVERNING WILD FOXES

Once Huoan was teaching publicly, gentry and common people came in droves to take refuge with him. A mendicant relayed this to Tiger Hill, where Xiatang said, "That mountain savage is using blind man's Chan to govern that bunch of wild fox ghosts."

When Huoan heard of this, he replied with a poem:

> You may dislike a mountain savage
> Leading a group, guiding an order, as though without doing so

Transcending convention, holding up a broom handle upside
down
Blind man's Chan governs the wild fox monks.

Xiatang just laughed.

RECORD OF THINGS HEARD

[209]

BALANCING

Huoan said to Minister of State Ceng Tai:
The essential point in studying the Way is like balancing stones to
weigh things: just get them even, that is all—it won't work if one side
is too heavy. Pushing ahead and lagging behind are both the same in
being one-sided. When you realize this you can study the way.

—A LETTER

[210]

TALENT AND CAPACITY

Chan Master Xiatang Yuan said to Huoan:
People's talent and capacity are naturally great or small, for these
things cannot be taught. Those whose paper is small cannot wrap up
large objects; those whose rope is short cannot draw from a deep well.
An owl can catch a louse and see a hair by night, but when the sun
comes out in daytime, it irritates the owl's eyes so much that it cannot even see a hill. It seems that the distribution is set.

ANNALS OF TIGER HILL

[211]

A MOMENT IN HISTORY

Chan Master Jiantang Ji lived on Mount Guan in Fanyang for some
twenty years, making soup of wild herbs and millet for his meals; he
had utterly severed his mind from glory and success.
Once when he went down the mountain he heard the sound of
weeping by the road. Feeling pity, Jiantang went to inquire. It turned

out that there was a whole family cold and sick; two members of the family had just died, and they were so poor they had nothing in which to put the bodies.

Jiantang made a special trip to town to obtain coffins to bury them. Everyone in the village was moved.

The minister, Mr. Li, said to the grandees, "Old Ji of our locality is a mendicant imbued with the Way; he bestows kindness as well as material goods. How can we let him stay forever on Mount Guan?"

At that time Military Inspector Wang, who was making a tour of the various highways, reported this in Jiujiang, and the district governor, Mr. Lin Shuda, had the teaching seat at Yuantong vacated and invited Jiantang there.

When Jiantang heard this order, he said, "My Way is going into effect," and gladly took up his staff and went there. To expound the Teaching, he said, "Yuantong doesn't open a fresh herb shop—to each I just sell a dead cat head. I don't know who doesn't think or figure—upon partaking the whole body runs with cold sweat."

The monastics and lay people were startled and considered this unusual. This teaching center now flourished greatly.

RECORDS OF LAZY HERMITAGE

[212]

SHARING

Jiantang said:

When the people of old cultivated themselves and conquered their minds, they shared the Way with others. When they undertook tasks and accomplished works, they shared the achievement with others. When the Way was accomplished and achievement revealed, they shared the fame with others. This is why nothing in the Way was not clear, no accomplishment was not consummated, no fame was not glorious.

People nowadays are not like that. They are exclusively concerned about their own ways, and just worry that others will surpass them. Also they cannot pursue the good and work for what is right, because they are aggrandizing themselves. Concentrating on their own achievement, they don't want others to have it.

Also they cannot trust in the wise or get along with the able, because they magnify themselves. They are solely concerned with their own fame, not sharing it with others. They cannot guide people with humility, because they consider themselves successful.

Therefore this Path cannot avoid obscurity, their achievement cannot avoid loss, their fame cannot avoid dishonor. This is the great distinction between students of ancient and modern times.

[213]

GROWTH

Jiantang said:

Studying the Way is like planting a tree—if you cut it just when it branches out, it can be used for firewood; if you cut it when it's about to reach full growth, it can be used for rafters; if you cut it when it's somewhat stronger, it can be used for beams; and if you cut it when it's old and huge, it can be used for pillars.

Could it not be that when you take the attainment over the long run the profit is greater?

Therefore the people of old saw to it that their Way was sure and great and not narrow, their determination and will was far-reaching and profound and not shortsighted, and their words were lofty and not mean.

Although they met with the contradictions of the times and experienced the extremes of starvation and cold, perishing in the mountains and valleys, because of the residual power of their bequest, spanning hundreds and thousands of years, people of later times still transmit it as religious law.

If in the past they had been narrow in their Way, opportunistic in admitting people, seeking rapprochement for immediate ambitions, talking slavishly, serving authority, their profit would have ended at glory in one lifetime. How could there have been enrichment left over to reach later generations?

—LETTER TO PRIME MINISTER LI

[214]

A SUCCESSOR TO THE ANCIENTS

Mr. Wu, the imperial official, said to Jiantang:

The ancients calmed their minds and obliterated their self-consciousness in mountains and valleys, drinking from streams and eating from trees, in the manner of those who have absolutely no thought of success and fame. Yet the time came when they were called upon by emperors.

They hid their light and concealed their tracks in the mills and at other menial chores. From the beginning they had no thought of glory or achievement, in the end they stood in the ranks of the transmitters of the lamp.

Therefore, when attained in unminding, the Path is great and the virtue universal; when sought with ambition, the fame is ignoble and the aspiration narrow.

But your measure and capacity are stable and far-reaching, succeeding in the footsteps of the ancients. Thus you could live on Mount Guan for seventeen years and finally become a good vessel of truth in the community.

Monks of the present have nothing to concentrate on within, while outside they pursue distracting frills. They have little foresight, and no sense of the great body. Therefore they cannot help spiritual teaching, and thus they are a long way from you.

RECOLLECTIONS OF ATTENDANT GAO

[215]

THE ORDINARY CONDITION OF HUMAN BEINGS

Jiantang said:

It is the ordinary condition of human beings that few are able to be free from delusion. Usually they are enshrouded by their beliefs, obstructed by their doubts, slighted by their contempt, drowned by their likes.

Once belief is biased, when people hear words they do not think about truth, until eventually it comes to words that exceed what is appropriate. When doubt is extreme, people do not listen to words even if they are true, until there is hearing that misses truth.

When people disrespect others, they lose sight of their worthy qualities. When people like something, they will keep around those who should be abandoned. These are all indulgence in private feelings without considering reason, eventually forgetting the Way of enlightened ones, losing the heart of the community.

So what ordinary feelings take lightly is what sages take seriously. An ancient worthy said, "Those who plan for what is ahead first check what is near at hand. Those who strive for the great must be careful about the small."

It should be a matter of a wide range of choice and careful use therein; it is surely not a matter of admiring the high and liking the unusual.

—LETTER TO MR. WU

[216]

A CHAN MASTER

Jiantang was pure and clear, and even-minded. He reached people with kindness and benevolence. If students made small mistakes, he would cover for them and protect them to develop their virtue. He once said of this, "Who has no faults? Excellence is a matter of reforming them."

When Jiantang was living on Mount Guan in Fanyang, once in the dead of winter it rained and snowed continuously so long that he ran out of food, yet the master behaved as if he weren't aware of it. He made a poem on this occasion that said:

The hearth's without fire, the knapsack empty,
The snow is like apricot blossoms falling at year's end.
Patch robe over my head, burning scraps of wood,
I am not conscious of my body in peaceful quietude.
In daily life I go on the Way by myself,
Not rushing after glory and fame.

On the day he answered the request to be teaching master of Yuantong monastery on holy Mount Lu, he came with only a staff and straw sandals. Those who saw him looked refreshed and felt relieved. The governor of the Nine Rivers region, Mr. Lin Shuda, said when he saw him, "This is a bridge of Buddhism."

Thenceforth his name was honored in all quarters. His behavior truly had the character of the masters of old. On the day he died, even the monastery servants and workers wept.

ZEN ESSENCE
The Science of Freedom

INTRODUCTION

Zen is the essence of Buddhism, freedom is the essence of Zen. At its simplest and most profound level, Zen is purely devoted to liberating the hidden potential of the human mind. The Chinese Zen master Ying-an said, "Zen living is a most direct shortcut, not requiring the exertion of the slightest bit of strength to attain enlightenment and master Zen right where you are."

The freedom that Zen proposes is not remote, but right in this world. It does not require anything extraneous, but can be put into practice in the midst of normal occupations and activities. It is applicable immediately, and develops naturally. Dahui, another great Chinese Zen master, said, "To attain Zen enlightenment it is not necessary to give up family life, quit your job, become a vegetarian, practice asceticism, or flee to a quiet place."

Yet even while effectively *in* the world, Zen freedom is not essentially *of* the world; it is not the same as a freedom that can be instituted or granted by a social or political system. According to Zen teaching, freedom that depends on things of the world can be undermined, and freedom that can be granted can be taken away. Aiming for freedom that cannot be undermined and cannot be taken away, Zen liberation reaches out from within. By its very nature it cannot enter in from outside the individual mind.

Zen liberation is essentially achieved by special knowledge and perception that penetrate the root of experience. This knowledge and perception free the mind from the arbitrary limitations imposed on it by conditioning, thus awakening dormant capacities of consciousness. Dahui explained:

> The realm of the enlightened is not an external realm with manifest characteristics; buddhahood is the realm of the sacred knowledge found in oneself. You do not need paraphernalia, practices, or realizations to attain it. What you need is to clean

out the influences of the psychological afflictions connected with the external world that have been accumulating in your psyche since beginningless time.

Zen cleans the mind for inner perception of its own essential nature; then inner perception of mind's essential purity enables one to remain spontaneously poised and free in all circumstances, so that one may go on clarifying daily experience. The old Japanese Zen master Bunan said,

> People think it is hard to perceive the essential human nature, but in reality it is neither difficult nor easy. Nothing at all can adhere to this essential nature. It is a matter of responding to right and wrong while remaining detached from right and wrong, living in the midst of passions yet being detached from passions, seeing without seeing, hearing without hearing, acting without acting, seeking without seeking.

Enlightened Zen freedom, being in the world yet not of the world, is traditionally likened to a lotus flower, rooted in the mud while blossoming over the water. It is not a negative detachment but a balance of independence and openness. Therefore it is not realized by formal effort but by direct experience and unfolding of the essence of the human mind.

The paradox of Zen freedom is that it is present and available, yet somehow elusive when deliberately sought. It responds to what Bunan called "seeking without seeking." Ying-an put it this way: "Zen has nothing to grab on to. When people who study Zen don't see it, that is because they approach too eagerly."

For this reason, classical Zen books are not manuals of doctrine or ritual to be followed as systematic courses of Zen that are supposed to lead one and all step by step to the inner sanctum. They are written to awaken sleeping dimensions of consciousness, not to inculcate ideas or beliefs.

Countless systems have been devised to approach Zen since the disappearance of the original schools, but none of them is complete or final, and none of them lasts. This is simply the nature of Zen, which speaks to the personal experience of each individual and each time. It is also true of all Buddhist schools, as their scriptures attest. Zen master Dahui said, "If you think there are any verbal formulations that are special mysterious secrets to be transmitted, this is not real Zen."

Zen adds extra dimension to consciousness in both rational and intuitive modes. It does so by deepening and sharpening thought, and by fostering a special kind of insight or knowledge more subtle than thought. Since it is axiomatic that this kind of mental development ultimately cannot be given and cannot be taken, Zen learning needs its own approach.

The essence of the Zen approach is deceptively simple, as explained by the Chinese master Yuanwu: "Set aside all the slogans you have learned and all the intellectual views that stick to your flesh." Zen is the freshest essence of mind, already gone by the time it becomes an idea. The Zen meaning of literature is impact, not ideology.

Because of the very nature of Zen, its essence is neither of the East nor of the West. The classical Zen masters have said that this essence does not belong to any particular culture or philosophy, let alone any particular social class or group. A Zen poet remarked, "On whose door does the moonlight not shine?" It is at the source of ideas, not a product of ideas; and this is what distinguishes the essence of Zen from all derivative philosophy, religion, art, and science.

There are many ways of entering into Zen, and the possibilities that emerge from Zen are even richer. This volume is a collection of hints on realizing and living the essence of Zen, drawn from the works of the greatest Zen masters of ancient China. Translated from the original Chinese records, these unique writings represent the most open and direct forms of instruction in the entire Zen canon. They are not religion or philosophy but a practical psychology of liberation.

This type of Zen literature has been public for centuries and can be enjoyed by anyone. It requires consciousness alone and does not depend on a particular background in Zen Buddhism or any form of Asian culture. It applies directly to the relationship between mind and culture itself, whatever that culture may be. Therefore it relates immediately to the way in which the world is experienced and life is lived, wherever one may be. This is the universal aspect of Zen, the essence of Zen.

NOTES ON SOURCES

The translations in this volume are from standard collections in the Zen portion of the Chinese Buddhist canon. The Zen masters quoted lived from the eighth to the fourteenth centuries. Further teachings of some of these masters, especially the earlier ones, are recorded in the translation and appendices of *The Blue Cliff Record* (in Volume Five of this series). The commentaries in the latter Zen classic are those of Yuanwu, who is also one of the major figures in the literature translated in the present volume.

Virtually all of the famed letters of Dahui, another important teacher in this collection, are in J. C. Cleary's translation *Swampland Flowers* (New York: Grove, 1977). A considerable amount of other material by and about Dahui is also translated in my *Zen Lessons: The Art of Leadership* (in this volume), in which Dahui is known by the epithet Miaoxi. This book also contains more on the teachings of some of the other Zen masters in *Zen Essence.*

Zen Master Mazu

The Normal Mind

The Way does not require cultivation—just don't pollute it.

What is pollution? As long as you have a fluctuating mind fabricating artificialities and contrivances, all of this is pollution.

If you want to understand the Way directly, the normal mind is the Way.

What I mean by the normal mind is the mind without artificiality, without subjective judgments, without grasping or rejection.

The Root

The founders of Zen said that one's own essence is inherently complete. Just don't linger over good or bad things—that is called practice of the Way. To grasp the good and reject the bad, to contemplate emptiness and enter concentration, is all in the province of contrivance—and if you go on seeking externals, you get further and further estranged.

Just end the mental objectivization of the world. A single thought of the wandering mind is the root of birth and death in the world. Just don't have a single thought and you'll get rid of the root of birth and death.

The Oceanic Reflection

Human delusions of time immemorial, deceit, pride, deviousness, and conceit, have conglomerated into one body. That is why scripture says that this body is just made of elements, and its appearance and disappearance is just that of elements, which have no identity. When successive thoughts do not await one another, and each thought dies peacefully away, this is called absorption in the oceanic reflection.

DELUSION AND ENLIGHTENMENT

Delusion means you are not aware of your own fundamental mind; enlightenment means you realize your own fundamental essence. Once enlightened, you do not become deluded anymore.

If you understand mind and objects, then false conceptions do not arise; when false conceptions do not arise, this is acceptance of the beginninglessness of things. You have always had it, and you have it now—there is no need to cultivate the Way and sit in meditation.

ZEN MASTER DAZHU

ARTIFICIAL ZEN

You are luckily all right by yourself, yet you struggle artificially. Why do you want to put on fetters and go to prison? You are busy every day claiming to study Zen, learn the Way, and interpret Buddhism, but this alienates you even further. It is just chasing sound and form. When will you ever stop?

YOUR TREASURE

My teacher said to me, "The treasure house within you contains everything, and you are free to use it. You don't need to seek outside."

Zen Master Linji

True Perception and Understanding

People who study Buddhism should seek real, true perception and understanding for now. If you attain real, true perception and understanding, birth and death don't affect you—you are free to go or stay. You needn't seek wonders, for wonders come of themselves.

Self-confidence

What I point out to you is only that you shouldn't allow yourselves to be confused by others. Act when you need to, without further hesitation or doubt.

People today can't do this—what is their affliction? Their affliction is in their lack of self-confidence.

If you do not spontaneously trust yourself sufficiently, you will be in a frantic state, pursuing all sorts of objects and being changed by those objects, unable to be independent.

Buddha Within

There is no stability in the world; it is like a house on fire. This is not a place where you can stay for a long time. The murderous demon of impermanence is instantaneous, and it does not choose between the upper and lower classes, or between the old and the young.

If you want to be no different from the buddhas and Zen masters, just don't seek externally.

The pure light in a moment of awareness in your mind is the Buddha's essence within you. The nondiscriminating light in a moment of awareness in your mind is the Buddha's wisdom within you. The undifferentiated light in a moment of awareness in your mind is the Buddha's manifestation within you.

No Obsessions

It is most urgent that you seek real, true perception and understanding, so you can be free in the world and not be confused by ordinary spiritualists.

It is best to have no obsessions. Just don't be contrived. Simply be normal.

You impulsively seek elsewhere, looking to others for your own hands and feet. This is already mistaken.

The Mind Ground

The mind ground can go into the ordinary, into the holy, into the pure, into the defiled, into the real, into the conventional; but it is not your "real" or "conventional," "ordinary" or "holy." It can put labels on all the real and conventional, the ordinary and holy, but the real and conventional, the ordinary and holy, cannot put labels on someone in the mind ground. If you can get it, use it, without putting any more labels on it.

Understanding People

When followers of Zen come to see me, I have already understood them completely. How can I do this? Simply because my perception is independent—externally I do not grasp the ordinary or the holy, internally I do not dwell on the fundamental. I see all the way through and do not doubt or err anymore.

Autonomy

Just be autonomous wherever you are, and right there is realization. Situations that come up cannot change you. Even if you have bad habits, you will spontaneously be liberated from them.

Spiritual Dilettantes

Zen students today are totally unaware of truth. They are like foraging goats that pick up whatever they bump into. They do not distinguish between the servant and the master, or between the guest and the host.

People like this enter Zen with distorted minds and are unable to enter effectively into dynamic situations. They may be called true initiates, but actually they are really mundane people.

Those who really leave attachments must master real, true perception to distinguish the enlightened from the obsessed, the genuine from the artificial, the unregenerate from the sage.

If you can make these discernments, you can be said to have really left dependency.

Professional Buddhist clergy who cannot tell obsession from enlightenment have just left one social group and entered another social group. They cannot really be said to be independent.

Now there is an obsession with Buddhism that is mixed in with the real thing. Those with clear eyes cut through both obsession and Buddhism. If you love the sacred and despise the ordinary, you are still bobbing in the ocean of delusion.

LABELS AND OBJECTIVE TRUTH

Because you grasp labels and slogans, you are hindered by those labels and slogans, both those used in ordinary life and those considered sacred. Thus they obstruct your perception of objective truth, and you cannot understand clearly.

THE FREE SELF

If you want to be free, get to know your real self. It has no form, no appearance, no root, no basis, no abode, but is lively and buoyant. It responds with versatile facility, but its function cannot be located. Therefore when you look for it you become further from it, when you seek it you turn away from it all the more.

NO CONCERN

Just put thoughts to rest and don't seek outwardly anymore. When things come up, then give them your attention; just trust what is functional in you at present, and you have nothing to be concerned about.

BLIND BALDIES

There are blind baldies who, after they have eaten their fill, do zazen and practice meditation, arresting thoughts leaking out to prevent them from arising, shunning clamor and seeking quiet. This is a deviated form of Zen.

UNCRITICAL ACCEPTANCE

You take the words of these ordinary Zen teachers for the real Way, supposing that Zen teachers are incomprehensible and as an ordinary person you dare not attempt to assess those old timers. You are blind if you take this view all your life, contrary to the evidence of your own two eyes.

TOURIST TRAPS

At Zen centers they say there is a Way to be practiced and a religious truth to be realized. Tell me, what religious truth is realized, what way is practiced? In your present functioning, what do you lack? What would you fix?

Younger newcomers, not understanding this, immediately believe these mesmerists and let them talk about things that tie people up.

SUPERNORMAL FACULTIES

The six supernormal faculties of the enlightened are the ability to enter the realm of form without being confused by form, to enter the realm of sound without being confused by sound, to enter the realm of scent without being confused by scent, to enter the realm of flavor without being confused by flavor, to enter the realm of feeling without being confused by feeling, to enter the realm of phenomena without being confused by phenomena.

OBJECTIVE PERCEPTION AND UNDERSTANDING

If you want to perceive and understand objectively, just don't allow yourself to be confused by people. Detach from whatever you find inside or outside yourself—detach from religion, tradition, and society, and only then will you attain liberation. When you are not entangled in things, you pass through freely to autonomy.

ZEN TEACHING

I have no doctrine to give people—I just cure ailments and unlock fetters.

ADDING MUD TO DIRT

There are Zen students who are in chains when they go to a teacher, and the teacher adds another chain. The students are delighted, unable to discern one thing from another. This is called a guest looking at a guest.

SLAVERY

When I say there is nothing outside, students who do not understand me interpret this in terms of inwardness, so they sit silent and still, taking this to be Zen Buddhism.

This is a big mistake. If you take a state of unmoving clarity to be Zen, you are recognizing ignorance as a slave master.

MOVEMENT AND STILLNESS

If you try to grasp Zen in movement, it goes into stillness. If you try to grasp Zen in stillness, it goes into movement. It is like a fish hidden in a spring, drumming up waves and dancing independently.

Movement and stillness are two states. The Zen master, who does not depend on anything, makes deliberate use of both movement and stillness.

Zen Master Yangshan

Zen Teaching

There is interaction if there is a call for it, no interaction if there is no call for it.

Deep and Shallow

If I were to explain the source of Zen, there wouldn't be a single person around, let alone a group of five hundred or seven hundred. If I talk about this and that, however, you race forward to pick it up. This is like fooling a child with an empty fist—there is no reality in it.

The Zen Essence

I explain to you matters pertaining to enlightenment, but don't try to keep your mind on them. Just turn to the ocean of your own essence and develop practical accord with its true nature.

Supernormal Capacities

You do not need supernormal capacities, because these are outgrowths of enlightenment. For now you need to know the mind and get to its source.

Root and Branches

Just get the root, don't worry about the branches, for someday you will come to have them naturally. If you have not attained the basis, even if you consciously study you cannot attain the outgrowths either.

The Inner Gaze

You should turn your attention within—don't memorize my words. You have been turning from light to darkness since before you can remember, so the roots of your subjective ideas are deep and hard to uproot all at once. This is why I temporarily use expedients to take away your coarse perceptions.

Zen Master Fayan

False Zen Teachers

It is wrong to act as a teacher of others before your own mind ground is clearly illumined.

The Basis of Zen

The teaching of the mind ground is the basis of Zen study. The mind ground is the great awareness of being as is.

Confusion

Due to confusion, people mistake things for themselves; covetousness flares up, and they get into vicious cycles that cloud perceptions and enshroud them in ignorance. The vicious cycles go on and on, and people cannot be free.

The Deterioration of Zen

The purpose of Zen is to enable people to immediately transcend the ordinary and the holy, just getting people to awaken on their own, forever cutting off the root of doubt.

Many people in modern times disregard this. They may join Zen groups, but they are lazy about Zen study. Even if they achieve concentration, they do not choose real teachers. Through the errors of false teachers, they likewise lose the way.

Without having understood senses and objects, as soon as they possess themselves of some false interpretation they become obsessed by it and lose the correct basis completely.

They are only interested in becoming leaders and being known as teachers. While they value an empty reputation in the world, they bring ill on themselves. Not only do they make their successors blind and deaf, they also cause the influence of Zen to degenerate.

SECTARIANISM

Zen is not founded or sustained on the premise that there is a doctrine to be transmitted. It is just a matter of direct guidance to the human mind, perception of its essence, and achievement of awakening. How could there be any sectarian styles to be valued?

There were differences in the modes of teaching set up by later Zen teachers, and there were both tradition and change. The methods employed by a number of famous Zen masters came to be continued as traditions, to the point where their descendants became sectarians and did not get to the original reality. Eventually they made many digressions, contradicting and attacking each other. They do not distinguish the profound from the superficial, and do not know that the Great Way has no sides and the streams of truth have the same flavor.

DISCERNMENT

Zen teachers need first to distinguish false and true, then they must clearly understand the time.

DEGENERATE ZEN

Zen teachers in recent times have lost the basis, so students have no way to learn. There is egotistical contention, and impermanent states are taken to be attainments.

PRINCIPLE AND FACT

Zen Buddhism includes both principle and fact. Fact is based on principle, principle is illustrated by fact. Principle and fact work together like eyes and feet.

SUBJECTIVE JUDGMENTS

If you make subjective, personalistic judgments of past and present events, not having been through the process of refining and purifying your insight, this is like trying to do a sword dance without having learned to handle a sword.

Understanding and Imagination

It is not possible to fathom the intention of the words or acts of the enlightened by indulging in fantasy.

Zen Succession

If you memorize slogans, you are unable to make subtle adaptations according to the situation. It is not that there is no way to teach insight to learners, but once you have learned a way, it is essential that you get it to work completely. If you just stick to your teacher's school and memorize slogans, this is not enlightenment, it is a part of intellectual knowledge.

This is why it is said, "When your perception only equals that of your teacher, you lessen the teacher's virtue by half. When your perception goes beyond the teacher, only then can you express the teacher's teaching."

The sixth ancestor of Zen said to someone who had just been awakened, "What I tell you is not a secret. The secret is in you."

Another Zen master said to a companion, "Everything flows from your own heart."

Zen Master Fenyang

The Work of a Teacher

Someone asked Fenyang, "What is the work of a teaching master?" Fenyang replied, "Impersonally guiding those with affinity."

Moon and Clouds

The original Buddha-nature of all living beings is like the bright moon in the sky—it is only because it is covered by floating clouds that it cannot appear.

Independent Knowing

You should know by yourself what is holy and what is ordinary, what is wrong and what is right—don't be concerned with others' judgments. How many people have ever managed to find out every subtlety? People arbitrarily follow material senses, running like idiots.

Time and Time Out

When will you ever stop competing? Before you realize, the scenery of spring has turned to autumn. The leaves fall, the geese migrate, the frost gradually grows colder. Clothed and shod, what more do you seek?

Devil, Buddha, and Mind

When you know the mind, mind is Buddha. If you don't know it, it is the devil. Devil and Buddha are products of one mind. Buddha is real, the devil is madness.

DIRECT POINTING TO BASIC MIND

Few people believe their inherent mind is Buddha. Most will not take this seriously, and therefore are cramped. They are wrapped up in illusions, cravings, resentments, and other afflictions, all because they love the cave of ignorance.

SUDDEN AWAKENING

When you suddenly realize the source of mind, you open a box of jewels. Honorable on earth and in the heavens, you are aloof even from the joy of meditation. The essence containing all flavors is the supreme delicacy, worth more than ten thousand ounces of pure gold.

COMMUNICATION THROUGH THE SOURCE

When you are deluded and full of doubt, even a thousand books of scripture are still not enough. When you have realized understanding, even one word is already too much.

Zen is communicated personally, through mental recognition. It is not handed on directly by written words.

SUMMARY OF ZEN PRACTICE

When you're settled in Zen, your mind is serene, unaffected by worldly distractions. You enter the realm of enlightenment, and transcend the ordinary world, leaving the world while in the midst of society.

REALIZING THE WAY

Once you realize universal emptiness, all situations are naturally mastered. You have perfect communion with what is beyond the world, while embracing what is within all realms of being.

If you miss the essence of Zen, after all there's nothing to it. If you get its function, it has spiritual effect.

The real Way of "nonminding" is not a school for petty people.

Zen Master Xuedou

The Living Meaning of Zen

Someone asked Xuedou, "What is the living meaning of Zen?" Xuedou said, "The mountains are high, the oceans are wide."

Where Do You Get It?

Someone asked Xuedou, "As it is said, 'The one road beyond is not transmitted by any of the sages.' Where did you get it?"

Xuedou said, "I thought you were a Zen practitioner."

An Eye-Opening Experience

Where the sword wheel flies, sun and moon lose their shine; when the jewel staff strikes, heaven and earth lose their color. Through this experience, all devils' guts burst; through this experience, all sages' eyes open.

Illuminating Perception

When you illuminate your perception, your eyes are like a thousand suns, so that nothing can escape notice. Ordinarily, people just have never been so observant, but they should not give up in frustration because of underestimating themselves.

Truth and Wisdom

The wise boldly pick up a truth as soon as they hear it. Don't wait for a moment, or you'll lose your head.

ZEN TEACHING

Someone asked Xuedou, "What is your manner of teaching?"
Xuedou replied, "When guests come, one should see them."

SPOILING THE BROTH

Once there was a Zen elder who didn't talk to his group at all during a retreat. One of the group said, "This way, I've wasted the whole retreat. I don't expect the teacher to explain Buddhism; it would be enough to hear the two words 'Absolute Truth.' "

The elder heard of this and said, "Don't be so quick to complain. There's not even a single word to say about 'Absolute Truth.' " Then when he had said this, he gnashed his teeth and said, "It was pointless to say that."

In the next room was another elder who overheard this and said, "A fine pot of soup, befouled by two rat droppings."

Whose pot hasn't one or two droppings in it?

THE ZEN RIVER

The river of Zen is quiet, even in the waves; the water of stability is clear, even in the waves.

ZEN MASTER HUANGLONG

TEACHERLESS KNOWLEDGE

The universal body of reality is so subtle that you do not hear it when you deliberately listen for it, and you do not see it when you look at it. As for the pure knowledge that has no teacher, how can it be attained by thought or study?

OPEN YOUR EYES

Seekers should open their own eyes—don't let yourselves in for regret later on. Zen cannot be reached by psychic powers or by cultivation of special experiences. Zen cannot be discussed by means of the knowledge or intelligence of the merely learned.

KNOWLEDGE AND FEELINGS

The basis of sentient existence is the ocean of knowledge, which is its source. The substance of the flow of conscious existence is the body of Reality.

But when feelings arise, knowledge is blocked, so true reality is unknown in everyday life. As mental images change, things differ, with people tending toward objects of habit and not returning.

THE ZEN WAY

The Way does not need cultivation—just don't defile it. Zen does not need study—the important thing is stopping the mind.

When the mind is stopped, there is no rumination. Because it is not cultivated, you walk on the Way at every step.

When there is no rumination, there is no world to transcend. Because it is not cultivated, there is no Way to seek.

SEEKING

To travel around to various schools looking for teachers is outward seeking. To take the inherent nature of awareness as the ocean and the silent knowledge of transcendent wisdom as Zen, is called inward seeking.

To seek outwardly busies you fatally; to seek inwardly while dwelling on mind and body binds you fatally.

Therefore Zen is neither inward nor outward, not being or nonbeing, not real or false. As it is said, "Inner and outer views are both wrong."

LEAVINGS

"When ordinary and sacred feelings are forgotten, Being is revealed, real and eternal. Just detach from arbitrary involvements, and you awaken to Being as it is."

Although these are the leavings of an ancient Zen master, there are many people who cannot partake of them. I've lost considerable profit just by bringing them up.

Can anyone discern? If you can, you will recognize the disease of "Buddhism" and the disease of "Zen."

LIVING ZEN

To drink up the ocean and turn a mountain upside down is an ordinary affair for a Zennist. Zen seekers should sit on the site of universal enlightenment right in the midst of all the thorny situations in life, and recognize their original face while mixing with the ordinary world.

REAL DETACHMENT

"Where people of today dwell, I do not dwell. What people of today do, I do not do." If you clearly understand what this really means, you must be able to enter a pit of fire with your whole body.

Golden Chains

Someone asked Huanglong, "It is said that someone who is uncontrived and unconcerned is still hindered by golden chains—what is wrong?"

Huanglong said, "When a word enters the public domain, it can't be withdrawn for nine years."

In and Out

All sages since remote antiquity have entered the pit of life and death, gone into the fire of ignorance, to help people out. What about you? How do you enter?

If people can enter, this can be called not burning in fire, not drowning in water.

If people cannot enter, they not only cannot help themselves, they cannot help others.

Zen Master Yangqi

Lost and Found

When body and mind are pure, all things are pure. When all things are pure, body and mind are pure.

"The coin lost in the river is to be retrieved from the river."

Still Worldly

When you detach from the whole universe, everywhere is dark. When you let go of the absolute, the rain is seasonal and the breeze is moderate. Even so, there is still worldliness there.

The Ancient Teaching

Someone asked Yangqi, "As it is said, 'If you want to escape from clamor in the mind, you should read the ancient teaching.' What is the ancient teaching?"

Yangqi replied, "The moon is bright in space, the waves are calm on the ocean."

The inquirer asked, "How does one read it?"

Yangqi said, "Watch your step."

The Supreme Vehicle of Zen

I am asked to expound the supreme vehicle of Zen, but if it is the supreme vehicle, even the sages stand aside, buddhas and Zen masters disappear.

Why? Because you are all the same as the buddhas of old.

But can you really believe and trust this?

If you really can, let us all disband and go our separate ways.

If you don't leave, I'll go on fooling you.

MIND AND PHENOMENA

Mind is the faculty, phenomena are the data: both are like scratches in a mirror.

When there are no scratches or dust, the clarity of the mirror shows.

When mind and phenomena are both forgotten, then your nature is real.

SILENT ZEN

Someone asked Yangqi, "When the founder of Zen came from India to China, he sat facing a wall for nine years—what does this mean?"

Yangqi said, "As an Indian, he couldn't speak Chinese."

Zen Master Wuzu

Zen Teaching

To be a Zen teacher, it is imperative to "drive away the plowman's ox, snatch away the hungry man's food."

When you drive away the plowman's ox, that makes his crops abundant; when you snatch away the hungry man's food, that frees him from hunger forever.

For most people that hear this saying, it is like the wind passing the ears. If you drive away the plowman's ox, how does that make his crops abundant? If you snatch away the hungry man's food, how does that free him from hunger?

At this point, you must have the ability to drive away the plowman's ox and snatch away the hungry man's food, then give a pressing thrust, causing people to reach their wit's end. Then you tell them, "Blessings are not received twice, calamities do not occur alone."

Something Indescribable

There is something in the world that is neither in the sphere of the ordinary nor in the sphere of the holy. It is neither in the realm of the false nor in the realm of the true.

Halcyon

When there is not a speck of cloud dotting the great clarity for ten thousand miles, sun and moon in the original sky are of themselves clear.

It is not permitted for a general to see great peace, but a general may establish great peace.

The Goal of Zen

To study Zen, first you must obtain directions to the ultimate goal. Hearing sound and seeing form are inconceivable. From the eternal sky every night the moon shines on every home; its reflection descends into a quiet pool, but how many know?

Seeking without Finding

Few seekers of Zen attain it. When will judgments ever cease? If you talk about high and low based on words, that is like before enlightenment.

Everyone Can Arrive

There is a road to emptiness by which everyone can arrive. Those who do arrive realize that its rich flavor is lasting. The ground of mind doesn't produce useless plants; naturally the body radiates light.

Talking about Zen

Talking about Zen all the time is like looking for fish tracks in a dry riverbed.

Zen Master Yuanwu

The Aim of Zen

When enlightened Zen masters set up teachings for a spiritual path, the only concern is to clarify the mind to arrive at its source. It is complete in everyone, yet people turn away from this basic mind because of their illusions.

Immediate Zen

If you have developed great capacity and cutting insight, you can undertake Zen right where you are. Without getting it from another, you understand clearly on your own.

The penetrating spiritual light and vast open tranquility have never been interrupted since beginningless time. The pure, uncontrived, ineffable, complete true mind does not act as a partner to objects of material sense, and is not a companion of myriad things.

When the mind is always as clear and bright as ten suns shining together, detached from views and beyond feelings, cutting through the ephemeral illusions of birth and death, this is what is meant by the saying, "Mind itself is Buddha."

Intellectual Egotists

Many worldly intellectuals just study Zen for something to talk about, something that will enhance their reputation. They consider this a lofty interest, and try to use it to assert superiority over others. This just increases their egotism.

MOTIVATION

When your original reason for studying Zen is not right, you wind up having labored without accomplishment. This is why ancients used to urge people to study Zen as if they were on the brink of death.

PEACE

Human lives go along with circumstances. It is not necessary to reject activity and seek quiet; just make yourself inwardly empty while outwardly harmonious. Then you will be at peace in the midst of frenetic activity in the world.

INSTANT ZEN

In Zen, it is not difficult for those of keen faculties and higher insight to attain a thousand understandings at one hearing.

FIRM FOOTING

It is necessary for your footing to be firm and solid, accurate and sure. Taking control and being the master, you become one with all different situations, like space without barriers. When profound, open clarity has no change, and is consistent at all times, only then can you be at peace.

CHANGING METHODS

Zen teachers of true vision and great liberation have made changes in method along the way, to prevent people from sticking to names and forms and falling into rationalizations.

THE PURPOSE OF ZEN

Over the course of centuries, Zen has branched out into different schools with individual methods, but the purpose is still the same—to point directly to the human mind.

Once the ground of mind is clarified, there is no obstruction at all—you shed views and interpretations that are based on concepts such as victory and defeat, self and others, right and wrong.

Thus you pass through all that and reach a realm of great rest and tranquility.

OPENING THE MIND

Zen requires opening the mind and losing all false cognition and false views. When nothing hangs on your mind and you have passed through cleanly, then you are ready for refinement.

BUDDHA'S TEACHINGS

When a buddha appears in the world and expounds various teachings according to people's inclinations, all of the teachings are expedients, just for the purpose of breaking through obsessions, doubts, intellectual interpretations, and egocentric ideas.

If there were no such false consciousness and false views, there would be no need for buddhas to appear and expound so many teachings.

RELEASE

In Zen, sudden release into realization isn't subject to either ruin or support by other people. Be totally aloof, and one day you will boldly pass through with penetrating senses to experience Zen directly.

Then you use it at will, you act at will, without so many things going through your mind.

When this is developed to maturity and you let go all at once, you immediately attain rest and comfort right where you are.

HALF-BAKED ZEN

What is most difficult to rectify is half-baked Zen, where you stick to quiet stillness and consider this the ultimate treasure, keeping it in your heart, radiantly aware of it all the time, carrying around a bunch of mixed-up knowledge and understanding, claiming to have vision and to have attained the approval of a Zen master, just increasing your egoism.

ZEN MIND

In those who attain Zen, mental machinations disappear, vision and action are forgotten, and there are no subjective views.

Zen adepts just remain free, and are imperceptible to anyone, either would-be supporters or would-be antagonists.

They walk on the bottom of the deepest ocean, uncontaminated, with free minds, acting normally, indistinguishable from the average person.

Though they liberate their minds directly and develop to this state, they still are unwilling to dwell here.

They sense the slightest thing as mountainous; anything that seems to cause obstruction they immediately push away.

Although this is purely the ground of noumenon, there is still nothing in it to grasp. If you grasp it, it becomes a sticky view.

Therefore it is said, "The Tao is mindless of union with humanity; when people are unminding, they unite with the Tao."

How could anyone show off and claim to have attained Zen?

LIVING AND DEAD WORDS

Study the living word of Zen, not the dead word. When you attain understanding of the living word, you never forget it. When you attain understanding of the dead word, you can't even save yourself.

THE SWORD OF DEATH, THE SWORD OF LIFE

It is said that you need the sword that kills in order to kill, and you need the sword that gives life in order to give life.

Once people have been killed, they should be brought to life, and once they have been brought to life they should be killed.

If either type of technique is used in isolation, there is an imbalance.

DON'T SEEK ZEN

If you want to attain intimate realization of Zen, first of all don't seek it. What is attained by seeking has already fallen into intellection.

The great treasury of Zen has always been open and clear; it has always been the source of power for all your actions.

But only when you stop your compulsive mind, to reach the point where not a single thing is born, do you pass through to freedom, not falling into feelings and not dwelling on concepts, transcending all completely.

Then Zen is obvious everywhere in the world, with the totality of everything everywhere turning into its great function.

Everything comes from your own heart. This is what one ancient called bringing out the family treasure.

DIRECT EXPERIENCE OF ZEN

Zen originally is not established on slogans, it just points directly to the human mind.

Direct pointing is just pointing to that which is inherent in everyone, though in a shell of unawareness.

When the whole being appears responsively, it is no different from that of the sages since antiquity.

This is what is called the originally pure subtle luminosity of naturally real essence, which swallows and spits out the whole universe, individually freed from the material senses.

Only by detaching from thoughts and cutting off feelings, utterly transcending ordinary parameters, with great perceptivity and great insight, using inherent power, can this be directly experienced in your present situation.

ZEN ATTAINMENT

An ancient master said, "Those who have attained Zen just keep free, desireless and independent all the time."

ZEN PRACTICE

Just still the thoughts in your mind. It is good to do this right in the midst of disturbance. When you are working on this, penetrate the heights and the depths.

LIBERATION

Let go of all your previous imaginings, opinions, interpretations, worldly knowledge, intellectualism, egoism, and competitiveness; become like a dead tree, like cold ashes. When you reach the point where feelings are ended, views are gone, and your mind is clean and naked, you open up to Zen realization.

After that it is also necessary to develop consistency, keeping the mind pure and free from adulteration at all times. If there is the slightest fluctuation, there is no hope of transcending the world.

Cut through resolutely, and then your state will be peaceful. When you cannot be included in any stage, whether of sages or of ordinary people, then you are like a bird freed from its cage.

RESOLVE

The Way is arrived at by enlightenment. The first priority is to establish resolve—it is no small matter to step directly from the bondage of the ordinary person into transcendent experience of the realm of sages. It requires that your mind be firm as steel to cut off the flow of birth and death, accept your original real nature, not see anything at all as existing inside or outside yourself, and make your heart perfectly clear, without any obstruction, so all actions and endeavors emerge from the fundamental.

THE ESSENTIAL POINT

The essential point in learning Zen is to make the roots deep and the stem firm. Twenty-four hours a day, be aware of where you are and what you do.

When no thoughts have arisen and nothing at all is on your mind, you merge with the boundless and become wholly empty and still. Then your actions are not interrupted by doubt and hesitation.

This is called the fundamental matter right at hand.

As soon as you produce any opinion or interpretation, and want to attain Zen and be a master, you have already fallen into psychological and material realms. You have become trapped by ordinary senses and perceptions, by ideas of gain and loss, by ideas of right and wrong. Half drunk and half sober, you cannot manage effectively.

Don't Linger

As soon as you sense any lingering or obstruction, all of it is false imagining. Just make your mind clean and free, like space, like a mirror, like the sun in the sky.

Autonomy and Integration

When you are free and independent, you are not bound by anything, so you do not seek liberation. Consummating the process of Zen, you become unified. Then there are no mundane things outside of Buddhism, and there is no Buddhism outside of mundane things.

Consulting Teachers

Step back on your own to look into reality long enough to attain an unequivocally true and real experience of enlightenment. Then with every thought you are consulting infinite teachers.

Substance and Function

Complete, tranquil, open, still—such is the substance of the Way. Expanding, contracting, killing, giving life—such is its subtle function.

Extremes

If you haven't attained clear true vision, this causes you to lapse into extremes, so that you lose contact with reality.

Tools

The words of buddhas and Zen masters are just tools, means of gaining access to truth. Once you are clearly enlightened and experience truth, all the teachings are within you.

Then you look upon the verbal teachings of buddhas and Zen masters as something in the realm of reflections or echoes, and you do not wear them around on your head.

MISUSE OF TOOLS

Nowadays many Zen students do not go to the root of the design of Zen, instead they just try to pick out sayings and discuss them in terms of familiarity and strangeness, of winning and losing. They interpret the ephemeral as being real.

SNOWFLAKES ON A FURNACE

You should refrain from dependence on anything at all, pure or impure. Then mindfulness and mindlessness, views and no view, will be like a snowflake on a red-hot furnace.

NONMINDING

When you are inwardly empty and quiet, while outwardly detached from perception, you naturally attain penetrating experience of nonminding, which means that even if everything happens at once, that cannot disturb your spirit, and even though all kinds of troubles face you, that does not affect your thoughts.

SERENE RESPONSE

When you can actively respond to changes in the midst of the hurly-burly of life while being inwardly empty and serene, and can also avoid infatuation with quietude when in a quiet environment, then wherever you are is where you live. Only those who have attained the fundamental are capable of being inwardly empty while outwardly harmonious.

ZEN LIFE AND DEATH

The capacity of speech is not only in the tongue, the ability to talk is not just a matter of words.

The enlightened know that spoken words are not to be relied on, so the sayings of the ancient Zen masters are only intended to induce people to directly witness the nexus of causes and conditions that constitute what has always been of greatest concern.

Therefore the teachings of the Buddhist scriptures are like fingers pointing to the moon. When you know this matter of greatest concern, then you stop formal study and apply this knowledge thoroughly, using it with comprehensive penetration.

Eventually you will reach the point of immovability, where you can pick up Zen and use it, putting it away and letting it out expertly.

Then you can see through ordinary situations and detach from them without leaving a trace.

And when you come to the border of life and death, when they interlock but do not mix, you depart serenely, unperturbed. This is the Zen of facing death.

Zen Teachers

Zen teachers should be compassionate, gentle, and skilled at adaptation, dealing with people impartially, minding their own business and not contending with anyone.

Dealing with Opposition

If people find fault with you and try to put you in a bad light, wrongly slandering and vilifying you, just step back and observe yourself. Don't harbor any dislike, don't enter into any contests, and don't get upset, angry, or resentful.

Just cut right through it and be as if you never heard or saw it. Eventually malevolent pests will disappear of themselves.

If you contend with them, then a bad name will bounce back and forth with never an end in sight.

Zen Enlightenment and Zen Work

An ancient Zen master said that Zen is like learning archery; only after long practice do you hit the bullseye.

Enlightenment is experienced instantaneously, but Zen work must be done over a long time, like a bird that when first hatched is naked and scrawny, but then grows feathers as it is nourished, until it can fly high and far.

Therefore those who have attained clear penetrating enlightenment then need fine tuning.

When it comes to worldly situations, by which ordinary people get suffocated, those who have attained Zen get through them all by being empty. Thus everything is their own gateway to liberation.

FALSE ZEN TEACHERS

Zen teachers without the methodology of real experts unavoidably cheat and deceive those whom they try to teach, leading them into confusion, fooling around with a bunch of curios.

ZEN DEVICES

The intention of all Zen devices, states, sayings, and expressions is in their ability to hook the seeker. The only important thing is liberation—people should not be attached to the means.

CLICHÉ

Although the great Zen teachers did not establish clichés and slogans, eventually seekers misapprehended this and turned this itself into a cliché and a slogan—they made a cliché of no cliché, and a slogan of no slogan. They should not cling to the means as an end.

PERCEPTION AND RESPONSE

Unless your heart is open and serene, with nothing touching your feelings, how can you respond completely without error and perceive things before they begin to act?

ESSENTIAL NATURE AND ULTIMATE TRUTH

Zen study requires you to see your essential nature and understand ultimate truth.

Immediately forget feelings and detach from perceptions, so your heart is clear and your mind is simple, not comparing gain and loss, not making a contest of better and worse.

UNCONCERN

Cut through all situations and don't allow yourself to continue with thoughts of whether these situations are favorable or adverse. Eventually you will naturally reach the realm of nondoing and unconcern. But if you have the slightest desire for unconcern, this has already become a concern.

PRIDE

If you have the idea of superiority and are proud of your ability, this is a disaster.

CONCEPTS AND TRAINING

To study Zen conceptually is like drilling in ice for fire, like digging a hole to look for the sky. It just increases mental fatigue. To study Zen by training is adding mud to dirt, scattering sand in the eyes, impeding you more and more.

PENETRATING ZEN

People who are sharp should have their feet on the ground, and need an iron spine, traveling through the world looking on everything as illusory, holding still and being the master, not following human sentiments, cutting through discrimination between others and self, and getting rid of intellectual interpretations of Zen.

Then, when it comes to practical function, responding to conditions, they don't fall into clichés. Developing single-minded persistence, keeping profound calm, lightening body and mind, while in the midst of the toil of the world they penetrate through to freedom.

TRUST AND INSIGHT

If you can give up your former knowledge and understanding, thus making your heart open, not keeping anything at all on your mind, so you experience a clear empty solidity where speech and thought do not apply, you will directly merge with the fundamental source, sinking into the infinite, spontaneously attaining inherent wisdom that has no attainment.

This is called thorough trust and penetrating insight. There is, moreover, still boundless, fathomless, measureless great potential and great function yet to be realized.

Stumbled Past

As soon as you try to chase and grab Zen, you've already stumbled past it.

Zen Experience

Set aside all the slogans you have learned and all the intellectual views that stick to your skin and cling to your flesh. Make your mind empty, not manifesting any thoughts on your own, not doing anything at all. Then you can attain thoroughgoing Zen experience.

But even when you reach this point, you should still realize that there is progressive action that transcends a teacher.

Direct Zen

If you have great perceptions and capacities, you need not necessarily contemplate the sayings and stories of ancient Zen masters. Just correct your attention and quiet your mind from the time you arise in the morning, and whatever you say or do, review it carefully and see where it comes from and what makes all this happen.

Once you can pass through right in the midst of present worldly conditions, the same applies to all conditions—what need is there to remove them?

Then you can go beyond "Zen," transcend all parameters, and magically produce a sanctuary of purity, effortlessness, and coolness, right in the midst of the turmoil of the world.

Nondualism

You do not have to abandon worldly activities in order to attain effortless unconcern. You should know that worldly activities and effortless unconcern are not two different things—but if you keep thinking about rejection and grasping, you make them into two.

Nonabiding

A scripture says, "All things are established on a nonabiding basis."

Another scripture says, "Activate the mind without dwelling on anything."

An ancient Zen master said, "Don't mind anything or dwell on anything, whether of the world or beyond the world."

If you dwell on anything, you get stuck, and cannot change effectively.

SUBJECTIVE ZEN

Many intelligent people understand Zen subjectively and are unable to let go of their subjectivity. They still their minds without experiencing their real nature, and think this is emptiness. They try to abandon existence to cling to emptiness. This is a serious malady.

DISSOLVING ILLUSIONS

It is necessary to detach from both rejection and clinging, from both being and nonbeing, so that you are unburdened, completely tranquil, empty and still, calm and peaceful.

Then you can trust this true pure ineffable mind, and when mundane conditions beckon involvement, you notice it doesn't go along with them.

You can only do this by long-term work on your own, empty and free, to dissolve away illusions and bring about your own insight.

BASIC MIND

When you are aware of the completeness, fluidity, and boundlessness of the basic mind, how can sense objects be partners to it? Basic mind is utterly free, open and pure, clear and ethereal; keep thoroughly aware of it, and do not allow superficiality. Then it is so high there is nothing above it, so broad it is boundless; clean and bare, perfectly round, this basic mind is without contamination or contrivance.

ZEN MASTER FOYAN

SAVING ENERGY

Zen practice requires detachment from thought. This is the best way to save energy. Just detach from emotional thought and understand that there is no objective world. Then you will know how to practice Zen.

MIND AND WORLD

Once there was a monk who specialized in the Buddhist precepts, and had kept to them all his life. Once when he was walking at night, he stepped on something. It made a squishing sound, and he imagined he had stepped on an egg-bearing frog. This caused him no end of alarm and regret, in view of the Buddhist precept against taking life, and when he finally went to sleep that night he dreamed that hundreds of frogs came to him demanding his life.

The monk was terribly upset, but when morning came he looked and found that what he had stepped on was an overripe eggplant. At that moment his feeling of uncertainty suddenly stopped, and for the first time he realized the meaning of the saying that there is no objective world. Then he finally knew how to practice Zen.

INHERENT ZEN

Why do you not understand your nature, when it is inherently there? There is not much to Buddhism—it just requires getting to the essential.

We do not teach you to annihilate random thoughts, suppress body and mind, shut your eyes, and say this is Zen. Zen is not like this.

You should observe your present state—what is the reason for it? Why do you become confused?

DISCRIMINATION AND NONDISCRIMINATION

You should become aware of the nondiscriminating mind without leaving the discriminating mind; become aware of that which has no perception without leaving perception.

INDEPENDENCE

What do you go to a "Zen center" for? You should make a living on your own, and not listen to what others say.

WHO IS IT?

Search back into your own vision—think back to the mind that thinks. Who is it?

MIND'S EYE

It is as though you have an eye that sees all forms but does not see itself—this is how your mind is. Its light penetrates everywhere and engulfs everything, so why does it not know itself?

RATIONALIZATIONS

As soon as you rationalize, it is hard to understand Zen. You will have to stop rationalizing before you will get it.

Some people hear this kind of talk and say there is nothing to say and no reason—they do not realize they are already rationalizing when they do this.

GOING IN CIRCLES

Why do you not understand your mind? First you make "your own mind" into a cliché, then you use your mind to seek its realization. This is called driving a spike into a stump and then running in circles around the stump.

RECOGNITION

Zen enlightenment is as if you have been away from home for many years, when you suddenly see your father in town. You know him right away, without a doubt. There is no need to ask anyone else whether he is your father or not.

ZEN PERCEPTION

You can be called a Zen student only when you perceive before signs appear, before falling into thought, before ideas sprout.

STEPPING BACK

You should step back and investigate. How do you step back? It is not a matter of sitting there ignoring everything, stiffly repressing body and mind so that they are like earth or wood—that will never do any good.

When you want to step back, if there are any sayings you do not understand, or any stories you do not comprehend, they are then right before you. Step back and see for yourself why you do not understand.

DOUBT AND UNDERSTANDING

If you want to understand Zen, you must question inwardly to study it deeply. If you question deeply, transcendental knowledge appears.

JUST YOU

An ancient Zen master, seeing a monk go down a staircase, called to him, "Reverend!" The monk turned around, whereat the Zen master said, "From birth to old age, it's just you—why turn your head and revolve your brains?"

The monk understood Zen at this remark.

What is this principle? "From birth to old age, it's just you." Tell me, who is this? As soon as you arouse the intention of seeing who you are, you don't see yourself. It is hard to see yourself—very difficult.

People today say, "I am myself—who else?" Ninety-nine out of a hundred understand in this way. What kind of grasp is this on the matter? If you understand in this way, how do you understand the matter of "from birth to old age"? How can you see it's just you?

PERSONALISTIC ZEN

People these days are just the same as they have been all along, and their capabilities are the same as they have been all along: continuously fluctuating. The reason they are uncertain is because they make up intellectual understandings of the words of ancient Zen teachers, using personalistic approaches.

MISUNDERSTANDING

Ancient Zen teachers were so compassionate that they said, "Activity is Buddha activity, sitting is Buddha sitting, all things are Buddha teachings, all sounds are Buddha voices." It is, however, a misunderstanding to think this means all sounds are actually the voice of enlightenment, or that all forms are actually forms of enlightenment.

FIXATION

The minute you fixate on the recognition that "This is 'it,' " you are immediately bound hand and foot and cannot move around anymore.

So as soon as it is given this recognition, nothing is right, whatever it may be. If you don't fixate on recognition, you can still be saved.

It's like making a boat and outfitting it for a thousand mile journey to a treasure trove; if you drive a stake and tie the boat to it before you jump in and start rowing, you can row till kingdom come and still be on the beach. You see the boat waving this way and that, and you think you are on the move, but you've never gone a single step.

KNOW YOURSELF

I tell people to get to know themselves. Some people think this means what beginners observe, and consider it easy to understand. Reflect more carefully, in a more leisurely manner—what do you call your self?

Misapplication

Buddhism is an easily understood teaching that saves energy, but people cause themselves pains. The ancients saw people helpless, and told them to try meditating quietly. This was good advice, but later people didn't understand what the ancients meant, and closed their eyes, suppressed body and mind, and sat like lumps waiting for enlightenment. How foolish!

Subjective Objects

Objects are defined subjectively. Since objects are defined arbitrarily, this gives rise to your arbitrary subjectivity.

Nonsubjectivity

When you see, let there be no seer or seen; when you hear, let there be no hearer or heard; when you think, let there be no thinker or thought.

Buddhism is extremely easy and saves the most energy. It's just that you yourself waste energy and cause yourself trouble.

The Veil of Light

Some senior Zen students say they don't rationalize at all, don't calculate and compare at all, don't cling to sound and form, don't rest on defilement and purity. They say the sacred and the profane, delusion and enlightenment, are a single clear emptiness. They say there are no such things in the midst of great light. They are veiled by the light of wisdom, fixated on wisdom. They are incurable.

Distorted by a Teacher

The second ancestor of Zen used to give talks wherever he happened to be, and all who heard him attained true awareness. He didn't establish any slogans or talk about causes and effects of practice and realization.

In his time there was a certain meditation teacher who sent a top disciple to listen in on the Zen ancestor. The disciple never came back. The meditation teacher was furious, and took the occasion of a congress to upbraid his former disciple for disloyalty.

The former disciple said, "My perception was originally true, but it was distorted by a teacher."

Later someone asked a Zen master, "Where is my power of perception?" The Zen master said, "It is not obtained from a teacher."

This is the way to attain Zen. An ancient said, "The Way is always with people, but people themselves chase after things."

TURNING THINGS AROUND

In the scriptures it says, "If you can turn things around, this is the same as enlightenment." How can things be turned around?

Scripture also says, "All appearances are illusory. If you see appearances are not the same as true characteristics, you see where enlightenment comes from."

An ancient Zen master said, "If you deny appearances as you see them, you do not see where enlightenment comes from."

Just step back, stop mental machinations, and try to become aware of all the implications of these sayings. If you suddenly see through, how can you be affected by anything?

WHAT DELUDES YOU?

Only when you actually get to the state where there is neither delusion nor enlightenment are you finally comfortable and conserving the most energy.

But for this you have to be someone who has neither delusion nor enlightenment.

During the twenty-four hours of the day, what is there deluding you? You should make a truthful assessment of yourself.

WHERE YOU CANNOT FOOL YOURSELF

When you sit meditating and enter into absorption, you should have no concerns or problems in yourself. Try to think independently, all by yourself. Other people don't know what you're doing all the time.

You reflect on yourself and see whether what you are doing accords with truth or not. Here you cannot fool yourself.

A Method of Sudden Enlightenment

Just don't arouse the mind or stir thoughts twenty-four hours a day. Then you will understand comprehensive realization all at once.

Seek without Seeking

If you seek, how is that different from pursuing sound and form? If you don't seek, how are you different from earth, wood, or stone? You must seek without seeking.

Misperception

Suppose a bit of filth gets stuck to a man's nose while he is sleeping. When he awakens, unaware of what has happened, he may notice an odor and start smelling his shirt. Thinking his shirt stinks, he takes it off. But then whatever he picks up smells bad to him. He doesn't realize the smell is on his nose.

Someone tells him, but he doesn't believe it. Told to wipe his nose, he refuses.

He'll realize sooner if he wipes off his nose, but when he eventually washes his face he'll find there is no odor. Then he'll find, when he smells things, that they do not stink after all.

Zen study is like this. Those who will not stop and look into themselves go on looking for intellectual understanding. That pursuit of intellectual understanding, seeking rationalizations and making comparisons, is all wrong.

If people would turn their attention back to the self, they would understand everything.

Rationalizations

At other places they either put you to work or sit you still. Here I neither put you to work nor sit you still. This is easy to understand, with a minimum of effort, so why don't you understand? Simply because of your countless clever rationalizations. This is what makes it hard for you to understand.

ORDINARY PERCEPTIONS AND ENLIGHTENMENT

How can you equate ordinary perceptions with actual sudden enlightenment?

Sudden enlightenment is like when a farmer plowing the fields finds one of the pills of immortality and goes to heaven with his whole family after taking it.

It is also like an ordinary person being made a prime minister.

In Buddhist teachings it says that ordinary perceptions are like a clay pot that has not been fired and therefore cannot be used. You have to bake it in a fire before you can use it. That is like attaining sudden enlightenment.

ZEN AND ENLIGHTENMENT

I once asked my teacher, "Is there effective enlightenment in Zen?"

He replied, "How could it be attained without enlightenment? But seek without haste or excitement."

WHAT'S WRONG?

For your part, obviously something is wrong with you—that's why you go to others for certainty. If you were all right, why would you go ask others?

WHAT'S RIGHT?

I just point out where you're right. If you're wrong, I'll never say you're right. I'll wait until you *are* right. I'll only agree with you when you're right.

I can see everything. When I see people come to me, I know whether they have enlightenment or not, and whether they have understanding or not, like a physician who recognizes an ailment at first sight and knows its nature and whether or not it can be cured.

Someone who has to ask about each symptom to find out what's wrong is a mediocre doctor.

A Doze of Zen

Nowadays there are people who just sit there as they are. At first they are alert, but after a while they get sleepy. Nine out of ten sit there dozing. If you don't know how to work, how can you sit there stubbornly expecting to understand?

Sleeping and Eating Zen

My teacher said, "When you are asleep, study Zen as you sleep. When you are eating, study Zen as you eat."

True, Imitation, and Remnant Zen

Usually it is said that there is true Buddhism, and then there are imitations and remnants. I say that Buddhism does not have true, imitation, and remnant versions. Buddhism is always in the world: if you get the point, it is true; if you miss the point, it is an imitation or a remnant.

Boundaries and Traps

You shouldn't set up limits in boundless openness, but if you set up limitlessness as boundless openness, you've trapped yourself.

This is why those who understand emptiness have no mental image of emptiness.

If people use words to label and describe the mind, they never apprehend the mind, but if they don't use words to label and describe the mind, they still don't apprehend the mind.

Transcending Subject and Object

Those who realize Zen enlightenment transcend subject and object. There is no other mysterious principle besides this.

In the course of ordinary daily activities, when you see colors it is a time of realization, and when you hear sounds it is a time of realization. When you eat and drink, this too is a time of realization. This means all these are times of realization when you transcend subject and object in everything.

This is not a matter of long practice, and doesn't need cultivation. It is right here, yet worldly people don't recognize it.

So it is said, "Only with experiential realization do you know the unfathomable."

Natural Revelation

The Way is not only evident after explanation and demonstration, because it is always being revealed naturally.

Explanation and demonstration are expedients used to enable you to realize intuitive understanding; they are only temporary byways.

Whether you attain realization through explanation, or enter in through demonstration, or reach the goal by spontaneous sensing through individual awareness, ultimately there is no different thing or separate attainment.

It is just a matter of reaching the source of mind.

A Sacred Cow

People studying Zen today think dialogue is essential to the Zen school. They do not realize this is grasping and rejecting, producing imagination.

Check Yourself

You must know how to check yourself before you can attain Zen. It is because of confused minds that people strive on the Way; they go to mountains and forests to see teachers, on the false assumption that there is a particular path that can give people peace and comfort.

They do not know it is best to work on finding out where they got confused.

OVERSIMPLIFIED ZEN

Many people today consider the immediate mirrorlike awareness to be the ultimate rule. This is why an ancient master said, "Does it exist where there are no people?"

THE POWER OF THE WAY

For those who arrive on the Way, everything is "it." This power is very great.

It is only the infection of endless false consciousness that makes the function of the power defective.

Zen Master Dahui

The Realm of the Enlightened

The Flower Ornament Scripture says, "If you want to know the realm of the enlightened, you should make your mind as clear as space; detach from subjective imaginings and from all grasping, making your mind unimpeded wherever it turns."

The realm of the enlightened is not an external realm with manifest characteristics; buddhahood is the realm of the sacred knowledge found in oneself.

You do not need paraphernalia, practices, or realizations to attain it—what you need to do is to clean out the influences of the psychological afflictions connected with the external world that have been accumulating in your psyche since beginningless time.

Make your mind as wide open as cosmic space; detach from graspings in the conceptual consciousness, and false ideas and imaginings will also be like empty space. Then this effortless subtle mind will naturally be unimpeded wherever it turns.

See Buddha Everywhere

The Flower Ornament Scripture says, "Do not see Buddha in one phenomenon, one event, one body, one land, one being—see Buddha everywhere."

Buddha means awake, being aware everywhere and always. Seeing Buddha everywhere means seeing your own inherent natural Buddha in the fundamental wellspring of your self.

There is not a single time, a single place, a single phenomenon, a single event, a single body, a single land, a single realm of being, where this is not present.

DISCONTINUING THOUGHTS

When you are studying Zen, as you meet with people and deal with situations, never let bad thoughts continue. If you come up with a bad thought unawares, immediately focus your attention and root the thought out. If you just follow that thought and continue such thinking uninterrupted, this will not only hinder Zen realization, it will make you a fool.

MIND YOUR OWN BUSINESS

"Don't draw another's bow, don't ride another's horse, don't mind another's business."

Although this is a common saying, it can also help you penetrate Zen.

Just examine yourself constantly—from morning to night, what have you done that is beneficial to others and to yourself?

If you notice any partiality, you should alert yourself and not overlook it.

NO MIND

"When you have no mind, Zen is easy to find."

In Zen terminology, "mindlessness" does not mean insensitivity or ignorance. It means that the mind is stable and does not get stirred up by the situations and circumstances one encounters; it means the mind does not grasp anything, it is clear in all situations, unimpeded and undefiled, not dwelling on anything, even nondefilement.

THE PURPOSE OF STILLNESS

Those who study Zen should be mentally quiet twenty-four hours a day. When you have nothing to do, you should also sit quietly, making the mind alert and the body tranquil.

Eventually, when you are thoroughly practiced in this, body and mind become spontaneously peaceful and calm, and you have some direction in Zen.

The perfection of mental silence is only to settle scattered and confused awareness. If you cling to stillness as ultimate, you will be taken in by the false Zen of silent illumination.

THE SOURCE OF MIND

Good and bad come from your own mind. But what do you call your own mind, apart from your actions and thoughts? Where does your own mind come from?

If you really know where your own mind comes from, boundless obstacles caused by your own actions will be cleared all at once.

After that, all sorts of extraordinary possibilities will come to you without your seeking them.

THE NATURAL STATE

If you want to empty all things, first clean your own mind. When your mind is clear and clean, all entanglements cease.

Once entanglements cease, both substance and function are in their natural state. "Substance" means the clear, pure, original source of your own mind; the "function" is your own mind's marvelous function of change and creation, which enters into both purity and defilement without being affected by or attached to either purity or defilement.

ADAPTATION

In ancient times, Zen teaching was sometimes abstract, sometimes concrete, sometimes based on a particular time, sometimes transcendental. There was no fixed standard at all.

REAL ZEN

If you think there are any verbal formulations that are special mysterious secrets to be transmitted, this is not real Zen.

Real Zen has no transmission. It is just a matter of people experiencing it, resulting in their ability to see each other's vision and communicate tacitly.

YOUR OWN BUSINESS

Zen is not in quietude, nor is it in clamor. It is not in thought and discrimination, nor is it in dealing with daily affairs. But even so, it is most important that you not abandon quiet and clamor, dealing with daily affairs, or thought and discrimination, in order to study Zen. When your eyes open, you will find all these are your own business.

FOUL WEATHER ZEN

Many people who study Zen are in a burning rush to learn Zen when their worldly affairs are not to their satisfaction, but then give up Zen when they become successful in the world.

PEACE AND QUIET

When you have attained mental and physical peace and quiet, don't get stuck in peace and quiet. Be independent and free, like a gourd rolling and bobbing on a river.

LIVING ZEN

To attain Zen enlightenment, it is not necessary to give up family life, quit your job, become a vegetarian, practice asceticism, and flee to a quiet place, then go into a ghost cave of dead Zen to entertain subjective imaginings.

DEGENERATE ZENNISM

In modern times, Zen and Buddhism have become extremely degenerate. There are incompetent teachers who basically lack enlightenment themselves and have chaotic, unreliable consciousness. Lacking true skills, they take in students and teach everyone to be like themselves.

Quiet Meditation

If you have been practicing quiet meditation but your mind is still not calm and free when in the midst of activity, this means you haven't been empowered by your quiet meditation.

If you have been practicing quietude just to get rid of agitation, then when you are in the midst of agitation, the agitation will disturb your mind just as if you had never done any quiet meditation.

Saving Energy

People are backwards—ignorant of the true self, they pursue things, willingly suffering immeasurable pains in their greed for a little bit of pleasure. In the mornings, before they've opened their eyes and gotten out of bed, when they're still only half awake, their minds are already flying about in confusion, flowing along with random thoughts. Although good and bad deeds have not yet appeared, heaven and hell are already formed in their hearts before they even get out of bed. By the time they go into action, the seeds of heaven and hell are already implanted in their minds.

Did not the Buddha say, "All faculties of sense are receptacles manifested by your own mind. Physical bodies are manifestations of your own minds' representations of forms as subjectively imagined. These manifestations are like the flow of a river, like seeds, like a lamp, like wind, passing away from instant to instant. Frenetic activity, attraction to impure things, and voracity are the causes of the useless, deceptive habits that seem to have always existed, like a waterwheel always turning."

If you really see through this, you understand the meaning of impersonality. You know that heaven and hell are nowhere else but in the heart of the half awake individual about to get out of bed—they do not come from outside.

While in the process of waking up, you should really pay attention. While you are paying attention, you should not make any effort to struggle with whatever is going on in your mind. While struggling you waste energy. As the third ancestor of Zen said, "If you try to stop movement and return to stillness, the attempt to be still will increase movement."

When you notice that you are saving energy in the midst of the mundane stress of daily affairs, this is where you gain energy, this is where you attain buddhahood, this is where you turn hell into heaven.

ZEN HOBBYISTS

There are intellectual professionals who think they know everything but Zen, so they call over a few incompetent old monks, give them a meal, and have them say whatever comes into their minds. The intellectuals then write this babble down and use it to judge everyone else. They trade sayings and call this Zen encounter, imagining they have gotten the advantage if they get in the last word.

They don't even know it if they happen to run into real perceptives. Even if they do notice the real ones, these intellectuals are not really sure, and will not sincerely seek understanding from the teachers. They just seek approval as before. Then when the teachers demonstrate the real developmental impact of Zen in the midst of all sorts of situations, the intellectuals are afraid to approach.

LOOKING FOR THE SHORTCUT

When you have even a single thought of looking for a shortcut in Zen, you have already stuck your head in a bowl of glue.

ATTUNEMENT

Many people today study Zen acquisitively—this is truly a false idea about what has no false ideas.

Just make your mind free. But don't be too tense, and don't be too loose—working this way will save you unlimited mental energy.

LIBERATION

People have been used by the mind's conceptual consciousness since before they can remember, flowing in the waves of birth and death, unable to be independent. If they want to leave birth and death to be joyfully alive, they must cut through decisively, stopping the course of mind's conceptual consciousness.

ZEN SECTS

In Zen, there are no sectarian differences, but when students lack a broad, stable will, and teachers lack a broad, comprehensive teaching, then what they enter into differs. The ultimate point of Zen, however, has no such differences.

PAST, PRESENT, AND FUTURE

Buddha said that when the mind does not grasp things of the past, does not long for things of the future, and does not dwell on things of the present, then one realizes that past, present, and future are empty.

Don't think about past events, whether good or bad, for if you think about them, this impedes the Way. Don't calculate future matters, for if you calculate, you go mad. Don't fix your attention on present affairs, whether unpleasant or pleasant, for if you fix your attention on them, they will disturb your mind.

Just deal with situations as they happen, and you will spontaneously accord with these principles.

Zen Master Hongzhi

The Subtlety of Zen

To learn the subtlety of Zen, you must clarify your mind and immerse your spirit in silent exercise of inner gazing. When you see into the source of reality, with no obstruction whatsoever, it is open and formless, like water in autumn, clear and bright, like the moon taking away the darkness of night.

Finding Out for Oneself

The mind originally is detached from objects, reality basically has no explanation. This is why a classical Zen master said, "Our school has no slogans, and no doctrine to give people." Fundamentally it is a matter of people arriving on their own and finding out for themselves; only then can they talk about it.

Zen Mind

Just wash away the dust and dirt of subjective thoughts immediately. When the dust and dirt are washed away, your mind is open, shining brightly, without boundaries, without center or extremes. Completely whole, radiant with light, it shines through the universe, cutting through past, present, and future.

This is inherent in you, and does not come from outside. This is called the state of true reality. One who has experienced this can enter into all sorts of situations in response to all sorts of possibilities, with subtle function that is marvelously effective and naturally uninhibited.

EVERYONE'S ZEN

Ever since the time of the Buddha and the founders of Zen, there has never been any distinction between ordained and lay people, in the sense that everyone who has accurate personal experience of true realization is said to have entered the school of the enlightened mind and penetrated the source of religion.

ZEN EXPERIENCE

When you are empty and spontaneously aware, clean and spontaneously clear, you are capable of panoramic consciousness without making an effort to grasp perception, and you are capable of discerning understanding without the burden of conditioned thought. You go beyond being and nothingness, and transcend conceivable feelings. This is only experienced by union with it—it is not gotten from another.

ZEN LIFE, ZEN ACTION

The wordly life of people who have mastered Zen is buoyant and unbridled, like clouds making rain, like the moon in a stream, like an orchid in a recondite spot, like spring in living beings. Their action is not self-conscious, yet their responses have order. This is what those who have mastered Zen do.

It is also necessary to turn back to the source, to set foot on the realm of peace, plunge into the realm of purity, and stand alone, without companions, going all the way through the road beyond the buddhas. Only then can you fully comprehend the center and the extremes, penetrate the very top and the very bottom, and freely kill and enliven, roll up and roll out.

AUTUMN AND SPRING

When Zen practice is completely developed, there is no center, no extremes; there are no edges or corners. It is perfectly round and frictionless.

It is also necessary to be empty, open, and unpolluted, so "the clear autumn moon cold, its shining light washes the night. Brocade clouds flower prettily, the atmosphere turns into spring."

THE LIGHT OF MIND

When material sense doesn't blind you, all things are seen to be the light of mind. You transcend with every step, on the path of the bird, no tarrying anywhere. You respond to the world with clarity, open awareness unstrained.

SPONTANEOUS KNOWLEDGE

All realms of phenomena arise from one mind. When the one mind is quiescent, all appearances end. Then which is other, which is self?

Because there arc no differentiated appearances at such a time, nothing at all is defined, not a single thought is produced—you pass beyond before birth and after death; the mind becomes a point of subtle light, round and frictionless, without location, without traces. Then your mind cannot be obscured.

This point where there can be no obscuration is called spontaneous knowledge. Just this realm of spontaneous knowledge is called the original attainment. Nothing whatsoever is attained from outside.

ZEN MASTERY

The action and repose of those who have mastered Zen are like flowing clouds, without self-consciousness, like the full moon, reflected everywhere. People who have mastered Zen are not stopped by anything: though clearly in the midst of all things, still they are highly aloof; though they encounter experiences according to circumstances, they are not tainted or mixed up by them.

ALOOF OF THE TUMULT

When you understand and arrive at the emptiness of all things, then you are independent of every state of mind, and transcend every situation. The original light is everywhere, and you then adapt to the potential at hand; everything you meet is Zen.

While subtly aware of all circumstances, you are empty and have no subjective stance towards them. Like the breeze in the pines, the moon in the water, there is a clear and light harmony. You have no coming and going mind, and you do not linger over appearances.

The essence is in being inwardly open and accommodating while outwardly responsive without unrest. Be like spring causing the flowers to bloom, like a mirror reflecting images, and you will naturally emerge aloof of all tumult.

NORMALCY

The time when you "see the sun in daytime and see the moon at night," when you are not deceived, is the normal behavior of a Zen practitioner, naturally without edges or seams. If you want to attain this kind of normalcy, you have to put an end to the subtle pounding and weaving that goes on in your mind.

ENLIGHTENED AWARENESS

Buddhas and Zen masters do not have different realizations; they all reach the point of cessation, where past, present, and future are cut off and all impulses stop, where there is not the slightest object. Enlightened awareness shines spontaneously, subtly penetrating the root source.

SHEDDING YOUR SKIN

The experience described as shedding your skin, transcending reflections of subjective awareness, where no mental machinations can reach, is not transmitted by sages. It can only be attained inwardly, by profound experience of spontaneous illumination. The original light destroys the darkness, real illumination mirrors the infinite. Subjective assessments of what is or is not are all transcended.

ZEN MASTER YING-AN

ZEN MIND

The mind of Zen adepts is straight as a bowstring, like a long sword against the sky cutting through confusion wherever they may be. Wordly wealth and status, hauteur and extravagance, mundane desires, and all the ups and downs of life, cannot affect them. Fame and profit, judgments of right and wrong, and all the possible states of being, cannot trap them.

FREEDOM

When you pass through, no one can pin you down, no one can call you back.

DESTROYING ZEN

Some people gain an insight and then sit fast on this insight, so their perception is not free. They talk about mystery and marvel, setting forth byways and thinking they are thus helping people. They are destroying Zen.

There is another type of person who cultivates a state of quietude, so their bodies and minds feel somewhat light and calm, and then sit fanatically in the realm where there are no people. When they see others telling of good things, they get irritated and upset, and counter that there is basically nothing in the way of Zen to explain.

This is what an ancient master called a sickness characterized by lack of clarity in all places, in which there appears to be something present. This malady is most miserable.

There are those who get this point of view and then deny everything—there are no buddhas, no Zen masters, no sages. They go on denying, doing whatever they want and calling that "unobstructed Zen."

This is what another ancient master called "Having a vast realization of emptiness, then trying to deny the effects of causes, becoming wild and unrestrained, bringing on disaster."

There is also a type whose point of view is oblivious silence, not hearing anything. After they have eaten of the community's food, they just sit there as if dead, waiting for enlightenment.

People like this are clumps of clay in ramshackle huts in the deep mountains and broad wastelands. They might think they are Buddhist masters with unchanging wisdom, but they are just using up the alms of the faithful.

Real Zen students never have any such resorts; they have in themselves a life transcending religious or sectarian "Zen," with independent perception.

THE FIRST STEP

The beginning of cultivating yourself is right in yourself; on a thousand mile journey, the first step is the most important. If you can do both of these well, the infinite sublime meanings of hundreds of thousands of teachings will be fulfilled.

THE SUBTLETY OF ZEN

In Zen, your eyes are looking southeast while your attention is in the northwest. It cannot be sought by mindlessness, it cannot be understood by mindfulness. It cannot be reached by talking, it cannot be understood by silence.

NOTHING TO GRAB

Zen has nothing to grab onto. When people who study Zen don't see it, that is because they approach too eagerly.

If you want to understand Zen easily, just be mindless, wherever you are, twenty-four hours a day, until you spontaneously merge with the Way.

Once you merge with the Way, inside, outside, or in-between cannot be found at all—you experience a frozen emptiness, totally independent.

This is what an ancient worthy called "The mind not touching things, the steps not placed anywhere."

ORIGINAL ZEN

Early on, Zen was mastered and borne by exceptional people, because unperceptive and impulsive people cannot work it or hold it. All the original adepts were unique in their speech and activity, never willing to sink into stagnancy, as if there were a final form of Zen.

ZEN UNDERSTANDING

First of all, don't establish a preconceived understanding of Zen, yet don't rationalize Zen as "not understanding" either.

It's just like learning archery: eventually you reach a point where ideas are ended and feelings forgotten, and then you suddenly hit the target.

You should also know, furthermore, that there is a subtlety breaking through the target, which is attained spontaneously.

ZEN PRACTICE

Zen cannot be attained by lectures, discussions, and debates. Only those of great perceptive capacity can clearly understand it.

For this reason the ancient adepts did not waste a moment. Even when they weren't calling on teachers to ascertain specific truths, they were involved in real Zen practice, so they eventually attained mature serenity in a natural way. They were not wrapped up in the illusions of the world.

If you can do this, at some point you will suddenly turn the light of your mind around and see through illusions to the real self. Then you will understand where everything comes from—mundane passions and illusions, the material world, form and emptiness, light and darkness, principle and essence, mystery and marvel.

Once you understand this clearly, then you will not be caged or trapped by anything at all, mundane or transmundane.

False Zen, True Zen

There are two kinds of Zen students who won't let go. One kind consists of those who did not meet real teachers at the outset of their quest, plunged into the fires of false teachers, and having been poisoned by their venom, they think their Zen study is done.

Another kind consists of those who join Zen groups and call themselves Zen students but really lack the correct basis. They just usurp what they hear, eager to be known for it, trying to prove themselves, only saying that Zen is just this.

These two kinds of people are fatally ill, unless they recognize their error someday and let go of it sometime.

But what are people in these conditions to let go of, after all? Just let go of the burden of "others" and "self," of ideas of gain and loss, right and wrong, Buddha and Buddhism, mystery and marvel.

As soon as you let go this way, you feel body and mind light and easy, thoroughly pure inside and out. Then your heart is clear all the time. In a cool flash of insight, you go free.

Now you are ready for refinement. If you just keep to the insight you've attained and consider it ultimate, you are still clinging to something. Zen people free from convention are very different from this.

Chills and Fever

If mature people want to cut off the road of birth and death, they should relinquish what they have been holding dear, so that their senses become clean and naked. One day they will gain insight, and the road of birth and death is sure to end.

If you don't practice this in reality, but desire a lot of intellectual knowledge, thinking this is the wonder of self-realization, your chills and fever will be increased by the wind of intellectual knowledge; your nose will always be stuffy and your head will always be foggy.

Lone Lamp Zen

If people want to learn Zen, let them learn the Zen of a lone lamp shining in a death ward.

Do not set up any limit, with the idea that you want to realize Zen for sure by such and such a time.

IMITATION ZEN

There are people who go wrong because they do not comprehend Zen methodology. Some think stonewalling is great, some think utter silence is the ultimate rule, some think literary activity is versatility.

ZEN LIVING

Zen living is a most direct shortcut, not requiring the exertion of the slightest bit of strength to attain enlightenment and master Zen right where you are.

But because Zen seekers are searching too eagerly, they think there must be a special principle, so they try to describe it to themselves mentally, in a subjective way.

Thus they are swept by the machinations of emotive and intellectual consciousness into something that is created and will perish.

They cling to this created, perishable law, rule, principle, or way of life, as something ultimate. This is a serious misstep.

This is why it is said, "Do not talk about ultimate reality with your mind on what is created and destructible."

PERSONALISTIC ZEN

Many Zennists cling to personalistic views as ultimate realities or final truths, and do not believe there can be anything better. As soon as they are put to a real Zen test, they are lost.

This happens when they finally never meet a real Zen master, so their realization is crude. They sit in a nest of "win or lose," fearing to be disturbed by anyone, afraid they'll lose Zen.

Some Zennists say their viewpoints are all correct, and when experienced masters tell them it is not so, they say this is just a deliberate ploy to entrap them and pull them around.

These paranoid Zennists stop after they have merely managed to hold still. This is a fatal disease, which is of its own nature incurable. Therefore all Zen seekers can do is to be careful to avoid it.

The Zen of Essence

When the essence of seeing is everywhere, so is the essence of hearing. When you clearly penetrate the ten directions, there is no inside or outside. This is why it is said, "Effortless in all circumstances, always real in action and stillness." Action like this is the function of complete real wisdom.

Greatness

The ancient Zen masters did not have a single thought of trying to become great people. Only thus did they attain mastery of life and death, and after that greatness came of itself.

If you have a single thought of eagerness to attain Zen mastery, this burns out your potential, so you cannot grow anymore.

Looking for Approval

Nowadays when Zennists see respected masters, they don't ask what to do—all they want is to be told they have some insight. It delights them to hear themselves recognized, unaware that by indulging in this delight they are asking for trouble.

Ancient Zen Practice

The classical masters of Zen were people who had above all let go.

As soon as they showed up, they overturned the sky and wrapped up the earth.

How was it that they were like this?

Simply because their final thought was correct and they couldn't be trapped by false teachers or mountebanks and mesmerists, so their mentalities were beyond clannishness and transcended conventional parameters.

They did not associate with people at random, and they did not dwell on anything ephemeral.

They only kept life and death uppermost in their minds, and yet as they did so they did not suppose there is anything that dies or does not die.

This is how the ancients worked. In this it is essential to penetrate clearly and extend it to full application.

After that, one can undergo radical Zen treatment, lest one still be at a loss in the midst of complex changes and developments.

Needless to say, when one is still at a stage where the mind is "half dark and half light, half clear and half raining," one cannot "walk alone in the vastness" even if one wants to.

GRADUATE ZEN

"Enlightenment is beyond words, and no person has ever attained it."

A classical Zen master said, "Zen has no sayings, nothing at all to give people."

Another classical master said, "I don't like to hear the word 'Buddha.'"

See how they sprayed sand and hurled stones this way. This can already blind people. If you still look for a living road on a staff or search for a representative expression in a shout, this is no different from catching a rat and looking in its mouth for elephant tusks.

This is why the classical Zen masters preserved a certain state, in which no time whatsoever is wasted twenty-four hours a day.

This state is to be maintained until you reach the point where there is nowhere to grasp and nowhere to anchor.

Then you should let go and make yourself empty and quiet, clear and calm, to the point where former intellectual interpretation, rationalization, misknowledge, and misperception, cannot get into your mind or act on it at all.

This is the essential shortcut to the Way. Do this, and one day you will clearly understand what's going on where you are.

EMPOWERING WILL

Generally speaking, Zen requires a decisive, powerful will, because you are going to be cleaning your six senses all the time, so that even if you are in the midst of all the stresses and pleasures of the world, it is like being in a pure, uncontrived realm of great liberation.

Profoundly stable and calm, like a gigantic mountain, you cannot be disturbed by cravings or external conditions, you cannot be held back by interference and difficulty.

This is a shortcut to the Way by empowered work.

The Subtle Mind of Zen

If you want to see the subtle mind of Zen, that is very easy. Just step back and pick it up with intense strength during all of your activities, whatever you are doing, even as you eat, drink, and talk, even as you experience the stress of attending to the world.

Zen Master Mi-an

The Living Road

All people have their own living road to heaven. Until they walk on this road, they are like drunkards who cannot tell which way is which.

Then when they set foot on this road and lose their confusion, it is up to them which way they shall go—they are no longer subject to the arbitrary directions of others.

Totally Alive

When you are totally alive and cannot be trapped or caged, only then do you have some independence. Then you can be in the ordinary world all day long without it affecting you.

Deluded Zen

Many people study Zen, but encounter Zen teachers without clear perception of truth. They make arbitrary explanations and take their subjective interpretations of Zen sayings for final truths. Their aim is to be recognized as understanding Zen. This is a most serious malady.

Zen Malfunctions

When people study Zen diligently but do not attain enlightenment, their problem may be in a number of places.

It may be in getting bogged down in Zen sayings.
It may be in sitting transfixed in a realm of surpassing wonder.
It may be in empty formlessness.
It may be in keeping Zen or Buddhism on one's mind.
It may be in trying to reject illusion for enlightenment.

ZEN MASTER MI-AN   201

It may be in not having met a real enlightened teacher at the outset and thus having been drawn into a nest of complications.

These problems are not experienced only by beginners. Even ancient Zen masters who had thoroughly understood the basic mind and seen into its fundamental nature realized the original state but still did not understand the whole truth.

THE ZEN SHORTCUT

The shortcut of Zen is to leave the present and directly experience the state before birth, before the division of wholeness.

When you accomplish this, you are like a dragon in the water, like a tiger in the mountains. You are very clear and calm everywhere, free to enliven or kill everywhere, spontaneously able to "rouse the wind and stir the grasses" everywhere. You do not cling to any activity, you do not sit inactive.

This is like cutting a skein of thread, and dyeing a skein of thread—when one is cut all are cut, when one is dyed all are dyed. From top to bottom, the whole thing is a huge door of liberation. Now Buddhist truths and things of the world have become one—where is there any external thing at all to constitute an impediment?

Zen Master Xiatang

The Perception of Sages

The Scripture on Infinite Light says, "Rivers, lakes, birds, trees, and forests all invoke Buddha, Truth, and Communion."

In a moment of awareness without discrimination, great wisdom appears. This is like pouring water into the ocean, like working a bellows in the wind.

Furthermore, how do you discriminate? "Buddha" is a temporary name for what cannot be seen when you look, what cannot be heard when you listen, whose place of origin and passing away cannot be found when you search.

It covers form and sound, pervades sky and earth, penetrates above and below. There is no second view, no second person, no second thought. It is everywhere, in everything, not something external.

This is why the single source of all awareness is called "Buddha."

It doesn't change when the body deteriorates, it is always there. But you still cannot use what is always there. Why? Because, as the saying goes, "Although gold dust is precious, when it gets in your eyes it obstructs vision." Although buddhahood is wonderful, if you are obsessed with it it becomes a sickness.

An early Zen master said, "It is not mind, not Buddha, not a thing—what is it?" This says it all. It has brought us the diamond sword that cuts through all obsessions.

Another classical Zen master said, "The slightest entangling thought can cause hellish actions; a flash of feeling can chain you indefinitely. Just end ordinary feelings, and there is no special perception of sages to seek—the perception of sages appears where ordinary feelings end."

Breaking Habits

To learn to be a Buddha, first you should break through the seeds of habit with great determination, and then be aware of cause and effect so that you fear to do wrong. Transcend all mental objects, stop all rumination. Don't let either good or bad thoughts enter into your thinking, forget about both Buddhism and things of the world. Let go of body and mind, like letting go over a cliff. Be like space, not producing subjective thoughts of life and death, or any signs of discrimination. If you have any views at all, cut them right off and don't let them continue.

Zen Master Yuansou

The Crowning Meditation

If you do not listen truly, you will call the bell a pitcher, and inevitably wind up adding error to error, talking about "Buddha," "Zen masters," "mind," and "essence." How is this different from gouging a wound in healthy flesh?

Real Zennists set a single eye on the state before the embryo is formed, before any signs become distinct. This opens up and clears the mind, so that it penetrates the whole universe. Then they are no different from the Buddha and the founder of Zen.

This is called the crowning meditation, the jewel that reflects all colors, the inexhaustible treasury, the gateway to spiritual powers, the diamond sword, the crouching lion, the blaze—there are various names for it.

Now there is nothing in the universe, nothing mundane or transmundane, to be an object, an opposite, a barrier, or a hindrance to you.

Expedients and Reality

The mountains, rivers, earth, grasses, trees, and forests, are always emanating a subtle, precious light, day and night, always emanating a subtle, precious sound, demonstrating and expounding to all people the unsurpassed ultimate truth.

It is just because you miss it right where you are, or avoid it even as you face it, that you are unable to attain actual use of it.

This is why Buddhism came into being, with its many expedients and clever explanations, with temporary and true, immediate and gradual, half and full, partial and complete teachings. These are all simply means of stopping children from whining.

IT

Those who meditate in silent stillness regard silent stillness as final, but it is not something to finalize in stillness. Those who assert mastery in the midst of busyness are satisfied with busyness, but it is not something to be satisfied with in the midst of busyness. Those who learn from the scriptures consider the scriptures basic, but it is not learned from the scriptures. Those who work with teachers and colleagues regard this as a profound source, but it is not attained from working with teachers and colleagues.

It is a formless, indestructible being that has always been like a fish hidden in a spring, that drums up waves and dances by itself. When you look for it in the east, it goes west; when you look for it in the south, it goes north. It can give names to everyone, but no one can give it a name. In all places and all times it is the master of myriad forms, the teacher of myriad phenomena.

DISTORTION BY TEACHERS

The "one road beyond" is vast as cosmic space times ten; it cannot be sought with mind, it cannot be attained by mindlessness. It cannot be reached by words, it cannot be understood by silence. The essential point is for the individual to be firm in faith and see right through the state before the embryo is formed, before any signs become distinct.

Passing through the heights and the depths, escaping all traps, ranging over all time, totally without attachment and repulsion, free in all ways, when you attain great independence you have some measure of accord with the one road beyond.

If you rely on the differences in teachers and see the differences in persons, you are misled by blind teachers into reifying Buddha, Dharma, Zen, Tao, mysteries, marvels, functions, and states. One way and another this glues your tongue down, nails your eyes shut, and constricts your heart.

Like oil getting into flour, this becomes deeply ingrained, until you eventually become a sprite or a ghoul, emanating countless "lights" and manifesting countless "psychic powers," thinking you are peerless in all the world. This is what is meant by the saying, "Our perception is originally correct, but it is distorted by teachers."

LIBERATION

This inconceivable door of great liberation is in everyone. It has never been blocked, it has never been defective. Buddhas and Zen masters have appeared in the world and provided expedient methods, with many different devices, using illusory medicines to cure illusory illnesses, just because your faculties are unequal, your knowledge is unclear, you do not transcend what you see and hear as you see and hear it, and you are tumbled about endlessly in an ocean of misery by afflictions due to ignorance, by emotional views and habitual conceptions of others and self, right and wrong.

The various teachings and techniques of buddhas and Zen masters are only set forth so that you will individually step back into yourself, understand your own original mind and see your own original nature, so that you reach a state of great rest, peace, and happiness.

BAD HABITS

In the root and stem of your own psyche there is an accumulation of bad habits. If you cannot see through them and act independently of them, you will unavoidably get bogged down along the way.

SPONTANEOUS ZEN

In Buddhism there is no place to apply effort. Everything in it is normal—you put on clothes to keep warm and eat food to stop hunger—that's all. If you consciously try to think about it, it is not what you think of. If you consciously try to arrange it, it is not what you arrange.

EXPEDIENTS

Buddhist teachings are prescriptions given according to specific ailments, to clear away the roots of your compulsive habits and clean out your emotional views, just so you can be free and clear, naked and clean, without problems.

There is no real doctrine at all for you to chew on or squat over. If you will not believe in yourself, you pick up your baggage and go around to other people's houses looking for Zen, looking for Tao, looking for mysteries, looking for marvels, looking for buddhas, looking for Zen masters, looking for teachers.

You think this is searching for the ultimate, and you make it into your religion, but this is like running blindly to the east to get something that is in the west. The more you run, the further away you are, and the more you hurry the later you become. You just tire yourself, to what benefit in the end?

ZEN MIND

The mind of people of the Way is straight as a bowstring. Simply because they are not burdened by ideas of others and themselves, of right and wrong, of sacred and profane, of better and worse, or by deception, falsehood, flattery, or deviousness, they spontaneously gain access to the substance of mind that dwells on nothing.

Fundamentally this is not another, not oneself, not ordinary, not holy, not mind, not Buddha, not a thing, not Zen, not Tao, not a mystery, not a marvel.

It is only because of a moment of subjectivity in discrimination, grasping and rejecting, that so many horns are suddenly produced on your head and you are turned about by those myriad objects all the time, unable to be free and independent.

Afterword

Reflections on the Science of Freedom

Someone asked one of the early Zen masters to teach him a way to liberation.

The Zen master said, "Who binds you?"
The seeker of liberty said, "No one binds me."
The Zen master said, "Then why seek liberation?"

Liberation of the human mind from the inhibiting effects of mesmerism by its own creations is the essence of Zen. This liberation is seen on the one hand in terms of freeing the mind from uncomfortable and unnecessary limitations and on the other in terms of freeing the "great potential and great function" dormant in the unknown realm of conscious action beyond those limitations. Early Zen masters revived the teaching of Buddha that liberation is the essential criterion of spiritual authenticity, not tradition or convention.

In modern times it has become customary to think of bondage primarily in social, political, or economic terms. Emotional, intellectual, and more subtle forms of bondage are commonly associated with side effects or secondary developments of more obvious forms of oppression, such as those visible in material or institutional terms. Bondage is often seen primarily as something imposed from without, while its internal manifestations are regarded as reactions or adaptations to the external condition.

Buddhist thought, on the other hand, sees mind as the ultimate source of bondage, whether imposed by others or self-imposed. If this is true, it explains why social liberation and reform movements that work on the symptoms of bondage and injustice without effectively addressing their source are never completely or finally effective. History tells of political liberators who became oppressors in turn; of organizations originally set up to protect rights turning into usurpers of rights; of institutions ostensibly established to free people from ignorance becoming little more than tools for the imprisonment of minds within the boundaries of received opinion.

According to Zen teaching, the quest for freedom itself has the power to bind, whether it be acted out in psychological, political, or religious terms. Buddhism insists that real freedom is possible, even if its price includes the very myths and illusions that may have once inspired this aspiration. Just as mind is considered by Buddhists to be the source of bondage, it is also considered to be the source of enlightenment. Buddhists believe that unimaginable capacities for fulfillment lie hidden in the mind, concealed by the preoccupations of day-to-day concerns and worries.

Who binds us? Buddhism says we bind ourselves in the web of our individual and collective ideas, words, and acts. This is held true of everything from personal neuroses to massive oppressions, from self-inflicted suffering to the suffering that people impose on their neighbors. Furthermore, these ideas, words, and acts are observed to emerge from subtle attitudes or mental postures that unconsciously potentiate them and sustain their continuity.

Since these postures are rarely given conscious critical examination, screened as they are by their own subjectivity, the beginning of bondage, from the development of the characteristic inclinations these inner attitudes foster and the reinforcement they attract, is in Zen terminology called "tying yourself up without rope."

From a Zen point of view, the problem underlying diverse manifestations of bondage is a fundamental confusion. In classic Zen terms, this is expressed as mistaking the servant for the master, or taking a guest for the host. Even obvious forms of bondage, such as the political and economic enslavement of peoples, begin and develop into repetitious cycles from the domination of minds by ideas, words, and acts. Buddhist thinking recognizes the susceptibility of the mind to suggestion and conditioning, hence the proverb, "Be master of mind rather than mastered by mind."

While it is understood that nothing can be said about an absolute objectivity totally beyond the mind that supposes it, Buddhism strives for the greatest possible objectivity in understanding humanity, free from the biases and prejudices that blight human relations and prevent humankind from seeing itself as it is. In order to accomplish this, Buddhism examines the relationship between subjectivity and objectivity from every possible angle to arrive at the limits of what can be known about what is real and what is true.

Until one reaches the point where this critical discernment can be made, Zen liberation is not really possible. People may feel liberated when all they have had is a change of concern. They may feel justified when they are only convinced they are right, and these feelings may be all they really want. Then again, people may feel relieved to be having things to do, think about, and talk about, without this really satisfying them or nourishing them inwardly; they may be, in Zen terms, stuffed but not fulfilled. People may feel impelled by conscience to act in ways that do not achieve what they envision because they cannot master the will and knowledge of which their impulses are echoes. All the problems of psychological and spiritual inauthenticity are placed under the rigorous scrutiny of the Zen eye. Zen drives at the reality of freedom, not the image of freedom.

An age-old Zen observation has been that whatever stimulates or motivates people, whether it be expressed in economic, political, social, psychological, or religious terms, may in fact be inhibiting them from fulfilling the very needs and desires that stimulate and motivate them. In Zen terms this does not mean that the object in itself thwarts anyone, but that the individual's conception of the object and attitude toward it are unfulfilling.

Here is the crux of the Zen approach to liberation. The shackles of poverty and oppression are visible to the ordinary eye, and it is not hard to find agreement in sympathy for those thus afflicted. Often, however, people—and peoples—are chained by shackles that they in fact treasure. As one Zen master said, it is hard for people to see anything wrong with what they like, or to see anything good in what they do not like. Another Zen master noted that familiarity itself is a quality that people are generally inclined to like. This means that predilections and habits with which people feel comfortable at a given time may serve them for comfort but may in fact be holding them back from greater capacity for progress and fulfillment.

Like Taoism, its ancient predecessor, Zen has long observed that one of the predilections contrary to real progress in social and individual development is the desire for rapid and visible results. Countless studies have shown that the results of haste in social and political affairs are similar to the results of haste in psychological studies— depression, resentment, regret, and longing, which eventually consume any temporary gains that might have been made. What is finally left of this process, after emotions are exhausted, is a collection of rationalizations, in themselves as ineffective as emotions alone.

It is sometimes asked, for example, why massive hunger and oppression continue to exist in spite of large quantities of surplus wealth and elaborate systems of law and government. Searching for an answer to this conundrum, a political thinker might focus mainly on the interplay of conflicting material interests involved and the influence of interlopers. A social scientist might advance theories resorting to peculiarities of culture and history to explain the persistence of involutionary social patterns. A Zen observer would, however, have to consider the entire nexus of conditions impartially, without isolating any one element because of emotional associations.

In order to understand truthfully what is really possible in a given situation, the would-be illuminate may have to stand aside from inculcated ideals and sacrifice sentimental compassion. This is part of the "great death" Zen practitioners seek in order to clarify their minds and see what is before them impersonally and impartially, so that they may start life fresh without the burden of past illusions.

One of the most attractive illusions of modern times has been the popular myth that freedom can be gained and safeguarded simply by appropriately designed systems of organization and government. While one system may prove more effective than another under given conditions, nevertheless the fact remains that people still create and operate the systems, making individual human development critical to any process of social improvement. This is taken for granted in Buddhist political thought.

Emphasis in Buddhism on individual liberation, even in schools whose express aim is collective liberation, has given rise to the misconception that it is a socially passive, even escapist, religion. While passivism and escapism are well-documented corruptions of certain practices, these attitudes are far from the spirit of Buddhism. Importance is placed on the commonweal even in the schools that focus primarily on individual liberation; the liberation of individuals is seen as an integral part of the welfare of society, reducing sources of conflict and enabling people to work for the benefit of others unhindered by personal ambition.

According to Buddhist teaching, even a simple act of generosity is not really genuine as long as it is tainted by personal feelings, even the desire to give or the satisfaction of giving. This does not mean that Buddhists withhold social action until they reach the ultimate objectivity, but that they do not use social action to mollify their own personal human feelings. Rather, Buddhists use action as a means of knowledge, and use knowledge to guide action. According to "The Book on the Ten Stages" in *The Flower Ornament Scripture*, one of the seminal texts of universalist Buddhism, when practitioners reach the stage where they are perfecting meditation, they "practice whatever in the world would benefit sentient beings." Among the activities mentioned in the scripture are writing, teaching, mathematics, natural science, medicine, performing arts, engineering, horticulture, and psychology.

History shows traces of Buddhist activity in a wide variety of cultural, social, economic, and political operations in Asia. Buddhist contributions to fine and applied arts, literature, philosophy, medicine, and education are comparatively well known. Buddhists also played an important part in reclamation and conservation of land, water, and human resources, as well as in the development of banking, trade, crafts, hostelry, communications, printing, and publishing. Buddhists participated in government at all levels, particularly local administration, but they also intervened from outside, sometimes arranging mass amnesties for political prisoners and even leading armed uprisings against oppressive regimes. Buddhism also established a socially acceptable means whereby women could exercise the right to divorce, as well as the first public facilities for orphans in the clan-oriented societies of old Asia.

The social activities of Buddhists of the past are not always noticed by Western observers who expect such activities to be invariably accompanied by a great deal of publicity as well as the constitution of official or quasi-official institutes and organizations for the discharge of these functions. Buddhism, in its purest sense, is based on the fluidity of events, and its programs are local and specific even if they are based on universal principles or a higher understanding of humanity. Zen Buddhism is particularly strident in its warnings against trying to institutionalize the "good" or the "holy" because of the sentimental attachments built up around these ideas, and the hypocrisy that feeds on these attachments.

Buddhism confronts the individual and society as a whole with the problems of self and mind, and does not allow for escapism—whether that escapism be by nihilism and quietism, or by immersion in movements that provide people with ready-made ideas, activities, and interests in which the devotee can "forget the self." Buddhist literature contains many warnings about the seductive delusions presented by these attempts to avoid the questions of self, mind, and true reality. Yet it is precisely these forms of escapism which because of their conspicuous nature are often mistaken for legitimate expressions of Buddhism and not recognized as deviations.

The first step of the Buddhist approach to liberation is to determine the source of bondage. According to a Zen proverb, "The answer is in the question," and the art of useful questioning is a key to Zen. The proverb also says, however, "The question is in the answer," in that it is not enough to know the answer, it is essential to work the answer out in life; thus the question becomes how to apply the answer to living situations.

The opening statement of the *Dhammapada*, perhaps the oldest written record of Buddha's teaching, provides a classic presentation of the problem of bondage, in which the answer and the question clearly contain each other: "Everything is based on mind, is lead by mind, is fashioned by mind. If you speak and act with a polluted mind, suffering will follow you, as the wheels of an oxcart follow the footsteps of the ox. Everything is based on mind, is lead by mind, is fashioned by mind. If you speak and act with a pure mind, happiness will follow you, as a shadow clings to a form."

Pursuing this basic theme, *The Flower Ornament Scripture*, the most comprehensive of Buddhist texts, says, "Mind is like an artist, able to paint the worlds." Contrasting the possibilities of mentally fashioned worlds, the scripture also says, "Some lands have no light; they are dark and full of fear, with pains like the wounds of weapons. Those who see them suffer by themselves. . . . Some worlds are terrifying, with great howls of pain, those voices most bitter and harsh, frightening all who hear. . . . In some lands are always heard heavenly sounds of various gods, pure sounds of celestial realms, or the voices of leaders of the worlds."

In a more detailed analysis of the root of involution, the "Ten Stages" book of *The Flower Ornament Scripture* says,

> Because of continually slipping into erroneous views, because of minds shrouded by the darkness of ignorance, because of being

puffed up with pride, because of conceptions, because of mental fixations of desires caught in the net of craving, because of hopes pursued by actions in the tangle of deceit and falsehood, because of deeds connected with envy and jealousy producing mundane states, because of accumulation of actions rife with passion, hatred, and folly, because of the flames of mind bound up with delusion, because of seeds in the mind, intellect, and consciousness bound to the flows of lust, existence, and ignorance, therefore ignorant people produce sprouts of subsequent life in the world.

Over the course of centuries, Zen developed a science of freedom, dealing with both the subtle but knowable and coarse but ignorable psychological bases of limitation and growth. This science was not a new creation of Zen schools, however, for Zen inherited extremely rich amalgams of Indian, central Asian, and Southeast Asian developments in the search for mental freedom. According to conditions, however, the science of liberation always remained esoteric to a greater or lesser degree, for three main reasons: first, because it is by its very nature difficult for the conditioned mind to grasp; second, because of the possibility of misuse; and third, because it was inevitably perceived as a threat by people with proprietary interests in ideology and custom, who naturally had considerable influence in society.

In accordance with tradition, generations of early Zen teachers reexamined the principles and practices of this science and encoded it in an immense body of anecdotes, aphorisms, and poetry, all designed to protect the science and reproduce its desired effect, mental freedom. In reality, there is some Zen in all schools of Buddhism, and there is something of all schools of Buddhism to be found in Zen; in spite of vast theoretical and methodological differences, where the aim of freedom is realized there can be no difference in essence.

The basis for the symbolic Zen language of mind was constructed within three or four centuries of the beginning of Zen in China. During this time, many of the fundamental teachings and approaches of Zen were put into groups of stories about the early masters. There is, for example, the figure of the unfathomable Baozhi, a mendicant meditation master of extraordinary attainments who taught mainly by symbolic acts and laconic statements, which led to his being now imprisoned for "disturbing the masses" with his miraculous powers, now invited to court to enlighten the emperor. He is one of the first adepts to leave writings prized in the Zen traditions.

Then there is the story of Fu Shanhui, a small farmer and family man who by dint of his own study and effort attained higher consciousness and became a renowned philanthropist, teacher, and social activist. He is known for converting many of his relatives and people of his locality and for his extraordinary acts of charity. He even tried to gain an interview with the emperor to offer him some advice on ameliorating the wretched conditions of the times, but because of his low social status he was unable to make any headway until Baozhi, who knew of Shanhui's enlightenment, intervened at court.

Both of these characters, Baozhi and Fu Shanhui, figure prominently in Zen lore; neither belonged to any perceptible school, but both represent prototypes of freedom and independence. Even the radical differences between them are typical of Zen, for as the saying goes, "If all the waves of the Zen stream were alike, innumerable ordinary people would get bogged down."

Both Baozhi and Fu Shanhui are said to have met Bodhidharma, who is usually called the founder of Zen and is one of the most important symbols of Zen tradition. Bodhidharma is represented as an Indian prince (like Buddha himself) who abandoned a life of luxury in order to seek a more permanent reality. According to the legend, his teacher was the leading Buddhist master in India of that time. This teacher instructed Bodhidharma to go to China sixty-seven years after the teacher's death, the story goes, so he traveled by the sea route from south India to China in his old age to carry out his mission.

Bodhidharma is represented as having drawn the distinction between sociocultural manifestations of religion and the ultimate understanding of Zen. To cross the broad cultural gap between India and China, Bodhidharma used the Buddhist doctrine of consciousness, which cuts through cultural and historical differences to the essence of the human mind. Much later, his teaching was referred to as "direct pointing to the human mind to see its essence and attain enlightenment."

The doctrine of consciousness is a useful tool for understanding what Zen does, and this is one reason for its traditional association with the Zen founder Bodhidharma. According to this teaching, things have three natures: imaginary, relative, and absolute. The es-

sence and practice of Zen lie in these three natures and their interplay.

The imaginary nature of things means things as we conceive of
them, as we represent them to ourselves subjectively. The imaginary
nature of things is known by the way we think and talk about things.
Thus the imaginary nature of things is conditioned by cultural and
personal history and custom.

The relative nature of things is the nature of phenomena as existing only in relation to one another. According to the doctrine, the
inherent reality of this continuous interaction of interdependent conditions is ultimately beyond the scope of human conception, because
all conceptions of it are mental images superimposed on it, not the
thing in itself.

The absolute reality, the doctrine concludes, is the emptiness of
reality, or the ultimate unreality, of the imaginary nature of things. It
may also be described as the relative nature of things being empty of
real correspondence to their imagined natures. The classical Zen
master Baizhang said, "If you realize there is no connection between
your senses and the external world, you will be liberated on the spot."

The doctrine says that absolute reality can be witnessed, but not
by ordinary sense or thought. According to Buddhist texts that analyze the reception of Buddhism in human communities, when the
doctrine is stated this far, there inevitably arises the idea that the aim
of Buddhism is to depart from the fiction of imaginary reality to unite
with the ultimate nature of absolute reality. According to these diagnostic texts, this misunderstanding is one of the main problems of
practical Buddhism. It is dealt with very frequently in Zen writings.

According to the doctrine of consciousness, the imaginary reality
of the present becomes incorporated into the available dimension of
the relative reality of the future. In ordinary terms, views and attitudes condition deeds that influence environments, which in turn
affect views and attitudes. The purpose of realization of absolute reality is not to annihilate imaginary reality but to attain the practical
freedom to affect it deliberately, not just reinforce it by automatic
habit.

The *Sandhinirmocana-sutra,* a classic of the consciousness-only
doctrine, says that the essential means by which absolute reality is
known is nonattachment to the imaginary reality. The Zen teachings
of "mindlessness," "no thought," "stopping the mind," and so on, are

all representations of this exercise of letting go of the image of the world to witness the absolute. This is why making the mind blank is rejected in Zen, since this state is just another image and not detachment from imagination.

One of the early classical Zen masters is often quoted as teaching this formula for Zen: "First you go over to the other side (the absolute) to find out it exists, then you come back to this side (the relative as it is perceived in common) to act." After a certain degree of experience, direct knowledge of absolute reality replaces meditation as the means to control one's relationship to imaginary reality.

Using the freedom this brings, the Zen Buddhist can then gain access to a greater range of consciousness of relative reality than is permitted by a closed system of attitudes and concepts. This increases potential for effective cultivation or reconstruction of imaginary reality in ways that will bring about improvements in future relative reality.

In the Flower Ornament School of Buddhism, from which Zen freely borrowed, this two-sided process is referred to in terms of "returning objects to mind" (realizing images are mental) and "realizing true emptiness" (fictional nature of images), then "projecting objects from mind" (working out viable, constructive images) and "realizing subtle being" (the concretization of thought in action).

Both of these steps have specific practical guidelines, or natural laws for working with the absolute and the relative. These are presented in many different ways throughout the Buddhist canon. One of the most explicit descriptions of the rule for the absolute, one that clarifies a basic attribute of Zen, is to be found in the *Sandhinirmocana-sutra.* According to this scripture the Buddha said,

> The ultimate truth of which I speak is that which is inwardly realized by sages, while the scope of thought and deliberation is what unenlightened people testify to among themselves. Therefore you should know that ultimate truth transcends all objects of thought and deliberation. The ultimate truth of which I speak has no form to which to relate, whereas thought and deliberation operate only in the sphere of forms. Therefore you should know that ultimate truth transcends all objects of thought and deliberation. The ultimate truth of which I speak cannot be expressed in words, whereas thought and deliberation only operate

in the realm of verbalization. Therefore you should know that ultimate truth transcends all objects of thought and deliberation. The ultimate truth of which I speak has no representation, whereas thought and deliberation only operate in the realm of representation. Therefore you should know that ultimate truth transcends all objects of thought and deliberation. The ultimate truth of which I speak puts an end to all controversy, whereas thought and deliberation only operate in the realm of controversy. Therefore you should know that ultimate truth transcends all objects of thought and deliberation.

Thus classical Zen teachers insist that Zen cannot be understood or attained by ordinary cognition. The scripture goes on to illustrate how mental habits inhibit the awakening of the subtle formless perception and knowledge activated in Zen realization:

Someone accustomed to pungent and bitter flavors all his life cannot think of or assess or believe in the sweetness of honey or sugar. Someone who in ignorance takes an overwhelming interest in desires because of passionate craving and is therefore inflamed with excitement, as a result, cannot think of or assess or believe in the marvelous bliss of detachment and inward effacement of sense data. Someone in ignorance who, because of overwhelming interest in words, clings to rhetoric, cannot, as a result, think of or assess or believe in the pleasure of holy silence with inner tranquillity. Someone in ignorance who, because of overwhelming interest in perceptual and cognitive signs, clings to the appearances of the world, cannot, as a result, think of or assess or believe in ultimate nirvana that obliterates all signs so that reification ends.

Just as people in ignorance, because of their various controversies and beliefs involving attachments to self and possessions, cling to mundane contentions and therefore cannot think of or assess or believe in an ideal state in which there is no egotism, no possessiveness, no attachment, and no contention, in the same way those who pursue thoughts cannot think of or assess or believe in the character of the ultimate truth that is beyond the sphere of all thought and deliberation.

Because of the radical difference between Zen knowledge and ordinary knowledge, the emphasis placed on this absolute law in Zen teaching often draws so much attention that an imbalance is created. Nevertheless, in spite of the drawbacks of emphasizing the absolute—drawbacks mainly deriving from exaggerated reactions such as irrational yearning or fear—it is axiomatic that the relative rule itself cannot be made fully effective without realization of the absolute. Zen proverb says, "Let go over a cliff, die completely, and then come back to life—after that you cannot be deceived." Knowledge of the absolute is thus used to cut through subjective illusions or sentiments about what is indicated, or what is possible, in the realms of the relative and imaginary rules.

Perhaps the most concise yet inclusive definition of the relative rule—which is relative to the realm in which it is carried out—is articulated in the *Flower Ornament Scripture:* the rule states that enlightening action includes all "that which is conducive to the benefit and well being of all creatures." The steps taken to carry out this rule are summarized in two classical Zen stories: two masters were asked what one should do in daily life; one said, "I do not ask about daily life, I only require that your vision be true," and the other said, "Each step should tread on this question." Together these stories illustrate the harmonization of the two facets of Zen realization, following the traditional approach that avoids both dogma and denial.

One of the greatest tasks of Zen, therefore, is to make the transition between the imagined, relative, and absolute levels of reality as fluid as possible. The doctrine of consciousness uses another model for this purpose, that of "three subtle and six coarse aspects" of conscious representation. An excellent tool for self-observation, this model is also useful for understanding the purposes of Zen procedures.

The first of the three subtle aspects is called ignorant conditioned consciousness. This gives rise to what is called the state of excitement, which is the appearance of subjectivity. This second aspect produces the third, which is the objectivization of the views of this subjective state of excitement. Herein lies the imperceptible link between the relative and the imaginary. The appearance of the objectivization of subjectivity is further subjected to the treatment known as the six coarse aspects of consciousness.

The first of these six coarse aspects of consciousness is cognition, cognition of the characteristics of the mental constructs projected to define the world. The second aspect is continuity, or repetition of these constructs. The third is attachment to the specific appearances thus construed. The fourth coarse aspect of consciousness is assignment of labels. The fifth is action based on the ideas and attitudes thus engendered. The sixth and final aspect of conditioned consciousness is that of the pain caused by bondage to habit.

There are various Zen techniques used to interrupt the mental formation of vicious cycles at critical points in this chain of subtle and coarse aspects of conditioning. The stories and images of Zen tradition are themselves means of affecting the quality of consciousness by their impact on certan links of the chain.

Bodhidharma is said to have founded Zen in China based on the doctrine of consciousness without any organizational ties. According to one legend, Bodhidharma spent over fifty years in China, teaching whenever the occasion arose. Other sources say he was there for a much briefer period and was much more limited in his activity. It is generally believed that he communicated the innermost secrets of Zen to four people, including one woman. It is also said that he was poisoned six times by rivalrous Buddhist priests, and finally allowed himself to die, at a very advanced age, when his teaching mission was completed.

As so often happens in Zen tradition, most of Bodhidharma's heirs disappear from center stage into the historical unknown. Most of the lore of later generations focuses on only one of the first Chinese Zen masters, a man named Huike. There are several key stories about Huike, representing such topics as the triumph of mind over matter, the Zen exercise of looking for the source of mind, the use of hectic environments to test mental stability, and the continuity of Zen work in the midst of ordinary work. Huike used to go to the outer gates of great urban monasteries and give talks on the formless teaching of Zen mind, drawing large crowds. As a result, like Bodhidharma he was persecuted by sectarians, finally to die by execution at a very advanced age.

Three hundred years later, a famous Zen master was to say, "Our ancestors were driven out wherever they went," referring to the psychological reality that the radical independence of Zen is anathema to ordinary human sentiment, leaving the individual with the solitary struggle of lifting sensibility above the rationalization and emotion that regard familiarity as the fundamental criterion of reality.

Huike is said to have had ten private students, nearly half of them lay people, to whom he communicated the essence of Zen. In view of the intensity and weight of the illustrative tales of early Zen, concentrating whole lifetimes and generations into a few vignettes, it is noteworthy that this lore claims that women and lay people were included in Zen Buddhism from its very inception.

Very many Buddhist scriptures and other writings are regularly addressed to lay men and women, and contain many examples of male and female lay adepts and teachers. Zen history also says that the lineages of the so-called Five Houses of Zen, the major classical schools of Zen in China, were all patched by women at critical junctures during their formative generations.

The prospect of liberation for women and the common person in general was, as usual, regarded by entrenched political interests as a threat to the constituted order of society. This was a major reason why mendicants, who in their true form were people who had abandoned personal interest in wordly gain or loss, were commonly chosen to represent Buddhism publicly, in order to calm the irrational fears of politicians and academics. When some monks became potentates themselves, however, and politics invaded the monasteries, this particular function diminished considerably.

Zen master Huike is also represented as caring for the sick, part of the overall tradition of Buddhist practice. His most famous healing was of Sengcan, a man with a dreaded disease who was eventually to become Huike's Zen successor. In this case Huike is said to have used purely spiritual means of healing to release the hold of the illness on the man and enable him to recover his health naturally and spontaneously.

Mental healing in Zen, important enough to be included among the tales of the founders, appears here and there throughout Zen history but is seldom singled out for emphasis. The mental healing of Huisi, another early Zen master reckoned as one of the founders of Tiantai Buddhism, is also documented in Zen history. His student Zhiyi, the definitive author of the highly articulated Tiantai system of Buddhism, included teachings on healing methods in his famous works on meditation.

Huike's successor Sengcan, is traditionally credited with authorship of "The Trusting Heart," one of the earliest and most enduringly popular works on Zen. Quotations from this favorite work appear throughout later Zen literature. Generally speaking, it is a guide to

Zen meditation, but the unifying theme is mental balance. Many of the Zen instructions translated in the present volume are very much in the spirit of this early Zen classic.

Sengcan's successor Daoxin was the first great Chinese Zen master to establish a special commune for intensive Zen study. Like numerous other Zen masters, he is represented as refusing the honors bestowed on him by the emperor of China, illustrating the transcendence of Zen over wordly ambitions.

Now that Zen was in the public eye, Daoxin articulated a wide variety of methods and strictly exacting criteria for Zen teachers. He emphasized the natural law of Zen transmission, that no one could possibly teach Zen to another without having already attained perfect clarity of mind. He himself is said to have given only one of five hundred students permission to teach. This student, a man of unknown origin named Hongren, attracted a following of seven hundred students, eleven of whom became recognized as enlightened successors and public Zen teachers.

Hongren is formally designated as the author of a short treatise on the Zen technique of preserving the original mind, but this work is little noted in Zen tradition. More commonly Hongren is associated with the transcendent wisdom teaching of Buddhism, which distinguishes mind from mental states and separates the essence of religion from emotion and sentimentality. The transcendent wisdom teaching, also central to Tiantai Buddhist praxis, came to be used in Zen schools to such an extent that some observers have identified Zen with a development of this particular phase of Buddhism.

With the career of Hongren's foremost successor, the renowned Zen master Huineng, the history of what shortly became the mainstream of Zen began. Huineng, who died in the early eighth century, is portrayed as an illiterate young woodcutter from a backward region of China who suddenly awoke to the truth of Zen when he happened to hear someone reciting a popular transcendent wisdom scripture. According to legend, he stayed in the community of the great Zen master Hongren for a brief time as manual laborer, received recognition of his enlightenment, then fled in secret to avoid the hostility of the scholars in the community. He spent fifteen years living in the mountains with bands of hunters, and finally reappeared in southern China as a mature Zen master who attracted seekers of truth from all over China.

The legend of Huineng typifies a number of basic Zen themes. Being from a backward area, without social status or formal education, he represents the same transcendence of caste and custom that the original Buddha represented when he declared the ancient Indian caste system invalid in Buddhism and told people not to believe in anything just because it is a traditional belief, or because it is written in books or pronounced by authorities. And just as Buddhism produced the first great sacred Indian literature in vernacular languages, so did Zen Buddhism produce, in the three centuries after Huineng, a sacred literature in vernacular Chinese.

Enlightened as a young man without the benefit of any previous training or education, Huineng responded to a test devised by Hongren to illustrate something to his large community of students. Zen tradition represents these students as highly learned and well-trained Buddhist monks—and history affirms that many such advanced Buddhists of other schools flocked to Zen in its early centuries. The young, uninitiated but enlightened Huineng is portrayed as surpassing even the greatest of these distinguished scholars and practitioners, with the supreme wisdom known as teacherless knowledge.

Throughout mainstream Zen there is the idea that Zen understanding may be provoked by cultivation, but no amount of deliberate cultivation can absolutely guarantee Zen realization. There is, according to tradition, an indefinable element necessary to potentiate the Zen effect. This is a thing that is not a thing, the ineffable wisdom called teacherless knowledge. This is held to be inherent in everyone, but Huineng is especially singled out as the master of teacherless knowledge to show how enlightenment does not depend on conditioning.

This independent knowledge is also called "the subtlety that cannot be passed on, even from father to son." It is not like ritual transmission of formal knowledge or authority, nor like a doctrine or creed. Several of the classical masters are most emphatic on this point, and one of the major controversies of Zen history was in effect caused by people who denied the necessity of enlightenment on one's own but claimed there was a secret transmission. The medium of this "secret transmission" naturally became contaminated with personal views, and then with personal feelings.

The legendary attack of one faction of monks against Huineng is a classic model of what happens when proprietary feelings attach themselves to religion. From the very beginning of Zen when the founder Bodhidharma told the emperor of China his pious acts had no merit, through the ages Zen has dealt with this problem of ulterior egoism in religion. According to a Zen proverb, "If you have no feelings about wordly things, they are all Buddhism; if you have feelings about Buddhism, it is a wordly thing."

According to traditional Zen history, Huineng had thirty-three enlightened disciples who became local teachers, while "the others who hid their names and concealed their tracks could not all be counted." This also becomes a recurring theme in Zen lore, where people who come to understand Zen disappear into the fabric, while only a few appear to continue the public teaching of Zen. In China, at least, this was matched in concrete history by a virtually continuous scattering and reformation of Zen schools, and by the emergence of successive phases of Zen teaching under different names in different guises.

After the completion of Huineng's teaching and the dismantling of his school, Zen quietly and informally penetrated the ancient Buddhist establishments, then burst into bloom under the guidance of two extraordinary Zen masters of the eighth century, Shitou and Mazu. These two teachers, known as "the two doors of immortality," and almost all of the known Zen masters of the following generation were taught by both of them.

Shitou, whose lifetime spanned nearly the entire eighth century, is particularly well known for his remarkable didactic poem entitled "Merging of Difference and Sameness." This is one of the most compact statements of Buddhism on record, written at a high level of concentration. Many attempts have been made to elucidate its inner meanings, with commentaries dating all the way back to the late classical period of Zen, only a few generations removed from the original composition.

In the typical manner of texts written in a concentrated Zen style, Shitou's work says a great deal about the fundamental premises of Zen right in the opening statement: "The mind of the great immortal of India is intimately communicated East and West." The great immortal of India refers to Buddha, and that mind refers to the enlightened mind. The term used for immortal here is a Taoist term, and the characters in the title of the work are identical to an early Taoist classic of spiritual alchemy. Here Shitou is not just using literary embellishment or approximation of concepts; the message is that the enlightened mind cuts through and goes beyond distinctions of religious format, is deeper than and unimpeded by cultural differences such as those between East and West.

Shitou's great contemporary Mazu, whose lifetime also spanned nearly the entire eighth century, is the first of the Zen masters whose instructions are translated in this volume. Most of what is known about Mazu is to be found in the records of his interactions with other people, recounting tales of sudden awakenings said to have been provoked by his words, acts, and charismatic influence. Mazu had one hundred and thirty-nine enlightened disciples, eighty-four of whom became public teachers. His spiritual descendants created a major impact over the next few hundred years.

Mazu's recorded teaching is extremely simple yet encompassing, emphasizing psychological normalcy in the Zen sense of freedom from the fluctuation of mental contrivances and artificialities. To accomplish or restore this normalcy, Mazu taught people not to cling to subjective views; by this means, he claimed, it is possible to transcend the ordinary world without isolation or rejection of everyday life. Mazu said that thoughts and feelings congeal over individual and cultural lifetimes, forming the substance of the apparent world.

His basic Zen technique involved using this realization to impersonalize oneself and society, relaxing the grip of mind on its creations and letting go of thought trains, thus arriving at an inconceivable perception of reality. According to Mazu, enlightenment means realization of the essence of mind and objects, and its fruition is beyond the practices that lead to its attainment.

One of Mazu's many outstanding spiritual heirs was Dazhu, whose sayings follow those of Mazu in this collection. Dazhu presents a prime example of the profound simplicity of this early Zen. He elucidates the shortcoming of the religious ego or religious passion so typically criticized in later Zen writings; making a business of Buddhist studies, Dazhu says, may incapacitate people for authentic experience of liberation, insofar as studies are pursued in a frame of mind affected by ordinary subjectivity and object-fascination.

In somewhat later times, when Zen was even more well established, teachers often noted links between sterile approaches to Zen and ordinary material greed, as Zen communes were transformed into wordly institutions and walks of life, complete with social and material systems of rewards and punishments, bailiwicks, factions, and all that proceeds from them. The roots of this problem, however, were already articulated in the early generations of Zen Buddhism by Dazhu and other successors of Mazu's school.

The next Zen master whose instructions appear in this volume is Linji, a redoubtable teacher of the ninth century. Taught by a spontaneously enlightened man who had also associated with Baizhang, one of Mazu's outstanding disciples, Linji consummated the structural representation of the Zen teaching that had come down to him, and brought it to life with his own extraordinary enlightenment. The record of his sayings, originally compiled by an immediate disciple, became one of the outstanding classics of Zen. It is from this famous record that the selections here are translated.

Like other Zen masters teaching normalcy, Linji warned students not to seek extraordinary powers. He did not deny such powers, but implied that subjective imaginations and personal desires were not sound bases for developing the higher potentials of mind. Linji insisted that what people really need is true perception and understanding; attain this, he said, and wonders come of themselves. He emphasized the importance of independence, refusing to take on other's confusions and delusions, trusting in the innermost self. Linji told people to do whatever they had to do, without being changed by external influences.

Like other Zen masters, Linji referred to Zen as the teaching of the mind ground, the most fundamental level of awareness. He taught that the mind ground can go freely into both sacred and profane realms without being identified with either. Be independent, he said, not dwelling even on the mind ground, not leaning on either internal states or external conditions; then situations that arise cannot change you, and this radical independence releases you even from vicious habits.

Linji also warned that indiscriminate study is ineffective, likening it to a goat nosing around and chewing on whatever it finds. Special discernments are essential if study is to progress beyond a certain point, he explained; professional religionists who cannot distinguish obsession from enlightenment consequently form what are in effect social organizations rather than spiritual bodies. This is not independence in the Zen sense of the word. As Linji says, "If you love the scared and despise the ordinary, you are still bobbing in the ocean of delusion."

Linji taught that mental blocks hindering both spiritual as well as social life are caused by clinging to labels and slogans. These mental blocks inhibit perception of objective truth, he said, by trapping the mind within the walls of ideas and attitudes continually reinforced by what the doctrine of consciousness calls "the lull of words." To be free from such influences, Linji insisted, it is imperative to know the real self; but this real self cannot be deliberately sought, because the deliberation is already artificial. Herein lies the subtlety of Zen.

According to the history as described by Zen masters, the subtlety of Zen, of its very nature impossible to grasp by the ordinary intellect, was eventually used as a veil by meddlers, charlatans, and would-be teachers fascinated by the power of mystification. According to Linji, many Zennists who are not really enlightened climb to the position of teachers as an anticipated career step. Imposters hide behind mysterious sayings or ritualized religiosity. Pious but naive people may be deceived by pretenders of this sort, whose "teaching" is not liberative but is, on the contrary, binding. Again like many other authentic masters, Linji speaks out clearly against false Zen transmitters, showing how to recognize and avoid the aggressive mental suggestion of imitation Zen.

Like the Buddha, Linji maintains that to attain liberation it is necessary to detach emotion and intellect from preconceptions formed by social conditioning, including traditional and religious beliefs, in order to recover the mental spaciousness and objectivity needed for a universal perspective on reality. Typically, in this connection Linji asserts that there is no doctrine in Zen, because Zen is just a matter of "curing ailments and unlocking fetters."

Following Linji in this volume are sayings of his contemporary Yangshan. Yangshan was noted as one of the great geniuses of Zen, and many high officials called themselves his disciples. Numerous anecdotes of Yangshan are found in standard collections of Zen stories. Yangshan is noted for emphasizing the nondogmatic nature of Zen teaching, which operates by response to need rather than by profession and assertion. Yangshan stated that absolute Zen is beyond human feeling and does not appeal to the sensation seeker.

This perspective is itself sometimes regarded as dogmatic by people who are accustomed to dogma, but the inaccessibility of absolute

Zen to ordinary thought and feeling is not considered by Buddhists to be a doctrine but a quality of its inherent nature, as explained in the *Sandhinirmocana-sutra.*

Like Linji, Yangshan warned people not to seek the miraculous but to get at the essential, the basic true mind; all marvels are outgrowths, he said, which come of themselves when the basis is established. Subjective attraction to the unusual or extraordinary is not regarded as a sound basis for Zen practice, since it still imprisons the mind within its own images. This does not mean that Zen masters do not develop extraordinary capacities, only that they do not strive for them for their own sake.

The next Zen master presented in this collection is Fayan, who died in the mid-tenth century. Fayan was the last of the great classical masters whose schools perfected the early articulation of Buddhism in Zen terms. His school, particularly known for its demonstration of what Zen scholarship is and how it functions, had an especially great impact on Korea during its first three generations. One of Fayan's successors was instrumental in reviving the ancient Tiantai school of Buddhism. Among the latter's heirs was the ninth patriarch of Pure Land Buddhism, a master of Zen and all the schools, pioneer of a new pan-Buddhist movement.

Fayan himself is mainly known for teaching advanced students, but he also wrote a succinct treatise on general guidelines for Zen schools, criticizing the decadent trends he observed in Zen sects even at that time, and plainly outlining the true ideals of Zen. In this Fayan continued and further articulated a critical tradition that is strongly marked in the teachings of the successors and descendants of Mazu and was to become highly intensified in Zen as taught during the Song dynasty (960-1278), when Zen influence on Chinese culture was paramount. The selections translated here are from this treatise, one of the earliest Zen writings.

The first point Fayan made in his guidelines is the need to be enlightened oneself before teaching others. He wrote that degeneration in Zen was caused by people seeking to become Zen teachers and group leaders. It is therefore imperative, he taught, to clarify the basis of mind and detach oneself from vicious cycles that imprison the attention and perception within artificially conditioned limitations. Fayan also said that true Zen clarity and enlightenment cannot be accomplished by meditation without correct guidance.

Among the deteriorations in Zen schools to which Fayan's treatise makes special reference is sectarianism. Fayan wrote that while Zen has no sectarian ways to value, eventually followers became traditionalistic, sectarian, and competitive. To counteract this tendency, Fayan taught people not to simply memorize slogans and not to just follow the format of a school in the manner of political stooges following a party line. As models of the true approach to Zen, Fayan's treatise cites some of the famous sayings of earlier masters in this regard, saying, "The secret is in you," and "Everything flows from your own heart."

Fayan also warned people not to mistake impermanent states for real attainments, and not to allow theory and practice, or principle and fact, to become alienated from one another. The misperception of cultivated states as enlightenment experiences is rather typical of deteriorated Zen schools with a taste for excitement, while the alienation of theory and practice is typical of doctrinal schools using standardized systems. Both of these extremes are well documented in Zen diagnostic lore, as is the subjective interpretation of Zen stories, another common deterioration also condemned by Fayan in his treatise.

These translations from the sayings and writings of the classical masters Mazu, Dazhu, Linji, Yangshan, and Fayan are followed by selections from the writings of two pioneers in the literary projection of Zen during the tenth and eleventh centuries, Fenyang and Xuedou, and sayings of two teaching masters who accelerated the mid-Song dynasty development of Zen, Huanglong and Yangqi.

The literary projection of Zen was instrumental in penetrating the general fabric of Chinese and Chinese-influenced cultures and societies, but it only represents one part of the total impact of Zen. Fenyang and Xuedou were also successful teachers as well as exceptionally talented writers, but their contribution to Zen literature stands out most prominently. Fenyang had met more than seventy Zen masters, and incorporated the teachings of all the major lines of Zen into his writings, also adding his own comments and creating new forms of ancient Zen linguistic devices.

Fenyang emphasized the basic Buddhist idea that enlightenment is inherent in the mind but is obscured by acquired habits of perception and thought. Delusion and enlightenment are both rooted in the mind, Fenyang writes, but most people do not really take the idea of inherent buddha-nature seriously because they are wrapped up in personal thoughts, feelings, and moods. This is the reason for the existence of Zen teaching in spite of the fact that it is ultimately imperative, as Fenyang says, to "know for yourself."

According to Fenyang, although Zen teaching is impersonal, it needs the affinity or attunement of the seeker with Zen itself. The relationship between Zen teacher and apprentice is critical, but it is not the same as the relationship between teacher and student in conventional systems of education, particularly in that Zen cannot be fully explained or conveyed in ordinary terms. As Fenyang says, a thousand books are not enough, yet even one word is too much.

Furthermore, Zen education is distinguished from ordinary learning in that competition, a well-recognized element of conventional systems, only wastes time in Zen. While Zen awakening is key to peace of mind in the midst of the world and unlocks hidden capacities, the freedom of Zen is not useful for the unprepared. Thus Zen education places extraordinarily high levels of responsibility on both teachers and students, requiring what is from the point of view of secular schools an unusual degree of maturity.

Xuedou is considered the reviver of what was perhaps the most arcane and elaborate of the classical schools of Zen, which employed techniques that had always required special genius. He is particularly noted for three outstanding literary works: a collection of verses on one hundred Zen stories, a collection of prose comments on another set of one hundred Zen stories, and an anthology of poetry. His living successors also grew into one of the most powerful schools of Zen during the late Song dynasty, and his writings even influenced the early Complete Reality School of Taoism.

Xuedou wrote that the living meaning of Zen is the design of life itself, and that really intimate understanding cannot be obtained from another person. This principle of Zen—that it is ultimately realized within oneself—also came to be used as a mask for all sorts of personalistic versions of Zen, but Xuedou warned that it is necessary to strip the mind of acquired illusions before seeing reality directly. This caveat is similar to that articulated by Fayan in regard to Zen stories, which he said required mental purification to understand and employ.

In contrast to Fenyang and Xuedou, Huanglong and Yangqi are examples of Zen masters who are famed mainly for the effects of their schools rather than for their literary remains, their own personal teachings being relatively little known. There is a collection of Huanglong's letters extant, but they are largely concerned with current events and seldom contain overt Zen instructions.

Analyzing the condition of bondage from which Zen proposes to liberate people, Huanglong uses a famous expression from Flower Ornament Buddhism: knowledge of reality is blocked by feelings, and things are shaped by images; people tend to fall into habits based on these feelings and images, and hence unconsciously bind themselves. To arrive at spontaneous Zen awakening for the solution of this problem, Huanglong continues, it is necessary to stop the restless mind. Going around to schools looking for teachers, he says, "busies you fatally."

According to Huanglong, the supreme Zen knowledge, knowledge that cannot be taught, is beyond ordinary intellectual exercise or study. The essence of Zen, he said, is beyond the material senses and cannot be reached by sensory experiences. This does not mean, however, that ordinary experience is to be avoided or rejected to seek Zen, for "Zen seekers should sit on the site of universal enlightenment right in the midst of all the thorny situations in life, and recognize their original face while mixing with the ordinary world." Freedom on earth, he taught, means to be ready for anything; people who are stuck in detachment and cannot enter the realm of passions unscathed can help neither themselves nor others.

Hardly anything is known of Yangqi, despite the fame of his school and the powerful influence of the line of teachers descended from him. Yangqi said that the condition of the environment depends on the individual and collective mentalities and actions of its inhabitants, but the individual and collective mentalities and actions of the inhabitants are also conditioned by the environment. From inside, this circle is the suffocating wheel of bondage itself, but with extradimensional consciousness able to deliberately transform thought and behavior it becomes a field of progressive action.

Detachment from the images formed by the process of conditioning, Yangqi said, undermines their spellbinding power and enables the mind to recover the autonomy that makes fresh progress possible. Nothing is destroyed by this experience, however, except the force of illusion; Yangqi taught that there is still human feeling, corresponding to the design and reason of the natural world.

Yangqi also said that there are ultimately no teachers of absolute

Zen. When you understand Zen, he claimed, there is no more need for schools—you can go on your way freely, independent and whole. When the mind is "open and clear as space," he explained, the original intelligence is clear; and when consciousness is "broad and deep as the ocean," there is equanimity in the midst of events. In order to achieve this, he said, presence of mind in action is necessary.

The next four teachers appearing in this collection—Wuzu, Yuanwu, Foyan, and Dahui—were distinguished representatives of the so-called East Mountain School of Zen, which was descended from the classical master Linji through Yangqi. Noted for its great influence among the secular intelligentsia, the East Mountain School is among the most extensively documented branches of Zen.

Wuzu had already reached middle age when he entered Zen specialization under the tutelage of one of the Zen prodigies of the time, Baiyun, a direct heir of Yangqi who became a Zen teacher at an unusually young age and passed away early. Baiyun sent Wuzu to run the mill operated by the Zen monastery in a town below the mountain on which the monastery was located. It is said that whenever monks would come down the mountain snooping around, Wuzu would scandalize them by flirting with the young women who came to the mill.

Wuzu was later known for a skill in teaching that was unique in his time, using graphic stories, colorful metaphors, earthy poetry, profound abstractions, paradoxical actions, and forthright statements to open the minds of his hearers. Much of the dynamic of the East Mountain School's influence can be traced to the great capacity of Wuzu. He was outspoken in his criticism of the Zen institutions of his era, which he declared to have become infected by elements of human behavior inconsistent with the true aims and practices of Zen. Consequently he was also explicit in his descriptions of what he considered appropriate criteria for authentic Zen, for both the generalist and the specialist. His disciples and descendants in the East Mountain School followed him in this.

Wuzu made a point of the need for Zen guides to strip away even seekers' most cherished conceptions in order for them to reach the subtlety of Zen that cannot be categorized or defined in any conventional terms, cannot be imagined, and cannot be reached by thought. Later certain sayings of his were especially used for this purpose. But even this subtlety is not, he said, to be made into a "nest" in mature

Zen, and it is not to be taken personally as an attainment—as the Zen proverb has it, "A general may establish peace, but it is not for the general to see peace."

Yuanwu, one of Wuzu's three most illustrious disciples, is distinguished as the author of *The Blue Cliff Record*, an outstanding Zen literary classic. There is also a large collection of records of his talks, verses on Zen subjects, and letters of Zen instruction. These letters of instruction, particularly esteemed by later students of Zen mind, were collected under the title "Essentials of Mind." It is from this famous text that the selections here are taken.

Yuanwu affirmed the expedient nature of Zen teachings and practices, which are not supposed to be fixed dogmas and rites, but means of helping people arrive at the source of mind and be free from illusions. Zen is in you, Yuanwu said; its penetrating insight and profound calm always exist. Look for the level of mind that is not dancing with objects and hanging around with things, he instructed; clear the mind, forget about subjective opinions and feelings, and you see what is meant by the Zen saying "Mind is Buddha."

Like his teacher Wuzu, Yuanwu was highly critical of deteriorated Zen studies. He noted that many intellectuals and educated people study Zen as a hobby and conversation piece. Zen was used as a status symbol and became the basis for a great deal of snobbery because of its honored position in Chinese culture. This kind of interest in Zen increases rather than decreases egotistic attachments. Thus Yuanwu insisted on the right purpose and inspiration for Zen study, particularly recommending the exercise of looking at death to clarify the will. Yuanwu also affirmed that quietude is not necessary for Zen study and practice—be empty inside while harmonizing with the environment, he said, and you will be at peace even in the midst of busy activity in the world.

Yuanwu explained that the changes made in Zen method over the ages by truly perceptive and free guides were needed to prevent people from clinging to outward faces of the teaching and rationalizing them into inflexible principles. "All of the teachings are expedients," he wrote, "just for the purpose of breaking through obsessions, doubts, intellectual interpretations, and egocentric ideas." This is of a different order from ritualistic sectarian cults claiming to be Zen schools in later times.

Yuanwu also affirmed that real Zen does not need social support and is not vulnerable to destructive social pressures. He explained both fallacies and realities of Zen, how to avoid the fallacies and how to usefully employ the realities. In these discussions he included remarks on such topics as the so-called living and dead word of Zen, the sterility of creeds, dogma, and slogans, and the need for balance in the types of techniques employed.

A basic aspect of this balance is summarized by Yuanwu in terms also familiar in Taoism: "If you want to attain intimate realization of Zen, first of all don't seek it. What is attained by seeking has already fallen into intellection. . . . Only when you stop your compulsive mind . . . do you pass through to freedom." He also quotes the ancient master Dazhu on the subject of external seeking: "Everything comes from your own heart. This is what an ancient called bringing out the family treasure."

In terms of method, Yuanwu taught people to still their thoughts, adding that "it is good to do this right in the midst of disturbance." He told people to let go of "previous imaginings, opinions, interpretations, wordly knowledge, intellectualizing, egoism, and competitiveness" to make the mind "clean and naked," thus to open up to Zen. After that, however, he said it is still necessary to develop consistency. For both stages he insisted on the importance of will, in that it requires extraordinary resolve to purify the heart and keep it clean, because one needs constant awareness of inner and outer states and actions. "Only those who have attained the fundamental," he wrote, "are capable of being inwardly empty while outwardly harmonious."

Detachment and cessation of thought are means, not ends, of Zen. Yuanwu said that when the process of Zen is consummated, "There are no mundane things outside Buddhism, and there is no Buddhism outside mundane things." After awakening to reality, he stated, "With every thought you are consulting infinite teachers."

If even deep meditations are only tools in Zen, how much the more so are words. They have enormous potential as expedient means of stimulating perceptions, but they are not liberative when transformed into totems. Yuanwu wrote that when you realize the verbal teachings of the enlightened are within you, "you do not wear them around on your head." He was constantly warning people about faddish and cultish behavior, which may provide some emotional satisfactions but does not produce Zen awakening.

Yuanwu also mentioned another specific abuse of artifacts like writings, well documented in Zen diagnostic lore, characterized by judgment of the artifacts in ordinary sentimental and intellectual terms based upon subjective comparisons. As tools, these writings are precision instruments designed to measure and to guide. Although one of their functions is to reveal defective or incomplete mentation, the value of this effect depends on other factors, such as the attitude of the individual. One of the persistent themes of Zen is to note imbalances and flaws in one's own mind and thought, in order to deliberately counterbalance or overcome them, and avoid their future appearance.

According to Yuanwu, thorough independence means that mindfulness and mindlessness leave no impression on your soul. Then even troublesome events do not affect your thoughts; you are inwardly serene while outwardly adaptable. Yuanwu also discussed Zen teacherhood, emphasizing compassion, tact, impartiality, being unobtrusive and noncompetitive. He added that opposition could cause no personal feelings, and followed the ancient Taoist teaching that "no one can contend with one who does not contend." Eventually, Yuanwu said, "malicious pests will disappear of themselves."

Yuanwu cautioned seekers that time and practice are needed to reach the possibilities indicated by Zen guides, and in this interval all sorts of false teachers may try to teach the uncertain. He described one major characteristic of spiritual charlatans as leading people into "fooling around with curios." In this respect real Zen teaching is anathema to religious cultists and literary dilettantes.

Explaining Zen teaching methods, Yuanwu said that devices of real Zen teachers are geared to "hook" people, or bring out their dominant confusion or controlling attitude, in order to liberate them from these limitations. Imagining these devices to represent the beliefs of the masters themselves, turning them into articles of faith or slogans of a school, results in the creation of ineffective and often thoroughly absurd interpretations of Zen teaching.

Yuanwu was one of the outstanding Zen masters commonly associated by historians with a watershed in the history of the use of Zen stories in the process of Zen learning and teaching. Although he said it was a serious mistake not to wonder about the sayings of the ancients after awakening oneself, thus taking advantage of the perceptual leverage they provide, he also said that the use of sayings and stories is not absolutely essential for some people: "Just correct your attention and quiet your mind from the time you arise in the morning, and whatever you say or do, review it carefully and see where it comes from and what makes it all happen."

Mind watching may itself become an unproductive and confusing activity without the detachment necessary to objectivity. Yuanwu stressed that it is not necessary to abandon action in the world in order to attain freedom. Stilling the mind, he taught, at best an expedient, may give the subjective impression of emptiness, but is not in itself the emptiness that Buddhism calls the ultimate truth. Real Zen emptiness, or openness, he said, is alive and cannot be pinned down; it is neither in being nor in nonbeing, it is beyond the attitudes of rejection or attachment. Eventually, Yuanwu wrote, "You can trust this true, pure ineffable mind, and when mundane conditions beckon involvement, you notice that the mind does not go along with them."

With Yuanwu, Zen master Foyan was one of the so-called "Three Buddhas" of the early East Mountain School under the tutelage of the great Wuzu. There is an immense record of his teachings, including one of the largest collections of direct instructions in the Zen canon. The selections translated in this volume are taken from these direct instructions, which utilize one of the most subtle forms of Zen wisdom.

Foyan taught people to detach from thought, an exercise that does not require stopping the mind but is used to achieve the same purpose. "We do not teach you to annihilate random thoughts, suppress body and mind, close your eyes, and consider this Zen," he said, stressing the importance of what he called "saving energy," effortlessly preserving the integrity of the original mind. Foyan also emphasized independence and self-observation, explaining that subjective feelings, or subjective interpretations of the objective world, are not themselves the real, objective world.

Foyan talks about a wide range of practical matters in a simple and straightforward manner that while easy to understand shows the true difficulty of Zen. "You must know how to check yourself before you can attain Zen," he said, illustrating a number of ways to approach this activity. One thing Foyan does not recommend is that confused people go rushing around looking for gurus when they should first be looking into where they became confused. Like other Zen masters, he says, "It is just a matter of reaching the source of mind."

The liberation proposed by Zen, realized by arriving at the source of mind, is not only liberation from unnecessary limitation and suffering, but liberation of a vast reserve of power inherent in reality. This is a very important point, connecting with Foyan's recurrent warning not to think that Zen involves suppression of mind and body. It is customary for Zen masters to refrain from discussing the higher powers latent in the human mind (although they are described at length in certain Buddhist texts), and to avoid making a display of such powers. This custom is observed to discourage people from seeking Zen for reasons of personal ambition, but it has also encouraged the mistaken identification of "normalcy" as understood in Zen with "normalcy" as defined in the terms accepted by social systems which do little or nothing to foster the development of human consciousness beyond the limits of those systems.

So useful did the Foyan's general talks prove to later seekers that they were collected into a book ranked among one of the three so-called incomparables of Zen literature. Another one of these three "incomparables" is the famous collection of the letters of Dahui, a successor of Yuanwu whose impact as a Zen teacher was so extraordinary that he is sometimes described as a reincarnation of Linji, the redoubtable spiritual ancestor of the whole East Mountain School of Zen. Selections from these letters follow Foyan's talks in the translations contained in this volume.

Dahui was particularly noted for his ability to explain Zen in plain terms, his extraordinary capabilities in provoking Zen awakening, and his practice of collecting rare and unusual Zen lore. While still in the circle of his teacher Yuanwu, Dahui was given the special assignment of dealing with the lay people who come seeking advice, and later as a teacher he also carried out extensive correspondence with lay seekers.

Dahui made extensive use of the teaching of *The Flower Ornament Scripture* and the meditation known as the "oceanic reflection," from which this scripture is said to derive. He stressed that buddahood is not an externally perceptible form, but is an inner knowledge. Teaching the expedient of being like aware space, seeing Buddha everywhere in everything, Dahui stated that there is no need for the trappings of religion or spirituality in studying Zen. What is essential, he said, is awakeness; examine yourself, he taught, beware of distraction and partiality. Find out the source of mind, he continued, and when it is necessary to change things, do so by changing the mind. According to Dahui, impartiality is the true meaning of Zen "mind-lessness," and this part of his teaching was incorporated verbatim into a secular handbook on civil service and statecraft.

Like Foyan and others, Dahui said that it is important not to abandon the ordinary world to study Zen. Many study Zen earnestly only when they have troubles, he observed, then slack off when they become successful in the world. For Zen enlightenment, he stated, it is not necessary to give up family and friends and retire from one's occupation, not necessary to be a vegetarian, an ascetic or an eremite. People who outwardly abandoned society while inwardly retaining ordinary sentiments were those who transformed Zen communities into families, societies, and occupations that may have differed from wordly organizations in external trappings and professed ideologies but nevertheless were based on a thoroughly worldly psychology.

Dahui said that teachers without enlightenment, careerists in monastic society, just make clones of themselves and do not communicate enlightenment. In this way the transformation of Zen into a mundane counterfeit proceeded apace during the Song dynasty, inspiring Dahui and others to come forth with their cutting criticism. According to the real adepts, reputed Zen masters and schools may in reality be creations of hobbyists who record and enshrine what they like. One of the telltale signs of self-deceived Zennists, however, is that they usually do not recognize real seers if they do happen to meet them, and even if they recognize them it is useless because the self-deceived are seeking agreement and approval, not understanding.

Zen master Hongzhi, a great contemporary of Dahui, was one of the last living representatives of his lineage of Zen, and is considered by some to have completed the articulation and refinement of the Song dynasty Zen literary project. Extracts from his Zen instructions are translated in this volume, following the selections from Dahui's letters.

Hongzhi made altogether extraordinary contributions to Zen literature in every form. His poetry is among the most refined work of its kind, and even his prose has a poetic quality that is rarely equaled. He compiled two famous collections of one hundred Zen stories each, adding his own comments, one set in poetry and the other in prose, paralleling those of the earlier Xuedou. There is also a considerable collection of Hongzhi's other talks, sayings, poems, and writings.

Translated here are selections from his instructions, which are written in prose of the most exceptional grace and beauty, adding a matchless artistic quality to the scientific precision found in corresponding works of Yuanwu, Foyan, and Dahui.

In his teachings on mental freedom, Hongzhi affirmed that the mind is originally unattached to objects. To actualize this as a practical affair, however, he taught what he calls the "silent exercise of inner gazing." He reiterates the Zen dictum that there is no way to explain reality, that it must be experienced on one's own; to do this, he said, "Just wash away the dust and dirt of subjective thoughts immediately." Success in this allows the practitioner to progress to an effortless type of Zen exercise in which there is spontaneous awareness and panoramic consciousness.

Enlightened life, Hongzhi writes, is natural and spontaneous, yet orderly and not arbitrary. He presents exercises for eliminating arbitrariness and perfecting attunement of the human mind, keeping this true inward spirituality intact even while participating in the ordinary world. Dahui maintained that when quiet sitting does not result in serenity in the midst of turbulence, that means it is not really effective even in quietude; similarly, Hongzhi criticized some students for sitting in meditation too long and losing the capacity for effective integration.

The selections from Hongzhi's work translated in this volume are followed by excerpts from the instructions of Ying-an, another distinguished teacher from the East Mountain School. Ying-an became a disciple of the great Yuanwu after having had an initial enlightenment under the tutelage of another Zen master. Later, on Yuanwu's own recommendation, Ying-an became a student of Huqiu, one of Yuanwu's successors, known as the "Sleeping Tiger" of Yuanwu's circle. Huqiu eventually recognized Ying-an as a Zen master and gave him permission to teach.

In his presentation of Zen, Ying-an emphasized immunity to the ordinary economic, social, and mental influences that ordinarily coerce humanity. Zen freedom, he said, cannot be pinned down and cannot be second-guessed. Real perception is the essence of Zen, he maintained; genuine Zen students have no resorts, no fixed creed or religion.

Ying-an cites several types of degenerate Zen, including those deriving from attachment to temporary insights and isolated elaborations of limited views. He also describes multiple personalities of both quietism and nihilism, which sometimes masquerade as Zen. One type of false Zen is characterized by Ying-an as promoted by people whose minds have been poisoned by false teachers into thinking that they are themselves Zen masters. Another type of false Zen is promoted by camp followers who pick up Zen lingo and try to become known for their Zennism. To be cured of these forms of madness, people may need to give up deliberate involvement in spiritual studies.

A familiar Taoist proverb says, "The journey of a thousand miles begins with the first step." According to Ying-an, the first step must be the right step, in the right direction, if it is to lead to arrival at the destination. This is why ancient Zen masters left behind so many directions, or at least indications as to how and where seekers might find direction.

In his instructions, Ying-an also notes that eagerness to learn is often a prime barrier to real Zen perception. Not the least of the drawbacks of such eagerness is that it may foster the impulsive tendency to take the "first step of a thousand mile journey" at random. Don't approach Zen with preconceptions, Ying-an teaches, yet don't think there is no Zen understanding. It takes practice, he says, but the purpose of the practice is to arrive at naturalness and spontaneity.

One of the most general observations made by Zen masters is that activities that once had a specific purpose tend to be diverted to other purposes or transformed into ends in themselves. Virtually all of the methods of Zen that can be defined have been thus diverted or transformed at various times, as have most ordinary educational methods. This is one reason for periodic changes in tactics.

"Zen cannot be attained by lectures, discussions, or debates," says Ying-an, referring no doubt to the highly ritualized remnants of interactional education popularized in baroque Zen schools. On the other hand, he continues, if people can do as the ancient Zen masters themselves did, "at some point you will suddenly turn the light of your mind around and see through illusions to the real self."

Overly intellectualized versions of quasi Zen evidently abounded in Song-dynasty China, undoubtedly contributing to the ossification of such formats as those Ying-an renounced. Of the desire for intellectual knowledge, Ying-an says, "Your chills and fever will be increased by the wind of intellectual knowledge, your nose will always be stuffed up and your head will always be foggy."

Many of the stumbling blocks and blind alleys that Ying-an notes are related in some way either to excessively intellectual or anti-intellectual approaches to Zen. Intellectualism is found among many academic, literary, artistic, and priestly attitudes toward Zen; but then again so is anti-intellectualism, or the idea that because Zen denies the supremacy of intellect it must be anti-intellectual.

Ying-an also reemphasizes the point that people interested in Zen should not approach it with the idea of achieving greatness, or with eagerness for success, or with desire for recognition. According to Zen teaching, all of this is the work of vanity, not real aspiration for enlightenment. It is therefore counterproductive and blocks the way of Zen.

Because Zen enlightenment is ultimately beyond words, teachers have been known to use other means of communicating impressions. Among the more dramatic of their techniques were various shock tactics. Surprising blows and shouts, for example, are known to have been employed by some ancient Zen masters to produce specific effects in the minds of seekers. These devices are also known to have been widely mimed. Used imitatively and at random, they lost their original intended effects. Thus they were transformed into forms of pretense and mystification. There are many references to this phenomenon in Zen literature.

Ying-an says that blows and shouts—which in the popular mind came to be associated with Zen mysticism—do not really represent Zen. Instead of being concerned with doctrines, literary expressions, or pantomime, Ying-an recommends what he calls "a certain state in which no time whatsoever is wasted, twenty-four hours a day," a state to be "maintained until you reach the point where there is nowhere to grasp and nowhere to anchor."

Then, he says, "You should let go and make yourself empty and quiet, clear and calm, to the point where former intellectual interpretations, rationalizations, misknowledge and misperception, cannot get into your mind or act on it at all." Ying-an also stresses the need for a strong will to accomplish this; even though seeing the Zen mind is easy, he said, strength is needed to use it.

Following the sayings of Ying-an in this collection are extracts from the talks of one of his Zen successors, master Mi-an. According to Mi-an, Zen is a matter of being "totally alive and free," for only thus is it possible to be in the world without being affected by it. This possibility is inherent in everyone, he says, but many people who try to attain it through Zen are misled by false teachers. When Zen study is also motivated by a desire for recognition, he warns, this makes people so much the more susceptible to such deception.

Mi-an cites half a dozen typical problems that inhibit Zen enlightenment in spite of intensive study. He adds that these are problems encountered not only by beginners, but even by people with basic Zen experience. Mi-an emphasizes, however, that when Zen is realized, "Buddhist truths and things of the world have become one—where is there any external thing to constitute an impediment?"

Mi-an's sayings are followed by Zen instructions of Xiatang, another of Yuanwu's noted disciples. Xiatang gives a detailed explanation of nondiscursive knowledge, considered basic to Zen. He points out that the awareness in this knowledge is inherently nondiscursive; it is not reached by suppression of reason, but by a level of attention beyond that of ordinary sense. Xiatang also hints that the source of awareness is in fact the "spiritual immortality" sought by the higher ranks of Taoists.

Xiatang makes it clear, however, that attaining experience of this nondiscursive knowledge is not the same thing as utilizing it. "Glimpsing" followed by obsession spells trouble, he says, using the classic metaphor of "gold dust in the eyes" to describe the problem of spiritual attachment. As usual, Xiatang also quotes ancient masters on ways out of this impasse.

Xiatang stresses the primary importance of breaking the hold of compulsive or coercive habituation and conditioning mechanisms. He follows this up with emphasis on the need to be aware of the consequences of actions. The realm beyond the tyranny of external influences is sometimes called emptiness, or nothingness, in the sense that reality is seen without a mind full of preconceptions.

Many of the Song dynasty Zen masters urgently addressed the attitudinal and behavioral problems associated with imperfect realization of emptiness. A later master explained that the Zen stage of "no good or evil" does not mean that evil is good, and does not mean that one can do ill and not suffer the consequences. It means, he said, that one is not touched by either good or evil. Only then, according to classical Zen teaching, is one capable of distinguishing real good and evil from supposed good and evil, without subjective biases implanted by conditioning.

This volume concludes with excerpts from the sayings of Yuansou, one of the most illustrious Zen masters of the fourteenth century. At this time China was ruled by Mongol usurpers, who generally favored the Tibetan schools of Buddhism over the Chinese schools. Kubilai Khan (grandson of the notorious Jenghiz Khan), who extended the Mongol conquest to include the whole of continental China, was for a time interested in Zen Buddhism, but few Mongolians seem to have gone into Zen studies. One of the rare Mongolian Zen masters, however, was a student of Yuansou.

Yuansou was a fourth generation heir of the Zen lineage of the great Dahui, but he also worked with one of the last masters of Hongzhi's line as well. Yuansou is said to have given many evidences of paranormal powers, and he attracted thousands of seekers during his many years as a public teacher. Although much of the record of his teaching is said to have been lost during the civil disturbances of the latter fourteenth century as the Mongolian Yuan dynasty crumbled, nevertheless a considerable amount of material has survived, including a number of instructional letters, from which the present selections are translated.

Yuansou presents a fairly detailed description of the essence of Zen meditation, showing how different terms used through the ages refer to the same thing. He emphasizes the expedient nature of the Buddhist teachings, noting something of their wide variety. He also mentions a number of very general and very common approaches to Zen realization, and states that the aim is not actually confined to, or within, any particular approach.

Yuansou confirms the elusive omnipresence of Zen experience, which is made elusive only by attempts to pin it down. Yuansou says that when you try to pin Zen down, it pins you down; as you allow yourself to be "misled by blind teachers into reifying Buddha, Dharma, Zen, Tao, mysteries, marvels, functions, and states, one way and another this glues your tongue down, nails your eyes shut, and constricts your heart."

Explaining the reasons for use of expedient methods, Yuansou says that the "various teachings and techniques of Buddhas and Zen masters are only set forth so that you will individually step back into yourself, understand your own original mind and see your original nature, so that you reach a state of great rest, peace, and happiness."

Adding that accumulated bad habits hinder people along the way, Yuansou warns that just as this is true in ordinary life it is even more so when trying to reach sophisticated Zen perceptions, which cannot be consciously arranged even with good intentions. What is more, he says, bad habits may well lay beneath a veneer of good intentions. This is the pattern of pretended religionists and spiritual hobbyists characterized by Yuansou in these terms: "You pick up your baggage and go to other people's houses looking for Zen, looking for Tao, looking for mysteries, looking for marvels, looking for buddhas, looking for Zen masters, looking for teachers. You think this is searching for the ultimate and make it into your religion, but this is like running blindly to the east to get something in the west. The more you run the further away you are, and the more you hurry the later you become."

Yuansou also speaks of the straightforwardness of Zen mind, unburdened by confusing and deluding thoughts and ideas. He says it is impersonal and does not belong to any culture or system or idea. Subjectivity in discrimination, he warns, grasping and rejecting, makes people lose their independence and fall under the mesmeric influence of "things." Thus from first to last his total emphasis, like that of all the classical Zen masters, is on liberation—the freedom to see, the freedom to be, the freedom to live deliberately.

THE FIVE HOUSES OF ZEN

INTRODUCTION

When Buddhism took root in China after the end of the Han dynasty (206 B.C.E.–219 C.E.), it triggered the release of enormous waves of creative energy from a people who had been spiritually imprisoned for centuries. For four hundred years the mainstream Chinese culture had been kept within the suffocating confines of narrow-minded Confucian orthodoxy, imposed by the ruling house of Han as part of its handle on political power.

Not the least of the effects of Buddhism on China was the development of Taoism, China's native spiritual tradition, in highly elaborated religious and literary formats emulating the extraordinarily rich intellectual and aesthetic expressiveness of Buddhism. Yet even with the rapid expansion of Taoism, the more internationalized China of the post-Han centuries found Buddhist teachings immensely attractive, and the two religions grew side by side in the lively syncretic culture evolving in the new China.

While Buddhist literature and learning expanded the minds of the Chinese intelligentsia, Buddhist adepts took an active role in the resettlement and reconstruction of war-torn territories in the aftermath of the breakup of the old order. As relatively local and short-lived dynasties rose and fell over the following centuries, eventually Chinese warlords emulated their central Asian counterparts and began adopting Buddhism as a kind of state religion.

In contrast to Confucianism, Buddhism was an international religion, without ethnic or cultural bias. Like Druidism in pre-Roman Europe, in addition to being a repository of many kinds of knowledge, Buddhism served as a medium for international cultural and diplomatic exchange throughout most of Asia, even—perhaps especially—in times when warfare ravaged the world at large.

There was, naturally, a drawback to the flourishing of Buddhist religion in China. As a Zen saying goes, "One gain, one loss." Having become well established, well funded, and well thought of, Buddhism came to attract many idlers and many greedy and ambitious poseurs. Some sought material support, some sought intellectual diversion, some sought political power. The abundance of ritual, literature, and organizational methods that Buddhism offered was intoxicating to many Chinese aristocrats and warlords.

A result of the bewildering volume and variety of Buddhist literature pouring into China from south and central Asia was the development of schools of Chinese Buddhism based either on certain important texts or on certain arrangements of the whole body of canonical teachings. This process was already beginning by the early fifth century, and by the end of the sixth century the first syncretic school, T'ien-t'ai, had absorbed a number of earlier schools that had been more limited in scope.

The next three centuries saw the most distinctive and most sophisticated stage of evolution, not only of Chinese Buddhism but of Chinese culture as a whole. This was the age of the T'ang dynasty (619–906), the zenith of the civilization and the greatest expression of its complex genius.

T'ang culture was highly stimulated by the vigorous policies of the Empress Wu Tse-t'ien (r. 684–701), a highly accomplished individual who promoted Confucianism, Taoism, and Buddhism to enrich the spiritual resources of the entire civilization. Discussion and debate among the three ways of thought were promoted, in order to discourage complacency under state sponsorship and bring out the best in each of the philosophies.

It was during the T'ang dynasty that the Buddhist schools of Pure Land, T'ien-t'ai, Hua-yen, Chen-yen (Mantra) and Ch'an (Zen) were given their definitive expression by the great masters of the age. The Pure Land school was taken to new heights of mystic experience by the ecstatic writings of Shan-tao; the T'ien-t'ai meditation exercises were elaborately facilitated in the technical commentaries of Chan-jan; the Hua-yen universe was brilliantly illuminated in the essays of Fa-hsiang; the secrets of Tantric Buddhism were encapsulated in the esoteric art of Hui-kuo; and the inner mind of Ch'an or Zen Buddhism was straightforwardly revealed in the lectures of Hui-neng.

Certain hallmarks distinguished Zen from other schools. One of the most evident of these is the greater diversity of Zen expression, which is rooted in the fact that classical Zen was stricter in observance of the Mahayana Buddhist axiom that particular systems cannot be fixed as universal prescriptions for everyone's enlightenment. While Zen and other schools of Buddhism share a vast range of teachings, their modes and methods of expedient selection, organization, and presentation differ greatly.

To be practical, approaches and methods have to be adjusted to the needs and capacities of communities and individuals. This is not a Zen idea but is basic to Buddhism as a whole. Buddhist principles and practices vary over a wide spectrum for this reason, and their breadth and flexibility were also reflected in the custom of original Zen teachers to encourage and stimulate direct individual experience and avoid dogmatic cliché.

In accord with its pragmatic nature, Zen interpretation of Buddhist scripture dropped mythological thinking in favor of analogical thinking. Buddhist scriptures were not treated by Zen adepts as holy writ that was necessarily regarded as literally true, but as compendia of potentially useful ideas, outlooks, and exercises, commonly couched in sometimes dazzling symbolic language. Insisting on understanding the scriptures in practical terms, not just reciting them piously, the leading masters of Zen interpreted Buddhist symbolism by a special kind of structural analysis based on aspects and phases of Buddhist experiences of awakening and awareness. This discipline was also applied to the growing body of special Zen lore, particularly stories and poems.

Because of its nature and history, there is no fixed curriculum and no standard textbook of genuine classical Zen. Most of the material that would be required for a real history of Zen does not actually exist. This is part of the original teaching of Zen, which has to be experienced personally to be understood and whose masters consequently spoke to the needs of others and did not talk much about themselves.

Although there is no fixed canon as such in Zen, some writings and remnants of classical teachings have been preserved. Parts of this lore were used in various ways from time to time in Zen revivals, and an immense secondary literature of interpretation and elaboration also came into being, parts of which were picked up in yet later movements and revivals. This eventually resulted in extremely convoluted, indeed involuted, literary mannerisms, which contributed to the decline and demise of experiential illuminist Zen.

Within the vast body of recognized Zen literature emanating from countless teachers and schools appearing and disappearing over the centuries, the work that stands out preeminently as the mother lode of classical examples of Zen is that which is associated with the so-called Five Houses of Zen. Historically represented by several groups of outstanding Zen teachers, the Five Houses arose in China during the ninth and tenth centuries.

The Five Houses were not sects or schools, but later they came to be thought of that way. Although the grand masters of the Five Houses were eminent teachers, and the theoretical concept of the Houses seems to center around their teachings, in fact virtually nothing is known of the inner or outer lives of these individuals, and no organizations can actually be traced to them. In short, the original Houses were not institutionalized, their teachings were not dogmatized, and their guides and exemplars were not idolized.

The Five Houses of Classical Zen, in order of historical emergence, were the Kuei-Yang, named after the masters Kuei-shan Ling-yu (771–854) and Yang-shan Hui-chi (813–890); the Lin-chi, named after the master Lin-chi I-hsuan (d. 866); the Ts'ao-Tung, named after the masters Tung-shan Liang-chieh (807–869) and Ts'ao-shan Pen-chi (840–901); the Yun-men, named after the master Yun-men Wen-yen (d. 949); and the Fa-yen, named after the master Fa-yen Wen-i (885–958).

The present collection of teachings from the Five Houses of Zen begins with sayings of Pai-chang Huai-hai (720–814), who was the teacher of Kuei-shan Ling-yu of the House of Kuei-Yang. Also a direct forerunner of the House of Lin-chi, Pai-chang is credited with the early Zen rule "A day without work, a day without food," which fostered independence from secular patronage. Pai-chang's sayings are strongly infused with scriptural Buddhist teachings, and this characteristic also marks the subsequent works of the masters of the Kuei-Yang and Lin-chi Houses.

Following Pai-chang's sayings are extracts from the *Admonitions* of Kuei-shan, one of the earliest Zen writings. During the Sung dynasty (960–1278), this work was incorporated into a popular primer of Buddhism and subsequently was made the object of much study and commentary. Orally transmitted sayings of Kuei-shan and his successor Yang-shan appear in many classical anthologies of Zen works, and numerous dialogues between them are used as examples in major collections of teaching stories.

Relatively little is known or recorded of later masters of the House of Kuei-Yang, which returned to quiescence after a few generations. An exception to this is found in a rare record of the work of Sun-chi, a successor of Yang-shan, who came from Korea and whose sayings are found only in the *Annals of the Halls of the Ancestors,* an early Zen collection lost in China but preserved (and apparently augmented) in Korea.

This material is particularly valuable in that it contains the most extensive and most clearly explained usages of circular symbols, for which the House of Kuei-Yang is said to have been famous. Yang-shan is supposed to have inherited a unique book of symbols from an ancient master. To avoid attachment to the concrete, Yang-shan burned this book but later made a copy from memory to return to the master from whom he received it. Nothing more is known of this system, except for fragments appearing here and there. Sun-chi's explanations clarify the mystery of the circular symbols to some degree, particularly in demonstrating the connection between scriptural Buddhism and Zen.

After the Kuei-Yang, the next of the Five Houses of Zen was the Lin-chi. The selection of materials presented here begins with extracts from *Essential Method of Transmission of Mind* by Huang-po (d. 850), who was the Zen teacher of Lin-chi, after whom the House is named. Huang-po is said to have been enlightened by nature, but he is also considered a Zen successor of the great Pai-chang.

Huang-po's sayings are followed by excerpts from the *Lin-chi Lu,* or "Record of Lin-chi," one of the most extensive collections of lectures and dialogues of an individual teacher to be made during the classical period of Zen. Reflecting the spirit of Pai-chang and Huang-po in his teaching, Lin-chi further refined some of their formal didactic constructs and also perfected the use of shock techniques to stimulate direct perceptual breakthrough outside of conventional thought patterns.

The Lin-chi House of Zen declined almost immediately and was nearly extinct after the fourth generation. It was revived by a sixth-generation master who studied with more than seventy teachers of Zen, including representatives of all the existing Houses as well as other Zen lineages. This revival of Lin-chi Zen was brought to its greatest level of sophistication in the tenth generation by the Zen master Yuan-wu (1063–1135), whose famous *Essentials of Mind* also became a Zen classic. Extracts of this work are presented here.

The Ts'ao-Tung House of Zen arose at more or less the same time as the Kuei-Yang and Lin-chi. The records of the masters of this House were scattered, and little remains but some dialogues and a few compositions attributed to Tung-shan and Ts'ao-shan. The selection presented here begins with sayings of Tung-shan's predecessors Yao-shan (745–828) and Yun-yen (781–841). The teaching embodied in Tung-shan's famed *Song of Focusing the Precious Mirror*, given here in translation, is said to have originated with Yao-shan and been transmitted to Tung-shan by Yun-yen.

The House of Ts'ao-Tung is particularly known for the teaching device of the Five Ranks, said to have been extracted from Yao-shan's teaching by Tung-shan and refined by his successor Ts'ao-shan. The present collection includes Ts'ao-shan's most remarkable exposition of this device, which primarily illustrates the integration of absolute and relative perspectives in Zen experience, extending its use to structural analysis of Zen sayings and stories to define the states and stages of realization they represent.

The Ts'ao-Tung school died out after the passing of the last of the sixth-generation masters but was revived by a seventh-generation master of the House of Lin-chi, who had been entrusted with the Ts'ao-Tung teaching methods by the last living master. A subsequent revival of the Ts'ao-Tung House of Zen ultimately climaxed in the teachings of Hung-chih (1091–1157), who turned out to be one of the greatest Zen writers of all time, in both poetry and prose. Selections from Hung-chih's remarkable writings cap this chapter on the Ts'ao-Tung House of Zen.

The fourth of the Five Houses is named after Yun-men, who studied with a disciple of Huang-po and attained enlightenment before meeting Hsueh-feng, who is traditionally regarded as his main Zen teacher. Hsueh-feng himself studied with Tung-shan of the House of Ts'ao-Tung Zen, and Yun-men later associated with Tung-shan's successor Ts'ao-shan. After completing his studies with Hsueh-feng, Yun-men also spent time with a successor of Kuei-shan of the House of Kuei-Yang Zen. Thus the Yun-men House of Zen had spiritual connections with each of the older Houses.

The selection of materials on Yun-men Zen presented here begins with sayings of Hsueh-feng (822–908), who was the teacher of Yunmen and of many other distinguished Zen masters of the age. Hsueh-feng attained his first Zen realization at the age of eighteen, but he did not reach complete Zen enlightenment until he was forty-five and is traditionally held up as a prime illustration of the proverb, "A good vessel takes a long time to complete." He subsequently attracted many followers and is said to have had fifteen hundred disciples. By the time he died, he had more than fifty enlightened successors already teaching Zen.

Yun-men, after whom the House is named, was one of the most brilliant and abstruse of all the classical masters. His talks include numerous examples of quotations and variations of existing Zen lore, and meditation on Zen stories and sayings was clearly one of the methods of his school. Tradition has it, nevertheless, that Yun-men forbade his followers to record his own words, so that they could not memorize sayings at the expense of direct experience of reality. The record we nonetheless have of Yun-men, more extensive than that of other original masters of the Five Houses, is said to have been surreptitiously written down by a longtime disciple on a robe made of paper. Such robes were sometimes worn by monks as an exercise in remembrance of the perishability of things. This anthology presents several of Yun-men's lectures, in which he gives orientation for Zen studies in relatively straightforward terms.

Yun-men had sixty-one enlightened disciples, but little is known of most of them. In the next generation, however, a successor of one of his disciples emerged as a leading writer and intellectual of his time as well as a distinguished Zen master. This was the great master Ming-chiao (1008–1072), who wrote extensively on secular subjects as well as religious and spiritual themes. Ming-chiao had many contacts among the Confucian intelligentsia, and he played a powerful role in the Zen influence on the emergence and development of Sung dynasty neo-Confucianism. Several of Ming-chiao's lucid essays on psychology and spirituality are presented here in the materials on the Yun-men House of Zen.

In the next, fourth, generation of this Zen House, another giant arose, the eminent Hsueh-tou, who was also a great writer and an outstanding poet. Traditionally regarded as the reviver of the House of Yun-men, Hsueh-tou is particularly famous as the author of the poetic commentaries on Zen stories of the classic collection *Blue Cliff Record*. Another collection of poetry is also attributed to Hsueh-tou, as well as an anthology of Zen stories with his own prose comments, the *Cascade Collection*, selections of which are presented here to cap the section on Yun-men Zen.

The last of the Five Houses of Zen was the Fa-yen. One of the earliest collections of classical Zen lore refers to this House as a revival of the Zen school of Hsuan-sha (835–908), one of the most redoubtable masters of the T'ang dynasty. Originally a fisherman, Hsuan-sha became an apprentice and colleague of the great Zen master Hsueh-feng, already mentioned as the forerunner of the Yun-men House.

The selection of materials presented here on the Fa-yen House of Zen begins with sayings of Hsuan-sha and his successor Kuei-ch'en, who was the teacher of Zen master Fa-yen. This is followed by the complete text of Fa-yen's classic composition *Ten Guidelines for Zen Schools*, in which the great master—who is said to have had a thousand disciples and more than sixty enlightened successors—analyzes the deterioration of contemporary Zen teaching and practice vis-à-vis the fundamental principles and original ideals of Zen.

Among Fa-yen's many spiritual heirs were numerous distinguished Zen masters, including a National Teacher of Koryo, unified Korea, where this House was to have a great impact. Another of his outstanding successors, a National Teacher of the Latter Han dynasty in post-T'ang China, was instrumental in the restoration and revival of the T'ien-t'ai school of Buddhism, one of the mother houses of ancient Zen. This master was in turn succeeded by the illustrious Yung-ming Yen-shou (905–976), who is also considered a patriarch of Pure Land Buddhism.

Yen-shou revitalized the study of pan-Buddhism in the Zen context and the study of Zen in the pan-Buddhism context. He was probably the most prolific Zen author of all time, especially noted for his hundred-volume compendium *Source Mirror Record*, in which he synthesizes the whole range of exoteric Buddhist doctrine, quoting extensively from more than three hundred classical sources.

This anthology of materials from the Five Houses of Zen closes with two selections from the work of Yen-shou of the House of Fa-yen. First is a summary critique of more than one hundred cultic deviations of Zen, following on the work of Fa-yen and others along these lines. This is followed by an instructive work on balancing the two basic aspects of meditation, commonly referred to as cessation and contemplation (or stopping and seeing) in the context of causative practice, and as concentration and insight (or stability and wisdom) in the context of effective realization. This is one of the most valuable guides to Zen meditation to be found among the literature of the Five Houses.

The House of Kuei-Yang

PAI-CHANG
Sayings

It is necessary to distinguish language referring to absolute truth from language referring to relative truth. It is necessary to distinguish general statements from particular statements. It is necessary to distinguish the language of a complete teaching from the language of an incomplete teaching.

The complete teaching deals with purity; the incomplete teaching deals with impurity. The incomplete teaching explains the defilement in impure things in order to eliminate the profane; the complete teaching explains the defilement in pure things in order to eliminate the sacred.

Before Buddha had expounded the elementary teachings, people had no vision, so they needed someone to refine them. If you are speaking to unhearing worldlings, you need to teach them to get over their attachments, live a disciplined life, practice meditation, and develop insight. But it is not appropriate to speak in this way to people beyond measure.

People in the process of self-purification have already willingly accepted discipline in full. Theirs is the power of discipline, concentration, and insight; therefore to preach to them in this way is called speaking at the wrong time, because it is not appropriate to the occasion. It is also called suggestive talk.

People in the process of purification must be told of the defilement in pure things. They must be taught to detach from all things, existent or nonexistent. They must be taught to detach from all cultivation and experience and even to detach from detachment.

The process of purification is to strip away influences of habit. If people in the process of purification cannot get rid of the diseases of greed and hatred, they are also unhearing worldlings and still have to be taught to practice meditation and cultivate insight.

, , ,

The two lesser vehicles put an end to the diseases of greed and hatred, removing them completely, yet dwell in desirelessness and consider that correct. This is the formless realm; this is obstructing the light of complete enlightenment, shedding the blood of Buddha. Here too it is still necessary to practice meditation and develop insight further.

, , ,

You have to distinguish references to purity and impurity. There are many names for impure things—greed, hatred, infatuation, and so on. There are also many names for pure things—enlightenment, nirvana, liberation, and so on. Yet even in the very midst of these twin streams, purity and impurity—in the midst of standards of profanity and holiness, in the midst of forms, sounds, smells, tastes, feelings, and things, in the midst of worldly things and transmundane phenomena—the immediate mirroring awareness should not get fixated on anything at all.

, , ,

Once you are free of obsession and fixation, if you abide in nonattachment and consider that correct, this is the elementary good. This is abiding in the subdued mind. This is what a disciple is. You are attached to the means and will not let go of it. This is the way of the two lesser vehicles. This is a result of meditation.

Once you are no longer grasping, and yet do not dwell in nonattachment either, this is the intermediate good. This is the Half Word Teaching. This is still the formless realm; although you avoid being trapped in the way of the two lesser vehicles and avoid being trapped by bedevilment, this is still a meditation sickness. This is the bondage of enlightening beings.

Once you no longer dwell in nonattachment and do not even make an understanding of nonabiding, this is the final good. This is the Full Word Teaching. You avoid being trapped in the formless realm, avoid being trapped in meditation sickness, avoid being trapped in the way of enlightening beings, and avoid being trapped by bedevilment.

, , ,

Because of barriers of knowledge, barriers of state, and barriers of action, seeing your own buddha nature is like seeing color at night. As it is said, in the stage of buddhahood, two kinds of ignorance are stopped: the ignorance of subtle knowledge and the ignorance of extremely subtle knowledge.

If you can pass through the three phases of beginning, intermediate, and final goodness, you will not be constrained by them. Buddhist teachings liken this to a deer leaping three times to get out of a net. Then you are called an enlightened one beyond confinement; nothing can capture or bind you. You are one of the buddhas succeeding to the Lamp Buddha. This is the supreme vehicle, the highest knowledge; this is standing on the Way of enlightenment. You are now a buddha, with enlightened nature; you are a guide, able to employ an unobstructed influence. This is unimpeded illumination.

＞　＞　＞

After enlightenment, you will be able to use causality of virtue and knowledge freely; this is building a car to carry causality. In life, you are not stayed by life; in death, you are not obstructed by death. Even though you are within the clusters of mental and physical elements, it is as if a door had opened up, so you are not inhibited by these clusters of mental and physical elements. You are free to leave or to remain, going out and entering without difficulty. If you can be like this, there is no question of stages or steps, of superior or inferior; everything, even down to the bodies of ants, is all the land of pure marvel. It is inconceivable.

＞　＞　＞

The foregoing is still just talk for the purpose of untying bonds. As scripture says, "They themselves are whole; don't injure them." Even terms like *Buddha* and *enlightening beings* are injuries. As long as you speak of anything at all, whether it exists or not, it is all injury. "Whether it exists or not" refers to all things.

＞　＞　＞

Enlightening beings of the tenth stage are still in the river of impure streams; they create a teaching of a pure stream, defining characteristics of purity and explaining the afflictions of impurity.

> , , ,

In ancient times, the ten great disciples of Buddha all had their individuality and characteristic condition; one by one they had their errors explained away by the Guide. In the four stages of meditation and eight concentrations, even the likes of saints dwell in absorption for as long as eighty thousand eons; clinging dependently to what they practice, they are intoxicated by the wine of pure things.

Therefore, disciples may hear the teaching of the Enlightened One but are not able to conceive the spirit of the supreme Way. That is why it is said that people who cut off roots of goodness have no buddha nature. A scripture says this is called the deep pit of liberation, a fearsome place; if the mind retreats for an instant, it goes to hell like an arrow shot.

> , , ,

We cannot speak only in terms of retreating or not retreating, since supernal enlightening beings like Manjushri, Avalokiteshvara, and Mahasthamaprapta come back to the stage of stream-entering, mingling with various kinds of people in order to guide them. We cannot say that they have retreated or regressed; all we can say at such times is that they have entered the stream.

As long as the immediate mirroring awareness is not concerned by anything at all, whether it exists or not, and can pass through the three stages and all things, pleasant or unpleasant, then even if you hear of a hundred, a thousand, or even a hundred million buddhas appearing in the world, it is as if you had not heard. And yet you do not dwell in not hearing, and you do not make an understanding of nondwelling. Then you cannot be said to retreat; measurements and calculations do not apply to you. This is what is meant by the saying that Buddha is always in the world without being habituated to things of the world.

> , , ,

To say the Buddha turns the Wheel of the Teaching and then retreats is to slander the Enlightened One, the Teaching, and the Community. To say the Buddha does not turn the Wheel of the Teaching and does not retreat is also to slander the Enlightened One, the Teaching, and the Community. As Seng Chao wrote, "The Way of enlightenment cannot be measured; it is so high that there is nothing above it, so vast that it cannot be limited, so profound that it is bottomless, so deep that it cannot be fathomed. Even to speak of it is like setting up a target, inviting an arrow."

’ ’ ’

When we speak of mirroring awareness, even this is not really right. Discern the pure by way of the impure. If you say the immediate mirroring awareness is right, or else that there is something beyond mirroring awareness, this is all delusion. If you keep dwelling in immediate mirroring awareness, this is also tantamount to delusion; this is what is called the mistake of naturalism.

If you say immediate mirroring awareness is your own Buddha, these are words of measurement, words of calculation; they are like the crying of a jackal. This is being stuck at the gate, like being stuck in glue.

Originally you did not acknowledge that innate knowing and awareness are your own Buddha, and so you went running elsewhere to seek Buddha. Therefore you needed a teacher to tell you about innate knowing and awareness, as a medicine to cure this disease of frantic outward seeking.

Once you no longer seek outwardly, this disease is cured, and it is necessary to remove the medicine. If you cling fixedly to innate knowing awareness, this is a Zen sickness, characteristic of a fanatical follower. It is like water turned to ice: all the ice is water, but it cannot be used to quench thirst. This is a mortal illness, before which ordinary physicians are helpless.

’ ’ ’

There has never been such a thing as "Buddha," so do not understand it as Buddha. "Buddha" is a medicine for emotional people; if you have no disease, you should not take medicine. When medicine and disease are both dissolved, it is like pure water; buddhahood is like a sweet herb mixed in the water, or like honey mixed in the water, most sweet and delicious. And yet the pure water itself is not affected.

’ ’ ’

It is not that there is nothing there, because it has always been there. This truth is originally present in everyone. All the buddhas and enlightening beings may be called people pointing out a treasure. Fundamentally, it is not a thing; you don't need to know or understand it; you don't need to affirm or deny it. Just stop dualism; stop suppositions of being and nonbeing, of neither being nor nonbeing.

When there are no traces of either extreme, then there is neither lack nor sufficiency; this is not profane or holy, not light or dark. This is not having knowledge, yet it is not lacking knowledge. It is not bondage and not liberation. It is not any name or category at all. Why is this not true speech? How can you carve and polish emptiness to make an image of Buddha? How can you say that emptiness is blue, yellow, red, or white?

, , ,

It is said, "Reality has no comparison, because there is nothing to which it may be likened; the body of reality is not constructed and does not fall within the scope of any category." That is why it is said, "The reality of the enlightened is nameless and cannot be expressed in speech; it is impossible to tarry in the empty door of truth as it really is." Just as insects can alight anywhere but on the flames of a fire, the minds of emotional people can form relations to anything except transcendent insight.

, , ,

When you visit teachers, seeking some knowledge or understanding, this is the demon of teachers, because it gives rise to talk and opinion.

If you take the four universal vows, promising to rescue all living beings before attaining buddhahood yourself, this is the demon of the knowledge of the way of enlightening beings, because the vow is never given up.

If you fast and discipline yourself, practice meditation, and cultivate insight, these are afflicted virtues. Even if you manifest attainment of complete, perfect enlightenment and rescue innumerable people, enabling them to attain individual enlightenment, this is the demon of virtues, since it arouses greed and attachment.

If you are completely undefiled by greed in the midst of all things, so that your aware essence exists alone, dwelling in extremely deep absorption without ever rising or progressing further, this is the demon of concentration, because you will be permanently addicted to enjoying it until you reach ultimate extinction, desireless, quiescent, and still. This is still demon work.

If your insight cannot shed so many demon webs, then even if you can understand a hundred books of knowledge, all of it is dregs of hell. If you seek to be like Buddha, there is no way for you to be so.

> , , ,

Now when you hear me tell you not to be attached to anything at all, whether good or bad, existent or nonexistent, you immediately take that to be falling into a void. You don't realize that abandoning the root to pursue the branches is falling into a void. Seeking buddhahood, seeking enlightenment, seeking anything at all, whether it exists or not, is abandoning the root to pursue the branches.

For now, eat simple food to sustain life, wear old clothing to keep off the cold, and when thirsty scoop up water to drink. Beyond this, if you harbor no thought of concern with anything at all, whether it is there or not, then you will in time have your share of ease and clarity.

> , , ,

Good teachers do not cling to being or nonbeing, having abandoned all kinds of demonic suggestion. When they speak, they do not entangle or bind others. Whatever they say, they do not call it a teacher's explanation; like echoes in a valley, their words fill the land faultlessly. They are worthy of trust and association.

If anyone should say, "I am capable of explaining, I am able to understand; I am the teacher, you are the disciples," this is the same as demonic suggestion and pointless talk. Once you have actually seen the existence of the Way, to say, "This is Buddha, this is not Buddha, this is enlightenment, this is extinction, this is liberation," and so on is to pointlessly express partial knowledge. To lift a finger and say, "This is Zen! This is Tao!" is to utter words that entangle and bind others endlessly. This only increases the ties of seekers. And there are still errors of speech even when they are unspoken.

> , , ,

Be master of mind; don't be mastered by mind. In the incomplete teaching, there is a teacher, there is a guide; in the complete teaching, there is no teacher, and doctrine is not the master. If you are still unable to resort to the mystic mirror, then for the time being resort to the complete teaching, and you will yet have some familiarity with it. As for the incomplete teaching, it is suitable only for unhearing worldlings.

For now, do not depend on anything at all, whether it is there or not; and do not dwell on not depending on anything, and also do not make an understanding of not depending or dwelling, either. This is called great wisdom.

, , ,

Only a buddha is a great teacher, because there is no second person. The rest are all called outsiders, and what they say is demonic suggestion.

Right now, the point is to explain away dualism. Do not be affected by greed for anything at all, whether it is there or not. As far as untying bonds is concerned, there are no special words or statements to teach people.

If you say there are some particular statements to teach people, or that there is some particular doctrine to give people, this is heresy and demonic suggestion.

, , ,

You must distinguish complete and incomplete teachings, prohibitive and nonprohibitive words, living and dead words, expressions of healing and sickness, negative and positive metaphors, and generalizing and particularizing expressions.

To say that it is possible to attain buddhahood by cultivation, that there is practice and there is realization, that this mind is enlightened, that the mind itself is Buddha, is Buddha's teaching. This is the incomplete teaching. These are nonprohibitive words, generalizing expressions, words of a one-pound or one-ounce burden. These words are concerned with weeding out impure things. These are words of positive metaphor. These are dead words. These are words for ordinary people.

To say that it is not possible to attain buddhahood by cultivation, that there is no cultivation and no realization, that it is neither mind nor Buddha, is also Buddha's teaching. These are words of the complete teaching, prohibitive words, particularizing words, words of a ten-thousand-pound burden, words of negative metaphor and negative instruction, words concerned with weeding out pure things. These are words for someone of rank in the Way. These are living words.

As long as there are verbal formulations, from entry into the stream all the way up to the tenth stage of enlightenment, everything is in the category of defilement by the dust of doctrine. As long as there are verbal formulations, everything is in the realm of affliction and trouble. As long as there are verbal formulations, everything belongs to the incomplete teaching.

The complete teaching is obedience; the incomplete teaching is transgression. At the stage of buddhahood, there is neither obedience nor transgression; neither the complete nor the incomplete teachings are admitted.

, , ,

Discern the ground by way of the sprouts; discern the pure by way of the impure. Just be aware, mirrorlike, right now. If you assess mirroring awareness from the standpoint of purity, it is not pure, but absence of mirroring awareness is not pure either, nor is it impure. Nor is it holy or unholy. It is not, furthermore, a matter of seeing the impurity of the water and talking about the problems of impurity in water. If the water were pure, nothing could be said; in fact, speech would defile the water.

, , ,

If there is a questionless question, there is also speechless explanation. A buddha does not explain truth for the sake of buddhas. In the world of reality where everything is equally suchness, there is no Buddha; no one rescues living beings. A buddha does not remain in buddhahood; this is called the real field of blessings.

, , ,

You must distinguish host and guest words. If you are affected by greed for anything at all, whether it is there or not, you will be confused and disturbed by everything. Your own mind then becomes the king of demons, and its perceptive functions are in the category of deluding demons.

If your immediate mirroring awareness does not dwell on anything, existent or nonexistent, mundane or transcendent; and yet does not make an understanding of nondwelling and does not even dwell in the absence of understanding, then your own mind is Buddha, and its perceptive functions are in the category of enlightening beings. Master of all mental conditions, its perceptive functions are in the realm of passing phenomena.

It is like waves telling of water; it illumines myriad forms without effort. If you can perceive calmly, you will penetrate the hidden essence and penetrate all time. As it is said, "When psychology has no influence on perception, the ultimate power remains, serving as a guide in all places."

, , ,

People's natural consciousness is sticky, because they have not trodden the steps to enlightenment. They have stuck fast to various things for a long time. Even as they partake of the hidden essence, they cannot use it as medicine. Even as they hear words beyond conception, they cannot believe completely.

This is why Gautama Buddha spent forty-nine days in silent contemplation under the tree where he was enlightened. Wisdom is obscure, difficult to explain; there is nothing to which it may be likened.

To say people have buddha nature is to slander the buddhas, their Teaching, and their Communities. To say people have no buddha nature is also to slander the buddhas, their Teaching, and their Communities.

To say there is buddha nature is called slander by attachment. To say there is no buddha nature is called slander by falsehood. As it is said, to say buddha nature exists is slander by presumption, and to say it does not exist is slander by repudiation; to say buddha nature both exists and does not exist is slander by contradiction, and to say buddha nature neither exists nor does not exist is slander by meaningless argument.

KUEI-SHAN
Admonitions

As long as you are subject to a life bound by force of habit, you are not free from the burden of the body. The physical being given you by your parents has come into existence through the interdependence of many conditions; while the basic elements thus sustain you, they are always at odds with one another.

Impermanence, aging, and illness do not give people a set time. One may be alive in the morning, then dead at night, changing worlds in an instant. We are like the spring frost, like the morning dew, suddenly gone. How can a tree growing on a cliff or a vine hanging into a well last forever? Time is passing every moment; how can you be complacent and waste it, seeing that the afterlife is but a breath away?

> , , ,

Inwardly strive to develop the capacity of mindfulness; outwardly spread the virtue of uncontentiousness. Shed the world of dust to seek emancipation.

> , , ,

Over the ages you have followed objects, never once turning back to look within. Time slips away; months and years are wasted.

> , , ,

The Buddha first defined precepts to begin to remove the veils of ignorance. With standards and refinements of conduct pure as ice and snow, the precepts rein and concentrate the minds of beginners in respect to what to stop, what to uphold, what to do, and what not to do. Their details reform every kind of crudity and decadence.

How can you understand the supreme vehicle of complete meaning without having paid heed to moral principles? Beware of spending a lifetime in vain; later regrets are useless.

> , , ,

If you have never taken the principles of the teachings to heart, you have no basis for awakening to the hidden path. As you advance in years and grow old, your vanity will not allow you to associate with worthy companions; you know only arrogance and complacency.

> , , ,

Dawdling in the human world eventually produces dullness and coarseness. Unawares, you become weak and senile; encountering events, you face a wall. When younger people ask you questions, you have nothing to say that will guide them. And even if you have something to say, it has nothing to do with the scriptures. Yet when you are treated without respect, you immediately denounce the impoliteness of the younger generation. Angry thoughts flare up, and your words afflict everyone.

One day you will lie in sickness, flat on your back with myriad pains oppressing you. Thinking and pondering from morning to night, your heart will be full of fear and dread. The road ahead is vague, boundless; you do not know where you will go.

Here you will finally know to repent of your errors, but what is the use of trying to dig a well when you're already thirsty? You will regret not having prepared earlier, now that it is late and your faults are so many.

When it is time to go, you shake apart, terrified and trembling. The cage broken, the sparrow flies. Consciousness follows what you have done, like a man burdened with debts, dragged away first by the strongest. The threads of mind, frayed and diffused, tend to fall to whatever is most pressing.

The murderous demon of impermanence does not stop moment to moment. Life cannot be extended; time is unreliable. No one in any realm of being can escape this. Subjection to physical existence has gone on in this way for untold ages.

> , , ,

Our regret is that we were all born in an era of imitation. The age of saints is distant, and Buddhism is decadent. Most people are lazy.

, , ,

If you pass your whole life half asleep, what can you rely on?

, , ,

If you only want to sit still with folded hands and do not value even a moment of time, if you do not work diligently at your tasks, then you have no basis for accomplishment. How can you pass a whole life in vain?

, , ,

When you speak, let it concern the scriptures; in discussion, follow your study of the ancients. Be upright and noble of demeanor, with a lofty and serene spirit.

On a long journey, it is essential to go with good companions; purify your eyes and ears again and again. When you stay somewhere, choose your company; listen to what you have not heard time and again. This is the basis of the saying, "It was my parents who bore me; it was my companions who raised me."

Companionship with the good is like walking through dew and mist; although they do not drench your clothing, in time it becomes imbued with moisture. Familiarity with evil increases false knowledge and views, creating evil day and night. You experience consequences right away, and after death you sink. Once you have lost human life, you will not return ever again, even in ten thousand eons. True words may offend the ear, but do they not impress the heart? If you cleanse the mind and cultivate virtue, conceal your tracks and hide your name, preserve the fundamental and purify the spirit, then the clamor will cease.

, , ,

If you want to study the Way by intensive meditation and make a sudden leap beyond expedient teachings, let your mind merge with the hidden harbor; investigate its subtleties, determine its most profound depths, and realize its true source.

, , ,

When you suddenly awaken to the true basis, this is the stairway leading out of materialism. This shatters the twenty-five domains of being in the three realms of existence. Know that everything, inside and outside, is all unreal. Arising from transformations of mind, all things are merely provisional names; don't set your mind on them. As long as feelings do not stick to things, how can things hinder people? Leaving them to the all-pervasive flow of reality, do not cut them off, yet do not continue them either. When you hear sound and see form, all is normal; whether in the relative world or in the transcendental absolute, appropriate function is not lacking.

, , ,

If there are people of middling ability who are as yet unable to transcend all at once, let them concentrate upon the teaching, closely investigating the scriptures and scrupulously looking into the inner meaning.

, , ,

Have you not heard it said, "The vine that clings to the pine climbs to the heights; only based on the most excellent foundation may there be widespread weal"? Carefully cultivate frugality and self-control. Do not vainly be remiss, and do not go too far. Then in all worlds and every life there will be sublime cause and effect.

, , ,

Cease conceptualization; forget about objects; do not be a partner to the dusts. When the mind is empty, objects are quiescent.

, , ,

Assert mastery; do not follow human sentimentality. The entanglements of the results of actions are impossible to avoid. When the voice is gentle, the echo corresponds; when the figure is upright, the shadow is straight. Cause and effect are perfectly clear; have you no concern?

, , ,

This illusory body,
this house of dreams:
appearances in emptiness.
There has never been a beginning;

how could an end be determined?
Appearing here, disappearing there,
rising and sinking,
worn and exhausted,
never able to escape the cycle,
when will there ever be rest?
Lusting for the world,
body-mind and the causal nexus
compound the substance of life.
From birth to old age,
nothing is gained;
subjection to delusion comes
from fundamental ignorance.
Take heed that time is passing;
we cannot count on a moment.
If you go through this life in vain,
the coming world will be obstructed.
Going from illusion to illusion
is all due to indulgent senses;
they come and go through mundane routines,
crawling through the triplex world.
Call on enlightened teachers without delay;
approach those of lofty virtue.
Analyze and understand body and mind;
clear away the brambles.
The world is inherently evanescent, empty;
how can conditions oppress you?
Plumb the essence of truth,
with enlightenment as your guide.
Let go of mind and objects both;
do not recall, or recollect.
With the senses free of care,
activity and rest are peaceful, quiet;
with the unified mind unaroused,
myriad things all rest.

KUEI-SHAN AND YANG-SHAN
Sayings and Dialogues

Kuei-shan said, "The mind of a Wayfarer is plain and direct, without artificiality. There is no rejection and no attachment, no deceptive wandering mind. At all times seeing and hearing are normal. There are no further details. One does not, furthermore, close the eyes or shut the ears; as long as feelings do not stick to things, that will do.

"Sages since time immemorial have only explained the problems of pollution. If one does not have all that false consciousness, emotional and intellectual opinionatedness, and conceptual habituation, one is clear as autumn water, pure and uncontrived, placid and uninhibited. Such people are called Wayfarers, or free people."

Kuei-shan was asked, "Is there any further cultivation for people who have suddenly awakened?"

Kuei-shan replied, "If they awaken truly, realizing the fundamental, they know instinctively when it happens. The question of cultivation or not is two-sided. Suppose beginners have conditionally attained a moment of sudden awakening to inherent truth, but there are still longstanding habit energies that cannot as yet be cleared all at once. They must be taught to clear away streams of consciousness manifesting habitual activity. That is cultivation, but there cannot be a particular doctrine to have them practice or devote themselves to.

"Having entered into the principle through hearing, as the principle heard is profound and subtle, the mind is naturally completely clear and does not dwell in the realm of confusion. Even if there are hundreds and thousands of subtleties to criticize or commend the times, you must gain stability, gird your loins, and know how to make a living on your own before you can realize them.

"In essence, the noumenal ground of reality does not admit of a single particle, but the methodology of myriad practices does not abandon anything. If you penetrate directly, then the sense of the ordinary and the sacred disappears, concretely revealing the true constant, where principle and fact are not separate. This is the buddhahood of being-as-is."

, , ,

Kuei-shan asked Yun-yen, "What is the seat of enlightenment?"

Yun-yen said, "Freedom from artificiality."

Yun-yen then asked Kuei-shan the same question. Kuei-shan replied, "The vanity of all things."

, , ,

Kuei-shan asked Yang-shan, "Of the forty scrolls of the *Nirvana Scripture*, how many are Buddha's talk, and how many are the devil's talk?"

Yang-shan replied, "They're all devil talk."

Kuei-shan said, "Hereafter no one will be able to do anything to you."

Yang-shan asked, "As a temporary event, where do I focus my action?"

Kuei-shan said, "I just want your perception to be correct; I don't tell you how to act."

, , ,

Kuei-shan passed a water pitcher to Yang-shan. As Yang-shan was about to take it, Kuei-shan withdrew it and said, "What is it?"

Yang-shan responded, "What do *you* see?"

Kuei-shan said, "If you put it that way, why then seek from me?"

Yang-shan said, "That is so, yet as a matter of humanity and righteousness, it is also my own business to pour some water for you."

Kuei-shan then handed Yang-shan the pitcher.

, , ,

Kuei-shan asked Yang-shan, "How do you understand origin, abiding, change, and extinction?"

Yang-shan said, "At the time of the arising of a thought, I do not see that there is origin, abiding, change, or extinction."

Kuei-shan retorted, "How can you dismiss phenomena?"

Yang-shan rejoined, "What did you just ask about?"

Kuei-shan said, "Origin, abiding, change, and extinction."

Yang-shan concluded, "Then what do you call dismissing phenomena?"

,   ,   ,

Kuei-shan asked Yang-shan, "How do you understand the immaculate mind?"

Yang-shan replied, "Mountains, rivers, and plains; sun, moon, and stars."

Kuei-shan said, "You only get the phenomena."

Yang-shan rejoined, "What did you just ask about?"

Kuei-shan said, "The immaculate mind."

Yang-shan asked, "Is it appropriate to call it phenomena?"

Kuei-shan said, "You're right."

,   ,   ,

Yang-shan asked Kuei-shan, "When hundreds and thousands of objects come upon us all at once, then what?"

Kuei-shan replied, "Green is not yellow, long is not short. Everything is in its place. It's none of my business."

,   ,   ,

A seeker asked Kuei-shan, "What is the Way?"

Kuei-shan replied, "No mind is the Way."

The seeker complained, "I don't understand."

Kuei-shan said, "You should get an understanding of what doesn't understand."

The seeker asked, "What is that which does not understand?"

Kuei-shan said, "It's just you, no one else!" Then he went on to say, "Let people of the present time just realize directly that which does not understand. *This* is your mind; *this* is your Buddha. If you gain some external knowledge or understanding and consider it the Way of Zen, you are out of touch for the time being. This is called hauling waste in, not hauling waste out; it pollutes your mental field. That is why I say it is not the Way."

,   ,   ,

Yang-shan asked Kuei-shan, "What is the abode of the real Buddha?"

Kuei-shan said, "Using the subtlety of thinking without thought, think back to the infinity of the flames of awareness. When thinking comes to an end, return to the source, where essence and form are eternal and phenomenon and noumenon are nondual. The real Buddha is being-as-is."

, , ,

Yang-shan said in a lecture, "You should each look into yourself rather than memorize what I say. For beginningless eons you have been turning away from light and plunging into darkness, so illusions are deeply rooted and can hardly be extirpated all at once. That is why we use temporarily set-up, expedient techniques to remove your coarse consciousness. This is like using yellow leaves to stop a child's crying by pretending they are gold; it is not actually true, is it?"

, , ,

Yang-shan said in a lecture, "If there is a call for it, there is a transaction; no call, no transaction. If I spoke of the source of Zen, I wouldn't find a single associate, let alone a group of five hundred to seven hundred followers. If I talk of one thing and another, then they struggle forward to take it in. It is like fooling children with an empty fist; there's nothing really there.

"I am now talking to you clearly about matters pertaining to sagehood, but do not focus your minds on them. Just turn to the ocean of your own essence and work in accord with reality. You do not need spiritual powers, because these are ramifications of sagehood, and for now you need to know your mind and arrive at its source.

"Just get the root, don't worry about the branches—they'll naturally be there someday. If you haven't gotten the root, you cannot acquire the branches even if you study, using your intellect and emotions. Have you not seen how Master Kuei-shan said, 'When the mentalities of the ordinary mortal and the saint have ended, being reveals true normalcy, where fact and principle are not separate; this is the buddhahood of being-as-is'?"

SUN-CHI
Symbolic Studies

Circles

The circle is a symbol of nirvana as the refuge. It is also called the sign of the noumenal buddha nature. All people, ordinary folk as well as sages, are related to this: though the sign does not differ, delusion and understanding are not the same; that is why there are ordinary mortals and there are sages. In other words, those who perceive the meaning of the symbol are called sages, while those who misperceive it are called ordinary people.

Thus when Nagarjuna was in south India, to expound the Teaching to a crowd he manifested a transformation of appearance, such that his body looked like the moon hovering over his chair; only his voice was heard teaching, and his bodily form was invisible.

A grandee in the crowd by the name of Aryadeva said to the people, "Do you recognize this sign?"

The people replied, "No. It would take an advanced sage to understand, wouldn't it?"

Now Aryadeva's mind sense was already quiet, and he in fact saw the sign, silently sharing in understanding. So he said to the crowd, "This auspicious sign is the teacher illustrating the buddha nature; it is not the teacher's own body. The image of formless concentration is like the full moon; it means buddha nature."

Before the grandee had even finished speaking, the teacher manifested his own body in the chair and said in verse,

> Physical manifestation of the full moon symbol
> Is used to illustrate the body of buddhas;
> Explaining that the Truth has no such form
> Is to make clear it's not an object of sense.

If someone uses the symbol of the moon orb to pose a question, the word *ox* is written inside the circle to reply.

A circle with an ox inside is the symbol of the ox eating the herb of tolerance. It is also called the symbol of attaining enlightenment by seeing essence.

What is the reasoning? Scripture says, "There is an herb in the Snowy Mountains called Tolerance; a cow that eats it produces ghee." It also says, "If people listen to exposition of great nirvana, then they see the buddha nature." So the herb symbolizes the sublime teaching, the ox symbolizes the potential for sudden enlightenment, and the ghee symbolizes buddhahood. Thus if the ox eats the herb, it produces ghee; if people understand the teaching, they attain correct awakening. Therefore the symbol of the ox eating the herb of tolerance is also called the symbol of perceiving essence and attaining enlightenment.

A circle with three animals beneath it is the symbol of the three vehicles seeking emptiness. Why? When people in the three vehicles hear exposition of true emptiness, they consciously aim for it, not having yet experienced true emptiness. Thus this is represented by three animals below the circle.

If this symbol is used to pose a question, it is answered by attainment of enlightenment through gradual perception of essence.

The circle with an ox inside is the symbol of the white ox on open ground. The open ground stands for the stage of buddhahood; it is also called ultimate emptiness, or emptiness in the absolute sense. The white ox stands for the subtle intelligence of the spiritual body. Thus it is represented by one ox gone into a circle.

Why are three animals placed beneath the moon orb symbol, then answered with one ox inside the moon orb symbol? The three animals below the moon orb symbol represent the three vehicles, while the one ox in the center of the moon orb symbol represents the unitary vehicle. Thus when the temporary vehicles are brought up, the response is manifestation of the reality, leading into experiential realization.

Previously it was said that an ox in the circle is the symbol of an ox eating the herb of tolerance; it was also said that an ox in the circle is a symbol of the white ox on open ground. The symbol is the same, but the explanations are different; yet in spite of the difference in explanations, the circle and the ox are not different. The question then is, if they are not different, why is the symbol expressed twice?

The answer is that even though the circle and ox does not differ, the relative swiftness of perceiving essence differs. That is why the same circle and ox appears in different contexts.

In terms of the difference in swiftness of perceiving essence between the ox that eats the herb of tolerance and the white ox on open ground, which is the slow one and which is the fast one?

The ox eating the herb of tolerance illustrates the sudden perception of reality, as in the *Flower Ornament Scripture*, so it is quick. The white ox on open ground illustrates the ultimate resolution of three vehicles into one. So even though the explanations are not the same, the principle that is realized is not different. So the same symbols are used, to show that principle and knowledge do not differ. It does not mean that the derivations are exactly the same.

A circle with an ox above it is a symbol of cultivating cause in conformity with the result. Why? Even though the initial inspiration may produce correct awakening, nevertheless one's actions and insight are not equal to those of buddhahood. This symbol is to illustrate how application does not go beyond stage; the ancient dictum about "walking in the footsteps of those who arrive at reality" is represented by this symbol.

If this symbol is used to pose a question, the response is a moon disk with a sign of well-being inside. The circle with the sign of well-being inside symbolizes the complete fulfillment of cause and result.

Why is the well-being sign inside the circle a reply to the ox above the circle? Because the ox over the circle symbolizes cultivating cause in accord with result, while the well-being sign inside the circle symbolizes completion of cause and fulfillment of result. When the cause is brought up, the result is illustrated in reply.

A circle with an ox below it symbolizes spiritual practice in quest of emptiness. This is called the reed hut in front of the gate. Enlightening beings seek emptiness, so scripture speaks of "cultivating enlightening practice for three incalculable eons, enduring the unendurable and carrying out the impossible, seeking unremittingly." That is what this symbol illustrates; if it is used to pose a question, the word *king* is written inside a circle in reply.

A circle with a king inside symbolizes gradual witness of reality. Why? If enlightening beings, through eons of practical cultivation, destroy all bedevilments, only then will they attain uncontaminated knowledge of reality and experientially enter the state of buddhahood. Then there are no more habits obstructing them. They are like wise kings who have overcome all rebels, so their countries are peaceful and they have no more enemies interfering with them.

The next two pairs of symbols represent dismissing the unreal to point to the real.

A circle with an ox above and a human inside symbolizes conceptual understanding of the teachings left behind by the Buddha. In other words, if people rely on the universal teaching of the unitary vehicle expounded by Buddha and are well able to analyze and explain it truly, without error, and yet do not realize their own noumenal insight, they are completely dependent on the explanations of another. That is the sense of this symbol.

If this symbol is used to pose a question, it is answered by removing the ox from above the circle, leaving a circle with a human inside.

A circle with a human inside symbolizes perceiving the root and returning to the source. Scripture says, "Return the spirit to abide in the cave of emptiness, overcoming what is difficult to subdue, shedding the bonds of bedevilment; sitting aloof on open ground, the cluster of consciousness is completely nirvanic." That is what this symbolizes.

Why remove the ox above but not the human within the circle? Because the human within the circle represents noumenal insight, while the ox above the circle represents conceptual understanding. Even if people rely on the teachings and analyze the works of the whole Buddhist canon, as long as they have not actualized their own noumenal insight, it is all conceptual understanding. When conceptual interpretation does not arise, then noumenal insight appears, so we erase the ox above the circle and not the human inside it. This is why scripture says, "Just get rid of the sickness, not the prescription."

Why can't ordinary people learn the truth by way of the teachings? If people have wisdom, what do they need with teachings? If they are ordinary people with discriminatory minds, they derive no benefit from depending on doctrines.

Then do the canonical Buddhist teachings have any use? It's not that no one can become enlightened through the teachings, but conceptual interpretation is simply unreal. This is why Buddha chided Ananda, "Even if you memorize the pure principles of the canons of all the buddhas of the ten directions fluently, that will just increase frivolous argumentation." So we should realize that conceptual interpretation of the teachings is of no benefit.

Why do the teachings say, "Those who hear Buddha's teachings all attain sagehood"? It is people of more highly developed faculties who wake right up by way of the teachings, directly actualizing noumenal insight, sure and clear. For those of lesser faculties who do not awaken through the Teaching, conceptual understanding is of no use. But if people of less-developed faculties let the Teaching influence their lives, waiting for another time, who would say there is no benefit? Those who hear the teachings all attain sagehood; the tiniest bit of goodness is a setting forth to arrive at buddhahood—how much more this is so of broad learning in scriptures and treatises!

A circle with a human inside and an ox below symbolizes mistaking your reflection for your head. What is the reasoning? If people do not realize their own inner Buddha and Pure Land but believe in a Buddha and Pure Land in some other realm, they wholeheartedly seek rebirth in the Pure Land to see the Buddha and hear the Teaching. Therefore they diligently practice good deeds and chant the names of the Buddha and the features of the Pure Land. That is what this symbolizes. This is what Master Chih ridiculed when he said, "Those who do not understand that mind itself is Buddha are as if mounted on a donkey looking for a donkey."

If this symbol is used to pose a question, the ox below is removed in reply.

The circle with a human inside symbolizes turning away from your reflection to recognize your head.

Why remove the ox below the circle and not the human inside? When people have not yet awakened true knowledge and have not arrived at true voidness., they focus on seeking a Pure Land and a Buddha in another dimension, so that they might be reborn in the Pure Land, see the Buddha, and hear the Teaching. If people would turn their attention inward, awaken knowledge, and attain true emptiness, then the Buddha and Pure Land within themselves would appear at once, without their having to seek a Pure Land or Buddha outside the mind. So the human inside the circle is not removed, only the ox below the circle.

What is the Buddha within oneself, and the Pure Land within oneself? If people awaken true knowledge and arrive at true emptiness, then true knowledge is Buddha, and emptiness is the Pure Land. If you understand this through experiencing it, where else would you seek a Pure Land and a Buddha? This is why scripture says, "If you're going to keep listening to an external Buddha, why does your inner Buddha not listen to its own listening?"

There are five more symbols, in four pairs.

A semicircle is a symbol of "bringing up a box, seeking a lid," also called the symbol of the half moon awaiting fullness. If this is used to pose a question, another half moon is added in response. Thus the question brings out a box seeking a lid, while the response puts a lid on the box. As the box and cover fit each other, they manifest the sign of the full moon, the circle representing the essence of all buddhas.

An empty circle is a symbol of holding a jade looking for a match. If this symbol is used to pose a question, a certain word is written inside the circle to reply. Thus the question brings a jade seeking its match, and the one who replies recognizes the gem and acts on that.

A circle with a hook inside symbolizes fishing for continuity. If this is used to pose a question, the character for *human* is added next to the character for *hook*, forming a character *buddha*. Thus the questioner fishes for continuity, and the one who answers follows up to complete a precious vessel.

A circle with *buddha* inside symbolizes having completed the precious vessel. If this is used to pose a question, the character for *land* is written inside the circle to reply.

A circle with *land* inside symbolizes the mystic seal. This is utterly beyond all the preceding symbols and is not contained in the concepts of the teachings.

THREE MEANINGS OF BUDDHAHOOD

1. Attaining buddhahood by realizing noumenon
2. Attaining buddhahood by fulfillment of application
3. Attaining buddhahood in manifestation

Attaining buddhahood by realizing principle, or noumenon, means that with a teacher's instruction you turn your attention around to focus it on the source of your own mind, where there is basically nothing concrete. This is attaining buddhahood without going through a gradual process of myriad practices. This is why scripture says that one attains true enlightenment at the first inspiration, and an ancient said that buddhahood is not far away—just turn your attention around, and there it is.

In the context of attaining buddhahood by realizing noumenon, if you speak of essence there is no thing there at all, but if you talk about the three embodiments, there is a buddha and two bodhisattvas, an enlightened one and two enlightening beings. Although there are three personifications, in the present case of attainment of buddhahood by perceiving essence, the achievement of buddhahood is therefore attributed to Manjushri. That is why the ancients said that Manjushri is the mother of all buddhas, because all buddhas are born from Manjushri, for Manjushri represents true knowledge. All buddhas realize enlightenment by means of true knowledge, so Manjushri is the mother of all buddhas.

As for attaining buddhahood by fulfillment of application, this means that even when you have discovered the true principle of noumenal reality, still you follow the practical commitments of Universal Good, practicing extensive cultivation of the bodhisattva path stage by stage. "Attaining buddhahood by fulfillment of application" refers to comprehensiveness of application and complete fulfillment of knowledge and compassion.

For this reason an ancient said, "The ultimate end of practical application is the original place." So we know that when practical application is complete, it returns to the origin. The origin is the principle, the noumenon.

This principle realized in attainment of buddhahood by fulfillment of practical application is no different from the principle realized in attainment of buddhahood by realization of noumenon. Even though the principle is no different, this latter is called attaining buddhahood by fulfillment of practical application because we arrive at the result by putting the cause into effect.

In referring to attainment of buddhahood by fulfillment of practical application, if we speak in terms of the qualities of fruition, we just speak of attaining buddhahood by the practice of Samantabhadra, or Universal Good. But if we speak in terms of the three embodiments, there is also one buddha with two accompanying bodhisattvas.

Nevertheless, though there are three personifications, now because we are dealing particularly with attainment of buddhahood by fulfillment of practice, the merit of attainment of buddhahood is in Samantabhadra, so the ancients said that Samantabhadra is the father of the buddhas. When it is said that all buddhas are born of Samantabhadra, this Samantabhadra or Universal Good means myriad practices; all buddhas realize enlightenment through their myriad practices, so Samantabhadra is the father of all buddhas.

When we speak of one buddha and two bodhisattvas, Vairochana Buddha stands for principle, or noumenon, while Manjushri bodhisattva stands for knowledge, and Samantabhadra bodhisattva stands for practice. Because this principle, knowledge, and practice are the same essence, none can be dispensed with.

The one buddha and two bodhisattvas, furthermore, are both central and auxiliary to each other. In terms of the supremacy of the basic essence, Vairochana is central. In terms of the accomplishment of knowledge seeing essence, Manjushri is central. In terms of the power of virtue of myriad practices, Samantabhadra is central. Thus Li T'ung-hsuan said, "All buddhas attain enlightenment through the great beings Manjushri and Samantabhadra," yet he also said, "Manjushri and Samantabhadra are the younger and elder sons of all buddhas." So obviously the three personifications are both central and auxiliary to one another.

As for attainment of buddhahood in manifestation, after one has realized the principle and one's practice is complete, now that one's own practical attainment of buddhahood is done, one manifests eight aspects of attainment of buddhahood for other people.

The eight aspects of attainment of buddhahood are: descent from the heaven of satisfaction into the womb; dwelling in the womb; emerging from the womb; living in a palace; leaving home; awakening; teaching; and passing away into nirvana. Attainment of buddhahood has eight aspects whereby this is called attainment of buddhahood in manifestation.

It should be realized that the eight aspects of attaining buddhahood are of the embodiments of enjoyment and projection, not of reality. This is why scripture says, "Buddhas do not emerge in the world, nor do they become extinct; it is by the power of their basic commitment that they manifest the state of freedom." This scripture points to the real Buddha within the buddhas of enjoyment and projection. Scripture also says, "It has been infinite eons since I attained buddhahood," indicating that Shakyamuni Buddha had already completed his practice and fully awakened infinite eons earlier and was manifesting the attainment of enlightenment for the sake of other people.

The House of Lin-chi

HUANG-PO
Transmission of Mind

The buddhas and all living beings are only one mind; there is no other reality. This mind, from beginninglessness, has never been born and never passed away. It is neither blue nor yellow; it has no shape and no form. It does not belong to existence or nonexistence; it does not count as new or old. It is neither long nor short, neither large nor small. It transcends all limiting measurements, all labels, all traces, all oppositions. This very being is it; when you stir thoughts, you turn away from it. It is like space, which has no boundaries and cannot be measured.

This one mind is itself Buddha. Buddha and sentient beings are no different; it's just that sentient beings seek externally, grasping appearances, losing the more they seek. If you try to have Buddha seek Buddha, or use mind to grasp mind, you will never succeed. What you don't realize is that if you stop thoughts and forget ruminations, the Buddha spontaneously appears.

This mind itself is Buddha; buddhas are sentient beings. As sentient beings, this mind is not diminished; as buddhas, this mind is not increased. Even the six perfections, myriad practices, and countless virtues are inherent and do not need to be added by cultivation; when the appropriate circumstances are encountered they are employed, and when those circumstances end they rest.

If you do not believe with certainty that this is Buddha, and want to cultivate practice bound up with forms in order to seek effective application, this is all illusion, contrary to the Way. This mind itself is Buddha; there is no other buddha and no other mind. This mind is clear and pure as space, with no appearance at all; when you arouse the mind and stir thoughts, you turn away from the essence of its reality. This is attachment to appearances; there has never been buddhahood attached to appearances. If you cultivate the myriad practices of six perfections in quest of buddhahood, this is a gradual procedure, but there never has been buddhahood as a gradual procedure. Just realize the one mind, and there is nothing else at all to attain. This is the real Buddha.

Buddhas, sentient beings, and the one mind are no different, like space without adulteration or corruption, like the orb of the sun illumining the four quarters. When the sun rises, its light pervades the land, but space is never bright. When the sun sets, darkness covers the land, but space is never dark. States of light and darkness alternate, but the nature of space remains open and empty, unchanging. So it is also with buddhas, sentient beings, and mind. If you contemplate buddhas as forms of pure illumination and liberation, and you contemplate sentient beings as forms of muddled living and dying in the dark, with this understanding you will never ever attain enlightenment, because you are attached to appearances.

It's just this one mind; there is nothing else at all to attain. Mind itself is Buddha. People who study the Way today do not understand the essence of this mind, so they conceive of another mind on top of this mind, seeking buddhahood externally, cultivating practices attached to appearances. All of this is wrong; it is not the way to enlightenment.

"Respectfully supporting all the buddhas in the universe is not as good as respectfully supporting a single mindless Wayfarer." Why is this so? Mindlessness means total nonsubjectivity, the essence of being-as-is. Inwardly one is immovable as a tree, unstirring as a rock; outwardly one is as free from blockage and resistance as space itself. There is neither subject nor object, no direction or location, no form or appearance, no gain or loss.

People who strive do not dare to enter into this teaching, fearing they will fall into voidness with no place to rest; they withdraw, intimidated. All of them search far and wide for knowledge. That is why those who seek knowledge are numerous as hairs, while those who realize the Way are rare as horns.

Manjushri stands for principle; Samantabhadra stands for practice. The principle here is the principle of true emptiness without resistance; practice here means infinite action detached from appearances. Avalokiteshvara stands for universal compassion; Mahasthamaprapta stands for universal knowledge. Vimalakirti means Pure Name: purity refers to essence; name refers to characteristics; essence and characteristics are not different, hence the title Pure Name. What the various major bodhisattvas represent is all within humanity. It is not apart from one mind; all you have to do is realize it.

People who study the Way today do not value enlightenment within their own minds, so they cling to appearances outside the mind and grasp objects; all of this is contrary to the Way.

As for the "sands of the Ganges River," Buddha explained that the sands do not rejoice when buddhas, bodhisattvas, Indra, Brahma, or any of the gods walk upon them, and the sands are not angered when oxen, goats, bugs, and ants walk on them. The sands have no craving for jewels and perfumes and no aversion to manure and filth. A mind like this is a mindless mind. This is the ultimate; if students of the Way do not plunge right into mindlessness, even if they cultivate practices for eons on end, they will never attain the Way. Captured by the practices of the Three Vehicles, they will be unable to attain liberation.

There are, however, differences in rapidity of realizing this mind. There are those who immediately attain mindlessness on hearing the teaching, and there are those who attain mindlessness only on reaching the Ten Faiths, the Ten Abodes, the Ten Practices, or the Ten Dedications. But whether it takes a long time or a short time, when you attain mindlessness, then you stop; there is nothing more to be cultivated or realized.

Actually, there is nothing attained, but this is actually true, not unreal. The accomplishment of attainment in one instant and attainment at the tenth stage are equal; there is no more deep or shallow.

It's just that when you go through eons you suffer painful toil unreasonably. Evildoing and doing good are both attachment to appearances. If you do evil attached to appearances, you subject yourself to vicious circles unreasonably. If you do good attached to appearances, you suffer the pains of laborious toil unreasonably. None of this is as good as immediately recognizing the basic reality on your own as soon as you hear of it.

This reality is mind; there is no truth outside of mind. This mind itself is truth; there is no mind outside of reality. Mind is inherently mindless; and there is no mindless one, either. If you mindfully try to be mindless, then minding is there.

It's just a matter of silent accord; it is beyond all conception. That is why it is said that there is no way to talk about it, no way to think about it.

This mind is pure at the source. Buddhas and ordinary human beings both have it. All living beings are one and the same body with all buddhas and bodhisattvas; it is only because of differences in their subjective thoughts that they create all sorts of activities, with their various results.

Basically there is nothing concrete in buddhahood; it is just open perception, serene clarity, and subtle bliss. When you realize it profoundly in yourself, this is directly it—complete fulfillment, with no further lack. Even if you exert yourself at spiritual exercises for three incalculable eons, going through all the stages and grades, when you reach that one instant of realization, you have just realized the Buddha within yourself; you have not added anything at all. Rather, you will see your eons of effort as the confused behavior of dreams.

This is why the Tathagata said, "In supreme perfect enlightenment I have not acquired anything. If I had acquired anything, Dipankara Buddha would not have given me direction." He also said, "This truth is impartial, without high or low; this is called enlightenment." This is the mind pure at the source, impartial in respect to sentient beings, buddhas, worlds, mountains and rivers, forms, formlessness, everything through the universe, with no image of other or self.

This mind pure at the source is intrinsically always completely clear and fully aware, but worldly people do not realize it; they only recognize perception and cognition as mind, so they are shrouded by perception and cognition. That is why they do not see the very essence of their spiritual luminosity. If they would just directly be mindless, that very essence would appear of itself, like the sun rising into the sky, lighting up everywhere, with no further obstruction.

So students of the Way, only recognizing the actions and movements of perception and cognition, empty out their perception and cognition, so their minds have no road to go on, and they attain no penetration. Just recognize the basic mind in perception and cognition, realizing all the while that the basic mind does not belong to perception and cognition and yet is not apart from perception and cognition.

Just do not conceive opinions and interpretations on top of perception and cognition, and do not stir thoughts on perception and cognition. Do not seek mind apart from perception and cognition, either, and do not try to get to reality by rejecting perception and cognition. When you are neither immersed nor removed, neither dwelling nor clinging, free and independent, then nothing is not a site of enlightenment.

Worldly people who hear it said that the buddhas all communicate the truth of mind think it means there is some special truth in the mind to realize or grasp, so they wind up using mind to search for mind. They do not realize that mind itself is the truth, and the truth itself is mind. It will not do to use mind to seek mind, for that way you will never realize it, even in a million years. It is better to be mindless right away, and then you find fundamental reality.

It is like the story of the wrestler who was unaware that a gem had been embedded in his forehead, and he looked elsewhere for it. He went all over the place but ultimately couldn't find it, until someone who knew pointed it out to him, whereupon he himself saw the original gem as it had been all along.

So it is that people who study the Way stray from their own original mind, not recognizing it as Buddha, and wind up seeking outwardly, undertaking practices and exercises, depending on a process for realization. Even though they seek diligently for eons, they never attain the Way. It is better to be mindless right away, realizing for certain that all things are originally without existence, ungraspable, based on nothing; they abide nowhere and are neither subjective nor objective. If you do not stir errant thoughts, you will immediately realize enlightenment.

LIN-CHI

Sayings

People who study Buddhism in the present day should for now seek truly accurate vision and understanding. Then life and death will not influence you, and you will be free to leave or to stay. You do not need to seek the extraordinary, for the extraordinary will come of itself.

The worthies of old all had means of emancipating people. What I teach people just requires you not to take on the confusions of others. If you need to act, then act, without any further hesitation or doubt.

When students today do not realize this, where is the problem? The problem is in not spontaneously trusting. If you do not trust yourself completely, you will then hurriedly go along with whatever happens in all situations; as you are caused to undergo changes by those myriad situations, you cannot be independent.

If you were able to put a stop to the mentality in which every thought is running after something, then you would be no different from a Zen master or a buddha. Do you want to know what a Zen master or a buddha is? Simply that which is immediately present, listening to the Teaching. It is just because students do not trust completely that they seek outwardly. Even if they get something by seeking, it is all literary excellence; they never attain the living meaning of the masters.

Make no mistake about it; if you do not find it now, you will repeat the same routines for myriad eons, a thousand times over again, following and picking up on objects that attract you, born in the bellies of donkeys and oxen.

According to my view, we are no different from Shakyamuni Buddha. Today, in your various activities, what do you lack? The spiritual light coursing through your six senses has never been interrupted. If you can see in this way, you will simply be free of burdens all your life.

The world is unstable, like a house on fire. This is not a place where you stay long. The murderous haunt of impermanence comes upon you in a flash, no matter whether you are rich or poor, old or young. If you want to be no different from a Zen master or a buddha, just do not seek outwardly.

The pure light of your mind in a single moment of thought is the reality-body Buddha in your own house. The nondiscriminatory light of your mind in a single moment of thought is the reward-body Buddha in your own house. The nondifferentiated light of your mind in a single moment of thought is the projection-body Buddha in your own house. These three kinds of embodiment are none other than the person who is listening to the teaching right here and now, but it is only by not seeking outwardly that one has these effective functions.

According to professors of scriptures and treatises, the three embodiments are the ultimate model, but in my view this is not so. These three embodiments are names, words; they are also three kinds of dependence. An ancient said, "Embodiments are established based on meaning; the lands are discussed based on substance." The embodiment of the nature of reality and the land of the nature of reality are obviously reflections of a light; now you should get to know the person who is manipulating the reflections of the light—this is the root source of the buddhas. Everywhere is your way home.

The fact is that your physical body cannot expound the Teaching or listen to the Teaching. Your lungs, stomach, liver, and gallbladder cannot expound the Teaching or listen to the Teaching. Space cannot expound the Teaching or listen to the Teaching. So what can expound the Teaching and listen to the Teaching? It is the immediately present, clearly obvious, completely formless solitary light; this is what can expound the Teaching and listen to the Teaching. If you can see in this way, you will be no different from a Zen master or a buddha.

Just do not allow any more interruptions at any time, and everything that you see is It. Just because feelings arise, knowledge is blocked; changes in conceptions result in changes in actualities. That is why you keep repeating the same routines in the world and suffer a variety of miseries.

In my view, nothing is not extremely profound; nothing is not liberated. The reality of mind has no form but pervades the ten directions. In the eyes it is called seeing, in the ears it is called hearing, in the nose it smells, in the mouth it speaks, in the hands it grips, and in the feet it steps. Basically it is a single spiritual light, differentiated into a sixfold combination. Once the whole mind is as nothing, you are liberated wherever you are.

What do I mean when I say this? It is just because you are unable to stop the whole mentality of seeking that you get hooked on useless actions and states of other people who lived a long time ago. If you take my view, you will sit at the head of the psychic and physical embodiments of Buddha: those at the tenth stage, with fulfilled hearts, will be like migrant laborers; those who have attained equivalent and ineffable enlightenment will be like people in fetters and chains; saints and self-illuminates will be like privy ordure; enlightenment and nirvana will be like donkey-tethering stakes.

Why so? You have these obstacles only because you have not realized the emptiness of the eons. Genuine Wayfarers are never like this; they just dissolve their history according to conditions, dressing according to circumstances, acting when they need to act, and sitting when they need to sit, without any idea of seeking the fruits of buddhahood.

Why are they like this? An ancient said, "If you are going to contrive activities to seek buddhahood, then buddhahood is a major sign of birth and death."

Time is to be valued! You just try to learn Zen or Tao on the surface as something outside yourself, learning to recognize terms and slogans, seeking "buddhahood," seeking "mastery," seeking "teachers," considering them conceptually. Make no mistake about it—you have but one father and mother, so what more are you seeking? Turn your attention back upon yourself and observe.

An ancient said "Yajnadatta lost his head, but when his searching stopped, then he had no troubles." What you should do is be normal; don't act imitatively.

There is a kind of shaveling who does not know good from bad, who sees spirits and ghosts, points out this and pictures that, and makes a fuss about sun and rain. All who are like this will have to pay back their debts, someday swallowing hot iron pills in front of the king of the underworld. Once men and women of good families get charmed by this kind of fox, they hoke up wonders, blind to the fact that one day they will be charged for their meals.

, , ,

It is absolutely necessary for you to seek to obtain genuinely accurate insight and understanding. Then you can travel freely anywhere and avoid being confused by the common sort of spiritual charmer.

It is the one without obsession who is noble. Just do not act in a contrived manner; simply be normal. When you go searching elsewhere outside yourself, your whole approach is already mistaken. You just try to seek buddhahood, but buddhahood is just a name, an expression—do you know the one who is doing the searching?

The buddhas and Zen masters of all times and places have emerged only on account of search for truth. Present-day seekers are also in search of truth. Only when you attain truth will you be done; until you have attained it, you will repeat your former ways.

What is the truth? The truth is the reality of mind. The reality of mind is formless and pervades the ten directions. It is being used presently, right before your eyes, yet people do not trust it sufficiently, so they accept terms and expressions, seeking to assess Buddhism conceptually in the written word. They are as far away as the sky is from earth.

What truth am I talking about? I am talking about the truth of the ground of mind, which can enter into the ordinary and the sacred, into the pure and the polluted, into the absolute and the conventional, and yet is not absolute or conventional, ordinary or sacred, but is able to give names to all the absolute, conventional, ordinary, and sacred. Someone who has realized this cannot be labeled by the absolute or the conventional, by the ordinary or the sacred. If you can grasp it, then use it, without labeling it any more. This is called the mystic teaching.

My teaching is different from that of everyone else. Even if Manjushri and Samantabhadra were to appear before me, each manifesting an embodiment to ask about the teaching, as soon as they addressed me I would already have distinguished them. As I sit in peace, if any more followers of the Way come to see me, I discern them all completely. Why is it like this? Because my view is distinct: externally I do not grasp the ordinary or the sacred; internally I do not dwell on the fundamental; seeing all the way through, I no longer doubt or err.

, , ,

There is no place for exertion of effort in Buddhism; it is just a matter of being normal and unobsessed, taking care of bodily functions, dressing and eating, lying down when tired. Fools laugh at me; it is the wise who understand this. An ancient said, "Those who work on externals are all ignoramuses."

For now, be the master wherever you are, and then wherever you stand is reality, and situations that come up cannot move you. Even if you have existing habit energy that would impel you to evil deeds, it naturally becomes an ocean of liberation.

Students today do not know the truth at all. They are like goats nosing around, taking whatever they find into their mouths. They cannot distinguish the servant from the master, the guest from the host. People like this enter the path with the wrong attitude; they cannot enter into clamorous situations, yet they call themselves genuine renunciants. In fact they are really worldlings.

As for renunciants, they must master constant truth and authenticity of insight and understanding. They must distinguish Buddha from the devil, they must distinguish the real from the false, and they must distinguish the ordinary from the holy. If they can make these distinctions, they can be called true renunciants.

Those who cannot distinguish devil from Buddha are actually leaving one house to enter another. They may be said to be creating karma; they cannot be called real renunciants. Now there is a confusion of Buddha and devil, like water and milk mixed together. They can only be separated by an expert.

As for Wayfarers with enlightened eyes, they strike down both devil and Buddha. If you love the holy and despise the ordinary, you are bobbing in the ocean of birth and death.

, , ,

What are the Buddha and the devil?

A moment of doubt in the mind is a devil. If you realize all things are unborn, and mind is like an illusory projection, so that there is no longer a single particle, a single phenomenon, but everywhere is immaculate purity, this is Buddha.

However, Buddha and devil represent the two realms of purity and defilement; in my own view, there is neither Buddha nor mortal being, there is neither antiquity nor present; those who get it do so at once, without taking a certain time. There is no cultivation, no realization, no gain, no loss. At all times there is nothing else. Even if there were something beyond this, I would say it is like a dream, like a projection. This is what I always say.

The immediate solitary light clearly listening is unobstructed everywhere, pervading the ten directions, free in the three realms, entering into the differentiations in objects without being changed. In an instant it enters the cosmos of realities: meeting buddhas, it talks about buddhas; meeting Zen masters, it talks about Zen masters; meeting saints, it talks about saints; meeting ghosts, it talks about ghosts. Within a single thought, it roams in lands everywhere teaching people; its omnipresent pure radiance pervades the ten directions.

Now you know there is basically nothing to be obsessed with. It's just because you do not trust completely that your thoughts run in search. Ignoring your own head, you look for another head, unable to stop yourself.

Bodhisattvas of the complete all-at-once path manifest their bodies in the cosmos of realities, disdaining the ordinary and seeking the holy within pure lands. Types like this have not yet forgotten grasping and rejection; mindfulness of pollution and purity is still there. The view of the Zen school is not like this; it is right now, no other time.

What I say is all temporary medicine for curing illness; there is no real doctrine at all. If you can see in this way, you are a true renunciant; you can use a thousand ounces of gold a day.

Do not hastily let teachers give you a stamp of approval, claiming, "I understand Zen, I understand Tao." They may talk glibly, but they are making hellish karma.

Genuine students of the Way do not look for the faults of the world; what is most urgent is to seek real true insight and understanding. If you attain real true insight, it must be complete and clear before you are finished.

YUAN-WU
Essentials of Mind

When the founder of Zen came to China from India, he did not set up written or spoken formulations; he only pointed directly to the human mind. Direct pointing just refers to what is inherent in everyone: the whole being appearing responsively from within the shell of ignorance, it is not different from the sages of time immemorial. That is what we call the natural, real, inherent nature, fundamentally pure, luminous and sublime, swallowing and spitting out all of space, the single solid realm alone and free of the senses and objects.

With great capacity and great wisdom, just detach from thought and cut off sentiments, utterly transcending ordinary conventions. Using your own inherent power, take it up directly right where you are, like letting go your hold over a mile-high cliff, freeing yourself and not relying on anything anymore, causing all obstruction by views and understanding to be thoroughly removed, so that you are like a dead man without breath, and reach the original ground, attaining great cessation and great rest, which the senses fundamentally do not know and which consciousness, perception, feelings, and thoughts do not reach.

After that, in the cold ashes of a dead fire, it is clear everywhere; among the stumps of dead trees everything illumines: then you merge with solitary transcendence, unapproachably high. Then there is no more need to seek mind or seek Buddha: you meet them everywhere and find they are not obtained from outside.

The hundred aspects and thousand facets of perennial enlightenment are all just this: it is mind, so there is no need to still seek mind; it is Buddha, so why trouble to seek Buddha anymore? If you make slogans of words and produce interpretations on top of objects, then you will fall into a bag of antiques and after all never find what you are looking for.

This is the realm of true reality where you forget what is on your mind and stop looking. In a wild field, not choosing, picking up whatever comes to hand, the obvious meaning of Zen is clear in the hundred grasses. Indeed, the green bamboo, the clusters of yellow flowers, fences, walls, tiles, and pebbles use the teaching of the inanimate; rivers, birds, trees, and groves expound suffering, emptiness, and selflessness. This is based on the one true reality, producing unconditional compassion, manifesting uncontrived, supremely wondrous power in the great jewel light of nirvana.

An ancient master said, "Meeting a companion on the Way, spending a life together, the whole task of study is done." Another master said, "If I pick up a single leaf and go into the city, I move the whole of the mountain." That is why one ancient adept was enlightened on hearing the sound of pebbles striking bamboo, while another was awakened on seeing peach trees in bloom. One Zen master attained enlightenment on seeing the flagpole of a teaching center from the other side of a river. Another spoke of the staff of the spirit. One adept illustrated Zen realization by planting a hoe in the ground; another master spoke of Zen in terms of sowing the fields. All of these instances were bringing out this indestructible true being, allowing people to visit a greatly liberated true teacher without moving a step.

Carrying out the unspoken teaching, attaining unhindered eloquence, thus they forever studied all over from all things, embracing the all-inclusive universe, detaching from both abstract and concrete definitions of buddhahood, and transcendentally realizing universal, all-pervasive Zen in the midst of all activities. Why necessarily consider holy places, teachers' abodes, or religious organizations and forms prerequisite to personal familiarity and attainment of realization?

Once a seeker asked a great Zen teacher, "I, so-and-so, ask: what is the truth of Buddhism?" The teacher said, "You are so-and-so." At that moment the seeker was enlightened. As it is said, "What comes from you returns to you."

An ancient worthy, working in the fields in his youth, was breaking up clumps of earth when he saw a big clod, which he playfully smashed with a fierce blow. As it shattered, he was suddenly greatly enlightened.

After this he acted freely, becoming an unfathomable person, often manifesting wonders. An old master brought this up and said, "Mountains and rivers, indeed the whole earth was shattered by this man's blow. Making offerings to the buddhas does not require a lot of incense." How true these words are!

,   ,   ,

The ultimate Way is simple and easy, yet profoundly deep. From the beginning it does not set up steps—standing like a wall a mile high is called the basic fodder. Therefore ancient buddhas have been known to carry out this teaching by silence.

Still there are adepts who wouldn't let them go at that, much less if they got into the marvelous and searched for the mysterious, spoke of mind and discoursed on nature, having sweaty shirts sticking to their flesh, unable to remove them—that would just seem all the more decrepit.

The example of the early Zen founders was exceptionally outstanding. The practical strategies of the classical masters were immediately liberating. Like dragons racing, tigers running, like the earth turning and the heavens revolving, in all circumstances they vivified people, ultimately without trailing mud and water.

As soon as they penetrated the ultimate point in truth, those since time immemorial who have realized great enlightenment have been fast as falcons, swift as hawks, riding the wind, dazzling in the sun, their backs brushing the blue sky.

Penetrate directly through to freedom and make it so that there is not the slightest obstruction at any time, twenty-four hours a day, with the realization pervading in all directions, rolling up and rolling out, capturing and releasing, not occupying even the rank of sage, much less being in the ordinary current.

Then your heart will be clear, comprehending the present and the past. Picking up a blade of grass, you can use it for the body of Buddha; taking the body of Buddha, you can use it as a blade of grass. From the first there is no superiority or inferiority, no grasping or rejection.

It is simply a matter of being alive to meet the situation: sometimes you take away the person but not the world; sometimes you take away the world but not the person; and sometimes both are taken away; and sometimes neither is taken away.

Transcending convention and sect, completely clear and free, how could you just want to trap people, to pull the wool over their eyes, to turn them around, to derail them? It is necessary to get to the reality and show them the fundamental thing in each of them, which is independent and uncontrived, which has nothing to it at all, and which is great liberation.

This is why the ancients, while in the midst of activity in the world, would first illuminate it, and as soon as there was the slightest obstruction, they would cut it off entirely. Even so they could hardly find anyone who could manage to learn this—how could they compare to these people who drag each other through the weeds, draw each other into assessments and judgments of words and deeds, make nests, and bury the sons and daughters of others?

Clearly we know that these latter people are "wetting the bed with their eyes open," while those other, clear-eyed people would never make such slogans and conventions. With a robust and powerful spirit that astounds everyone, you should aim to truly inherit this school of Zen: with every exclamation, every stroke, every act, every objective, you face reality absolutely and annihilate all falsehood. As it is said, "Once the sharp sword has been used, you should hone it right away."

When your insight penetrates freely and its application is clear, then when going into action in the midst of all kinds of complexity and complication, you yourself can turn freely without sticking or lingering and without setting up any views or maintaining any state, flowing freely: "When the wind blows, the grasses bend."

When you enter enlightenment in actual practice, you penetrate to the profound source, cultivating this until you realize freedom of mind, harboring nothing in your heart. Here even understanding cannot attain it, much less not understanding.

Just be this way twenty-four hours a day, unfettered, free from bondage. From the first do not keep thoughts of subject and object, of self and senses, or even of Buddhism. This is the realm of no mind, no fabrication, no object—how could it be fathomed or measured by worldly brilliance, knowledge, intelligence, or learning, without the fundamental basis?

Did the Zen founder actually "bring" this teaching when he came to China from India? He just pointed directly to the inherent nature in every one of us, to let us get out completely, clear and clean, and not be stained by so much false knowledge and false consciousness, delusory conceptions, and judgments.

Study must be true study. A true teacher does not lead you into a nest of weeds but cuts directly through so that you meet with realization, shedding the sweaty shirt sticking to your skin, making the heart empty and open, without the slightest sense of the ordinary or the holy. Since you do not seek outside, real truth is there, resting peacefully, immutable. No one can push you away, even a thousand sages—having attained a pure, clean, and naked state, you pass through the other side of the empty eon, and even the prehistoric buddhas are your descendants. Why even speak of seeking from others?

The Zen masters were all like this, ever since the founders. Take the example of the Sixth Grand Master: he was an illiterate woodcutter in south China, but when he came and met the Fifth Grand Master, at their first meeting he opened his heart and clearly passed through to freedom.

So even though the saints and sages are mixed in with others, one should employ appropriate means to clearly point out what is inherent in everyone, regardless of their level of intelligence.

Once you merge your tracks in the stream of Zen, spend the days silencing your mind and studying with your whole being, knowing this great cause is not gotten from anyone else. It is just a matter of bearing up bravely and strongly, ever progressing, day by day shedding, day by day improving, like pure gold smelted and refined hundreds and thousands of times.

As it is essential to getting out of the dusts and it is basic to helping people, it is most necessary to be thoroughly penetrating and free in all ways, reaching to peace without doubt and realizing great potential and great action.

This work lies in one's inner conduct: in everyday life's varied mix of myriad circumstances, in the dusty hubbub, amidst the ups and downs and conditions, appear and disappear without being turned around by any of it. Instead, you can actively turn it around. Full of life, immune to outside influences, this is your own measure of power.

On reaching empty, frozen silence, there is no duality between noise and quiet. Even when it comes to extraordinary words, marvelous statements, unique acts, and absolute perspectives, you just level them with one measure. Ultimately they have no right or wrong, it's all in how you use them.

When you have continued grinding and polishing yourself like this for a long time, you will be free in the midst of birth and death and look upon society's useless honor and ruinous profit as like dust in the wind, phantoms in dreams, flowers in the sky. Passing unattached through the world, would you not then be a great saint who has left the dusts?

Whenever the Zen master known as the Bone Breaker was asked a question, he would just answer, "Bone's broken." This is like an iron pill, undeniably strict. If you can fully comprehend it, you will be a true lion of the Zen school.

Once a great National Teacher of Zen asked another Zen master, "How do you see all extraordinary words and marvelous expressions?" The Zen master said, "I have no fondness for them." The National Teacher said, "This is your own business."

When Zen study reaches this point, one is pure, clean, and dry, not susceptible to human deceptions.

The House of Ts'ao-Tung

YAO-SHAN

Master guides only teach preservation; if greed or anger arises, you must ward it off, not letting it touch you. If you want to know how to do this, then you must bear up like a dead tree or a rock.

There are really no ramifications to be attained, but even so, you should still see for yourself. It will not do to deny verbal expression entirely. I am now speaking to you in order to reveal that which has no speech; that originally has no features like ears or eyes.

, , ,

Someone asked, "How is it that there are six courses of mundane existence?"

Yao-shan said, "Although I am within this circle, I am basically not affected."

, , ,

Someone asked, "How is it when one does not comprehend the afflictions within one's being?"

Yao-shan said, "What are the afflictions like? I want you to think about it. There is even a type who just memorizes words on paper; most of them are confused by the scriptures and treatises. I have never read the scriptures or treatises. You have fluctuating minds simply because you are confused by things and go through changes, at a loss, inwardly unstable. Even before you have learned a single saying, half an expression, a scripture, or a treatise, already you talk this way about 'enlightenment,' 'nirvana,' the mundane and the transmundane; if you understand in this way, then this is birth and death. If you are not bound by this gain and loss, then there is no birth and death. You see teachers of discipline talking about stuff like 'naihsargika' and 'dukkata'—this above all is the root of birth and death!

"Even so, when you examine birth and death thoroughly, it cannot be grasped. From the buddhas above to insects below, all have these differences of long and short, good and bad, big and small. If it doesn't come from outside, where is there some idler digging hells to await you?

"Do you want to know the path of hell? It is boiling and broiling right now. Do you want to know the path of hungry ghosts? It is presently being more false than true, so people cannot trust you. Do you want to know the path of animality? It is presently disregarding humanity and justice and not distinguishing friend from stranger—do you need to wear fur and horns, to be butchered and hung upside down? Do you want to know humans and angels? It is present pure conduct. To guarantee that you will escape falling into the other states, above all do not abandon this.

"This is not easily attained. You must stand atop the summit of the highest mountain and walk on the bottom of the deepest ocean. It is not easy to apply this, but only when you have done so will you have a little realization.

"All who come forward today are people of many obsessions; I am looking for a simpleton, but cannot find one. Don't just memorize sayings in books and consider that to be your own vision and knowledge, looking down on others who do not understand. People like this are all incorrigible heretics. This mentality simply does not hit the mark; you must examine carefully and understand thoroughly.

"This kind of talk is still within the bounds of the world. Don't waste your lives. At this point there is even more subtlety and detail; don't consider it idle, for you should know it. Take care."

YUN-YEN
Sayings

One day Yun-yen said to a group, "There is an offspring of someone's house who can answer any question."

Tung-shan asked, "How many books does he have in his house?"

Yun-yen said, "There is not even a single letter."

Tung-shan asked, "Then how did he get so much knowledge?"

Yun-yen said, "Never sleeping, day or night."

, , ,

As Yun-yen was sweeping the grounds, Kuei-shan said, "Too busy!"

Yun-yen said, "You should know there is one who is not busy."

Kuei-shan said, "Then there is a second moon."

Yun-yen stood the broom up and said, "Which moon is this?"

Kuei-shan lowered his head and left. Hsuan-sha heard about this and said, "Precisely the second moon!"

, , ,

As Yun-yen was making straw sandals, Tung-shan said to him, "If I ask you for perception, can I get it?"

Yun-yen replied, "To whom did you give away yours?"

Tung-shan said, "I have none."

Yun-yen said, "If you had, where would you put it?"

Tung-shan said nothing.

Yun-yen asked, "What about that which asks for perception; is that perception?"

Tung-shan said, "It is not perception."

Yun-yen disapproved.

, , ,

Yun-yen asked a nun, "Is your father still alive?"

She said, "Yes."

Yun-yen asked, "How old is he?"

She said, "Eighty years old."

Yun-yen said, "You have a father who is not eighty years old; do you know?"

She replied, "Is this not 'the one who comes thus'?"

Yun-yen said, "That is just a descendant!"

꙳ ꙳ ꙳

A monk asked, "How is it when one falls into the realm of demons the moment a thought occurs?"

Yun-yen said, "Why did you come from the realm of buddhas?"

The monk had no reply.

Yun-yen said, "Understand?"

The monk said, "No."

Yun-yen said, "Don't say you don't comprehend; even if you do comprehend, you're just beating around the bush."

TUNG-SHAN

Song of Focusing the Precious Mirror

The teaching of Being-As-Is
Has been intimated by the enlightened;
Now that you have gotten it,
You should keep it well.

A silver bowl full of snow
And a heron hidden in moonlight
Are similar but not the same;
Put them together, and they're distinct.

The meaning is not in words,
Yet responds to emerging potential.
There's a tendency to create clichés,
Slipping into retrospection, at a standstill.

Rejection and attachment are both wrong;
It is like a ball of fire.
Even to put it in literary form
Subjects it to defilement.

In the middle of night is just when it's bright;
At dawn it does not appear.
Acting as a guide for people,
Its function removes miseries.

Although it is not contrived,
It is not without speech.

It is like looking into a precious mirror,
Form and reflection beholding each other:
You are not it;
It is you.

It is like a baby,
With all its faculties,
Neither going nor coming,
Neither rising nor standing,
Babbling and babbling,
Speaking without saying anything,
Never getting concrete
Because its speech is not correct.

In the six lines of the Fire hexagram,
Relative and absolute integrate;
Stacked up, they make three;
Completion of the transformation makes five.
It is like the taste of a five-flavored herb,
Like the thunderbolt implement.

The subtle is contained within the absolute;
Inquiry and response arise together,
Conveying the source as well as the process,
Including integration as well as the way.

Merging is auspicious;
Do not violate it.
Naturally real, yet subtle,
It is not in confusion or enlightenment.

Under the right conditions, at the right time,
It shines bright in serene tranquillity.
It is so minute it fits where there's no room;
It is so immense it is beyond direction and location.
The slightest deviation
Means failure of attunement.

Now there are sudden and gradual,
On which are set up approaches to the source.
Once approaches to the source are distinguished,
Then there are guidelines and rules.
When the source is reached, the approach thus finished,
True eternity still flows.

To be outwardly still while inwardly stirring
Is to be like a tethered colt, a trapped rat.

Sages of yore took pity on this
And gave out teachings for it.

The way confusion goes,
Even black's considered white;
When confused imagination ends,
Mind in its simplicity realizes itself.

If you want to conform to the perennial way,
Please observe ancient precedent:
When about to fulfill buddhahood,
One meditated under a tree for ten eons,
Like a tiger wounded, like a horse tied.

Because of the existence of the lowly,
There are precious furnishings and fine clothes;
Because of the existence of the unusual,
There are house cats and cattle.

With skill an archer can hit a target
A hundred paces away,
But the meeting of arrow points
Has nothing to do with skill.

When a wooden man begins to sing,
A stone woman gets up to dance.
This cannot be reached by subjective perception;
How could it be thought about?

A minister serves the ruler,
A son obeys his father:
Not to obey is disobedience,
Not to serve is not helping.

Practice unknown, work in secret,
Being like one who is ignorant.
If you can achieve continuity,
This is called mastery of mastery.

Secret of the Mind Elixir

I have a medicine called elixir of mind;
For years it's been refined in the oven of afflictions,

Till I recognized its unchanging color in the matrix
Shining with radiance illuminating the universe.

It opens the eye of reality to see with minute precision;
It can change the ordinary mortal into a sage instantly.
To discern the real and the false to complete the work,
See to refinement at all times.

It has no shape or form; it is not square or round.
There are no things in words; there are no words in things.
Deliberate exploitation is contrary to true function;
When meditating with no intention, everything is Zen.

It neither goes dead nor gets aroused;
Everything is at its command.
Even the land, wherever the place,
When put in this oven is It.

My idea is to have no particular idea;
My knowledge is to have no particular knowledge.
There is no uniformity, no indifference;
When the appearance does not change, it's harder to discern.
When nothing more appears within,
Don't use anything to stabilize it;
Experiential merging with real emptiness
Is not cultivation.

Dialogues of Tung-shan

Tung-shan asked a monk, "Where have you come from?"
   The monk replied, "From a journey to a mountain."
   Tung-shan asked, "And did you reach the peak?"
   The monk said, "Yes."
   Tung-shan asked, "Was there anyone on the peak?"
   The monk answered, "No."
   Tung-shan said, "Then you didn't reach the peak."
   The monk retorted, "If I didn't reach the peak, how could I know there was no one there?"
   Tung-shan said, "I had doubted this fellow."

, , ,

As Tung-shan was eating some fruit with Tai, leader of the assembly, he posed this question: "There is one thing supporting heaven and earth; absolutely black, it is always in the midst of activity, yet activity cannot contain it. Where is the fault?"

Tai answered, "The fault is in the activity."

Tung-shan had the fruit tray removed.

, , ,

Yun-chu built a hut on the mountain peak and didn't come down to the communal hall for days. Tung-shan asked him, "Why haven't you been coming for meals recently?"

Yun-chu said, "An angel comes every day bringing me an offering."

Tung-shan said, "I thought you were an enlightened man, but you still have such a view. Come see me this evening."

That evening Yun-chu went to Tung-shan, who called him by name. When Yun-chu responded, Tung-shan said, "Don't think good, don't think bad—what is this?"

Yun-chu returned to his hut and sat in complete silence and stillness, so the angel couldn't find him. After three days like this, the angel disappeared.

, , ,

When Ts'ao-shan left Tung-shan, Tung-shan asked him, "Where are you going?"

Ts'ao-shan said, "To an unchanging place."

Tung-shan retorted, "If it is an unchanging place, how can there be any going?"

Ts'ao shan replied, "The going is also unchanging."

Tung-shan's Self-Admonition

Don't seek fame or fortune, glory or prosperity. Just pass this life as is, according to circumstances. When the breath is gone, who is in charge? After the death of the body, there is only an empty name.

When your clothes are worn, repair them over and over; when you have no food, work to provide. How long can a phantomlike body last? Would you increase your ignorance for the sake of its idle concerns?

Tung-shan's Five Ranks: Ts'ao-shan's Elucidation

The absolute state is relative; when it is discerned in the relative, this is fulfillment of both meanings.

The fact that the absolute state is relative is because it is not the opposite of any thing. But even though it is not the opposite of any thing, nevertheless it is there.

When there is no function in the absolute, then it is relative; total function is completeness. This is "both meanings."

What is "total"? One who does not look back is one who has attained. The absolute state does not come from illumination: it is so whether or not a buddha emerges in the world. That is why all sages resort to the absolute state to attain realization.

The relative within the absolute is inherent in this state; above all, don't cause disturbance.

When students choose solitary liberation outside things and stand up before the sages and declare that this is the absolute state, ultimately complete, in reality they are limiting the absolute state. Sayings like this are what the ancients referred to as the traces of passing still remaining. They have not yet attained the unspoken within the spoken. It is said, furthermore, that this is not the absolute state, because there is something said in the words. This could be called defective integration; it cannot be called mutual integration.

The relative state, though relative, still fulfills both meanings; discerned within conditions, this is the unspoken within the spoken.

This is because no aim is defined in function; when no aim is defined, that means it is really not fixed function.

The relative state, though relative, still fulfills both meanings in that there is no thing and no attachment in the function; this is both meanings. Although it is clarified in function, because it is not done violence in speech, here one can speak all day and yet it is as if one had not spoken.

The relative state is actually complete; this also involves being unattached in the midst of conditions.

There may be emergence in the absolute; this is the spoken within the unspoken.

Emergence in the absolute does not take in conditions; this is like Yao-shan's saying, "I have a statement that has never been spoken to anyone." Tao-wu said, "They come along together." Here he understood subtly. There are many examples like this. Things must come forth in combination, without confusion of noble and base. This is called the spoken within the unspoken. Also, in reference to "I have a statement that has never been spoken to anyone," when those who engage in dialogue come forth, they must avoid rejection and attachment; both rejection and attachment are due to ignorance of what's there.

The unspoken within statements does not define nobility, does not fall into left and right; therefore it is called emergence in the absolute.

Emergence in the absolute makes it clear that the absolute is not involved in conditions. To cite more sayings, it is like "How is it when the black bean has not sprouted?" or "There is someone who does not breathe" or "Before conception, is there anything to say?" This is where the buddhas of the ten directions emerge. These examples are referred to as speaking of the unspoken.

There is also borrowing phenomena for temporary use. In the state of emergence within the absolute, the one who responds must clarify the comprehension of things within the relative; one cannot clarify it while plunged into the absolute state.

If you want to know how this is expressed, it is like when my late teacher Tung-shan asked a student from Korea, "Where were you before you crossed the sea?" There was no reply, so Tung-shan himself said for him, " 'Right now I'm at sea, and where am I!' "

It is also like when Tung-shan said in behalf of an elder who held forth his staff and was asked where it came from, "It's being held forth right now! Is there anyone who can handle it?"

In these examples, though recognition is attained within conditional objects, it is not the same as the past, when mastery had not been attained. Later people may have relegated this to cultivated development, considering that to be the transcendental.

For example, students pick out this saying in answer to a question about the meaning of the founder of Zen—"I'll tell you when a lone cow gives birth to a calf"—and say that this is emergence within the absolute state. This kind of saying cannot under any circumstances be considered emergence within the absolute. It could be called dialogue on the mystic path; it's the same thing—this is a particular path. It cannot be called integration either, because it is obvious; even if guest and host interact, it can only be called defective integration.

There may be emergence within the relative; this is the unspoken within the spoken.

Emergence within the relative includes conditions, as in the saying "What can we call that which is right now?" As there was no answer, Tung-shan himself said, "Cannot but get it." There are many more such examples; this is referred to as the unspoken within the spoken.

Speech comes from elements, sound and flesh, which do not define place or direction, right or wrong. That is why it is said to be understood in relational context. This is emergence within the relative.

There are many corresponding sayings. For example, "What has come thus?" And, "When mind and objects are both forgotten, then what is this?" Also, "When concentration and insight are learned equally, you clearly see the buddha nature." These examples too, of which there are many, are referred to as the unspoken within the spoken.

Emergence within the relative is clarifying the essence within things, as in the saying "What has come thus?" and "When mind and objects are both forgotten, then what is this?" This category of saying refers to achievement to clarify state, illustrating the state in terms of the work.

Here too I used to cite corresponding examples. "What has come thus?" is one example of a saying: although it is recognized within conditions, in relational context, that is not the same as before. Also, with the example of " 'When concentration and insight are learned equally, you clearly see buddha nature'—what is this principle?" at first I would cite corresponding sayings. As for the saying "When mind and objects are both forgotten, then what is this?"—because this is an example from among the doctrines, it is not the same as mystical study. What one must do, in dealing with doctrinal examples, is to go through them into the gateway of the source. This is the exoteric side of mysticism.

In the case of the saying "Breathing out, I do not depend on conditions; breathing in, I do not abide in mental or material elements," this is all about work; it is not the same as recognition within conditions. Here too I used to cite corresponding examples of the host withdrawing into the absolute, saying, "There is someone who has no outgoing or incoming breath," to get others to know of the absolute.

There is, furthermore, an ultimate state of immaculate purity that includes work, which may also be called emergence within the relative. This is hard to discern; it must be picked out.

For example, a monk asked Tung-shan, "What is the mystic teaching?" Tung-shan replied, "Like the tongue of a dead man." Another asked, "What is presented as an offering twenty-four hours a day?" He said, "No thing." This is said to be emergence within the relative, but these two examples are not to be called emergence within the relative state. It is necessary to distinguish them individually. The saying about the "mystic teaching" could be considered the same as work and achievement, but neither saying can be referred to as the relative or as integration. It has already been made quite clear. This is using the work to illustrate the state; using the state to illustrate the work is the same as this.

There may be mutual integration: here we do not say there is the spoken or the unspoken. Here we must simply proceed directly. Here it is necessary to be perfectly fluid; things must be perfectly fluid.

With mutual integration, the force of words is neither relative nor absolute, implying neither being nor nonbeing, so they seem complete without being complete and seem lacking without lacking. One can only proceed directly; proceeding means we do not set up a goal. When they do not define a goal, words are at their most subtle. The incompleteness of the scene is a matter of ordinary sense.

An example is the saying of Tung-shan about the story of Wen-shu and tea drinking: "Would it be possible to make use of this?" And as Ts'ui-wei said, "What do you drink every day?"

However, words on the Way are all defective; people must master spoken expressions and proceed directly ahead. The spoken is coming thus; the unspoken is going thus. Among adepts, it is not that there is no speech, but it does not get into the spoken or the unspoken. This is called integrated speech. Integrated speech has no obvious aim at all.

Integration does not fall into the spoken or the unspoken, as in Yao-shan's saying on wearing a sword, which is an integrated saying. Observe the force of the words at the moment: sometimes it is immediate and direct, and sometimes it is emptiness within differentiation. If you do not understand this subtly, you are far, far away.

To cite examples of integrated sayings, there is the saying of Wen-shu about drinking tea, and also the saying, "Where is this man gone right now?" Yun-yen said, "So what? So what?" He also said, "How about right now?" There are very many such examples.

There is also integration within work and achievement, which resembles the transcendental. It is dealt with according to the situation: for example, if you get trapped in a state of pure ethereality, then you have to realize that there are still things happening; go when you need to go, stop when you need to stop. Adapting fluidly in countless ways, do not be crude.

Now then, the forces of the words of both the one who questions and the one who replies respond to each other. None is beyond the scope of the Five Ranks. Words can be coarse or fine, however, and answers may be shallow or deep. That is why Tung-shan articulated what is not in words; in every case this was considered a necessity in response to conditions, that is all.

"People of great ignorance," being complete in essence, are not the same as "incorrigibles." "Incorrigibles" suffer mentally when they know there is something to do; yet even though they suffer mentally, they accomplish service. To suffer mentally means not to keep thinking of Zen masters, buddhas, or one's own father and mother.

"Rotten people" do not resort to total burden-bearing, so they do not set up any idol.

"People of great conservation" have got their feet stuck deeply in the mud, so maintaining their discipline is not a small matter.

Integration should be like Wen-shu's saying on drinking tea and like Tung-shan's reply to Yun-yen's ginger-digging saying, as well as Master An's saying on the teaching hall and the conversation of Yao-shan and Ch'un Pu-na on washing Buddha. For the most marveous integration of all, nothing is better than Yao-shan's answer to Tao-wu on wearing a sword, or Pai-chang's saying "What is it?" when he was leaving the hall and the congregation was about to disperse. When Yao-shan heard this saying from far away, he said, "It's here."

Integration in the darkness uses work to illuminate things, and uses things to illuminate work; it uses errors to illustrate accomplishments, and uses accomplishments to illustrate errors, equally in this way. Whatever Yao-shan, Tung-shan, and all the other worthies produced that went beyond into the absolute were just marvelous expressions of mystic conversation, that is all. When they subsequently came to those who had attained a little power, they drew them into the absolute, in which context this type of saying is commonly used.

Because I have so much to do, I haven't had the time to go into details, and have only explained a little bit. You should not slight this; if you still get frozen or stuck anywhere, you should cut through to certainty then and there. You should practice diligently, so that this thing will never be allowed to die out. Don't reveal it carelessly, but if you meet someone who is pure and simple, who is an extraordinary vessel, then it is not to be concealed.

HUNG-CHIH
Sermons

Empty yet aware, the original light shines spontaneously; tranquil yet responsive, the great function manifests. A wooden horse neighing in the wind does not walk the steps of the present moment; a clay ox emerging from the sea plows the springtime of the eon of emptiness.
Understand?
Where a jade man beckons, even greater marvel is on the way back.

, , ,

One continuous clear void, the night precisely midway; the moon, cool, spews frost. When light and dark are merged without division, who distinguishes relative and absolute herein?
Thus it is said, "Although the absolute is absolute, yet it is relative; although the relative is relative, yet it is complete." At this precise moment, how do you discern?
How clear—twin shining eyes before any impulse!
How stately—the eternal body outside forms!

, , ,

Every atom of every land is self; there is nowhere to hide. Everywhere you go, you encounter It; such a person has eyes. On the hundred grasses, at the gates of a bustling city, impossible to mix up, you do not go along with the flow; impossible to categorize, you do not leak at all.

, , ,

When there is nowhere to place the mind, nothing to lean on, nothing to walk on, and nothing to say, this cannot be seen and described, cannot be grasped and manipulated. The totality of all forms is equal to its function; the whole of cosmic space is equal to its body. Ultimately free in action, it is the immortal being within species; skill-fully responsive, it is in the midst of the material world, yet different.

This is why a master teacher said, "True nature is the Earth Treasury of the mind. With neither head nor tail, it develops beings according to conditions; it is provisionally referred to as knowledge." Now what is the provisional knowledge that develops beings according to conditions? Understand? "Do not think it strange how I have offered you wine over and over since we sat down, for after we part we can hardly meet again."

, , ,

Standing alone and unchanging, acting comprehensively and inexhaustibly, do not disdain the phenomena filling your eyes. You must trust that in the world, which is only mental, the thousand peaks all point to the summit, and the hundred rivers all end in the sea.

If you understand in this way, you roll up the screens and remove the blinds. If you do not understand in this way, you shut the doors and create a barrier. Whether discussing understanding or nonunderstanding, ignoramuses are not quick.

, , ,

Hidden illumination inside the circle—a hibernating dragon murmurs in the clouds enveloping withered trees. True clarity beyond measurement—the pattern on the moon puts a soulful face on the nocturnal orb.

The route before the shuttle can be discerned by a stone woman; the talisman under the elbow can be used by a wooden man. Thus all of space can be sealed with one stamp, omitting nothing in the entire cosmos.

Understand? When the six senses convey clear meaning, the whole world is clear of any dust.

, , ,

When every particle of every land is the Self, there is no place to hide; when one encounters It everywhere, one is endowed with perception. Not mixed up by phenomena or swept away by events, not susceptible to categorization, totally free from leakage, know that the great function manifests in the action of Zen adepts.

One ancient master was half mad and half crazy. Another used to sing and dance by himself. Do you understand? When you use the wind to fan a fire, not much effort is needed. Inquire!

, , ,

When the six senses return to their source, they are thoroughly effective and clear, without compare. When the physical elements return to their source, the whole body is pure, without a particle of dust. Thus you manage to cut off causation, interrupt its continuity, merge all time, and obliterate all differences.

Understand?

> "The spiritual bird dreams on the branch that does not sprout;
> The flower of awakening blossoms on the tree that casts no
> shadow."

, , ,

A single particle of matter involves infinite worlds; a single instant of thought transcends infinite eons. A single body manifests infinite beings; a single actuality includes infinite buddhas. This is why it is said, "Universal complete awareness is my sanctuary; body and mind live at peace in the knowlege of essential equality."

This state cannot be limited spatially or temporally. Self and other combine, merging like water and milk; center and periphery interpenetrate, reflecting each other like images in mirrors.

How do you verbalize guarding your movements to avoid harming living beings?

When there is no fluctuation from one state of mind to the next, then there is no losing direction from one step to the next.

, , ,

Coming from nowhere, going nowhere, arriving at the equality of the principle of unity, we see the empty appearances of all things. Where the morning clouds have dispersed, the sun is bright; when the night rain has passed, the valley streams are swollen. The body of perception, independent, perpetually dwells on one suchness, responding to reality autonomously, a welter of myriad forms. Then you don't need to think deliberately anymore; there is naturally someone providing support to all alike.

Those of you who have attained the Great Rest: if you do not accept food, that is the fall of nobility.

, , ,

Extinct without passing away, you merge consciously with space; alive without being born, you function subtly in concert with all things. Traceless before time, you are at home after embodiment. The crane dreams in its nest, cold; faintly light, there's the moon in the dark green forest. When the dragon murmurs, the night lasts long; persistent are the clouds surrounding the withered tree.

At precisely such a time, there is no birth or death, no coming or going, but there subtly exists a way to act; do you get it?

> Mist engulfs the blue-green reeds—
> snow upon the sand.
> Wind plays with the white water plants—
> autumn on the river.

, , ,

The Boatman said to Chia-shan, "There should be no traces where you conceal yourself, but do not conceal yourself in the traceless. In thirty years with my teacher, I understood only this."

In the unusual grass on the cold cliff, you accomplish a task even while sitting; under the bright moon and white clouds, you emanate reflections with every step.

> At just such a time, how do you act?
> The recondite hollow has nothing to do
> with the very idea of a lock;
> What business have dualistic people
> with transcendental involvement?

, , ,

The clouds are naturally free, without intention; the sky is encompassing, without bounds. The Way responds universally, without image; the spirit is always at peace, without thinking. Follow this, and you do not see its tracks; go out to meet it, and you do not see it coming. The whole Buddhist canon only amounts to praises of it; the buddhas of all times can only watch from the side.

The lamp is bright, the hall is empty; as a weaving girl operates the loom, the path of the shuttle is fine. The water is luminous, the night quiet; a fisherman clutches his reed cloak around him, the moonlight in the boat cold.

Have you ever reached this state, this time? If not, don't bring it up in confusion.

, , ,

Pressing sesame seeds to get oil and cooking grain into cereal are matters for graduates of Zen. In practice of the Way it is important to be even-minded; why should it be necessary to struggle to shift at a moment's notice?

Our livelihood is naturalness; our family way is the matter at hand. Following the current, going along with the wind, the homeward boat lands on the shore. Free people laugh aloud; their mood is conveyed to those who understand.

, , ,

There is not so much to Buddhism. It just requires people to make body and mind empty all the time, not wearing so much as a thread, open, relaxed, and independent, the spiritual light of the original state not being dimmed at all.

If you practice in this way, such that you attain spontaneous harmony in all places and responsiveness at all times, without the slightest thing obstructing you, so you can put all the sages behind you, only then can you be called a Zen practitioner.

If you rely on others, accepting the judgments of others and allowing yourself to be confused by others, are you not a blind ass following a crowd?

This being the case, what is it all about, after all? It's just that you don't go back; if you return, you can. Who is there to contend with in the misty waves of the lakes?

, , ,

Subtle presence, profoundly calm, is not actually nothing; true perception, marvelously effective, is not actually something. Go ahead and take a step back between them and look: where the white clouds end, the green mountains are thin. Investigate!

, , ,

Open purity is boundless, yet knowledge accompanies it. Universal responsiveness has no conventional method, yet the spirit is coordinated with it. When knowledge is open, it perceives spontaneously, alert and awake; the function of the spirit is continuous, without deliberate effort. Then you can radiate great light all the time everywhere, doing enlightened work.

This is why it is said, "Mountains and rivers present no barrier; light penetrates everywhere." And haven't you read the saying "If people want to enter the realm of buddhas, they should make their minds clear as space, detaching from all appearances and fixations, causing the mind to be unobstructed where it turns"?

How do you act so as to attain this union?
Water and moon, calm, face one another;
The breeze in the pines, clear, has never stopped.

, , ,

Why is it that those who have swallowed the buddhas of all times cannot open their mouths? Why is it that those who have seen through the whole world cannot close their eyes?

I have removed many sicknesses for you all at once; but how can you get completely well? Understand? Breaking open the colors of Flower Mountain range soaring to the sky, releasing the sound of the Yellow River reaching the sea.

, , ,

If the host does not know there is a guest, then there is no way to respond to the world; if the guest does not know there is a host, then there is no vision beyond material senses.

, , ,

How is someone who has gone? Utterly silent, without a trace. How about someone who has come back? Perfectly clear; something is going on.

, , ,

Dig the pond, don't wait for the moonlight; when the pond is complete, the moonlight will naturally be there.

, , ,

In ephemeral objects, past, present, and future move from renewal to renewal. Within solid earth, initial positive energy subtly sprouts into movement. Sojourning without dwelling, one unobtrusively turns the wheel of potential; alive without birth, one ineffably transcends illusory phenomena.

This is how we borrow space for our body and use everything for our function, responding to the invitation of the whole world without stress, fully comprehending the void within the stamp of unity without exclusion.

But how do you experientially comprehend life without birth? Understand?

> If you want to know what will happen in spring,
> The winter plum blossoms simply do not know.

, , ,

Every flame of the eonic fire is an ember of events; in the emptiness of the eonic void there is a pedestal of awareness. There is no more beauty and ugliness to make flaws; beauty and ugliness both come from here.

, , ,

By the forms of combinations of objects and mind, puppets act out their parts on a stage. Breaking through the painted screen, come on back; the home fields are broad and clear.

, , ,

Use the light of the origin to wash away the darkness of the long night of ignorance; use the knowledge of the cosmos to break through the doubts of countless eons. Birth and death go on in profusion, but they do not reach the house of true purity; entangling conditions are troublesome, but they do not reach the realm of complete clarity. Let them change outside, while you as an individual remain empty within. Walking into the circle of the Way, you comprehend and forget illusory phenomena.

This is why an ancient said, "There is something before the universe; formless, originally quiescent, it is the master of myriad forms, never withering through the four seasons."

But tell me, what is this?
A whale drinks up the ocean water,
Exposing the coral branches.

, , ,

White is colorless, but it is placed before all colors; water is flavorless, yet all flavors are best with it. The Way has no root, but it pervades the universe; the Teaching has no fixed form, and can be this or that. A valley is always empty, but the echo can answer a call; a mirror is itself clear, while the reflections correspond to forms.

If you really attain such a body and mind, your great function, completely free, cannot be exploited. But tell me, who is it that cannot be exploited?

Understand?

Subtly transcending at the incipience of thought, standing independent before myriad impulses.

, , ,

The body is not a collection of atoms but a stately, wondrous being. The mind is not emotional and intellectual entanglements but an unknowable solitary awareness.

The substance is beyond all obstruction. The function is very independent. No going or coming, neither obvious nor occult, response to form and sound are void of opposition or dependence.

The saving grace in the cakes and cookies is up to us members of the guild doing our business.

, , ,

When rich in myriad virtues, even if ephemeral things are very prominent, you are entirely clear of dust.

Deliberately stopping speech and thought to plunge absolutely into tranquil silence, your inner way of being spontaneously shines, and you roam independent in the realm of true eternity.

When you take it up, it is crystal clear; a thousand differences and ten thousand distinctions cannot mix it up. When you put it down, it is free of all attributes; no trace can be found in any place or any time.

This is why ancients spoke of being impossible to trap, impossible to call back, not categorized even by the ancient sages, having no fixed place even now.

But tell me, how does one behave in order to attain such a realization?

Do you comprehend?

"Walking to where the stream ends, sitting and watching when the clouds arise."

, , ,

When people are even, they do not speak; when water is level, it does not flow. When the wind is calm, flowers still fall; when birds sing, the mountains seem even deeper.

Thus natural reality has no lack or excess; don't interpolate anything at all.

, , ,

In the realm of purity and coolness, the whole container of fresh air is steeped in autumn. When body and mind are clarified, the misty face of midnight embraces the moon. Spirituality spontaneous, open and always empty, you cut off the conditioning of birth and death and depart from subjective evaluations of what is and what is not.

Have you reached such a state, and are you capable of behaving in such a manner?

"When you have felled the cassia tree on the moon,
The pure light must be even more."

, , ,

Truly arrive at the emptiness of time, and you understand yourself; when you do not fall into being or nonbeing, you transcend birth and death.

The night boat, carrying the moon, fishes the river of freedom; the heritage of pure clarity is just like this.

, , ,

Affection congeals to form the body; thoughts settle to form the world; henceforth you bob around in the sea of birth and death.

When you see through to the spiritual source, whose profound stillness is unmixed, then you will know that illusions and bubbles present no obstacle.

When the weather is autumn in the senses and the conditions of the gross elements disintegrate, one reality always remains, with perfect clarity.

Merged in the bright moonlight, the snow and reeds are confusing to the eye; sent by a pure breeze, the night boat's return is swift.

, , ,

Color empties, thus taking up the seal of the lineage of buddhas and Zen masters; light dissolves darkness, perpetuating the lamp that illumines the world.

At this time you do not fall into thought; in this situation you can, however, turn freely.

This is why the Boatman said, "Let there be no traces where you hide, but do not hide where there are no traces. In thirty years with Yao-shan, I understood only this."

Now tell me, what was understood? Do you comprehend?

The tortoise returns to its ocean palace; the evening tide recedes; as the moon passes the river of stars, the soul of the night is clear.

, , ,

Intellect open and luminous, spirit calm and penetrating, clear cold transforms the night; a frosty moon traverses the sky.

This is how a Zen practitioner should behave, the four quarters and eight directions all crystal clear. Investigate!

, , ,

Empty, empty, absolutely trackless, not dimmed by even a dot; when profoundly still, free from words, unified potential spontaneously goes into operation.

At this point even the past and future buddhas do not presume to claim teacherhood; at this point even the founders of Zen do not claim to be masters.

Understand?

The golden needle is under double lock;
The road of harmonization is subtly all-inclusive.

, , ,

Magnificent, distinguished, it is revealed uniquely in myriad forms; clear, evident, it is encountered in all things. I do not see any external other; the other does not see any external me. Other is not outside of self, so objects of sense vanish; self is not outside of other, so feelings of perception are shed.

This is why it is said, "The world is thus, beings are thus; every particle is thus, and every thought is thus."

But tell me, how does one act so as to attain such a realization? Understand?

Unified potential subtly operating, the hub of the Way is still;
Myriad images' reflections flowing, the mind mirror is empty.

The House of Yun-men

HSUEH-FENG
Sayings

The whole universe, the whole world, is you; do you think there is any other? This is why the *Heroic Progress Scripture* says, "People lose themselves, pursuing things; if they could turn things around, they would be the same as Buddha."

, , ,

You must perceive your essential nature before you attain enlightenment. What is perceiving essential nature? It means perceiving your own original nature.

What is its form? When you perceive your own original nature, there is no concrete object to see.

This is hard to believe in, but all buddhas achieve it.

, , ,

Terms for the one mind are buddha nature, true suchness, the hidden essence, the pure spiritual body, the pedestal of awareness, the true soul, the innocent, universal mirrorlike cognition, the empty source, the ultimate truth, and pure consciousness.

The buddhas of past, present, and future, and all of their scriptural discourses, are all in your original nature, inherently complete. You do not need to seek, but you must save yourself. No one can do it for you.

, , ,

Look, look at these grown-ups traveling to the ends of the earth! Wherever you go, when someone asks you what the matter is, you immediately say hello, say good-bye, raise your eyebrows, roll your eyes, step forward, and withdraw. Broadcasting this sort of bad breath, the minute you get started you enter a wild fox cave. Taking the servant for the master, you do not know pollution from purity. Deceiving yourselves in the present, at the end of your lives you will turn out to be nothing more than a bunch of wild foxes.

Do you understand? How does this produce good people? Having received the shelter of Shakyamuni Buddha, you destroy his sacred heritage. What kind of attitude is this? All over China, Buddhism is dying out right before our eyes. Don't think this is an idle matter! As I sit here, I do not see a single individual who qualifies as an initiate in the Zen message of time immemorial. You are just a random collection, a gang ruining Buddhism. The ancients would call you people who repudiate wisdom. You will have to reject this before you can attain realization.

To attain this matter requires strength of character; don't keep on running to me over and over again, depending on me, seeking statements and asking for sayings. For a man of the required character, that is making fools of people. Do you know good from bad? I'll have to chase this bunch of ignoramuses away with my cane!

, , ,

If you immediately realize being-so, that is best and most economical; don't let yourself come to me for a statement. Understand? If you are a descendant of the founder of Zen, you will not eat food that another has already chewed.

What is more, you should not cramp yourself. Right now, what do you lack? The business of the responsible individual has been as clear as the bright sun in the blue sky for all time. There has never been anything at all obstructing it; so why don't you know it?

If I were to tell you that in order to understand you would have to take half a step, to exercise the slightest bit of effort, to read a single word of scripture, or to explicitly ask questions of others, I would be deceiving and threatening you.

What is this right here and now?

Unable to get it, and also unable to step back into yourself and examine thoroughly to see for yourself, you only know to go to ignorant and muddle-headed "old teachers" to memorize sayings. What relevance is there? Do you know this is not something verbal? I tell you, if you memorize a single phrase of a saying, you'll be a wild fox sprite for all time. Do you understand?

YUN-MEN
Sayings

The opportunity to preach the Way is certainly hard to handle; even if you accord with it in a single saying, this is still fragmentation. If you go on at random, that is even more useless.

Now then, there are divisions within the vehicles of the Teaching: the precepts are for moral studies, the scriptures are for learning concentration, and the treatises are for learning wisdom. The Three Baskets, Five Vehicles, Five Times, and Eight Teachings each have their goal. But even if you directly understand the complete immediate teaching of the One Vehicle, which is so hard to understand, this is still far from Zen realization.

In Zen, even if you present your state in a phrase, this is still uselessly bothering to tarry in thought. Zen methods, with their interactive techniques, have countless variations and differences; if you try to get ahead, your mistake lies in pursuing the expressions of others.

What about the perennial concern? Can you call this complete, can you call it immediate? Can you call it mundane or transcendental? Better not misconstrue this! When you hear me speaking this way, do not immediately turn to where there is neither completeness nor immediateness to figure and calculate.

Here, it is necessary for you to be the one to realize it; do not present sayings from a teacher, imitation sayings, or calculated sayings everywhere you go, making them out to be your own understanding.

Do not misunderstand. Right now, what is the matter?

, , ,

Better not say I'm fooling you today. To begin with, I have no choice but to make a fuss in front of you, but if I were seen by someone with clear eyes, I'd be a laughingstock. Right now I can't avoid it, so let me ask you all: What has ever been the matter? What do you lack?

Even if I tell you there's nothing the matter, I've already buried you, and yet you must arrive at this state before you will realize it. And don't run off at the mouth asking questions at random; as long as your own mind is unclear, you still have a lot of work to do in the future.

If your faculties and thoughts work slowly, then for now examine the methods and techniques set up by the ancients, to see what their principles are.

Do you want to attain understanding? The subjective ideas you yourself have been entertaining for measureless eons are so dense and thick that when you hear someone giving an explanation, you immediately conceive doubts and ask about the Buddha, ask about the Teaching, ask about transcendence, ask about accommodation. As you seek understanding, you become further estranged from it.

You miss it the moment you try to set your mind on it; how much more so when you talk! Would that mean that not trying to set the mind on it is right? What else is the matter? Take care!

> , , ,

If I were to bring up a single saying that enabled you to attain understanding immediately, this would already be scattering filth on your heads. Even if you understand the whole world all at once when a single hair is picked up, this is gouging out flesh and making a wound. Nevertheless, you must actually arrive at this state before you realize this. If you have not, then don't try to fake it in the meantime.

What you must do is step back and figure out your own standpoint: what logic is there to it?

There really is nothing at all to give you to understand, or to give you to wonder about, because each of you has your own business. When the great function appears, it does not take any effort on your part; now you are no different from the Zen masters and buddhas. It's just that your roots of faith are shallow and thin, while your bad habits are dense and thick.

Suddenly you get all excited and go on long journeys with your bowls and bags; why do you undergo such inconvenience? What insufficiency is there in you? You are adults; who has no lot? Even when you attain understanding individually on your own, this is still not being on top of things; so you shouldn't accept the deceptions of others or the judgments of others.

The minute you see some old monk open his mouth, you should shut him right up. Instead you act like green flies on a pile of manure, struggling to consume it. Gathering together in groups for discussion, you bore others miserably.

The ancients would utter a saying or half a statement for particular occasions, because of the helplessness of people like you, in order to open up ways of entry for you. If you know this, put them to one side and apply a bit of your own power; haven't you a little familiarity?

Alas, time does not wait for anyone; when you breathe out, there's no guarantee you'll breathe in again. What other body and mind do you have to employ at leisure somewhere else? You simply must pay attention! Take care.

> , , ,

Take the whole universe all at once and put it on your eyelashes.

When you hear me talk this way, you might come up excitedly and give me a slap, but relax for now and examine carefully the question of whether such a thing exists or not and what it means.

Even if you understand this, if you run into a member of a Zen school you'll probably get your legs broken.

If you are an independent individual, when you hear someone say that an old adept is teaching somewhere, you will spit right in that person's face for polluting your ears and eyes.

If you do not have this ability, as soon as you hear someone mention something like this, you will immediately accept it, so that you have already fallen into the secondary. Don't you see how Master Te-shan used to haul out his staff the moment he saw monks enter his gate, and chase them out? When Master Mu-chou saw monks come through his gate, he would say, "The issue is at hand; I ought to give you a thrashing!"

How about the rest? The general run of thieving phonies eat up the spit of other people, memorizing a bunch of trash, a load of garbage, then running off at the mouth like asses wherever they go, boasting that they can pose questions on five or ten sayings. Even if you can pose questions from morning till night and give answers from night till morning, on until the end of time, will you ever even dream of seeing? Where is the empowerment for people? Whenever someone gives a feast for Zen monks, people like this also say they've gotten food to eat. How are they worth talking to? Someday, in the presence of death, your verbal explanations will not be accepted.

One who has attained may spend the days following the group in another's house, but if you have not attained, don't be a faker! It will not do to pass the time taking it easy; you should be most thoroughly attentive.

The ancients had a lot of complex ways of helping out. For example, Master Hsueh-feng said, "The whole earth is you!" Master Chia-shan said, "Find me in the hundred grasses; recognize the emperor in the bustling marketplace." Luo-p'u said, "As soon as a single atom comes into existence, the whole earth is contained within it. There's a lion in every hair, and this is true of the whole body." Take these up and think them over, again and again; eventually, after a long, long time, you will naturally find a way to penetrate.

No one can do this task for you; it is up to each individual alone. The old masters who emerge in the world just act as witnesses to your understanding. If you have penetrated, a little bit of reasoning won't confuse you; if you have really not attained yet, then even the use of expedients to stimulate you won't work.

All of you have worn out footgear traveling around, having left your mentors and elders, your fathers and mothers. You must apply some perceptive power before you will attain realization. If you have no penetration, if you should run into someone with really effective methods who ungrudgingly devotes life to going into the mud and water to help others, someone who is worth associating with and who disrupts complacency, then hang up your bowls and bags for ten or twenty years to attain penetration.

Don't worry that you might not succeed, because even if you don't get it in the present life, you will still not lose your humanity in the future life. Thus you will also save energy in this quest; you will not betray your whole life in vain, nor will you betray those who supported you, your mentors and elders, your fathers and mothers.

You must be attentive. Don't waste time traveling around the countryside, passing a winter here and a summer there, enjoying the landscape, seeking enjoyment, plenty of food, and readily available clothing and utensils. What a pain! Counting on that peck of rice, you lose six months' provisions. What is the benefit in journeys like this? How can you digest even a single vegetable leaf, or even a grain of rice, given by credulous almsgivers?

You must see for yourself that there is no one to substitute for you, and time does not wait for anyone. One day the light of your eyes will fall to the ground; how can you prevent that from happening? Do not be like lobsters dropped in boiling water, hands and feet thrashing. There will be no room for you to be fakers talking big talk.

Don't waste the time idly. Once you have lost humanity, you can never restore it. This is not a small matter. Do not rely on the immediate present. Even a worldly man said, "If you hear the Way in the morning, it would be all right to die that night"—then what about ascetics like us—what should we practice? You should really be diligent. Take care.

> , , ,

It is obvious that the times are decadent; we are at the tail end of the age of imitation. These days monks go north saying they are going to bow to Manjushri and go south saying they are going to visit Mount Heng. Those who go on journeys like this are mendicants only in name, vainly consuming the alms of the credulous.

What a pain! When you ask them a question, they are totally in the dark. They just pass the days suiting their temperament. If there are some of you who have mislearned a lot, memorizing manners of speech, seeking similar sayings wherever you go for the approval of the elder residents, slighting the high-minded, acting in ways that spiritually impoverish you, then do not say, when death comes knocking at your door, that no one told you.

If you are a beginner, you should activate your spirit and not vainly memorize sayings. A lot of falsehood is not as good as a little truth; ultimately you will only cheat yourself.

Ming-chiao
Essays

That which has form emerges from that which has no form; that which has no form emerges from that which has form. Therefore the path of supreme spirituality cannot be sought in being and cannot be fathomed in nonbeing; it cannot be lost through movement and cannot be gained through stillness.

Is the path of sages empty? Then where does continual renewal of life come from? Is the path of sages not empty? What lives that does not die? To accurately comprehend both emptiness and nonemptiness in the path of sages would be desirable.

Now then, to prove emptiness experientially, there is nothing better than to understand that which has form. To understand that which has form, there is nothing better than to know that which has no form. If you know that which has no form, then you can see into the light of the spirit. When you can see into the light of the spirit, then you can talk about the path.

The path is where the spirit develops, and it is where consciousness comes from. Consciousness is a source of great problems. To say that the path of the sages is empty is to sink into a void of diffuseness, so that sickness becomes even sicker. Who in the world can cure this?

, , ,

The teaching of sages is in the path. The path of the sages is in awakening. Awakening means enlightenment; not awakening means not being enlightened. Not being enlightened is what separates the majority of consciousnesses from sagehood.

Awakening does not mean gradually waking up; it means being completely awake. Complete awakening is the consummation of the task of sages. Being awake is called buddhahood; it is likened to a vehicle. By awakening, one completes the path of sages; by this vehicle one reaches the realm of sages. This is true of all sages, past and future.

The awakening of sages lies within the normal awareness of ordinary people, but ordinary people wake up every day without ever realizing it. Even though they are awake, they are still dreaming; even though aware, they are still muddled. That is why the sages took the trouble to point it out to them, hoping that they'd seek awakening, inducing them to head for it, hoping they would attain it.

, , ,

Contemplating the mind is called the path; elucidating the path is called education. Education is the trail left by the sages; the path is the universal root of all living beings.

People have long misunderstood the root seriously; if sages did nothing about it, everyone would end up ignorant. That is why the sages have given people great illumination.

The mind has no outside, and the path has no inside, so there is no one who is not on the path. Sages are not selfish; the path does not abandon people; sages give everything that the path involves. Therefore their education penetrates both darkness and light, both the mundane and the transmundane; nothing is not penetrated.

Penetration means unification. Unification is a means of rectification, so that everyone will have the same virtues as sages.

For universal spiritual enlightenment, the path is supreme; for subtle functions of spiritual powers, the mind is supreme. When it comes to pursuing illusions and binding activities, nothing is worse that missing the root. When it comes to wandering in mundane routines, nothing is worse than death and rebirth. When it comes to recognizing the faults and ills of ordinary people, no one is more skilled than sages. When it comes to straightening the basis for all people, nothing is better than establishing education.

When correctness is stable, there is illumination. When illumination is stable, there is sublimation. When sublimation is stable, the path is consummated therein.

Therefore education is the great beginning of the sages' illumination of the path to save the world. Education is the inconceivable great function by which sages take advantage of timely opportunities to respond to potentials.

So it is that people of great potential go the immediate way, while those of lesser potential go the gradual way. The gradual way refers to the provisional; the immediate way refers to the real. The real is called the Great Vehicle, the provisional is called the Lesser Vehicle. The sages disseminated the great and the small among people of all kinds of potentials, so darkness and light were comprehended.

Hearing the immediate in the gradual teaching or hearing the gradual in the immediate teaching are also ways in which sages are more subtle than angels or humans and unfathomable to angels or humans. Sages teach the provisional to induce people to head for the real; sages illustrate the real so that people will avail themselves of the provisional. Therefore the provisional and the real, the partial and the complete, always concern one another.

Within the provisional, there is the manifest provisional and the hidden provisional. Sages' use of the manifest provisional involves shallow teaching, a small path, to provide a small resting place for believers. Sages' use of the hidden provisional involves other paths, other teachings, cooperating with the good and the bad, to provide nonbelievers with remote conditions for attaining enlightenment. The manifest provisional is obvious, but the hidden provisional is unfathomable.

As for the real, it is final truth. In the reality of final truth, others and self are one. Because others and self are one, sages are such because of all beings.

If we talk about the provisional teaching of sages, it would seem to be the great expediency that pervades all the goodness in the world, all the paths of the philosophers, for saving the world and helping people out. If we talk about the real teaching of sages, it would seem to be the universal path that pervades the universe and limits all things, finding out the truth and fulfilling nature for all the world.

As for sages, their sagacity is in not dying or being reborn yet showing death and showing birth, the same as other people, without anyone seeing why it is so. This does not only mean people of ancient times with highly developed spirituality and knowledge. That is why their education includes the spirit way as well as the human way; there are ordinary virtues, and there are extraordinary virtues—it is impossible to fit everything into one generalization, and this cannot be discussed in the same terms as worldly ways. Attainment lies in mental penetration; loss lies in comparison of traces.

＞　＞　＞

Feelings emerge from nature, whereas nature is concealed in feelings. When nature is concealed, the path of ultimate reality is inoperative. That is why sages use nature for their teaching to educate people.

Activities and movements in society start from feelings. The confusions of the masses are rectified by nature. How can society not examine the positive and negative aspects of feelings and nature? They know good and bad but not how good and bad begin and end; is that complete knowledge? Is it complete knowledge to know the end but not the beginning?

Only the consummate knowledge of sages knows the beginning and the end, knows the subtle and the nonexistent, and sees what pervades death and birth, dark and light, and makes images and forms.

The world is most extensive, but it arises from feelings. The universe is most enormous, yet it is contained within nature. Therefore nothing is more powerful than feeling and nature.

Feeling is the beginning of being. When there is being, then there is affection. When there is affection, then there is desire. When there is desire, then men, women, and all beings are born and die therein.

The experiences of death and life, good and bad, typically change; they begin and they end, cyclically passing away and regenerating unceasingly.

Nature is the attainment of nonbeing. Ultimate nonbeing does not mean nonexistence; it emerges at birth and submerges at death, without itself dying or being born.

The reason for the tranquillity of the path of sages is obvious: they only sense what is suitable.

Now then, feeling is artifice, and it is consciousness; when you have it, that makes for affection, sympathy, intimacy. But intimacy makes distance, and distance makes for inconsistent good and ill.

When you lose feeling, that makes for cheating, for cunning, for viciousness, for unruliness, for greed, for addiction, for loss of mind and destruction of nature.

As for nature, it is reality, it is suchness, it is perfection, it is innocence, it is purity, it is serenity. When you get near it, you become wise and upright. In the near term, it makes people decent and upright; in the long run, it makes sanctified spirits and great sages. This is what underlies the fact that sages educate people with teaching about nature, not feeling.

Feeling and nature exist in beings always, as ever. When you try to find them out, you cannot grasp them; even if you try to cut them off, they do not end. Sky and earth have an end, but the soul of nature does not die out.

Different states of mundane existence may alternate and change, but the burden of feeling does not dissolve. Therefore society has to distinguish between the meanings of feeling and nature. If people are educated on the basis of feeling, they remain within birth and death. If people are educated on the basis of nature, they get beyond death and birth. The education of feeling is short-ranged; the education of nature is long-ranged. If you pretend to be beyond death and rebirth and take a nihilistic view of them, then you are ignorant of the pattern of nature and you cut off the source of continual regeneration.

Small knowledge cannot reach great knowledge; the final destination of a game hen is the cooking pot, is it not?

When the mind stirs, that is called activity. Coordinated activity is called experience. Experience refers to both the internal and the external. Whose mind does not stir? Who does not experience the activities of myriad beings? The pattern of activity is recondite; the momentum of experience is far reaching. Therefore people do not notice and do not fear. The education of sages is to be careful of activity, so people will be on the alert, so that they will beware of stirring in the mind.

Internal experiencing is called beckoning, and external experiencing is called response. Beckoning is considered the cause; response is considered the result. The concrete and abstract forms of cause and effect are all involved.

Now then, movement in the mind may be perverse, or it may be harmonious; this is why good and bad feelings arise therein. Once good and bad feelings occur, then calamity and fortune come in response. To the degree that feelings are more or less shallow or deep, the consequences are more or less light or heavy. The light may be shifted, but the heavy cannot be removed.

Good and bad may precede or follow; calamity and fortune may be slow or swift. Even after ten generations, or even ten thousand generations, it is impossible to escape experiencing consequences. It is not only a matter of just one generation. Those who doubt this just because good and bad do not show results in one generation are ignorant of causality.

If rewards are not based on correct causality, then how can good people be encouraged in society? We do not see trees growing, yet they flourish day by day; we do not see a whetstone wearing down, yet it diminishes day by day. That is how it is with human actions, so how can we not be careful?

HSUEH-TOU
Stories

Te-shan Guides the Crowd

Te-shan said to a group, "Tonight I won't answer any questions. Anyone who asks a question gets a thrashing."

At that point, a monk came forward and bowed, whereupon Te-shan hit him.

The monk said, "I haven't even asked a question yet!"

Te-shan said, "Where are you from?"

The monk said, "Korea."

Te-shan said, "You deserved a thrashing before you stepped on the boat!"

Fa-yen brought this up and said, "The great Te-shan's talk is dualistic."

Yuan-ming brought this up and said, "The great Te-shan has a dragon's head but a snake's tail."

Hsueh-tou brought this up and commented, "Though the old masters Fa-yen and Yuan-ming skillfully trimmed the long and added to the short, gave up the heavy and went along with the light, this is not enough to see Te-shan.

"Why? Te-shan was as if holding the authority outside the door; he had a sword that would not invite disorder even when he didn't cut off when he should.

"Do you want to see the Korean monk? He is just a blind fellow bumping into a pillar."

Pai-chang and the Whisk

Pai-chang called on Ma-tsu a second time and stood there, attentive. Ma-tsu stared at the whisk on the edge of his seat.

Pai-chang asked, "Does one identify with this function or detach from this function?"

Ma-tsu said, "Later on, when you open your lips, what will you use to help people?"

Pai-chang picked up the whisk and held it up.

Ma-tsu said, "Do you identify with this function or detach from this function?"

Pai-chang hung the whisk back in its place.

Ma-tsu then shouted, so loudly that Pai-chang was deaf for three days.

Hsueh-tou brought this up and said, "Extraordinary, O Zen worthies! Nowadays, those who branch off in streams are very many, while those who search out the source are extremely few. Everyone says that Pai-chang was greatly enlightened at the shout, but is it really true or not?

"Similar ideographs resemble each other and get mixed up, but clear-eyed people couldn't be fooled one bit. When Ma-tsu said, 'Later on, when you open your lips, what will you use to help people?' Pai-chang held up the whisk—do you consider this to be like insects chewing wood, accidentally making a pattern, or is it breaking out of and crashing into a shell at the same time?

"Do you want to understand the three days of deafness? Pure gold, highly refined, should not change in color."

Hsueh-feng's Ancient Stream

A monk asked Hsueh-feng, "How is it when the ancient stream is cold from the source?"

Hsueh-feng said, "When you look directly into it, you don't see the bottom."

The monk asked, "How about one who drinks of it?"

Hsueh-feng said, "It doesn't go in by way of the mouth."

The monk recounted this to Chao-chou. Chao-chou said, "It can't go in by way of the nostrils."

The monk then asked Chao-chou, "How is it when the ancient stream is cold from the source?"

Chao-chou said, "Painful."

The monk said, "What about one who drinks of it?"

Chao-chou said, "He dies."

Hsueh-feng heard this quoted and said, "Chao-chou is an ancient buddha; from now on, I won't answer any more questions."

Hsueh-tou brought this up and commented, "Everyone in the crowd says that Hsueh-feng didn't go beyond this monk's question, and that is why Chao-chou didn't agree. If you understand literally in this way, you'll deeply disappoint the ancients.

"I dissent. Only one who can cut nails and shear iron is a real Zen master. Going to the low, leveling the high, one could hardly be called an adept."

Ts'ao-shu and the Nation of Han

Ts'ao-shu asked a monk, "Where have you recently come from?"

The monk said, "The nation of Han."

Ts'ao-shu asked, "Does the emperor of Han respect Buddhism?"

The monk said, "How miserable! Lucky you asked me! Had you asked another, there would have been a disaster!"

Ts'ao-shu asked, "What are you doing?"

The monk said, "I don't even see people's existence—what Buddhism is there to respect?"

Ts'ao-shu asked, "How long have you been ordained?"

The monk said, "Twenty years."

Ts'ao-shu said, "A fine 'not seeing people's existence'!" And he hit him.

Hsueh-tou commented, "This monk took a beating, but when he goes he won't return. As for Ts'ao-shu, while he carried out the imperative, he roused waves where there was no wind."

The House of Fa-yen

Hsuan-sha

Sayings

Have you attained the pure, original ocean of insight and knowledge of essence and forms? If you haven't attained it yet, now that you are gathered here, do you see the green mountains before you? If you say you see, how do you see? If you say you do not see, how can you say the green mountains are not visible? Do you understand?

The fact is that your pure, original ocean of insight and knowledge of essence and forms includes seeing and hearing. If you understand, it is just so, and even if you don't understand, it is still just so.

ʼ ʼ ʼ

Everything is always so; every essence is as such; just do not seek outside. If you have a great root of faith, then the buddhas are nothing but your own inner experience; whether you are walking, standing still, sitting, or reclining, never is it not so.

But now that I've told you this directly, already I am oppressing your freedom, making you slaves. Would you agree to say so? Whether you agree or not, how do you understand?

Now this talk is already showing ignorance of good and bad. How so? Because you discriminate this way and that way.

ʼ ʼ ʼ

What are you all taking such pains in search of? Don't tell me to flap my lips! Why? There is nothing accomplished by talk alone; it is not words that can bring people peace. You must experience unity and suchness before you attain harmony; don't just memorize sayings and expressions, for there is no end to that. It's just a matter of total concentration. Don't say you have to attain the function of the sages before you can be free; how are you unequal to them?

, , ,

The emergence of buddhas in the world exercising kindness and compassion has been all along like flowers in the sky, without solid reality. You should realize that there is that which has never emerged in the world and has never entered extinction.

Illusory manifestations and illusory names have no reality. Why? The essential nature of the material elements is fundamentally actually empty, so it has never passed away and never come to be, and it has never taught people.

Because the essential nature of beings is such, their material bodies are also such. Because the essential nature of beings is nirvanic, their material bodies are also nirvanic. But do you realize this?

If you do, then come forth and we'll all discuss it. If not, I now tell you that intrinsic essence does not produce intrinsic essence, and intrinsic essence does not annihilate intrinsic essence.

Then how can one attain understanding? Don't say this essential nature is as ever. If you understand, please express your understanding to the people; if you do not understand, then how are you not comparable to the buddhas?

This is how you must be before you attain. Those of higher faculties comprehend everything once they hear; those of middling faculties also comprehend once they hear; and those of lesser faculties also comprehend once they hear. What am I talking about with this reasoning? Do you know? Do you have insight?

It is inherent in everyone; it is manifest in everyone.

, , ,

The first axiom of Zen is to personally accept the completeness of present actuality. There is no other in the whole universe; it is just you. Who else would you have see? Who would you have hear? All of it is the doing of your mind monarch, fulfilling immutable knowledge. All you lack is personal acceptance of the realization. This is called opening the door of expedient methodology, to get you to trust that there is a flow of true eternity that pervades all time. There's nothing that is not it and nothing that is it.

This axiom only amounts to equanimity. Why? It is just using words to dismiss words, using principle to chase principle, teaching people equilibrium and constancy in essence and in manifestation for their own benefit. In terms of Zen, this is still understanding what comes before but not understanding what comes afterward. This is called uniform ordinariness, the experience of partial realization of the body of reality.

Without expression beyond patterns, you die at the statement and do not yet have any freedom. If you know experience beyond patterns, you will not be compelled by mental demons; they come within your power, and you can transform them effortlessly. Your words communicate the great Way, without falling into the view of even-mindedness. This is called the first axiom of Zen.

The second axiom is returning to causality and attending to effects, not sticking to the principle of constant oneness. This is expediently called turning from state to potential, enlivening and killing freely, granting and taking away as appropriate, emerging in life and entering in death, bringing benefits to all. Transcendently free of material desires and emotional views, this is expediently called the buddha nature that goes beyond the whole world all at once. This is called simultaneous understanding of two principles, equal illumination of two truths. Unmoved by dualistic extremism, subtle functions become manifest. This is called the second axiom of Zen.

The third axiom is to know that there is a root source of the nature and characteristics of great knowledge and to penetrate its infinite vision, understanding both the negative and the positive, comprehending the universe. The enhanced function of the one real essential nature becomes manifest, responding to developments without convention. Functioning completely without any effort, totally alive without any initiative, this is expediently called the method of concentration of compassion. This is the third axiom of Zen.

KUEI-CH'EN
Sayings

Don't lower your heads and think; thought cannot reach. If you then say you did not need to be discerning, do you understand enough to express it in words? Where will you begin your speech? Try to tell.

Is there anything that can get you nearer? Is there anything that can get you farther? Is there anything that can make you the same? Is there anything that can make you different? Then why do you particularly go to so much trouble? It is because you are weak and lack character, fretfully guarding the conceptual faculty, afraid that people will question you.

I always say, if you have any enlightenment, then reveal it without any sense of others or self; I will check it for you.

Why do you not accept what is right at hand? Don't take a puddle for an ocean. Buddhism pervades the universe; don't make the mistake of subjectively defining knowledge and views in your little heart and drawing the boundaries there. This is perception and cognition, thought and feeling. And yet it is not that this is wrong; but if you nod here and say you've found true reality, then you don't get it.

Now what about the ancient saying "Only I can know"—what perspective is this? Do you know? Is it not, "You see me, I see you"? Don't misunderstand! If it were this self, the self goes along with birth and death: as long as the body exists, it is there; but when the body is no longer, it is not there. That is why the ancient buddhas said, for the sake of you people of today, difference produces differences; when there is no difference, differences disappear.

Don't take this lightly; the matter of birth and death is serious. If you don't evaporate this mass, there will be plenty of discord wherever you are; if you don't break through sound and form, the same will be so of sensation, perception, conditioning, and consciousness. Even if your bones are sticking out, don't say that the five clusters are originally void. It does not depend on your claim to have understood emptiness. That is why it is said that you must personally attain penetration, and you have to be genuinely authentic.

I am not the first one to talk like this. The ancient sages have informed you of what they called the indestructible esoteric treasury of inconceivable light. It covers the whole universe, giving birth to the ordinary and nurturing the saintly, pervading all time. Who has none of it? Then who would you depend on anymore?

Thus the buddhas, in their compassion, seeing you helpless, opened up the door of expedient methodology, pointing out the characteristics of true reality. Now I am using expedient method; do you understand? If you do not understand, don't make up wonders in your conceptual faculty.

FA-YEN
Ten Guidelines for Zen Schools

Author's Own Preface

I shed the cage of entanglements in youth and grew up hearing the essentials of the Teaching, traveling around calling on teachers for nearly thirty years. The Zen schools, in particular, are widespread, most numerous in the South. Yet few in them have arrived at attainment; such people are rarely found.

Anyway, even though noumenal principle is a matter for sudden understanding, actualities must be realized gradually. The teaching methods of the schools have many techniques, of course, but insofar as they are for dealing with people for their benefit, the ultimate aim is the same.

If, however, people have no experience of the doctrines of the teachings, it is hard to break through discrimination and subjectivity. Galloping right views over wrong roads, mixing inconsistencies into important meanings, they delude people of the following generations and inanely enter into vicious circles.

I have taken the measure of this, and it is quite deep; I have made the effort to get rid of it, but I have not fully succeeded. The mentality that blocks the tracks just grows stronger; the intellectual undercurrent is not useful.

Where there are no words, I forcefully speak out; where there is no dogma, I strongly uphold certain principles. Pointing out defects in Zen schools, I briefly explain ten matters, using words critical of specific errors to rescue an era from decadence.

1. On False Assumption of Teacherhood without Having Cleared One's Own Mind Ground

The teaching of the mind ground is the basis of Zen study. What is the mind ground? It is the great awareness of those who arrive at suchness.

From no beginning, a moment of confusion mistaking things for oneself, craving and desire flare up, and you flow in the waves of birth and death. The radiance of awareness is dimmed, covered up by ignorance; routines of behavior push you on, so you cannot be free.

Once you have lost human status, you cannot restore it. That is why the buddhas emerged in the world with so many expedient methods; if you get stuck on expressions and pursue words, you will fall back into eternalism or nihilism. Through the compassion of the Zen masters, the mind seal was communicated unalloyed, so that people could transcend the ordinary and the sacred at once, without going through stages; it just got them to awaken on their own and sever the root of doubt forever.

People of recent times take a lot lightly. They may enter communes, but they are lazy about pursuing intense inquiry. Even if they develop concentration, they do not select a true master; through the mistakes of false teachers, like them they lose direction to the ultimate. They have not comprehended the faculties and fields of sense, so they have false understandings that lead them into deluded states, where they lose the true basis completely.

Concerned only with hurriedly striving for leadership, they are falsely called teachers; while they value an empty reputation in the world, how can they consider the fact that they are bringing ill upon themselves? Not only do they deafen and blind people of later times, but they also cause the current teaching to degenerate. Having climbed to the high and wide seat of a spiritual master, instead they lie on iron bedsteads, suffering the final shame of Chunda [whose offering caused the death of Buddha], forced to drink molten copper.

Beware! It is not good to be complacent with oneself. The punishment consequent on slandering the Great Vehicle is not minor.

2. On Factional Sectarianism and Failure to Penetrate Controversies

The Zen founder did not come from India to China because there is something to be transmitted. He just pointed directly to the human mind for the perception of its essence and realization of awakening. How could there be any sectarian style to be valued?

Nevertheless, the provisional teachings devised by the guides to the source had differences and accordingly came to differ from one another. For example, the two masters Hui-neng and Shen-hsiu had the same teacher, but their perceptions and understandings differed. Hence the world referred to them as the Southern School and the Northern School.

Once Hui-neng was gone, there were two teachers, Hsing-ssu and Huai-jang, who continued his teaching. Hsing-ssu taught Hsi-ch'ien, and Huai-jang taught Ma-tsu. Ma-tsu was also called Chiang-hsi, and Hsi-ch'ien was also called Shih-t'ou.

From these two branches diverged individual lineages, each occupying a region. The outflow of the original streams cannot be recorded in full. When it got to Te-shan, Lin-chi, Kuei-shan and Yang-shan, Ts'ao-shan and Tung-shan, Hsueh-feng, Yun-men, and so on, each school had established devices, with higher and lower gradations.

But when it came to continuation, their descendants maintained sects and factionalized their ancestries. Not basing themselves on reality, eventually they produced many sidetracks, contradicting and clashing with one another, so that the profound and the shallow became indistinguishable.

Unfortunately, they still do not realize that the Great Way takes no sides; streams of truth are all of the same flavor. These sectarians spread embellishments in empty space and stick needles in iron and stone, taking disputation for superknowledge and lip-flapping for meditation. Sword-points of approval and disapproval arise, and mountains of egotism toward others stand tall. In their anger they become monsters, their views and interpretations ultimately turning them into outsiders. Unless they meet good friends, they will hardly be able to get out of the harbor of delusion. They bring on bad results, even from good causes.

3. On Teaching and Preaching without Knowing the Bloodline

If you want to expound the vehicle to the source and bring out the essentials of the Teaching, unless you know the bloodline all you are doing is wrongly propagating heresies.

In this context, there is first extolling and then upholding, criticizing, or praising doctrines, snapping the thrust of intellect. When one is in charge of carrying out the imperative of Zen, enlivening and killing are in one's hands.

Sometimes one stands like a mile-high wall, totally inaccessible, or sometimes one may consent to let go temporarily and follow the waves. Like a king wielding a sword, the ideal is to attain autonomy.

Active function is a matter of appropriate timing; one grants or deprives like a grand general. Waves leap, peaks tower, lightning flashes, and wind rushes; the elephant king strolls, the true lion roars.

We often see those who do not assess their own strength but steal the words of others. They know how to let go but not how to gather in; they may have enlivening, but they have no killing. They do not distinguish servant from master or true from false; they insult the ancients and bury the essence of Zen.

Everyone figures and calculates in their conceptual faculties, speculating and searching within compounded elements of mind and matter. Since they are ignorant of the enlightenment right before their eyes, they attain only imitation insight.

How could it be an easy matter to set up the banner of the teaching on a nonabiding basis, to preach in the place of Buddha? Have you not seen how the great master Yun-men said, "In all of China it is hard to find anyone at all who can bring up a saying"?

And have you not seen how Master Huang-po said, "Grand Master Ma produced over eighty teachers; when questioned, each spoke fluently, but only Master Lu-shan amounts to anything"?

Thus we know that when one takes up this position, if one understands how to give direction and guidance, then one is a complete Zen master. How do we know this? Have you not seen how an ancient said, "Know the soil by the sprouts; know people by what they say"? One is already revealed at once even in blinking the eyes and raising the brows; how much the more in being an examplar. How could one not be careful?

4. On Giving Answers without Observing Time and Situation and Not Having the Eye of the Source

Anyone who would be a guide to the source first distinguishes the false from the true. Once the false and the true have been distinguished, it is also essential that the time and situation be understood.

It is, furthermore, necessary to speak with the eye of the source, able to make a point and to respond without inconsistency.

Thus, although there is nothing personal in a statement, we still make provisional use of discernment of the aim within words. The Ts'ao-Tung has "knocking and calling out" for its function, the Lin-chi has "interchange" for its working; Yun-men "contains, covers, and cuts off the flows"; while the Kuei-Yang silently matches square and round. Like a valley echoing melodies, like matching talismans at a pass, although they are different in their manners, that does not inhibit their fluid integration.

In recent generations, Zen teachers have lost the basis; students have no guidance. They match wits egotistically and take what is ephemeral for an attainment. Where is the heart to guide others? No longer do we hear of knowledge to destroy falsehood. Caning and shouting at random, they say they have studied Te-shan and Lin-chi; presenting circular symbols to each other, they claim they have deeply understood Kuei-shan and Yang-shan.

Since they do not handle the all-embracing source in their answers, how can they know the essential eye in their actions? They fool the young and deceive the sagacious. Truly they bring on the laughter of objective observers and call calamity upon their present state. This is why the Overnight Illuminate said, "If you do not want to incur hellish karma, do not slander the Buddha's true teaching."

People like this cannot be all told of. They just leave their teachers' heritage without any insight of their own. Having no basis upon which to rely, their restless consciousness is unclear. They are only to be pitied, but it is hard to inform them of this.

5. On Discrepancy between Principle and Fact, and Failure to Distinguish Defilement and Purity

The schools of the enlightened ones always include both principle and fact. Facts are established on the basis of principle, while principle is revealed by means of facts. Principles and facts complement one another like eyes and feet. If you have facts without principle, you get stuck in the mud and cannot get through; if you have principle without facts, you will be vague and without resort. If you want them to be nondual, it is best that they be completely merged.

Take the example of the manner of the House of Ts'ao-Tung: they have the relative and absolute, light and darkness. The Lin-chi have host and guest, substance and function. Although their provisional teachings are not the same, their bloodlines commune. There is not one that does not include the others; when mobilized, all are mustered. It is also like *Contemplation of the Realm of Reality*, which discusses both noumenal principle and phenomenal fact, refuting both inherent solidity and voidness.

The nature of the ocean is boundless, yet it is contained in the tip of a hair; the polar mountain is enormous, yet it can be hidden in a seed. Surely it is not the perception of saints that makes it thus; the design of reality is just so. It is not miraculous display of supernatural powers, either, or forced appellations of something false by nature. It is not to be sought from another; it all comes from mind's creation.

Buddhas and sentient beings are equal, so if you do not realize this truth, there will be idle discussion, causing the defiled and the pure to be indistinct and the true and the false to be undifferentiated. Relative and absolute get stuck in interchange; substance and function are mixed up in spontaneity. This is described in these terms: "If a single thing is not clear, fine dust covers the eyes." If one cannot eliminate one's own illness, how can one cure the diseases of others? You should be most careful and thoroughgoing; it is certainly not a trivial matter.

6. On Subjective Judgment of Ancient and Contemporary Sayings without Going through Clarification

Once people have joined an association for intensive study, they must select a teacher and then associate with good companions. A teacher is needed to point out the road; companions are valuable for refinement. If you only want self-understanding, then how can you lead on younger students and bring out the teaching of the school? Where is the will to deal with people to their benefit?

Observe how the worthies of the past traversed mountains and seas, not shrinking from death or life, for the sake of one or two sayings. When there was the slightest tinge of doubt, the matter had to be submitted to certain discernment; what they wanted was distinct clarity. First becoming standards of truth versus falsehood, acting as eyes for humanity and the angels, only after that did they raise the seal of the school on high and circulate the true teaching, bringing out the rights and wrongs of former generations, bearing down on inconclusive cases.

If you make your own subjective judgment of past and present without having undergone purification and clarification, how is that different from performing a sword dance without having learned how to handle a sword, or foolishly counting on getting across a pit without having sized it up? Can you avoid cutting your hand or falling?

One who chooses well is like a king goose picking out milk from water; one who chooses poorly is like a sacred tortoise leaving tracks. Especially in this context, where there is negative and positive activity and expression of mutual interchange, to come to life in a way that turns morbid is to relegate the absolute to the relative. It is not right to give rein to the unruly mind and use it as it is to try to fathom the meaning of the sages. This is especially true in view of the fact that the essence of the one-word teaching has myriad methods of setting up teachings. Can we not be careful of this, to prevent opposition?

7. On Memorizing Slogans without Being Capable of Subtle Function Meeting the Needs of the Time

It is not that there is no guidance for students of transcendent insight, but once you have gotten guidance, it is essential that expanded function actually appear; only then do you have a little bit of intimate realization. If you just stick to a school and memorize slogans, it is not penetrating enlightenment at all, but mere intellectual knowledge.

This is why the ancients said, "When your view equals your teacher, you have less than half your teacher's virtue. Only when your view is beyond your teacher can you bring out the teacher's teaching." The Sixth Patriarch, furthermore, said to Elder Ming, "What I have told you is not something secret; the secret is within you." And Yen-t'ou said to Hsueh-feng, "Everything flows forth from your own heart."

So we know that speaking, caning, and hollering do not depend on a teacher's bequest; how could the marvelous function, free in all ways, demand another's assent?

When you degrade them, pearls and gold lose their beauty; when you prize them, shards and pebbles shine. If you go when and as you should go, principle and fact are both mastered; if you act when and as you should act, there is not the slightest miss.

The stuff of a real man is not for sissies. Don't be a servile literalist and get stuck on verbal expressions as if this were the manner of Zen, or flap your lips and beat your gums as if this were sublime understanding. This cannot be penetrated by language or known by thought. Wisdom comes out in the village of infinite nothingness; spirituality is found in the realm of unfathomability. Where dragons and elephants tread is not within the capability of asses.

8. On Failure to Master the Scriptures and Adducing Proofs Wrongly

Whoever would bring out the vehicle of Zen and cite the doctrines of the Teaching must first understand what the Buddha meant, then accord with the mind of Zen masters. Only after that can you bring them up and put them into practice, comparing degrees of closeness.

If, in contrast, you do not know the doctrines and principles but just stick to a sectarian methodology, when you adduce proofs readily but wrongly, you will bring slander and criticism on yourself.

Yet the canon of sutras is nothing but pointing out tracks; the complete all-at-once Higher Vehicle is just like a signpost. Even if you can understand a hundred thousand concentrations and countless doctrines and methods, you only increase your own toil and do not get at the issue.

What is more, comprehending the provisional and returning to the absolute, gathering the outgrowths back to the source, not admitting a single atom in the realm of absolute purity while not rejecting anything in the methodology of enlightened activity, inevitably deciding the case on the basis of the facts, getting to the substance and removing the complications, has no connection whatsoever with the source of Zen.

There are many great people who are experts in the scriptures, real devotees of broad knowledge of the ancients, who flaunt their eloquence like sharp blades and set forth their wealth of learning like stocks in a storehouse; when they get here, they must be taught to be still and silent, so that the road of speech cannot be extended. Finding that all their memorization of words and phrases has been an account of others' treasures, for the first time they will believe in the specialty of Zen, which is the separate transmission outside of doctrine.

Younger people should not bog themselves down, incurring the derision of others and disgracing the way of Zen. Do not say you do not need cultivation, or consider a little bit enough. Since you do not even understand the outgrowths, how can you realize the root?

9. On Indulging in Making Up Songs and Verses without Regard for Meter and without Having Arrived at Reality

There are many styles of song and verse in Zen; some are short, some long, some modern, some ancient. They use sound and form to reveal practical application, or call on events to express states. Some follow principle to talk of reality; some oppose the trend of affairs to rectify customs and morals.

Thus, although their approaches are different—which is inevitable, since their inspirations were different—they all bring out the great cause. Together they extol the meditations of the Buddha, inspiring students of later times and criticizing the intelligent people of former times. In each case, the main meaning is in the words, so how could it be proper to compose them arbitrarily?

Sometimes I see established Zen teachers and advanced students of meditation who consider songs and verses to be leisure pursuits and consider composition to be a trivial matter. They spit out whatever they feel, and in many cases their works are similar to vulgar sayings. Composed on impulse, they are just like common talk.

These people say of themselves that they are not concerned by coarseness and are not picky about grubbiness; they are thus trying to suggest that theirs are words beyond worldly convention, advertising them as hearkening back to ultimate truth. The knowledgeable laugh in derision when they read them, while fools believe in them and circulate them. They cause the principles of names to gradually disappear, and add to the growing weakness of the doctrinal schools.

Have you not seen the tens of thousands of verses of the *Flower Ornament Scripture* and the thousands of poems of the Zen masters? Both are profuse and vivid, with elegant language; all of them are refined and pure, without padding. They are hardly the same as imitation of worldly customs with all their fripperies.

For writing to be a pathway in later times and true in the mouths of the multitudes, it is still necessary to study precedents, and then it is essential to suit it to the occasion. If you happen to have little natural ability, then you should be natural and content with simplicity; why pretend to genius or aspire to intellectual brilliance?

If you spout vulgar inanities, you disturb the influence of the Way. Weaving miserable misconceptions, you cause trouble. Unconvincing falsehoods will increase later disgrace.

10. On Defending One's Own Shortcomings and Indulging in Contention

As the land is full of religious communes and the Zen societies are extremely numerous, with communities numbering not less than half a thousand gathered there, are there not one or two working for the furtherance of the Teaching?

There are some people among them who embrace the Way, people of pure conduct, who agree to temporarily go along with the feelings of the community and exert their strength to continue the Zen teaching, gather colleagues from all over, and establish a site of enlightenment in one region. With morning questioning and even assembly, they do not shy away from toil and hardship, wanting only to continue the life of wisdom of the buddhas, guiding beginners.

They do not do it for the sake of increasing fame or out of greed for profit and support; rather, like a bell ringing when struck, they dispense medicine when they encounter illness. Showering the rain of the Teaching, they have no bias toward great or small; as they sound the thunder of the Teaching, far and near all respond. Their prosperity or austerity naturally varies, their activity and concealment differ; but this is not on account of choosiness or because of attachment and rejection.

There are those who inherit succession by sycophancy, who hold position by stealing rank and then claim to have attained the highest vehicle and to have transcended mundane things. They defend their own shortcomings and derogate the strengths of others. Fooling around in cocoons of ignorance, they smack their lips in front of meat markets. Emphasizing their temporal power, they take pride in glibness.

They gossip and call that compassion; they are sloppy and call that virtue in action. Violating Buddhist prohibitions and precepts, abandoning the dignity of the religious community, they disparage the Two Vehicles and wrongly dispense with the three studies. What is more, they fail to investigate the great matter, yet approve of themselves as masters.

Thus, at the end of the age of imitation, the demons are strong and the Teaching is weak. They use the Buddha's robe of righteousness to steal the benevolence and dignity of kings. Their mouths speak of the basis of liberation, but their minds play with the obsessions of ghosts and spirits. Since they have no shame or conscience, how can they avoid wrongdoing?

Now I have exposed these folks to warn people in the future. Meeting with a chance for wisdom is not a small matter; choosing a teacher is most difficult. If you can bear the responsibility yourself, eventually you will fulfill maximum potential. I am forcibly dispensing a stunning medicine, willing to be subjected to slander and hatred, so that people on the same path may be assisted in awakening.

Yung-ming

False Cults

Because of ignorance of the qualites of inherent nature, people fail to understand the true source. Abandoning enlightenment, they follow the dusts, giving up the root for the branches. They get hung up in the demonic web of being and nonbeing, and they wander in the forest of errors of oneness and differencc. Trying to master true emptiness, they become alienated from the nature of reality; based on the arising and disappearance of sense data, they follow the being and nothingness of objects. Clinging to nihilism, confused by eternalism, they pursue the conditional and forget the essential. Mistakenly developing intellectual interpretation, they cultivate practice wrongly.

Some mellow the spirit, nurture energy, and preserve naturalness. Some torture the body, mortifying the flesh, and consider that the ultimate path.

Some cling to nongrasping and stand rooted in the immediate environment. Some suppress the wandering mind in quest of quiet meditation.

Some get rid of feelings and negate phenomena in order to stabilize voidness. Some stick to reflections, get involved in objects, and embrace forms.

Some extinguish the true radiance of the spiritual source. Some eliminate the true causal basis of Buddhist principles.

Some cut off consciousness and freeze the mind, experiencing an inanimate state in consequence. Some clear the mind and ignore matter, abiding as a result in a kind of celestial state in which it is hard to become enlightened.

Some stick to phantasms, clinging to their existence. Some become complete nihilists.

Some eliminate all views and dwell in dark rooms. Some insist on perception and dwell on cognition.

Some consider having awareness to be the form of the true Buddha. Some imitate insentience, like wood or stone.

Some cling to illusion as if it were the same as the ultimate realization, like considering clay in itself to be a jar. Some seek ways of liberation wrongly focused, like seeking water while rejecting waves.

Some hasten outwardly and deludedly produce dream states. Some keep to inwardness and live in solemnity, embracing ignorance.

Some are devoted to oneness and consider everything the same. Some see differences and define individual reality-realms.

Some keep to ignorant nondiscrimination and consider that the Great Way. Some value the notion of voidness and consider denial of good and bad to be true practice.

Some interpret inconceivability to be insensate voidness. Some understand true goodness and subtle form to be really existent.

Some stop mental workings and cut off thoughts, like angels with polluted minds. Some contemplate with awareness and attention, falling within the bounds of intellectual assessment.

Some fail to investigate the nature of illusion thoroughly, interpreting it as the unknown beginning. Some are ignorant of illusory substance and make a religion of nothingness.

Some recognize reflections as realities. Some seek reality while clinging to falsehood.

Some recognize the nature of perception as a living thing. Some point to illusory objects as inanimate.

Some willfully entertain ideas and turn away from silent knowledge. Some cut off thoughts and thus lack enlightened function.

Some lose sight of natural qualities and conceive views of matter and mind. Some rely on ultimate emptiness and develop a nihilistic attitude.

Some cling to universal principle and immediately abandon adornment. Some misunderstand gradual teaching and become fanatical activists.

Some detach from objects by relying on essence but make their attachment to self stronger. Some ignore everything and maintain themselves in ignorance.

Some decide that persons and phenomena are as they are naturally, and fall into the idea that there is no causality. Some cling to the combination of objects and intellect and conceive the notion of collective causality.

Some cling to the mixing of mind and objects, confusing subjective and objective actualities. Some stick to distinguishing absolute and conventional, bound up in the folly of obstruction by knowledge.

Some adhere to unchanging oneness, thus falling into eternalism. Some determine the movement of origin, abiding, decay, and nothingness, thus sinking into nihilism.

Some cling to noncultivation and thus dismiss the ranks of sages. Some say there is realization, and thus turn away from natural reality.

Some delight in the environment and their own persons, thus following the routines of the world. Some reject life and death and thus lose true liberation.

Some, misunderstanding true emptiness, are devoted to causes and obsessed with results. Some, ignorant of ultimate reality, long for enlightenment and despise bewilderment.

Some cling to expedient statements, holding to them as literal truth. Some lose the reality of verbal expression and seek silence apart from words.

Some are devoted to doctrinal methods and disdain spontaneous meditation. Some promote meditative contemplations and repudiate the measuring devices of the complete teaching.

Some compete at being extraordinary while only being concerned with status, suddenly sinking in the sea of knowledge. Some contrive purity to find out hidden secrets, instead getting trapped within a realm of shadows.

Some produce extraordinary intellectual interpretations, gouging flesh and producing wounds. Some dwell on original essential purity but cling to the medicine so it becomes unhealthy.

Some pursue the literature, searching out meanings, and wind up drinking a flood. Some keep to stillness and live in isolation, sitting in the dust of dogma.

Some discuss the formless Great Vehicle with the idea of getting something. Some search for mystic truth outside of things by means of calculating thoughts.

Some reject explanation and conceive the notion of absolute nonverbalization. Some keep explanation and call on the criticism of clinging to the pointing finger.

Some approve of active function and remain at the root source of birth and death. Some concentrate on memorization, dwelling within the limits of conscious thinking.

Some lose the essence of complete awareness by modification and adjustment. Some let be whatever will be, and lack a method of entering the path.

Some initiate energetic physical and mental efforts and linger in contrivance. Some keep to letting be without concern and sink into the bondage of insight.

Some concentrate on focusing thoughts and contemplating diligently, thus losing correct reception. Some imitate uninhibited freedom and give up cultivation.

Some follow binding compulsions while presuming upon intrinsic emptiness. Some cling to bondage and try to eliminate it arbitrarily.

Some are so serious that they develop attachment to religion. Some are so flippant that they ruin the basis of enlightenment.

Some seek so aggressively that they turn away from the original mind. Some slack off and become heedless.

Some lack realism, their speech and their realization differing. Some violate the vehicle of enlightenment by disparity of being and action.

Some keep to tranquillity, dwelling in emptiness, thereby losing the nature of great compassion. Some ignore conditions and reject the temporal, thus missing the door of naturalness.

Some stick to the notion of self, thus being ignorant of the emptiness of person. Some confuse immediate experience and harden their attachment to doctrine.

Some interpret without having faith, increasing false views. Some have faith but no understanding, increasing ignorance.

Some affirm the subjective but deny the objective. Some claim states are deep while knowledge is shallow.

Some get confused about the nature of things by grasping. Some turn away from immediate reality by rejection.

Some violate cause because of detachment. Some forget consequences because of attachment.

Some repudiate reality by denial. Some ruin temporary expedients by affirmation.

Some hate ignorance but thereby turn their backs on the door of immutable knowledge. Some dislike varying states but thereby destroy absorption in the nature of reality.

Some base themselves on the principle of sameness but thereby develop conceit. Some dismiss differentiations, thus destroying the methods of expedient techniques.

Some affirm enlightenment but repudiate the cycle of true teaching. Some deny sentient beings and repudiate the true body of Buddha.

Some stick to basic knowledge and deny expedient wisdom. Some miss the true source and cling to temporary methods.

Some linger in noumenon, sinking into a pit of inaction. Some cling to phenomena, throwing themselves into the net of illusion.

Some annihilate boundaries and obliterate tracks, turning away from the door of dual illumination. Some maintain rectitude, keeping to the center, but lose the sense of expedient technique.

Some cultivate concentration or insight one-sidedly, without balance, thus rotting the sprouts of the path. Some carry out vows all alone, burying the family of the enlightened.

Some work on the practice of inaction to cultivate fabricated enlightenment. Some cling to the nonclinging mind, learning imitation insight.

Some aim for purity, misunderstanding the true nature of defilement. Some dwell on the absolute and lose the basic emptiness of the mundane.

Some practice formless contemplation, blocking true suchness. Some conceive a sense of knowing but thereby turn away from the essence of reality.

Some stick by true explanation but develop literalistic views. Some drink the elixir of immortality yet die young.

Some are so earnest about the principle of completeness that they develop an attitude of clinging attachment; they drink the nectar but turn it into poison.

The foregoing has been a brief notice of one hundred twenty kinds of views and understandings characteristic of false cults. All of them have lost the source and turned away from the essential message.

The Cooperation of Concentration and Insight

In Zen and the Teachings there are two methods, most honored of the myriad practices of ten perfections. At first they are called stopping and seeing, to help new learners; later they become concentration and wisdom, roots of enlightenment.

These are only one reality, which seems to have two parts. In the silence of the essence of reality is stopping by comprehending truth; when silent yet ever aware, subtle seeing is there.

Concentration is the father, insight the mother; they can conceive the thousand sages, developing their faculties and powers, nurturing their sacred potential, giving birth to buddhas and Zen masters in every moment of thought.

Concentration is the general, insight the minister; they can assist the mind monarch in attaining the unexcelled, providing forever means for all to realize the Way, in the manner of the enlightenment of the ancient buddhas.

Concentration is like the moonlight shining so brightly that the stars of errant falsehood vanish. If you can hold up the torch of knowledge, so much the clearer. Irrigating the sprouts of enlightenment, it removes emotional bondage.

Insight is like the sun shining, breaking up the darkness of ignorance. It is able to cause the Zen of the ignorant with false views to turn into transcendent wisdom.

A brief time of silence, a moment of stillness, gradually build up into correct concentration. The sages, making comparatively little effort, ultimately saw the subtle essence of the pedestal of the spirit.

As soon as you hear even a little bit of the Teaching, it can influence your subconscious such that seeds of awakening develop. The moment you turn the light of awareness around, accurate cognition opens up; in an instant you can accomplish Buddha's teaching like this.

The power of meditative concentration is inconceivable; it changes the ordinary into sages instantly. Boundless birth and death is thereby severed at the root; the nest of accumulated ages of mundane toils is destroyed. This is the water that stills the mind, the pearl that purifies the will; its light engulfs myriad forms, lighting a thousand roads.

When you open your own eyes, there are no obstructions; originally there is nothing in the world that constrains. When thieves of attention and reflection are quelled in a timely manner, then the sickness of obsession with objects suddenly clears up.

Washing away the dirt of thoughts and cleaning away the dust of confusion reveals the body of reality and strengthens the life of wisdom. Like an immutable mountain, like a still sea, even if the sky should flip and the earth overturn, you would not be changed. Bright as crystal imbued with moonlight, serene and unbound, you are independent.

No one can measure the insight of wisdom; it naturally manifests the light of the mind according to the occasion. It is the leader of myriad practices, the spiritual ruler at all times. It evaporates the ocean of misery and shatters the mountains of falsehood.

When the clouds of illusion withdraw completely for a while, the gold in the poor woman's house shows up all at once, and the pearl embedded in the wrestler's forehead re-emerges. Cutting through the web of folly, interrupting the flow of desires, the awesome power of the great hero has no peer; it can cool the iron beds and copper stakes of hell and cause the results of the actions of demons and antagonists to cease. Settling disputes, fulfilling honor and justice, everywhere it shows people the wisdom of the buddhas. Biased and perverted knowledge is all subordinated to the source; both the smallest and the greatest alike receive direction.

One-sided cultivation of concentration is pure yin; it corrodes people and erodes right livelihood. If you use accurate insight to illuminate meditation, all things will naturally be clear as a mirror.

One-sided cultivation of insight is pure yang; it withers people and makes them linger on the way. You should use subtle concentration to help contemplative exercise, like the clear light of the moon removing a film of mist.

I recommend equal cultivation of concentration and insight, not one-sided practice. They are originally one entity, not two things. It is like a bird flying through the sky with two wings, or like a chariot drawn on two wheels. Thus in the course of ordinary life you climb up onto the shore of awakening, then sail the boat of compassion on the ocean of karma.

There is concentration on the concrete, in which everything is accomplished by placing the mind on one point. There is concentration on the abstract, in which one must only look directly into the essential nature of mind.

There is contemplation of the concrete, in which one clarifies the characteristics of things and develops judgment. There is contemplation of the abstract, in which it is suddenly realized there is no One and no Beyond.

Insofar as concentration itself is insight, they are not one, not two, not any calculation of mind. Insofar as insight itself is concentration, they are not the same, not different, beyond looking and listening.

Sometimes they are operated together, so you are tranquil yet perceptive, penetrating the teaching of the real. Sometimes they both disappear; neither concentration nor insight, this transcends ordinary standards.

Entering concentration in one atom and arising from it in a multitude of atoms is something natural in the context of transcendent insight. While absorbed in the state of a child, you discuss the laws of reality in the state of an elderly person. If you can see into a single object, all objects are the same; an atom near at hand or a land far away—all are comprehended. On the road of true suchness, you discourse on birth and death; in the ocean of ignorance, you expound the complete religion. The eye can do the enlightened work of the nose; entering concentration in an atom of matter, you arise from concentration in an atom of scent.

Mind and objects are always the same; it is views that differ. Who speaks of not working on cultivation—waves are originally water. Neither silent nor shining, beyond words and thought, yet tranquil and perceptive, effective without compare: temporal and true both carried out, you open the right road; substance and function helping each other, you embody the subtle message.

I urge you not to throw away time, for it's swift as an arrow, fast as a stream. Distraction is entirely due to lack of concentration; stupidity and blindness are caused by lack of true knowledge.

Genuinely true words should be admitted into the ears. A thousand scriptures and ten thousand treatises indicate the same thing: the total effect of concentration and insight should never be forgotten—in a single moment you return at once to the state of real awakeness.

Concentration needs practice; insight needs learning. Don't let the spiritual pedestal be dimmed at all.

A massive tree grows from a tiny sprout; effective work gradually accumulated produces value and excellence. Even an ape that learns concentration is born in a heavenly realm; a little girl, with a moment's thought, enters the door of the Way.

When you can help yourself and also help others, then cause and effect are fulfilled; no one can talk of doing this without concentration and insight.

Glossary of Proper Names, Technical Terms, and Zen Stories

Sanskrit Names

ANANDA One of Buddha's major disciples, particularly noted for learning. See *Transmission of Light*, chapter 3.

ARYADEVA Reckoned as the fifteenth Indian patriarch of Zen, Aryadeva (also called Kanadeva) was a disciple of the great Buddhist philosopher Nagarjuna and also a distinguished metaphysician himself. See *Transmission of Light*, chapter 16.

AVALOKITESHVARA A prototypical bodhisattva, or enlightening being. The name literally means "the capacity of objective observation." This figure represents compassion. See *The Flower Ornament Scripture*, "Entry into the Realm of Reality."

BRAHMA A Hindu god, especially associated with creation.

DIPANKARA BUDDHA Also referred to in Chinese by a translation of the name, "Lamp," Dipankara was, according to illustrative tradition, a buddha of high antiquity in whose presence Shakyamuni Buddha was originally inspired to seek buddhahood.

INDRA "King of gods," Indra is a Hindu deity presiding over thirty-three celestial domains.

MAHASTHAMAPRAPTA A prototypical bodhisattva, representing spiritual power, popular in Pure Land Buddhist tradition. The name means "Imbued with Great Power."

MANJUSHRI A prototypical bodhisattva, representing wisdom and knowledge. The name means "Glorious One." See *The Flower Ornament Scripture*, books 9 and 10.

NAGARJUNA Sometimes considered the greatest Buddhist thinker after Buddha himself, Nagarjuna is the author of the seminal work on emptiness and the Middle Way. He is also traditionally said to have been responsible for recovering the *Prajnaparamita* and *Avatamsaka* scriptures from another realm of consciousness. Nagarjuna is traditionally considered the fourteenth Indian patriarch of Zen and also a patriarch or "patron saint" of T'ien-t'ai, Pure Land, and Tantric Buddhism. See *Transmission of Light*, chapter 15.

SAMANTABHADRA   A prototypical bodhisattva, "Universal Good," representing practical commitment and action. Also represents the totality of the bodhisattva work. See *The Flower Ornament Scripture*, pages 176–181 and 1503–1518.

SHAKYAMUNI   This name refers to Gautama, the historical Buddha.

TATHAGATA   An epithet of buddhas, meaning those who have arrived at suchness, or objective reality.

VAIROCHANA   The primordial "Cosmic Sun Buddha," Vairochana represents pure awareness or the "body of light."

VIMALAKIRTI   A scriptural figure, a completely enlightened buddha who is also a householder. Vimalakirti, whose name means "Pure Name" or "Undefiled Repute," stands for the Dharma itself. See *The Blue Cliff Record*, story 84.

YAJNADATTA   This name refers to an illustrative story commonly used in Zen. A man named Yajnadatta looked in the mirror one day and didn't see his face. Not realizing the mirror had been reversed and he was looking at the unreflective back side, Yajnadatta rushed around in a frenzy, thinking he had lost his head. This represents the way we tend to get lost in objects and influenced by situations and so forget our real minds and real selves.

Chinese Names

GRAND MASTER MA   Ma Tsu, a brilliant eighth-century master, disciple of Huai-jang (q.v.) and teacher of most of the Zen masters of the generation succeeding him. Ma Tsu and Hsi-ch'ien (Shih-t'ou) were considered the greatest teachers of their time, and many of their students studied with both of them.

HSI-CH'IEN   More commonly referred to as Shih-t'ou. An outstanding master of the eighth century, author of the early classic *Ts'an T'ung Ch'i*, or "Integration of Differentiation and Unity."

HSING-SSU An eighth-century master, disciple of Hui-neng, the Sixth Patriarch of Zen according to the reckoning of the Southern School. Hsing-ssu was the teacher of Shih-t'ou and is regarded as the common ancestor of the Zen Houses of Ts'ao-Tung, Yun-men, and Fa-yen.

HUAI-JANG An eighth-century master, disciple of Hui-neng, the Sixth Patriarch of Zen. Huai-jang was the teacher of Ma Tsu and is regarded as the common ancestor of the Zen Houses of Kuei-Yang and Lin-chi.

HUI-NENG The Sixth Patriarch or Grand Master of Zen, according to the reckoning of the Southern School of Zen, which followed him and ultimately grew to overwhelming predominance over other schools of Zen, such as the Northern School and the Ox Head School. According to tradition, Hui-neng, who died in the early eighth century, was an illiterate woodcutter who attained the highest degrees of enlightenment spontaneously, through "the knowledge that has no teacher."

LI T'UNG-HSUAN An eighth-century lay Buddhist expert on the *Avatamsaka* or *Hua-yen* scripture, author of one of the most famous commentaries. See *The Flower Ornament Scripture*, appendix 3.

LU-SHAN Zen master Pao-yun, a successor of the eighth-century great Ma Tsu.

MA TSU See Grand Master Ma.

MASTER CHIH Pao Chih, an uncanny fifth- to sixth-century mystic, author of didactic poetry prized by Zen Buddhists; also figures in didactic stories.

SENG CHAO A fourth- or fifth-century Buddhist scholar and mystic, disciple of the famous translator Kumarajiva, author of a number of unusual essays highly esteemed by Zen students.

SHEN-HSIU A seventh-century Zen master, considered the sixth patriarch of Zen according to the Northern Tradition.

SHIH-T'OU See Hsi-ch'ien.

SIXTH PATRIARCH Refers to the Southern Tradition: see Hui-neng.

TE-SHAN A ninth-century Zen master, teacher of the great Hsueh-feng, ancestor of the Yun-men House of Zen. In Zen lore, Te-shan is represented as occasionally hitting seekers in order to jar them out of closed-circuit thought habits.

YEN-T'OU An unusual ninth- to tenth-century master, conventionally referred to as a successor of Te-shan; inspired the final enlightenment of Hsueh-feng.

Technical Terms

AGE OF IMITATION According to Buddhist tradition, the teaching goes through three general periods: true, imitation, and degenerate. There are different reckonings of historical epicycles of the teaching; the one that places the classical Zen masters of China at the end of the age of imitation figures the true teaching to last five hundred years, followed by a thousand years of imitation teaching.

BODHISATTVAS Enlightening beings; may refer to people who are dedicated to universal enlightenment, or to supernal beings reflecting the essential principles of Buddhism.

CLUSTERS OF MENTAL AND PHYSICAL ELEMENTS Form, sensation, perception, conditioning, and consciousness.

COMPLETE ALL-AT-ONCE The most advanced mode of teaching and learning, according to the T'ien-t'ai school of Buddhism, in which the totality of truth is represented as a whole and apprehended in a nonsequential mode.

CONCENTRATION AND WISDOM Essential ingredients of Zen meditation. Without wisdom, concentration exaggerates and perpetuates flaws of character; without concentration, wisdom is unstable and hard to apply.

CONTEMPLATION OF THE REALM OF REALITY A seminal contemplation guide by Tu Shun (557–640), considered the founder of the Hua-yen or Flower Ornament school of Buddhism in China, based on the scripture by that name. Tu Shun's work was also valued by Zen Buddhists. The work in question, with a detailed explanation by a later master, is translated in full in my *Entry into the Inconceivable: An Introduction to Hua-Yen Buddhism* (University of Hawaii Press, 1983).

EIGHT CONCENTRATIONS A system of meditation consisting of the four stages of meditation (q.v.) plus the four formless attainments of absorption in infinity of space, absorption in infinity of consciousness, absorption in infinity of nothingness, and absorption in neither perception nor nonperception.

EIGHT TEACHINGS A classification scheme of T'ien-t'ai Buddhism for encompassing the diverse totality of Buddhist teachings within a single framework. The Eight Teachings refer to four levels of doctrine and four modes of teaching. The four levels of doctrine are called Tripitaka, referring to the elementary teachings; Common, referring to the teaching of emptiness common to all bodhisattvas; Separate, referring to unitarian teachings perceptible only to higher bodhisattvas; and Complete, for the highest bodhisattvas, in which the totality of truth is reflected all at once. The four modes are gradual, sudden, unfixed, and secret.

FACE A WALL This represents ignorance and inability to cope with differentiation.

FIRE HEXAGRAM A symbolic figure from the ancient Chinese *I Ching*. The Fire trigram consists of two solid lines with a broken line between them; the Fire hexagram consists of two Fire trigrams, one on top of the other. In Zen usage, this figure symbolizes integration of the relative and the absolute, and integration of the discursive and intuitive modes of cognition through which the relative and absolute are discerned.

FIVE TIMES A T'ien-t'ai Buddhist classification scheme, designed to group scriptures categorically according to a particular type of teaching proper to a particular time envisioned in the teaching career of Buddha. The first time is that of the *Flower Ornament Scripture*, when Buddha first revealed his whole enlightenment after his awakening. The second time is called that of the shallows, when Buddha backtracked to teach elementary methods of self-purification, in view of the inability of the vast majority to understand the *Flower Ornament* at first. The third time is called that of rebuke, or turning from the small to the great. This is when attachment to elementary methodology is rebuked and the perspective of Mahayana Buddhism is introduced. The fourth time is that of the perfection of wisdom, in which all attachments are resolved in emptiness. The fifth is the time of the Lotus and Great Demise, in which Buddha preached the unity and eternity of truth and the universality of the essence of buddhahood.

FIVE VEHICLES Variously defined in T'ien-t'ai and Hua-yen Buddhism, these represent different levels of aspiration and action, ranging from social morality, enhancement of consciousness, and inner peace to higher enlightenment and complete awakening of mind.

FOUR STAGES OF MEDITATION The first stage is defined by attention, reflection, joy, bliss, and single-mindedness. The second stage is defined by inner purity, joy, bliss, and single-mindedness. The third stage is defined by equanimity, recollection, insight, bliss, and single-mindedness. The fourth stage is defined by neither pain nor pleasure, equanimity, recollection, and single-mindedness.

GHEE A symbol of buddha nature, which is considered a latent potential within the human mind, just as ghee (clarified butter) is a latent potential in milk.

LAMP BUDDHA Dipankara Buddha (q.v.); symbolizes primordial awareness.

MOUNT HENG One of the five sacred mountains of China.

ONE VEHICLE Sanskrit *Ekayana*; this term refers to the most comprehensive manifestations of Buddhism. The One Vehicle is perceived, understood, and defined in different ways. Of particular interest is the complementary contrast between the "centripetal" unitarianism of the *Saddharmapundarika-sutra*, or Lotus scripture, and the "centrifugal" unitarianism of the *Avatamsaka-sutra*, or Flower Ornament scripture. The *Sandhinirmocana-sutra*, which gives the philosophy and technology of Buddhist yoga, expounds the Ekayana concept in terms of the unity of absolute truth. The unitarianism of Zen is rooted in what is called One Mind, or a unified mind, from which perspective it is able to accommodate both Lotus and Flower Ornament visions of unity as well as the unity of absolute truth.

SIX COURSES OF MUNDANE EXISTENCE Animals (symbolizing folly), ghosts (symbolizing greed), titans (symbolizing aggression), hells (symbolizing folly, greed, and hatred together), humanity (symbolizing social virtues), and heavens (symbolizing meditation states).

SIX PERFECTIONS Generosity, morality, tolerance, diligence, meditation, and insight.

STOPPING AND SEEING The two sides of meditation; stopping delusion and seeing truth.

TATHAGATA An epithet of buddhas.

TEN ABODES Initial determination; preparing the ground; practical action; noble birth; fulfillment of skill in means; correct state of mind; nonregression; youthful nature; prince of the teaching; and coronation. See *The Flower Ornament Scripture*, book 15.

TEN DEDICATIONS Dedication to saving all sentient beings without having any mental image of sentient beings; indestructible dedication; dedication equal to all buddhas; dedication reaching all places; dedication of inexhaustible treasuries of virtue; dedication causing all roots of goodness to endure; dedication equally adapting to all sentient beings; dedication with the character of true thusness; unattached, unbound, liberated dedication; and boundless dedication equal to the cosmos. See *The Flower Ornament Scripture*, book 25.

TEN FAITHS Elements of mental preparation: faith, mindfulness, diligence, intelligence, concentration, perseverance, stability, dedication, discipline, and commitment.

TEN GREAT DISCIPLES OF BUDDHA A group of Buddha's disciples, including often-mentioned names like Shariputra, Kasyapa, Subhuti, Ananda, Maudgalyayana, and so on, representing a variety of personalities and psychological types of students.

TEN PERFECTIONS The six perfections (q.v.), plus vowing, skill in means, power, and knowledge.

TEN PRACTICES Giving joy; beneficial action; nonopposition; indomitability; nonconfusion; good manifestation; nonattachment; overcoming difficulty; good teaching; and truth. See *The Flower Ornament Scripture*, book 21.

TENTH STAGE The highest stage of bodhisattvahood. See *The Flower Ornament Scripture*, pages 789–799.

THREE BASKETS A term for the Buddhist canon.

THREE REALMS OF EXISTENCE The realm of desire, the realm of form, and the formless realm.

THREE STUDIES The overall Buddhist curriculum: studies in discipline, concentration, and wisdom.

THREE VEHICLES Followers, Self-Enlightened, and Bodhisattva; the first two are called lesser; the third is called greater. The first two culminate in individual liberation, and the third is dedicated to universal enlightenment.

THUNDERBOLT IMPLEMENT A ritual implement used in Tantric Buddhism; in Ts'ao-Tung Zen, it stands for "five in one," referring to the five ranks of Zen as five facets of one reality.

TRIPLEX WORLD The conditioned world, called triplex in reference to the three realms of desire, form, and formlessness.

TWENTY-FIVE DOMAINS OF BEING A representation of the spectrum of conditioned mentalities or psychological states.

TWO LESSER VEHICLES The courses of followers and self-enlightened individuals, whose goal is personal salvation; also called simply "two vehicles."

TWO TRUTHS Relative truth and absolute truth; all Buddha's teachings are based on the assumption of two truths, often shifting point of reference from relative to absolute and absolute to relative.

UNITARY VEHICLE See One Vehicle.

WHITE OX ON OPEN GROUND A symbol of buddha nature revealed.

WRESTLER WITH A GEM EMBEDDED IN HIS FOREHEAD A symbol of buddha nature concealed.

Zen Stories

MASTER AN'S SAYING ON THE TEACHING HALL A monk entered the teaching hall of Master Ta-An, looked around, and said, "A fine teaching hall, but there's no one here." The master came through the door and said, "How so?" The monk had no reply.

PAI-CHANG'S SAYING "WHAT IS IT?" Master Pai-chang drove everyone from his teaching hall, then just as they were leaving, he called to them and said, "What is it?"

TUNG-SHAN'S REPLY TO YUN-YEN'S GINGER-DIGGING SAYING As Tung-shan was hoeing a ginger plot with Yun-yen, the latter made reference to a Zen master of the past. Tung-shan asked,

"Where has this man gone?" Yun-yen remained silent for a good while, then said, "What? What?" Tung-shan said, "Too late!"

WEN-SHU AND TEA DRINKING As Wen-shu was drinking tea with Wu-cho, he held up a crystal cup and asked Wu-cho, "Do they also have *this* in the South?" Wu-cho replied, "No." Wen-shu said, "Then what do they usually use for drinking tea?" Wu-cho had no reply. Later Tung-shan brought up this story: in behalf of Wu-cho he held out his hand and said, "Leaving 'yes' and 'no' aside for the moment, can I borrow this?"

YAO-SHAN AND CH'UN PU-NA ON WASHING BUDDHA Ch'un Pu-na was performing the ceremony of washing an icon of Buddha: Yao-shan asked, "You may wash *this one*, but can you wash *that one?*" Ch'un replied, "Bring me *that one.*" Yao-shan then stopped.

YAO-SHAN'S SAYING ON WEARING A SWORD As Yao-shan was traveling in the mountains with Yun-yen, his sword rattled at his side. Yun-yen said, "What's making that sound?" Yao-shan drew his sword and made a cutting gesture. Later Tung-shan remarked on this story, "See how Yao-shan lays himself down for this task; if people of the present want to understand the transcendental, it is necessary to understand the meaning of this first."

Further Readings

Scriptural Sources

T. Cleary. *Dhammapada: The Sayings of Buddha.* New York: Bantam Books, 1995.

Buddhist Yoga: A Comprehensive Course. Boston: Shambhala Publications, 1995.

The Flower Ornament Scripture. Boston: Shambhala Publications, 1993.

Zen Works

T. Cleary. *Transmission of Light: Zen in the Art of Enlightenment.* Classics of Buddhism and Zen, vol. 4. Boston: Shambhala Publications, 2001.

Zen Essence: The Science of Freedom. Classics of Buddhism and Zen, vol. 1. Boston: Shambhala Publications, 2001.

Zen Lessons: The Art of Leadership. Classics of Buddhism and Zen, vol. 1. Boston: Shambhala Publications, 2001.

T. & J.C. Cleary, *The Blue Cliff Record.* Boston: Shambhala Publications, 1977, 1992.

Zen Letters: Teachings of Yuanwu. Classics of Buddhism and Zen, vol. 2. Boston: Shambhala Publications, 2001.

J.C. Cleary, *Zen Dawn.* Boston: Shambhala Publications, 1996.

MINDING MIND
A Course in Basic Meditation

INTRODUCTION

Let the wise one watch over the mind,
    so hard to perceive, so artful,
    alighting where it wishes;
a watchfully protected mind
will bring happiness.

        —DHAMMAPADA

Sages use the mind deliberately,
    based on its essence.
With the support of the spirit,
    they finish what they begin.
Thus they sleep without dreams
    and wake without troubles.

        —HUAINANZI

Conscious cultivation of consciousness has been practiced by human beings for thousands of years, giving rise to many traditional sciences of mental development whose origins are lost in the dimness of the early dawn twilight of human awareness. Buddhist tradition is based on a breakthrough made by Siddhartha Gautama twenty-five hundred years ago in his attempts to rediscover the essential way to *moksha*, liberation, and *bodhi*, enlightenment, lost ideals of ancient tradition.

The mental science of Buddhism is extremely rich and complex. It is not simply an outgrowth, reformulation, or development of ancient Indian religion. According to Buddhist lore, there are five general categories of practice by which the relations and differences among orientations and methods of meditation can be distinguished.

The first type is called the meditation of the ordinary mortal. The intention and purpose of this type of meditation is to enhance the ordinary perceptions and faculties of the individual. The desired result is greater efficacy and efficiency in the ordinary activities of life, leading to a sense of confidence and well-being.

The second type of meditation is quite different from the first, focusing on transcending the world rather than dealing with the world in conventional terms. The desired result is quiescent nirvana, a profound peace of mind characterized by extinction of psychological afflictions. Exceptional psychic capacities are also commonly associated with people who attain quiescent nirvana in this way, but because they habitually remain in the quiescence of individual nirvana they do not ordinarily exercise these capacities in a concerted manner.

The third type of meditation focuses on the cultivation of altered states of consciousness. Those who practice meditation for the sake of attaining nirvana may also use these altered states for the purpose of breaking attachments to conceptual and perceptual conventions, but they are thereby exposed to the danger of addiction to intoxicating trances. Buddhist teaching emphasizes sobriety to avoid being obsessed, or as it is said, "reborn under the sway" of unusual states, taking care to use them for specific pragmatic purposes rather than for self-indulgence.

The fourth kind of meditation is dedicated to development of extraordinary capacities in the service of other people and the world at large. Practitioners of this type of meditation may use any or all of the methods and techniques characteristic of the first three kinds of meditation, but with a different orientation, in a different manner, and in a broader context. The range and scope of meditational states and experiences in this fourth category, furthermore, exceed those of the lower types of meditation by many orders of magnitude.

The fifth and highest type of meditation, according to this ancient classification, is called pure clear meditation arriving at being-as-is. This is considered the most penetrating insight and the nearest that an individual consciousness can come to true objectivity. The realization of pure clear meditation also enables its master to employ all the other types of meditation method deliberately and freely, without becoming fixated or obsessed.

Minding Mind is a compendium of instruction manuals dealing primarily with ways of attaining to the mode of experience characteristic of the last-named type of meditation, pure clear meditation arriving at being-as-is.

The first manual, *Treatise on the Supreme Vehicle*, is attributed to Hongren (602–675), who is known as the Fifth Patriarch of Chan Buddhism in China. There appears to be no historical trace of this text previous to the sixteenth century, and its origins are obscure. Although Hongren, like his teacher and several of his own disciples, was an illustrious Chan master of his time, little is really known for sure about his teaching or the activities of his school.

The language of this meditation manual would also suggest that it was in fact written in the sixteenth century, although certain passages, especially the quotations, do not reflect typical sixteenth-century Buddhist scholarship or language, and they give the impression that the text as we know it today is based on an older model. It may also be a product of a Korean branch of the ancient school. The method taught in this manual is basic and quintessential in theory and practice, setting the stage for the texts that follow.

The second manual, *Models for Sitting Meditation*, was composed by Chan Buddhist Master Cijiao of Changlu in late eleventh-century China. Little is known of Cijiao, except that he was not only a master of the powerful Linji school of Chan Buddhism but also a patriarch of popular Pure Land Buddhism. The combination of Chan and Pure Land Buddhism, especially in the domain of concentration technique, is commonly found in the records of early meditation schools of China, Korea, Japan, Tibet, and Vietnam.

The next manual, *Guidelines for Sitting Meditation*, was written by Foxin Bencai, a younger contemporary of Cijiao. The instructions of Foxin and Cijiao, both quite brief, address problems of deterioration in the quality of meditation practices and prescribe simple remedies to counteract confusion and misalignment in order to foster the proper state of mind.

These two texts are followed by another short manual for general audiences, *A Generally Recommended Mode of Sitting Meditation*, by the Japanese Zen Master Dōgen. Dōgen (1200–1253) was one of the pioneers of Zen Buddhism in Japan. Scion of a distinguished and powerful family, Dōgen was originally trained as a Confucian and groomed for ministerial service in the imperial government. He also began to study Buddhism at an early age, however, and ran away from home to become a Buddhist monk, on the eve of his debut at court.

Dōgen was an intellectually brilliant individual and mastered the theories of the exoteric and esoteric branches of the old Tendai school of Japanese Buddhism in a comparatively short time. Even before his Tendai studies were over, Dōgen began to look into Zen, newly imported from continental China. Eventually he came to concentrate on Zen, and even though he was locally recognized as a master at an early age, Dōgen decided to cross over into China to study Chan, the precursor of Zen, as it was then being practiced on the continent.

After five years in China, Dōgen returned to Japan with a more complete understanding of Zen than he had been able to acquire earlier. He spent nearly ten more years observing the situation in Japan before beginning to teach. One of the main concerns of Dōgen's teaching activity was to alert people to the shortcomings and dangers of incomplete Zen meditation and partial Zen experience. This manual, one of Dōgen's first written works, reflects this concern and outlines an approach to its resolution.

The next manual presented here, *Secrets of Cultivating the Mind*, was composed by Chinul (1158–1210), founder of the Chogye order of Korean Buddhism. Ordained as a monk at the age of eight, Chinul had no teacher. His first awakening occurred as he read a Chan Buddhist classic when he was twenty-five years old. After that, Chinul went into seclusion in the mountains. Later on, he perused the whole Buddhist canon, then went back into solitude in a mountain fastness. During this period, Chinul experienced another awakening while reading the letters of one of the great Chinese masters.

Eventually Chinul began to instruct others, establishing a number of teaching centers. He attracted the attention of the Buddhist king of Koryo Korea and was honored with the title National Teacher after his passing. Based on classical teachings, Chinul's *Secrets of Cultivating the Mind* is a highly accessible primer of basic Buddhist meditation, defining and contrasting the principles and methods of sudden and gradual enlightenment.

The next manual translated here, *Absorption in the Treasury of Light*, was written by the Japanese Zen Master Ejō (1198–1282). Born into an ancient noble family, Ejō became a Buddhist monk at the age of eighteen. After studying Tendai Buddhism, Ejō concentrated on Pure Land Buddhism, then turned to Zen. Eventually he became an apprentice of Zen master Dōgen, who soon appointed Ejō his teaching assistant and spiritual successor.

Most of Ejō's later life was devoted to perpetuating the works of his teacher Dōgen, whom he survived by thirty years. The unusual

Absorption in the Treasury of Light is Ejō's own composition. Reflecting Ejō's background in the esoteric branch of Tendai Buddhism as well as his classical Zen studies, this work shows how to focus on the so-called Dharmakāya, or Reality Body teaching of Buddhism, underlying a wide variety of symbolic expressions. This type of meditation, using scriptural extracts, poetry, and Zen koans, or teaching stories, to register a specific level of consciousness, is called *sanzen*. There is a great deal of Zen literature deriving from centuries of *sanzen*, among which Ejō's *Absorption in the Treasury of Light* represents a very unusual blend of complexity and simplicity, depth and accessibility.

The last meditation manual, *An Elementary Talk on Zen*, is attributed to Man-an, an old adept of a Sōtō school of Zen who is believed to have lived in the early seventeenth century. The Sōtō schools of Zen in that time traced their spiritual lineages back to Dōgen and Ejō, but their doctrines and methods were not quite the same as the ancient masters', reflecting later accretions from other schools.

Man-an's work is very accessible and extremely interesting for the range of its content. In particular, it reflects a modern trend toward emphasis on meditation in action, which can be seen in China particularly from the eleventh century, in Korea from the twelfth century, and in Japan from the fourteenth century.

A few years ago, the central authority of the Roman Catholic Church issued a statement about meditation, warning that altered mental and physical states could be mistaken by the unwary for authentic spiritual experiences. Although this statement provoked a negative reaction from certain meditation groups, the fact is that the same warning is traditional in authentic Buddhism.

The fact that many Westerners have been left confused and even mentally and physically injured by supposed Eastern meditation methods is not because they were not good Catholics but because they failed to observe all the requirements of traditional meditation science. The psychopathology of meditative malpractice is well known and thoroughly described in Buddhist literature, but certain cults regularly plunge people into intensive meditation without sufficient background knowledge, understanding, and experience. Sometimes this is not done out of sheer ignorance but as a calculated recruitment tool, because people become extremely vulnerable to fixation and conditioning under these circumstances.

It was for this reason that the Tibetan Gelugpa, or Virtuous school, whose head is the Dalai Lama, reformed the practice of meditation to prevent such abuses. In that school the practitioner is expected to become thoroughly familiar with the science of meditation before plunging into intense concentration. The Chan-Taoist Master Liu I-ming similarly encouraged people to study for ten years before starting intensive meditation. The early modern Japanese Zen master Kōsen prescribed a course of study requiring about three years before he allowed students to participate in concentrated Zen work with a teacher.

Preparatory study is also useful for recognition and evaluation of teachers, an issue of serious concern to Westerners. If you go to a real teacher unprepared, you will be wasting the teacher's time and unconsciously demonstrating your own greed and laziness as well; if you go to a false teacher unprepared, you will be wasting your own time and putting yourself and your dependents in danger besides. Hence the classical Chan saying, "First awaken on your own, then see someone else." That is the purpose for which the instruction manuals presented in this book were originally composed and published.

CHAN MASTER HONGREN
Treatise on the Supreme Vehicle

In aiming for the enlightenment of sages to understand the true 1
source, if the essential issue of cultivating the mind is not kept pure,
there is no way for any practice to yield realization. If any good
friends copy this text, be careful not to omit anything, lest you cause
people of later times to err.

The basic essence of cultivating enlightenment should be dis- 2
cerned: it is the inherently complete and pure mind, in which there is
no false discrimination, and body and mind are fundamentally pure,
unborn, and undying. This is the basic teacher; this is better than
invoking the Buddhas of the ten directions.

Question: How do we know that the inherent mind is fundamen- 3
tally pure?

Answer: According to *The Ten Stages Scripture*, there is an indestructible Buddha-nature in the bodies of living beings, like the orb of
the sun, its body luminous, round and full, vast and boundless; but
because it is covered by the dark clouds of the five clusters, it cannot
shine, like a lamp inside a pitcher.

When there are clouds and fog everywhere, the world is dark, but
that does not mean the sun has decomposed. Why is there no light?
The light is never destroyed; it is just enshrouded by clouds and fog.
The pure mind of all living beings is like this, merely covered up by
the dark clouds of obsession with objects, arbitrary thoughts, psychological afflictions, and views and opinions. If you can just keep the
mind still so that errant thought does not arise, the reality of nirvana
will naturally appear. This is how we know the inherent mind is originally pure.

Question: How do we know the inherent mind is fundamentally 4
unborn and undying?

Answer: *The Scripture Spoken by Vimalakīrti* says that suchness has no birth and suchness has no death. Suchness is true thusness, the Buddha-nature that is inherently pure. Purity is the source of mind; true thusness is always there and does not arise from conditions.

The scripture also says that all ordinary beings are *thus*, and all sages and saints are also *thus*. "All ordinary beings" refers to us; "all sages and saints" refers to the Buddhas. Although their names and appearances differ, the objective nature of true thusness in their bodies is the same. Being unborn and undying, it is called *thus*. This is how we know the inherent mind is fundamentally unborn and undying.

5   Question: Why call the inherent mind the basic teacher?

Answer: This true mind is natural and does not come from outside. It is not confined to cultivation in past, present, or future. The dearest and most intimate thing there could be is to preserve the mind yourself. If you know the mind, you will reach transcendence by preserving it. If you are confused about the mind and ignore it, you will fall into miserable states. Thus we know that the Buddhas of all times consider the inherent mind to be the basic teacher. Therefore a treatise says, "Preserve the mind with perfect clarity so that errant thoughts do not arise, and this is birthlessness." This is how we know the mind is the basic teacher.

6   Question: What does it mean to say that the inherent mind is better than invoking other Buddhas?

Answer: Even if you constantly invoke other Buddhas, you will not escape birth and death; but if you preserve your own basic mind, you will arrive at transcendence. *The Diamond Cutter Scripture* says that anyone who views Buddha in terms of form or seeks Buddha through sound is traveling an aberrant path and cannot see the real Buddha. Therefore it is said that preserving the true mind is better than invoking other Buddhas.

The word *better*, nevertheless, is only used to encourage people. In reality, the essence of the ultimate realization is equal, without duality.

7   Question: Since the true essence of Buddhas and ordinary beings is the same, why do Buddhas experience infinite happiness and unhindered freedom, without birth or death, while we ordinary beings fall into birth and death and suffer all sorts of pains?

Answer: The Buddhas of the ten directions realized the true nature of things and spontaneously perceive the source of mind; errant imagining does not arise, accurate awareness is not lost. The egoistic, possessive attitude disappears, so they are not subject to birth and death. Because they are not subject to birth and death, they are ultimately tranquil; so obviously all happiness naturally comes to them.

Ordinary people lose sight of the nature of reality and do not know the basis of mind. Arbitrarily fixating on all sorts of objects, they do not cultivate accurate awareness; therefore love and hatred arise. Because of love and hatred, the vessel of mind cracks and leaks. Because the vessel of mind cracks and leaks, there is birth and death. Because there is birth and death, all miseries naturally appear.

The Mind King Scripture says that true thusness, the Buddha-nature, is submerged in the ocean of cognition, perception, and sense, bobbing up and down in birth and death, unable to escape. Effort should be made to preserve the basic true mind, so that arbitrary thoughts do not arise, egoistic and possessive attitudes vanish, and you spontaneously realize equality and unity with the Buddhas.

Question: If the Buddha-nature that is truly *thus* is one and the same, then when one is deluded, everyone should be deluded, and when one is enlightened, everyone should be enlightened. Why is it that when Buddhas awaken to this nature, the ignorance and confusion of ordinary people remain the same? 8

Answer: From here on, we enter the domain of the inconceivable, beyond the reach of ordinary people. Enlightenment is realized by knowing mind; confusion happens because of losing touch with nature. If conditions meet, they meet; no fixed statement can be made. Just trust in the truth and preserve your inherent basic mind.

This is why *The Scripture Spoken by Vimalakīrti* says that there is neither selfhood nor otherness, that reality has never been born and does not presently perish. This is realizing the dualistic extremism of identification and alienation, thus entering into nondiscriminatory knowledge. If you understand this point, then preserving the mind is foremost among the essentials of the teachings on practical knowledge. This practice of preserving the mind is the basis of nirvana, the essential doorway into enlightenment, the source of all the scriptures, and the progenitor of the Buddhas of all times.

Question: How do we know that preserving the fundamental true mind is the basis of nirvana? 9

Answer: The essence of nirvana is tranquil, uncontrived bliss. Realize your own mind is the true mind, and errant imagining ceases. When errant imagining ceases, you are accurately aware. By virtue of accurate awareness, dispassionately perceptive knowledge arises. By dispassionately perceptive knowledge, one finds out the nature of reality. By finding out the nature of reality, one attains nirvana. This is how we know that preserving the fundamental true mind is the basis of nirvana.

10   Question: How do we know that preserving the fundamental true mind is the essential doorway into enlightenment?

Answer: "Even if you draw a figure of a Buddha with your finger, or perform countless virtuous deeds . . ."—teachings like this are just Buddha's instructions for ignorant people to create causes for better future states, and even for seeing Buddha. As for those who wish to attain Buddhahood quickly on their own, they should preserve the basic true mind. The Buddhas of past, present, and future are infinite, but not one of them attained Buddhahood without preserving the basic true mind. Therefore a scripture says that if you keep the mind on one point, there is nothing that cannot be accomplished. This is how we know that preserving the basic true mind is the essential doorway into enlightenment.

11   Question: How do we know that preserving the basic true mind is the source of all the scriptures?

Answer: In the scriptures, the Buddha explains all the causes and conditions, results and consequences, of all sins and virtues, drawing upon even the mountains, rivers, earth, grasses, trees, and other beings for countless parables, similes, and metaphors, on occasion manifesting countless varieties of spiritual powers and emanations. This is all because Buddha teaches people who lack insight but have all sorts of desires and innumerable different mentalities.

On this account, the Buddha uses means suited to individual mentalities in order to lead people into universal truth. Once we know that the Buddha-nature in all beings is as pure as the sun behind the clouds, if we just preserve the basic true mind with perfect clarity, the clouds of errant thoughts will come to an end, and the sun of insight will emerge; what is the need for so much more study of knowledge of the pains of birth and death, of all sorts of doctrines and principles, and of the affairs of past, present, and future? It is like wiping the dust off a mirror; the clarity appears spontaneously when the dust is all gone.

Thus whatever is learned in the present unenlightened mind is worthless. If you can maintain accurate awareness clearly, what you learn in the uncontrived mind is true learning.

But even though I call it real learning, ultimately there is nothing learned. Why? Because both the self and nirvana are empty; there is no more two, not even one. Thus there is nothing learned; but even though phenomena are essentially empty, it is necessary to preserve the basic true mind with perfect clarity, because then delusive thoughts do not arise, and egoism and possessiveness disappear. *The Nirvana Scripture* says, "Those who know the Buddha does not preach anything are called fully learned." This is how we know that preserving the basic true mind is the source of all the scriptures.

Question: How do we know that preserving the basic true mind is the progenitor of the Buddhas of all times? 12

Answer: The Buddhas of all times are born from the essence of mind. First preserve the true mind so that errant thoughts do not arise; then, after egoism and possessiveness have vanished, you can attain Buddhahood.

The foregoing dialogues could be expanded endlessly; my hope for now is that you will become conscious that your own basic mind is Buddha. This is why I exhort you so earnestly; nothing in the thousands of scriptures and myriads of treatises surpasses preserving the basic true mind—this is essential. 13

Now I will make further effort to instruct you by reference to *The Lotus of Truth Scripture*'s symbols of the great chariot, the treasure trove, the bright pearl, the wondrous herb: it's just that you yourself do not take and use them; that is why you suffer misery. 14

What should you do? When errant thoughts do not arise, and egoism and possessiveness disappear, then all virtuous qualities come to fulfillment naturally; you need not seek externally, for that brings you back to the miseries of birth and death. Wherever you are, examine your mind with accurate awareness. Do not plant seeds of future misery by attachment to present pleasure, fooling yourself and deceiving others, not getting free of birth and death. 15

Work, work! Although the present is transitory, together make the basis of future Buddhahood. Do not let past, present, and future go to waste, uselessly killing time. A scripture speaks of "being in hell as though it were a pleasure garden" and "being in other bad states as though in your own house." That we ordinary mortals are presently 16 like this unconsciously amazes people totally, but nothing is beyond mind. How wonderful! How miserable!

17   If there are beginners learning to sit and meditate, follow the directions in *The Scripture on Visualization of Infinite Life:* sit straight, accurately aware, with eyes closed and mouth shut. Mentally gaze evenly before you, as near or far as you wish: visualize the sun, preserving the true mind, keeping your attention on this uninterruptedly. Then tune your breathing, not letting it fluctuate between coarseness and fineness, for that causes illness and pain.

18   When you sit and meditate at night, you may see all sorts of scenes, good and bad. Or you may become totally absorbed in blue, yellow, red, white, and so on. You may perceive your body radiating tremendous light, you may see the form of a Buddha, or you may see all sorts of miraculous productions. Just know enough to collect your mind and not be attached to any of that, for all of it is empty, seen only because of subjective imagination. A scripture says, "All lands in the ten directions are like space; all worlds are illusory, just construed by mind."

19   If you do not enter trance and do not see all sorts of visions, do not wonder; just keep the basic true mind perfectly clear at all times, whatever you are doing, so that errant thoughts do not arise and egoism and possessiveness disappear.

20   Nothing is outside the inherent mind; the Buddhas expounded so many doctrines and parables because the patterns of ordinary people's behaviors are not the same. Eventually this caused the frameworks of the teaching to differ, but in reality the substance of the states of the eighty-four thousand doctrines, the three vehicles, and the eightfold path, the source of the seventy-two grades of illuminates, are not beyond the inherent mind, which is the basis. If you know the basic mind firsthand and continue to polish it moment to moment, then you will naturally see the Buddha-nature; at every moment you will be presenting offerings to countless Buddhas of the ten directions, while all the scriptures of the canon will be "recited" in every moment.

21   If you comprehend the mind source, then all meaningful mental phenomena spontaneously appear, all vows come to fulfillment, all practices are completed. Everything is done; you are no longer subject to becoming. It is necessary that errant thoughts do not arise and

egoism and possessiveness disappear; after you relinquish this body, you will certainly attain the uncreate, the inconceivable.

Work! Don't waste a moment. Words as true and undeceptive as these are hard to get to hear; those who hear them and actually put them into practice are extremely rare, and those who practice and actually attain them are even more rare.   22

Calm yourself, quiet yourself, master your senses. Look right into the source of mind, always keep it shining bright, clear and pure. Do not give rise to an indifferent mind.   23

Question: What do you mean by an indifferent mind?   24

Answer: When people who concentrate their minds focus on external objects, and their coarse mentalities cease for a while because of it, they inwardly refine the true mind; when the mind is not yet pure and clear, and they examine the mind constantly, whatever they are doing, and yet are unable to clearly perceive the mind source independently, this is called an indifferent mind.

This is still a contaminated mind, which does not as yet escape the great illness of birth and death. How about those who don't preserve the true mind at all! Such people sink into the bitter sea of birth and death; when will they ever get out? What a pity! Work, work!

Scripture says that if people's true sincerity does not emerge from within, even if they meet countless Buddhas past, present, and future, they can do nothing. Scripture also says that when people know the mind, they liberate themselves; Buddhas cannot liberate people. If Buddhas could liberate people, why have people like us not attained enlightenment in spite of the fact that there have been countless Buddhas in the past? It is just that true sincerity does not come from within; therefore people sink in a sea of bitterness.

Work, work! Diligently seek the basic mind; do not allow random contamination. What is past is not our concern; we cannot catch up with what has already gone by. I urge those who have now, in the present, gotten to hear the subtle teaching, to understand these words: realize that preserving the mind is the foremost path.

If you are unwilling to exercise utmost sincerity in the quest for enlightenment and its experience of infinite freedom and happiness, and instead start making a lot of noise, following the mundane, greedily seeking honor and profit, you will fall into a vast hell and suffer all kinds of misery. What can you do about this? How will you manage? What will you do?   25

26   Work, work! Just dress in old clothes, eat simple food, and preserve the basic true mind with perfect clarity. Feign ignorance, appear inarticulate. This is most economical with energy, yet effective. This is characteristic of very diligent people.

27   Deluded worldly people who do not understand this principle undertake many hardships in ignorance to carry out apparent good on a large scale. They hope to attain liberation, but return to birth and death. As for those who maintain accurate awareness with perfect clarity and liberate other people, they are powerful enlightening beings.

28   I tell you all clearly, preserving the mind is number one; if you do not make any effort to preserve the mind, you are extremely foolish. By not accepting the present, you suffer a lifetime of misery; by wishing for the future, you suffer calamity for myriad aeons. If I indulge you, I don't know what more I can tell you.

29   The one who is unmoved by the blowing of the eight winds is the real mountain of jewels. One who knows the result just acts and speaks with skillful fluidity to adapt to all situations, giving out remedies in accordance with illnesses; one who can do this and yet not conceive false thoughts, so that egoism and possessiveness are extinct, has truly transcended the world.

30   When the Buddha was alive, he had no end of praise for this; I speak of it to encourage you earnestly. If you do not create false ideas and are void of egoism and possessiveness, then you are beyond the world.

31   Question: What is the disappearance of egoism and possessiveness?

Answer: If you have any desire to surpass others, or any thought of your own ability, this is egoism and possessiveness. These are sicknesses in the context of nirvana, so *The Nirvana Scripture* says, "Space can contain everything, but space does not entertain the thought that it can contain everything." This is a metaphor for the disappearance of egoism and possessiveness, by which you proceed to indestructible concentration.

32   Question: Practitioners seeking true eternal peace who care only for the transient crude virtues of the world and do not care for the truly eternal subtle virtues of ultimate truth have not seen the principle, and just want to arouse their minds to focus on doctrines to pursue in thought; as soon as conscious awareness occurs, it is contaminated. But if one wants only to forget the mind, this is the

darkness of ignorance; it is not in accord with true principle. If one just wants to neither stop the mind nor focus on principles, this is wrongly grasping emptiness, living like an animal in spite of being human. At such times, if one has no methods of concentration and insight and cannot understand how to see the Buddha-nature clearly, the practitioner will only get bogged down—how can one transcend this to arrive at complete nirvana? Please point out the true mind.

Answer: You need to have complete confidence and effective determination. Gently quiet your mind, and I will instruct you again.

You should make your own body and mind unfettered and serene, not entangled in any objects at all. Sit straight, accurately aware, and tune your breathing so that it is properly adjusted. Examine your mind to see it as not being inside, not being outside, and not being in between. Observe it calmly, carefully, and objectively; when you master this, you will clearly see that the mind's consciousness moves in a flow, like a current of water, like heat waves rising endlessly.

When you have seen this consciousness, you find it is neither inside nor outside: unhurriedly, objectively, calmly observe. When you master this, then melt and flux over and over, empty yet solid, profoundly stable, and then this flowing consciousness will vanish.

Those who get this consciousness to vanish thereby destroy the obstructing confusions of the enlightening beings of the ten stages. Once this consciousness has vanished, then the mind is open and still, silent, serene and calm, immaculately pure, and tremendously steady.

I cannot explain this state any further. If you want to attain it, take up the chapter in *The Nirvana Scripture* on the indestructible body, and the chapter in *The Scripture Spoken by Vimalakīrti* on seeing the Immovable Buddha: contemplate and reflect on them unhurriedly, search them carefully and read them thoroughly. If you are completely familiar with these scriptures and can actually maintain this mind whatever you are doing, in the face of the five desires and eight winds, then your pure conduct is established and your task is done; in the end you will not be subjected to a body that is born and dies.

The five desires are desires for form, sound, fragrance, flavor, and feeling. The eight winds are profit and loss, censure and praise, respect and ridicule, pain and pleasure. This is where practitioners polish and refine the Buddha-nature; it's no wonder if one does not attain independence in this body. Scripture says, "If there is nowhere for a

Buddha to sojourn in the world, enlightening beings cannot actually function."

If you want to be free of this conditional body, do not discriminate between the past sharpness or dullness of human faculties; the best require but a moment, the least take countless aeons.

33   If you have the strength and the time to develop altruistic roots of virtues according to people's natures, thus to help yourself and others as well, adorning a Buddha-land, you must understand the Four Reliances and find out what reality is actually like. If you rely on clinging to the letter, you will lose the true source.

34   For mendicants learning to study the Way as renunciants, the fact is that "leaving home" means getting out of the fetters of birth and death: that is called "leaving home."

When accurate mindfulness is completely present and cultivation of the Way is successful, even if you are dismembered, as long as you do not lose right mindfulness at the moment of death, you will immediately attain Buddhahood.

35   I have composed the foregoing treatise simply by taking the sense of scriptures according to faith; in reality, I do not know by perfectly complete experience. If there is anything contrary to the Buddha's principles, I will willingly repent and eliminate it; whatever is in accord with the Buddha's path, I donate to all beings, hoping that everyone will get to know the basic mind and attain enlightenment at once. May those who hear this work become Buddhas in the future; I hope you will liberate my followers first.

36   Question: From beginning to end, everything in this treatise reveals that the inherent mind is the Way; does it belong to the category of actualization, or to the category of practice?

Answer: The heart of this treatise is to reveal the One Vehicle. Its ultimate intent, therefore, is to guide the deluded so that they may extricate themselves from birth and death; only then can they liberate others. Speaking only of self-help and not of helping others is characteristic of the category of practice; whoever practices in accord with the text will be the first to attain Buddhahood. If I am deceiving you, in the future I will fall into eighteen hells. I promise to heaven and earth: if I am not being truthful, let me be devoured by tigers and wolves lifetime after lifetime.

Chan Master Cijiao of Changlu
Models for Sitting Meditation

Those who aspire to enlightenment and who would learn wisdom should first arouse an attitude of great compassion and make an all-encompassing vow to master concentration, promising to liberate other people, not seeking liberation for your own self alone. 1

Then and only then should you let go of all objects and put to rest all concerns, so that body and mind are one suchness, and there is no gap between movement and stillness. 2

Moderate your food and drink, taking neither too much nor too little. Regulate your sleep, neither restricting it too much nor indulging in it too much. 3

When you are going to sit in meditation, spread a thick sitting mat in a quiet, uncluttered place. Wear your clothing loosely, but maintain uniform order in your posture and carriage. 4

Then sit in the lotus posture, first placing the right foot on the left thigh, then placing the left foot on the right thigh. The half-lotus posture will also do; just put the left foot on the right leg, that is all. 5

Next, place the right hand on the left ankle, and place the left hand, palm up, on the palm of the right hand. Have the thumbs of both hands brace each other up. 6

Slowly raise the body forward, and also rock to the left and right, then sit straight. Do not lean to the left or right, do not tilt forward or backward. Align the joints of your hips, your spine, and the base of the skull so that they support each other, your form like a stupa. Yet you should not make your body too extremely erect, for that constricts the breathing and makes it uncomfortable. The ears should be aligned with the shoulders, the nose with the navel. The tongue rests on the upper palate, the lips and teeth are touching. 7

The eyes should be slightly open, to avoid bringing on oblivion and drowsiness. If you are going to attain meditation concentration, that 8 power is supreme. In ancient times there were eminent monks specializing in concentration practice who always kept their eyes open when they sat. Chan Master Fayun Yuantong also scolded people for sitting in meditation with their eyes closed, calling it a ghost cave in a mountain of darkness. Evidently there is deep meaning in this, of which adepts are aware.

9   Once the physical posture is settled and the breath is tuned, then relax your lower abdomen. Do not think of anything good or bad. When a thought arises, notice it; when you become aware of it, it disappears. Eventually you forget mental objects and spontaneously become unified. This is the essential art of sitting Zen meditation.

10   In spite of the fact that sitting Zen meditation is a scientific way to peace and bliss, many people do it in a pathological manner that brings on sickness. This is because they do not apply their minds correctly. If you get the true sense, then your body will naturally feel light and easy, while your vital spirit will be clear and keen. True mindfulness is distinctly clear, the savor of truth sustains the spirit, and you experience pure bliss in a state of profound serenity.

11   For those who have already had an awakening, this can be said to be like a dragon finding water, like a tiger in the mountains. For those who have not yet had an awakening, it is still using the wind to blow on the fire; the effort required is not much. Just make the mind receptive and you will not be cheated.

12   Nevertheless, when the Way is lofty, demons abound; all sorts of things offend and please. As long as you keep true mindfulness present, however, none of this can hold you back.

13   The *Shūrangama-sūtra*, the Tiantai manuals of "stopping and seeing," and Guifeng's *Guidelines for Cultivation and Realization* fully explains bedevilments. Those whose preparation is insufficient should not fail to know these.

14   When you want to come out of concentration, slowly rock the body and rise calmly and carefully, avoiding haste.

15   After coming out of concentration, at all times use whatever means expedient to preserve the power of concentration, as if you were taking care of a baby. Then the power of concentration will be easy to perfect.

16   Meditation concentration is a most urgent task. If you do not meditate calmly and reflect quietly, you will be utterly at a loss in this domain. So if you are going to look for a pearl, it is best to still the

waves; it will be hard to find if you stir the water. When the water of concentration is still and clear, the pearl of mind reveals itself.

Therefore *The Scripture of Complete Awakening* says, "Unhin-   17 dered pure wisdom all comes from meditation concentration." *The Lotus Scripture* says, "In an unoccupied space, practice collecting the mind, stabilizing it so that it is as immovable as the Polar Mountain." So we know that in order to transcend the ordinary and go beyond the holy, one must make use of quiet meditation; to die sitting or pass away standing, one must depend on the power of concentration.

Even if you work on it all your life, you still may not succeed; how   18 much the more so if you waste time! What will you use to counteract karma? This is why the ancients said that if one lacks the power of concentration one willingly submits to death, living out one's life in vain, unseeing, like a wandering vagrant.

I hope that companions in meditation will read this tract over and   19 over, to help themselves and help others alike to attain true awakening.

CHAN MASTER FOXIN BENCAI
Guidelines for Sitting Meditation

1   In sitting meditation, make the heart upright and the mind straight and true. Purify the self and empty the heart. Sitting cross-legged, look and listen inward; clearly awake and aware, you are permanently removed from oblivion and excitement. If something comes to mind, do your best to cast it away.

2   In quiet concentration, examine clearly with true mindfulness. What is cognizant of sitting is mind, and what introspects is mind. What knows being and nonbeing, center and extremes, inside and outside, is mind. This mind is empty yet perceptive, silent yet aware. Round and bright, perfectly clear, it does not fall into ideas of annihilation or eternity. Spiritual awareness radiantly bright, its discrimination is not false.

3   Nowadays we see students who sit diligently but do not awaken. Their problem derives from their dependence on conceptions, their feelings sticking to bias and falsehood. In their confusion they turn their backs on the true basis and mistakenly go along with quietism or activism. This is why they fail to attain enlightenment.

4   If you can concentrate and clarify your mind such that you harmonize intimately with the uncreate, the mirror of knowledge will be cleared and the flower of mind will suddenly burst into bloom. Infinite attachments to conceptions will directly melt away, and accumulated aeons of ignorance will open up all at once.

5   This is like forgetting, then suddenly remembering; like being sick, then all at once recovering. A sense of joy arises within, and you know you will become a Buddha. Then you know that there is no separate Buddha outside of mind.

6   After that you increase cultivation in accord with enlightenment, experiencing realization by cultivation. The source of realization of enlightenment is the identity of mind, Buddha, and living beings.

This is called absorption in unified understanding and unified action. It is also called the effortless path.

Now you can turn things around without alienation from senses   7
and objects. Picking up what comes to hand, you alternate as host and guest. The eye of the universe clear, present and past are renewed. The spiritual capacity of direct perception is naturally attained. This is why Vimalakīrti said, "To live an active life without emerging from absorption in extinction is called quiet sitting."

So we should know that the moon appears when the water is still,   8
the shine is complete when the mirror is clean. For people who study the Way, it is essential to sit and meditate. Otherwise, you will be going around in circles forever.

Although this is unpleasant, I cannot keep silent. I have written   9
some generalities to help people discover the true source. If you do not neglect practice, then you will attain the same realization.

ZEN MASTER DŌGEN

A Generally Recommended Mode of Sitting Meditation

1   The Way is fundamentally complete and perfect, all-pervasive; how could it depend upon cultivation and realization?

2   The vehicle of the source is free; why expend effort?

3   The whole being is utterly beyond defiling dust; who would believe in a method of wiping it clean?

4   The great whole is not apart from here; why go someplace to practice?

5   Nevertheless, the slightest discrepancy is as the distance between sky and earth: as soon as aversion and attraction arise, you lose your mind in confusion.

6   Even though you may boast of comprehension and wallow in understanding, having gotten a glimpse of insight, and though you find the Way and understand the mind, inspired with the determination to soar to the skies, although you may roam freely within the bounds of initial entry, you are still somewhat lacking in a living road of emancipation.

7   Even Gautama Buddha, who had innate knowledge, sat upright for six years; this is a noteworthy example. When referring to the transmission of the mind seal at Shaolin, the fame of nine years facing a wall is still mentioned. Since the ancients did so, why should people today not do so?

8   Therefore you should stop the intellectual activity of pursuing words and chasing sayings, and should learn the stepping back of turning the light around and looking back. Body and mind will naturally be shed, and the original countenance will become manifest.

9   If you want to attain something, you should set right about working on it. For intensive Zen meditation, a quiet room is appropriate. Food and drink are to be moderate. Letting go of all mental objects, taking a respite from all concerns, not thinking of good or evil, not

being concerned with right or wrong, halt the operations of mind, intellect, and consciousness, stop assessment by thought, imagination, and view. Do not aim to become a Buddha; and how could it be limited to sitting or reclining?

Spread a thick sitting mat where you usually sit, and use a cushion on top of this. You may sit in the full-lotus posture, or in the half-lotus posture. For the full-lotus posture, first place the right foot on the left thigh, then the left foot on the right thigh. For the half-lotus posture, just place the left foot on the right thigh. Wear loose clothing, and keep it orderly.   10

Next place the right hand on the left leg, and the left hand on the right hand, with palms facing upward. The two thumbs face each other and hold each other up.   11

Now sit upright, with your body straight. Do not lean to the left or tilt to the right, bend forward or lean backward. Align the ears with the shoulders, and the nose with the navel. The tongue should rest on the upper palate, the teeth and lips should be closed. The eyes should always be open. The breathing passes subtly through the nose.   12

Once the physical form is in order, exhale fully through the mouth once, sway left and right, then settle into sitting perfectly still.   13

Think of what does not think. How do you think of what does not think? It is not thinking.   14

This is the essential art of sitting Zen meditation.   15

What I call sitting Zen meditation is not practice of *dhyāna*. It is just a method of comfort, a practical way of experiencing thoroughgoing investigation of enlightenment: objective reality becomes manifest, beyond any trap.   16

If you can get the meaning of this, you will be like dragons taking to the water, like tigers in the mountains. You will know that the truth has spontaneously become evident, while oblivion and distraction will already have been overcome.   17

When you are going to rise from sitting, move your body gradually, getting up gently. Do not be hasty or careless.   18

We have seen stories of transcending the ordinary and going beyond the holy, shedding the mortal coil while sitting or passing away while standing upright: all of these depend on the power in this.   19

And how about the transformations of state upon the lifting of a finger, a pole, a needle, a hammer? How about the realizations of accord on the raising of a whisk, a fist, a cane, a shout? These have   20 never been susceptible to understanding by thought and conceptualization; how could they be known by cultivated realization of supernatural powers?

21   It could be called dignified behavior beyond sound and form; is it not a guiding example prior to knowledge and views? Being such, it is not an issue whether one has more or less intelligence, making no distinction between the quick and the slow. Focused, unified concentration is what constitutes work on the Way.

22   The practice and realization are spontaneously undefiled; the process of heading for the aim, furthermore, is being normal.

23   Whatever they are, one's own world and the realms of others, West and East, they equally hold the seal of Buddha, based as one on the way of the source.

24   Just work on sitting, remaining in an immobile state. Even though it seems there are myriad differences and a thousand distinctions, just attend to intensive meditation to master the Way.

25   Why abandon a seat in your own house to idly roam in the dusty realms of alien countries? Take a single misstep, and you blunder past what's right in front of you.

26   Having gotten the key of the human body, do not pass time uselessly: preserve and uphold the essential potential of the Buddha Way.

27   Who has the folly to look forward to what lasts but a moment? Add to this consideration the fact that the physical body is like a dewdrop on the grass, a lifetime is like a lightning flash: all of a sudden they are void, in an instant they are gone.

28   May those high-minded people who participate in this study and have long learned to feel an elephant by hand not be suspicious of a real dragon. Proceed energetically on the straightforward path of direct pointing, and honor people who have transcended learning and gone beyond effort. Join in the enlightenment of the Buddhas, inherit the state of mind of the Zen founders.

29   Having long been thus, we should be thus. The treasury opens of itself, to be used at will.

SON MASTER CHINUL
Secrets of Cultivating the Mind

The triple world with its irritating vexations is like a house afire; who   1
could bear to stay there long, willingly suffering perpetual torment?

If you want to avoid going around in circles, nothing compares to   2
seeking Buddhahood. If you want to seek Buddhahood, Buddha is
mind. Need mind be sought afar? It is not apart from the body.

The material body is temporal, having birth and death. The real   3
mind is like space, unending and unchanging. Thus it is said, "When
the physical body decays and dissolves back into fire and air, one
thing remains aware, encompassing the universe."

Unfortunately, people today have been confused for a long time.   4
They do not know that their own mind is the real Buddha. They do
not know that their own essence is the real Dharma. Wishing to seek
the Dharma, they attribute it to remote sages; wishing to seek Buddhahood, they do not observe their own mind.

If you say that there is Buddha outside of mind, and there is   5
Dharma outside of essence, and want to seek the Way of Buddhahood
while clinging tightly to these feelings, even if you spend ages burning your body, branding your arms, breaking your bones and taking
out the marrow, wounding yourself and copying scriptures in your
own blood, sitting for long periods of time without sitting down,
eating only once a day, reading the whole canon and cultivating various austere practices, it will be like steaming sand to produce cooked
rice; it will only increase your own fatigue.

Just know your own mind and you will grasp countless teachings   6
and infinite subtle meanings without even seeking. That is why the
World Honored One said, "Observing all sentient beings, I see they
are fully endowed with the knowledge and virtues of Buddhas." He
also said, "All living beings, and all sorts of illusory events, are all

born in the completely awake subtle mind of those who realize suchness."

7   So we know that there is no Buddhahood to attain apart from this mind. The Realized Ones of the past were just people who understood the mind, and the saints and sages of the present are people who cultivate the mind; students of the future should rely on this principle.

8   People who practice the Way should not seek externally. The essence of mind has no defilement; it is originally complete and perfect of itself. Just detach from illusory objects and it is enlightened to suchness as is.

9   Question: If Buddha-nature is presently in our bodies, it is not apart from ordinary people. Then why do we not perceive Buddha-nature now?

10   Answer: It is in your body, but you do not perceive it yourself. At all times you know when you are hungry, you know when you are thirsty, you know when you are cold, you know when you are hot; sometimes you get angry, sometimes you are joyful—ultimately, what is it that does all this?

11   Now then, the material body is a compound of four elements: earth, water, fire, and air. Their substance is insentient; how can they perceive or cognize? That which can perceive and cognize has to be your Buddha-nature.

12   This is why Linji said, "The four gross elements cannot expound the Teaching or listen to the Teaching. Space cannot expound the Teaching or listen to the Teaching. Only the solitary light clearly before you, that which has no form, can expound the Teaching or listen to the Teaching."

13   What he called that which has no form is the stamp of the truth of all Buddhas, and it is your original mind. So the Buddha-nature is presently in your body; what need is there to seek outside? If you do not believe it, let me mention some stories of how ancient sages entered the Way, to enable you to clear up your doubts. You should believe with clear understanding of truth.

14   In ancient times a king asked a Buddhist saint, "What is Buddhahood?"

The saint said, "Seeing essence is Buddhahood."

The king asked, "Do you see essence?"

The saint said, "I see the essence of enlightenment."

The king asked, "Where is essence?"

The saint said, "Essence is in function."

The king asked, "What function is this, that it is not now visible?"

The saint said, "It is now functioning; it is just that you yourself do not see it."

The king asked, "Does it exist in me?"

The saint said, "Whenever you act, that is it. When you are inactive, the essence is again hard to see."

The king asked, "When it is to be employed, in how many places does it appear?"

The saint said, "When it appears, there must be eight places."

The king said, "Please explain those eight manifestations."

The saint said, "In the womb, it is called the body. In society, it is called the person. In the eyes, it is called seeing. In the ears, it is called hearing. In the nose, it distinguishes scents. In the tongue, it talks. In the hands, it grabs and holds. In the feet, it walks and runs. It manifests all over, including everything; countless worlds are collected in a single atom. Perceptives know this is the Buddha-nature, the essence of enlightenment. Those who do not know call it the soul."

On hearing this, the mind of the king was opened up to understanding.

Also, a monk asked Master Guizong, "What is Buddha?"   15

Guizong said, "If I tell you right now, I'm afraid you won't believe it."

The monk said, "If you speak truly, how dare I not believe?"

Guizong said, "You yourself are it."

The monk asked, "How can I preserve it?"

Guizong said, "When there is a single obstruction in the eye, there is a shower of flowers in the sky."

That monk attained insight at these words.

These stories I have quoted about the circumstances of ancient   16
sages' entry into the Way are clear and simple. They certainly save energy. If you gain true understanding by these stories, then you walk hand in hand with the ancient sages.

Question: You speak of seeing essence. Those who have really seen   17
essence are then sages. As such, they should be different from other people, manifesting spiritual powers and miracles. Why is there not a single practitioner today manifesting spiritual powers and miracles?

Answer: You shouldn't be too quick to speak wild words. Those   18 who do not distinguish the false from the true are confused and deluded people. Students of the Way today talk about truth, but in their hearts they get bored and fall back into the error of being indiscriminate—these are the ones you doubt. To study the Way without knowing what goes before and what comes later, to speak of principle without distinguishing root and branch, is called false opinion, not cultivation of learning. You not only cause yourself to go wrong, you also cause others to go wrong. Should you not be careful?

19   There are many avenues of entry into the Way, but essentially they all fall within the two categories of sudden enlightenment and gradual practice. Even though we speak of sudden enlightenment and immediate practice, this is how those of the very highest faculties and potential gain entry; and if you look into their past, they have already practiced gradual cultivation based on sudden enlightenment for many lifetimes, so that in the present life they realize enlightenment immediately upon hearing the truth, suddenly finished all at once. In reality, these people are also included in the category of those who are first enlightened and then practice.

20   So these two aspects, sudden and gradual, are the guidelines followed by all sages. Sages since time immemorial have all first awakened and then cultivated practice, attaining experiential proof based on practice. So-called spiritual powers and miracles are manifested by the gradual cultivation of practice based on enlightenment; it is not that they appear immediately upon enlightenment. As scripture says, "The abstract principle is understood all of a sudden; concrete matters are cleared up by means of this understanding. They are not cleared away all at once but worked through in an orderly manner."

21   This is why Guifeng said, in a profound explanation of the meaning of first awakening and then cultivating practice, "Consciousness is an ice pond: though it is all water, it needs the energy of the sun to melt. When ordinary people are awakened, they are Buddhas; but they rely on the power of the Dharma for cultivation. When ice melts, then water flows and moistens; only then can it perform its irrigating function. When delusion is ended, then the mind is open and penetrating, responsively manifesting the function of the light of spiritual powers."

22   So factual spiritual powers and miracles cannot be accomplished in one day; they appear after gradual cultivation. And what is more, from the point of view of those who have arrived, concrete supernatu-

ral powers are still apparitional affairs, and they are minor things to sages; even if they manifest, it is not right to want to use them.

Confused and ignorant people today imagine that countless subtle 23 functions, spiritual powers, and miracles will immediately appear upon an instantaneous awakening. If you entertain this understanding, this means you do not know what comes first and what follows afterward, and cannot distinguish the root from the branches. If you try to seek enlightenment without knowing what comes first and what follows afterward, what is basic and what is derivative, that is like trying to put a square peg in a round hole. Is it not a big mistake?

Since you do not know expedient technique, you imagine you are 24 facing a sheer precipice, and thus lose interest. Many are those who cut off their potential for enlightenment in this way. Since they themselves have not attained enlightenment, they do not believe that others have realized any enlightenment. Seeing those without spiritual powers, they become contemptuous and make the sages and saints out to be cheaters and deceivers. This is pitiful indeed.

Question: You say that the two categories of sudden enlighten- 25 ment and gradual practice are guidelines followed by all sages. If enlightenment is sudden enlightenment, what is the need for gradual practice? If practice is gradual practice, why speak of sudden enlightenment? Please explain the meanings of sudden and gradual further, to eliminate remaining doubts.

Answer: As for sudden enlightenment, as long as ordinary people 26 are deluded, they think their bodies are material conglomerates and their minds are random thoughts. They do not know that inherent essence is the true body of reality. They do not know that their own open awareness is the real Buddha. Seeking Buddha outside of mind, they run randomly from one impulse to another.

If a real teacher points out a way of entry for you, and for a single 27 instant you turn your attention around, you see your own original essence. This essence originally has no afflictions; uncontaminated wisdom is inherently complete in it. Then you are no different from the Buddhas; thus it is called sudden enlightenment.

As for gradual practice, having suddenly realized fundamental es- 28 sence, no different from Buddha, beginningless mental habits are hard to get rid of all at once. Therefore one cultivates practice based on enlightenment, gradually cultivating the attainment to perfection, nurturing the embryo of sagehood to maturity. Eventually, after a long time, one becomes a sage; therefore it is called gradual practice. It is like an infant, which has all the normal faculties at birth, but as yet undeveloped; only with the passage of years does it become an adult.

29   Question: By what expedient means can we turn our minds around instantly to realize our inherent essence?

30   Answer: It is just your own mind; what further expedient means would you apply? If you apply expedient means to go on to seek intellectual understanding, this is like wanting to see your own eyes because you think you have no eyes if you cannot see them. Since they are your own eyes, how can you see them? As long as you have not lost them, that is called seeing eyes. If you have no more desire to see, does that mean you imagine you are not seeing? So it is also with one's own open awareness. Since it is one's own mind, how can one yet seek to see it? If you seek understanding, then you do not understand it. Just know that which does not understand; this is seeing essence.

31   Question: The most superior people easily understand upon hearing; middling and lesser people are not without doubt. Please give further explanations of means to enable confused people to gain direction and access.

32   Answer: The Way is not in the province of knowing or not knowing. Get rid of the mind that uses confusion to anticipate enlightenment, and listen to what I say. All things are like dreams, like illusions or magical effects; therefore errant thoughts are basically silent, while material objects are basically empty. The emptiness of all things is not obscure to open awareness; so this mind with open awareness of silence and emptiness is your original countenance. It is also the seal of Dharma esoterically transmitted by the Buddhas of past, present, and future, the Zen Masters of successive generations, and all genuine teachers in the world.

33   If you realize this mind, this is really what is called ascending directly to the stage of Buddhahood without climbing up the steps. Your every footstep transcends the triple world; returning home, you put an end to doubt all at once. Then you are a teacher of the human and the celestial. With compassion and wisdom supporting each other, you fulfill both self-help and help for others. Worthy of human and celestial support, you are able to use ten thousand ounces of gold

in a day. If you are like this, a great person in the real sense, your task in life is done.

Question: In terms of my present state, what is the mind of open   34
awareness of silence and emptiness?

Answer: What enables you to ask me this question is your mind of   35
open awareness of emptiness and silence; why do you still seek outside instead of looking within? I will now point directly to the original mind in you, to enable you to awaken; you should clear your mind
to listen to what I say.

Throughout the twenty-four hours of the day, you operate and act   36
in all sorts of ways, seeing and hearing, laughing and talking, raging
and rejoicing, affirming and denying: now tell me, ultimately who is
it that can operate and act in this way?

If you say it is the physical body operating, then why is it that   37
when people's lives have just ended and their bodies have not yet
decomposed at all, their eyes cannot see, their ears cannot hear, their
noses cannot smell, their tongues cannot talk, their bodies do not
move, their hands do not grip, their feet do not step? So we know that
what can see, hear, and act must be your basic mind, not your physical body.

Indeed, the gross elements of this physical body are inherently   38
empty, like images in a mirror, like the moon reflected in water; how
can they be capable of perfectly clear and constant awareness, thoroughly lucid, sensitive and effective, with countless subtle functions?
Thus it is said, "Spiritual powers and subtle functions—drawing
water and hauling wood."

But there are many ways of access to the principle. I will point out   39
one entryway, by which you can return to the source. Do you hear
the cawing of the crows and the chattering of the jays?

[Student's response:] I hear them.   40

Now turn around and listen to your hearing essence; are there still   41
so many sounds in it?

[Student's response:] When I get here, all sounds and all discrimi-   42
nations are ungraspable.

Marvelous, marvelous! This is the Sound Seer's gateway into the   43
principle. Now let me ask you further: You say that when you get
here all sounds and all discriminations are totally ungraspable. Since
they cannot be grasped, does that not mean that there is empty space
at such a time?

44   [Student's response:] Originally not empty, it is clearly not obscure.

45   What is the substance that is not empty?

46   [Student's response:] It has no form; there is no way to express it in words.

47   This is the life of the Buddhas and Zen masters; do not doubt anymore. Since it has no form, could it have size? Since it has no size, could it have bounds? Because it has no bounds, it has no inside or outside. Having no inside or outside, it has no far or near. With no far or near, there is no there or here. Since there is no there or here, there is no going or coming. Because there is no going or coming, there is no birth or death. Having no birth or death, it has no past or present. With no past or present, there is no delusion or enlightenment. There being no delusion or enlightenment, there is no ordinary or holy. Since there is nothing ordinary or holy, there is no pollution or purity. Because there is no pollution or purity, there is no judgment of right and wrong. With no judgment of right and wrong, all terms and statements are ungraspable. Once there are no such subjective states and false ideas, then all sorts of appearances and all sorts of labels are ungraspable. Is this not original empty silence, original nothingness?

48   However, in the state where all things are empty, open awareness is not obscured; this is not the same as being insentient. The release of your own spirit is the pure substance of your mind, with open awareness of empty silence. And this pure, open, tranquil mind is the supremely pure luminous mind of the Buddhas of past, present, and future. It is also the essence of awareness that is the root source of all living beings.

49   Those who realize this and keep to it sit in one suchness and are immutably liberated. Those who stray from this and turn away from it traverse the six courses and go round and round for eternity. Therefore it is said that straying from the One Mind to traverse the six courses is "departure," or "disturbance," while awakening to the realm of reality and returning to the One Mind is "arrival," or "tranquillity."

50   Even though there is a difference between whether one strays from it or realizes it, nevertheless the basic source is one. That is why it is said that the Dharma refers to the minds of the living beings. This open, silent mind is not more in sages or less in ordinary people. Thus

it is said that in sages it is knowledge that is nevertheless not flashy, and while it is hidden in the ordinary mind, yet it is not dimmed.

Since it is not more in sages or less in ordinary people, how could the Buddhas and Zen masters be different from other people? What makes them different from other people is simply that they are able to guard their own minds and thoughts. If you can trust completely, your feelings of doubt will stop all at once, allowing a healthy will to emerge, so that you can discover real true vision and understanding, personally tasting its flavor, so that you naturally arrive at the stage of spontaneous acknowledgment.   51

This is the understanding of someone who is going to cultivate the mind; there are no more stages or steps, so it is called sudden. It is like the saying that real faith is attained only when there is conformity to perfect Buddhahood in the basis of your faith.   52

Question: If there are no more stages after having realized this principle, why the need for subsequent practice, gradual cultivation, and gradual perfection?   53

Answer: I have already explained the meaning of gradual practice after enlightenment, but seeing that your doubts have not yet been resolved, I will explain it again. You should purify your mind so as to listen truly and hear accurately.   54

Ordinary people have been revolving in circles since time immemorial, being born and dying in five courses of existence. Because of clinging fixedly to self-images, false ideas, and misperceptions, the habits of illusion eventually become second nature to them. Even if they suddenly awaken in this life and realize that their essential nature is fundamentally empty and silent, no different from the Buddhas, nevertheless past habits are difficult to remove all at once.   55

Therefore they rage and rejoice as they encounter irritating and pleasing situations; judgments of right and wrong arise and pass away in profusion, and afflictions caused by outside influences are no different from before. If they do not make use of the power within transcendent insight, how can they quell ignorance and reach the state of great rest and tranquillity? As it is said, "When suddenly awakened, although you are the same as Buddha, the energy of many lifetimes of habits is deep seated. Though the wind stops, the waves still billow; though noumenon is manifest, thoughts still invade."   56

Master Gao also said, "Time and again those who have sharp faculties awaken without much effort, then they become complacent and   57 neglect further cultivation. Eventually they drift back into their former confusion, unable to escape revolving in circular routines." So how can we neglect subsequent cultivation because of a single awakening?

58   Therefore, after awakening it is necessary to always observe and examine yourself. When errant thoughts suddenly arise, do not go along with them at all; reduce them, reduce them, until you reach the point of noncontrivance, which alone is the ultimate end. This is the ox-herding practice carried out by all illuminates after their enlightenment. Even though there is subsequent cultivation, they have already realized sudden enlightenment.

59   Errant thoughts are fundamentally empty; the essence of mind is fundamentally pure. To stop evil over and over without any stopping, and cultivate goodness over and over without any cultivating, is true stopping and cultivation. Therefore it is said that even as you fully cultivate myriad practices, only no thought is to be considered a basis.

60   In making a general distinction between the meanings of attaining enlightenment first and then cultivating it afterward, Guifeng said, "You suddenly realize this essence is originally free from afflictions; the essence of uncontaminated knowledge is inherently complete, no different from Buddha. To cultivate practice based on this is called the Zen of the highest vehicle, and it is also called the pure Zen of those who realize suchness. If you can cultivate its practice moment to moment, in a gradual manner you will naturally attain hundreds and thousands of spiritual states. This is the Zen that has been transmitted in the school of Bodhidharma." Thus sudden enlightenment and gradual cultivation are like the two wheels of a chariot; it will not work if one is missing.

61   Some people, not knowing the essential emptiness of good and evil, think practical cultivation of mind means to sit rigidly immobile, subduing body and mind, like a rock placed on top of grass. This is ludicrous. That is why it is said that followers cut off confusion in every state of mind, yet the mind that does the cutting off is a brigand.

62   Just clearly observe that killing, stealing, rapine, and falsehood arise from nature, arising without any arising, and they will immediately be annulled. Then what further need to stop them is there? That is why it is said that we should not fear the arising of thoughts, just

fear being slow to notice. It is also said, "When thoughts arise, immediately notice them; once you become aware of them, they are no longer there."

Thus in the experience of enlightened people, even if there are afflictions associated with the external world, all of them produce the most subtle and refined flavor. Just be aware that confusion has no basis, that the illusory triple world is like smoke swirling in the wind, that the phantasmagoric six sense fields are like hot water melting ice.   63

If you can practice this moment to moment, not neglecting to be attentive, seeing to it that concentration and insight are equally sustained, then love and hate will naturally lighten and thin out, while compassion and wisdom will naturally increase in clarity; sinful deeds will naturally end, while meritorious actions will naturally progress.   64

When afflictions are ended, then birth and death stop. If subtle flowings are permanently ended, the great knowledge of complete awareness alone remains, radiantly clear. Then you manifest millions of emanation bodies in the lands of the ten directions, responding to potential as sensed, like the moon appearing in the highest skies with its reflection distributed throughout myriad waters, functioning adaptively to liberate boundless beings with affinity, joyful and happy, without sorrow. This is called great enlightenment, honored by the world.   65

Question: The meaning of equally sustaining concentration and insight in the process of gradual cultivation is not really clear yet. Please explain further, with detailed instruction to break through confusion and lead us into the door of liberation.   66

Answer: If we set up principles for entry into inner truth, there may be a thousand methods, but all of them are within the categories of concentration and insight. To sum up their essentials, they are just the substance and function of our own essential nature. These are the aforementioned empty silence and open awareness.   67

Concentration is the substance, insight is the function. Being function identical to substance, insight is not apart from concentration; being substance identical to function, concentration is not apart from insight. As Caoqi said, "The ground of mind has no confusion, it is inherently stable; the mind of ground has no folly, it is inherently wise."   68

69   If you awaken like this, then the detachment and illumination of silence and awareness are not two. This is the sudden way, in which one cultivates both concentration and insight together as a pair.

70   If we speak of first using profound silence to quell conditioned thinking and then using alert awareness to quell oblivion, these initial and subsequent remedies balanced and harmonized to lead into tranquillity, this is considered the gradual way. This is the practice of those of inferior potentials; although they say alertness and silence are equally maintained, nevertheless they hold to tranquillity as a practice. How could they be considered people who have completed their work, who are never apart from fundamental silence and fundamental awareness, naturally practicing simultaneous cultivation of both? As Caoqi said, "Spontaneous enlightenment and cultivation of practice are not in quietude; if you are a quietist from beginning to end, you are confused."

71   Thus for adepts the principle of equally maintaining concentration and insight is not a matter of effort; it is spontaneous and effortless, with no more particular time frame. When seeing and hearing, they are just so; when dressing and eating, they are just so; when defecating and urinating, they are just so; when conversing with people, they are just so; whatever they are doing, walking, standing, sitting, reclining, speaking, silent, rejoicing, raging, at all times and in everything they are thus, like empty boats riding the waves, going along with the high and the low, like a river winding through the mountains, curving at curves and straight at straits, without minding any state of mind, buoyantly going along with nature today, going along with nature buoyantly tomorrow, adapting to all circumstances without inhibition or impediment, neither stopping nor fostering good or evil, simple and straightforward, without artificiality, perception normal.

72   Then there is not a single atom to make into an object; so why bother to work to clear anything away? Without a single thought producing feelings, there is no need for the power to forget mental objects.

73   However, those who obstructions are thick, whose habits are heavy, whose vision is lowly, and whose mind is unstable, those in whom ignorance is powerful and insight is weak, those who cannot avoid being altered by disturbance and quietude in dealing with good and bad situations, whose minds are not peaceful, cannot do without the work of forgetting mental objects and clearing up the mind.

As it is said, when the six sense faculties are in a controlled state 74 so that the mind does not go along with objects, that is called concentration; when mind and environment are both empty and radiant awareness is free from confusion, that is called insight.

Although this is a formal approach, a gradual approach to concentration and insight, something practiced by those of inferior potential, nevertheless it cannot be omitted in the context of remedial teachings and practices. 75

If there is a lot of excitement, you first use concentration to conform to noumenon and rein in the scattered mind; by not going along with mental objects, you merge with original silence. 76

If there is a lot of oblivion, then next you use insight to analyze things and contemplate emptiness; when consciousness is free from confusion, you merge with original awareness. 77

You quell random imagination by concentration, and quell insensibility by insight. When disturbance and quietude are both forgotten, curative work is done. Then when dealing with things, each passing thought returns to the source; encountering situations, each state of mind merges with the Way. 78

Only when you spontaneously practice both together are you considered free. If you are like this, you can truly be called one who maintains concentration and insight equally, and clearly sees Buddha-nature. 79

Question: According to the distinctions you have made, there are two meanings to equal maintenance of concentration and insight in the process of cultivation in the aftermath of enlightenment. One of them involves spontaneous concentration and insight, the other involves formal concentration and insight. 80

In reference to spontaneous concentration and insight, you have said that naturally occurring silent awareness is originally uncontrived and there is not a single atom to make into an object; so why bother to work to clear anything away? Without a single thought producing feelings, there is no need for the power to forget mental objects. 81

In describing formal concentration and insight, you have spoken of conforming to principle, concentrating the scattered mind, analyzing phenomena, contemplating emptiness, balancing and tuning the mind to eliminate oblivion and distraction, so as to lead into noncon- 82 trivance. In making the distinction, you say that this is the gradual approach, which is practiced by those of lesser potential.

83   I am not without doubt about the two approaches to concentration and insight. If you say that they are to be practiced by one and the same individual, does that mean that one first relies on the dual practice of spontaneous concentration and insight, then after that also applies the curative work of formal concentration and insight? Or is it that one first relies on the formal approach to balance and tune out oblivion and distraction, and then after that enters thereby into spontaneous concentration and insight?

84   If we first rely on spontaneous concentration and insight, they are natural silence and awareness, so there is no more curative work; why should we then also take up formal concentration and insight? This would be like losing the quality of white jade by carving a design on it.

85   If we first use formal concentration and insight until their curative effect is achieved, and then proceed to spontaneous concentration and insight, then this is the same as the gradual cultivation practiced prior to enlightenment in the gradual approach by those of inferior faculties; how could it be called a sudden approach, which is to first awaken and then cultivate practice afterward, using effortless effort?

86   If they are simultaneous, with neither preceding the other, yet the two kinds of concentration and insight, sudden and gradual, are different, how could they be practiced at once? Thus the individual taking the sudden approach relies on the spontaneous way, effortlessly going along with the flow; those of lesser potential taking the gradual approach follow the formal way, exerting effort at curative measures. The potentialities for which the two approaches are suited, the sudden and the gradual, are not the same; it is clear that one is superior to the other. How can initial enlightenment and subsequent practice both be analyzed into two types? Please give us a comprehensive explanation to enable us to put an end to doubt.

87   Answer: The analysis is perfectly clear; you are producing your own subjective doubts. Pursuing the words and creating interpretations, you create more and more doubt and confusion. When you get the meaning, you forget the words and do not bother to press the issue. But let me address the individually distinct modes of practice within the two approaches.

88   To practice spontaneous concentration and insight is the sudden

approach, using effortless effort, both operative yet both tranquil, spontaneously cultivating intrinsic essence, naturally fulfilling the Way of Buddhas. To practice formal concentration and insight is the gradual approach taken before enlightenment by those of lesser potential, using curative work, striving to direct each thought toward cutting off confusion and grasping quietude.

The practices of these two approaches, sudden and gradual, are individually different and not to be mixed up. When we also discuss formal curative practices within the process of gradual cultivation after enlightenment, this does not include everything that is practiced by those whose potentialities require a gradual approach. It is just a matter of temporarily taking expedient ways. 89

And why is this? Because among those who are suited to the sudden approach, there are also those whose potentials are superior and those whose potentials are inferior. Thus their practice cannot be judged by the same standard. 90

As for those whose afflictions are slight, who are light and easy in body and mind, who are detached from good in the midst of good and detached from evil in the midst of evil, who are unmoved by the eight winds and calmly accept the three kinds of sensations, they rely on spontaneous concentration and insight, which they cultivate simultaneously without effort, naturally real and uncontrived, always in meditation whether active or still, and fulfill the design of nature. Why should they pursue formal practices for curative purposes? When there is no illness, one does not seek medicine. 91

As for those who, in spite of having first realized sudden awakening, have deep afflictions and rigid mental habits, who give rise to feelings toward objects thought after thought, who create confrontations with situations in every state of mind, who are thereby befuddled and confused, killing and obscuring the normalcy of their silent awareness, it is appropriate for them to make provisional use of formal concentration and insight, not neglecting curative measures, balancing and tuning their minds to eliminate oblivion and distraction, thereby to enter into noncontrivance. Even though they make temporary use of curative practices to tune out their habit energies, because they have already attained sudden realization of the fundamental purity of the essence of mind and the fundamental emptiness of afflictions, therefore they do not fall into the affected practice of those with inferior potentialities who take the gradual approach. 92

93   Why is this? When practice is cultivated before awakening, then even if you work unremittingly, cultivating practice every moment, you will conceive of one doubt after another as you go along and will be as yet unable to attain nonobstruction. It will be like having something stuck in your chest; signs of uneasiness will always be present. If curative practices are developed to maturity over a long period of time, then body and mind seem lightened and eased of acquired pollution, but even though you are light and easy, as long as you have not cut through the root of doubt, curative practices are like stones placed on grass; you have still not attained freedom in the realm of birth and death. That is why it is said that when practice is before enlightenment, it is not real practice.

94   As for people who have realized enlightenment, even though they may have expedient techniques as curative measures, they never have a thought of doubt and do not fall into affected habits; over a period of time they naturally attain perfect accord. The naturally real subtle essence is spontaneously silently aware, focusing on all objects with each passing thought while annihilating all afflictions in each passing state of mind. This is not distinct from fulfilling supreme enlightenment by equal maintenance of spontaneous concentration and insight. So even though formal concentration and insight are practiced by those with potential suited for the gradual approach, for people who have realized enlightenment they can be said to transmute iron into gold.

95   If you know this, then how can you entertain doubts based on dualistic views, just because the two approaches to concentration and insight have an order of precedence? I hope that people who study the Way will examine and savor these words and stop entertaining doubts and inhibiting themselves. If they have a strong will to seek supreme enlightenment, what other recourse do they have if they reject this?

96   Do not cling to the letter, just comprehend the meaning, referring each point to your own self, so as to merge with the original source. Then the knowledge that has no teacher will spontaneously appear, the pattern of natural reality will be perfectly clear, unobscured, and you will attain the body of wisdom, attaining enlightenment without depending on anyone else.

97   However, even though this sublime teaching is for everyone, unless they have already planted seeds of wisdom and have the faculties and capacity for the Great Vehicle, they cannot conceive a thought of

genuine faith. And not only will they not believe in it, from time to time there are even those who slander and revile it, calling uninterrupted hell upon themselves.

Even if you do not believe or accept the teaching, once it passes by your ears it temporarily forms a connection. The merit of this, the virtue of this, cannot be measured. As it says in *The Secret of Mind Alone*, "If you hear but do not believe, that still forms a cause of Buddhahood; if you study but do not attain, that still increases the blessings of humans and celestials, not losing the true foundation of Buddhahood. How much the more infinite are the merit and virtue of those who hear and believe, study and attain, preserve intact and do not forget? How can their merit and virtue be measured?"   98

When we think back to past routine actions, who knows for how many thousands of aeons we have gone by way of darkness into uninterrupted hell, experiencing all sorts of misery of who knows how many kinds. So if we want to seek the Buddha Way, unless we meet good friends we will be forever sunk in darkness, unconsciously doing evil deeds.   99

Sometimes we may reflect on this and unconsciously heave a sigh of lament. How can we relax and take it easy, when it means experiencing the same troubles all over again? And who knows who may ever again enable us to find this path of cultivating realization open and unobscured? This can be called a blind tortoise finding a piece of driftwood, a minute seed hitting a needle.   100

What is more felicitous than the Way? If we get bored and backslide now, or if we get lazy and are always looking back, the minute we lose our lives we will fall back into evil dispositions and suffer all sorts of pains; then even if we wish to hear a single line of Buddhist teaching, believe and understand it, accept and hold it, in order to escape from the agony, how could that be possible?   101

When you are on the brink of destruction, it is useless to have regrets. I pray that people who practice the Way will not become heedless and not cling to greed and sensuality but will strive as diligently as if they were saving their heads from burning, not forgetting to notice that impermanence is swift, the body is like the morning dew, life is like the setting sunlight. Although we are here today, tomorrow cannot be guaranteed. Keep this in mind! Keep this in mind!   102

Even if you temporarily rely on mundane created goodness, you can still escape from the miserable routines of the worst states of   103 being and attain exceptional rewards in higher states of being, experiencing all sorts of bliss. How much the more of this most profound teaching of the supreme vehicle; the merit and virtue produced just by momentarily conceiving faith in it are such that no simile can convey the slightest amount thereof.

104   As scripture says, "If someone fills the worlds of a billion-world galaxy with precious substances and gives them as offerings to the living beings of those worlds, causing them all to be fulfilled, and also teaches all the living beings of those worlds to attain the four realizations, the merit of that would be measureless and boundless but would not be equal to the merit and virtue attained by thinking about this Teaching correctly for even the time it takes to eat a meal."

105   So we know that this teaching of ours is most noble, most valuable, beyond comparison to any merit or virtue. Therefore scripture says, "A moment of pure consciousness is the site of enlightenment; it is better than building countless jewel shrines. The jewel shrines will eventually crumble into dust, whereas an instant of pure consciousness attains true awakening."

106   I pray that people who practice the Way will study and savor these words, keeping them earnestly in mind. If you do not liberate yourself in this lifetime, then in what lifetime will you liberate yourself? If you do not cultivate practice now, you will miss out for myriad aeons; but if you do cultivate practice now, even if it is difficult, it will gradually become easier, until the work progresses of itself.

107   How unfortunate it is that people today are starving, and yet when they encounter a royal feast, they do not have the sense to partake of it. They are sick, and yet when they meet a master physician, they do not have the sense to take the medicine prescribed. "I cannot do anything for those who do not ask themselves what to do."

108   Furthermore, constructed worldly affairs have forms that can be seen and effects that can be tested. When people attain one thing, it is regarded as wonderful. This mind-source of ours has no perceptible shape or visible form; there is no way to talk about it, no way to think about it. Therefore demons and outsiders have no opening to slander it, while the gods cannot adequately praise it. So how can ordinary people with shallow perception describe it?

109   What a pity! How can a frog in a well know how wide the ocean is? How can a jackal roar the lion's roar? So we know that people in this age of derelict religion, who when they hear this teaching marvel

at it, believe and understand it, accept and hold it, have already worked for many sages and planted roots of goodness over countless aeons; they are those of highest potential, who have formed a profound affinity with the true basis of wisdom.

Therefore *The Diamond Scripture* says, "Those who are capable of engendering faith in these statements obviously have already planted roots of goodness in the company of infinite Buddhas." It also says, "This is expounded for those who set out on the Great Vehicle; it is expounded for those who set out on the Supreme Vehicle."   110

I pray that those who seek the Way will not be timid and weak but courageous and bold. The good causes of past aeons cannot yet be known; if you do not believe in excellence and are willing to be wretched, you will conceive ideas of difficulty and obstruction. If you do not cultivate this teaching now, even if you have good roots from former lifetimes, you are cutting them off now. Therefore you are in ever deeper difficulty, becoming even more alienated.   111

Now you have already arrived at the abode of the treasure; you should not go back empty-handed. Once you lose the human body, you cannot get it back even in ten thousand aeons; please make sure to be prudent with it! Could anyone with wisdom who knew where the treasure is paradoxically fail to seek it, instead spending an eternity lamenting poverty? If you want to get some treasure, let go of the skin bag.   112

ZEN MASTER EJŌ

Absorption in the Treasury of Light

1   There is a chapter on light in the *Shōbōgenzō:* the reason for writing this essay now in addition is just to bring out the essential substance, the fact that the countenance of Buddhism is absorption in the treasury of light.

2   This is the unobtrusive application of inconspicuous practice, carried out by oneself and influencing others, proper to people who have studied Zen for a long time and have entered its inner sanctum.

3   The so-called treasury of light is the root source of all Buddhas, the inherent being of all living creatures, the total substance of all phenomena, the treasury of the great light of spiritual powers of complete awareness. The three bodies, four knowledges, and states of absorption numerous as atoms in every aspect of reality, all appear from within this.

4   *The Flower Ornament Scripture* says, "The great light of the Lamplike Illuminate is supreme among auspicious signs: that Buddha has entered this hall, so this place is most auspicious."

5   This great light of the Lamplike Illuminate pervades the universe, without differentiating between the mundane and the sacred: thus "that Buddha has entered this hall." The reception of "thus once I heard" is itself "having entered this hall."

6   Because "this place is therefore most auspicious," Shākyamuni Buddha received indications of future direction from the Lamplike Illuminate.

7   Because this one light extends throughout all time, if there were any attaining it, then it would have to be twofold.

8   *The Scripture on the Miraculous Empowerment of Vairochana Attaining Buddhahood* says, in the book on entering the state of mind of the method of mystical spells, "At that time the Blessed One said

to the Thunderbolt Bearer, 'The will for enlightenment is the causal basis, great compassion is the root, skill in means is the ultimate.

" 'O Master of the Secret, what is enlightenment? It means know- 9 ing your own mind as it really is. This is unexcelled complete perfect enlightenment, in which there is nothing at all that can be attained. Why? Because the form of it is enlightenment; it has no knowledge and no understanding. Why? Because enlightenment has no form. Master of the Secret, the formlessness of all things is called the form of space.' "

The same scripture also says, "Master of the Secret, the practice 10 of the Great Vehicle awakens the mind that transports you to the unconditioned, guided by selflessness. Why? Those who have culti- vated this practice in the past have observed the basis of the clusters of mental and physical elements, and know they are like illusions, mirages, shadows, echoes, rings of fire, castles in the air. Master of the Secret, thus they relinquish the selfless, and the host of the mind autonomously awakens to the fundamental nonarousal of the essen- tial mind. Why? Because what is before mind and what is after mind cannot be apprehended. Thus knowing the nature of the essential mind, you transcend two aeons of yoga practice."

The fact that "before and after cannot be apprehended" means that 11 the light of great knowledge of Vairochana is like this because the essential mind is fundamentally unaroused.

The Flower Ornament Scripture also says, "The body of Buddha 12 radiates great light of infinite colors perfectly pure, like clouds cover- ing all lands, everywhere extolling the virtues of Buddhahood. All who are illumined by the light rejoice; beings with pains have them all removed. Everyone is inspired with respect and develops a com- passionate heart. This is the independent function of enlightenment."

The same scripture says, in "The Book on Awakening by Light," 13 "At that time the light passed a hundred thousand worlds and illu- mined a million worlds in the East. The same thing occurred in the south, west, north, four intermediate directions, the zenith, and the nadir. Everything in all of those worlds was clearly revealed. At that time, the enlightening being Mañjushrī in each place spoke up simul- taneously before the Buddha in each place, uttering this verse:

'The Enlightened One is supremely independent,
transcending the world, relying on nothing,

imbued with all virtuous qualities,
liberated from all that exists,
undefiled, unattached,
free from imagination, without fixations.
His substance and essence cannot be measured;
those who see him all utter praise.
His light is everywhere, clear and pure;
the burdens of the senses are washed away.
Without moving, he detaches from the two extremes;
this is the knowledge of the Enlightened One.' "

So the knowledge of the enlightened is light, a concentration of the light of immutable knowledge beyond the two extremes of ordinary and holy, or absolute and conventional. It is the light of the nonconceptual knowledge of Mañjushrī, who represents great knowledge. This becomes manifest in the effortlessness of simply sitting.

14   For this reason Vairochana said to the Master of the Secret, "The practice of the Great Vehicle awakens the mind that transports you to the unconditioned, guided by selflessness." The Third Patriarch of Zen said, "Do not seek reality, just stop views." Obviously there is no ego in the treasury of light of the vehicle of the unconditioned, no opinionated interpretation. Ego and opinions are different names of spirit heads and ghost faces. This is just the light alone, not setting up any opinions or views, from the idea of self and ego to the ideas of Buddha and Dharma. Let us clearly hear transcendent wisdom being likened to an enormous mass of fire.

15   *The Lotus of Truth Scripture* says, "At that time the Buddha radiated a light from the white hair between his eyebrows, illuminating eighty thousand worlds in the East, pervading them all, to the lowest hells below as well as the highest heavens above." So this auspicious sign of light is the foremost, rarest of spiritual lights perfected by Buddhas.

16   The great being Mañjushrī said, in answer to the question of Maitreya, "This very auspicious sign of light appeared in ancient times when the Buddha named Illuminate like a Lamp made of the Sun and Moon expounded the Great Vehicle, entering into absorption in the sphere of infinite meaning. Now Shākyamuni Buddha must be going to expound the teaching of the Lotus Blossom of Sublime Truth, which is for enlightening beings and kept in mind by Buddhas."

17   So we should know that this light is the universal illumination of

matchless, peerless great light completely filled with infinite meaning. The great being Mañjushrī was at that time called the enlightening being Sublime Light, and was the eighth son of the Buddha called Illuminate like a Lamp made of the Sun and Moon, who enabled him to stabilize unsurpassed enlightenment. The last one to attain Buddhahood was called Burning Lamp Buddha.

Hence we know that the sitting meditation of our school is absorption in the treasury of light inherited directly from Burning Lamp and Shākyamuni. What other doctrine might there be? This is the light that is not two in ordinary people and sages, that is one vehicle in past and present. It does not let anything inside out and does not let anything outside in: who would randomly backslide into cramped boredom within the context of discriminatory social and personal relationships? It cannot be grasped, cannot be abandoned: why suffer because of emotional consciousness grasping and rejecting, hating and loving?

Furthermore, in "The Book on Comfortable Behavior" [in *The Lotus Scripture*] Mañjushrī is told, "Great enlightening beings dwell in a state of forbearance, gentle, docile, and not rough, their minds undisturbed. And they do not ruminate over things, but see the real character of things, and do not act indiscriminately." This is simply sitting: without acting indiscriminately, one thereby goes along in conformity with the great light.

A verse from the same book says,

"Delusion conceives of things as existent or nonexistent,
as being real or unreal, as born or unborn.
In an uncluttered place, concentrate your mind,
remain steady and unmoving, like a polar mountain.
Observe that all phenomena have no existence,
that they are like space, without solid stability,
neither being born nor emerging.
Unmoving, unflagging, abide in oneness:
this is called the place of nearness."

This is a direct indication, "only expounding the unexcelled Way, getting straight to the point, setting aside expedients."

In China, the great master Bodhidharma replied to the question of an emperor about the ultimate meaning of the holy truths, "Empty, nothing holy." This is the great mass of fire of the light of the Zen of the founding teachers: crystal clear on all sides, there is nothing in it at all. Outside of this light, there is no separate practice, no different principle, much less any knowledge or objects; how could there be any practice and cultivation, or deliberate effort to effect specific remedies?

21   The emperor said to Bodhidharma, "Who is it replying to me?" Bodhidharma said, "Don't know." This is simply the single light that is empty.

22   Later Zen master Xuedou wrote a eulogy of this anecdote:

> " 'Empty, nothing holy'—
> how to discern the point?
> 'Who is replying to me?'—
> 'Don't know,' he says."

23   If you can attain freedom and ease by absorption in this koan, the entire body is luminous, the whole world is luminous.

24   The great master Yunmen, thirty-ninth generation from the Buddha, said to a group in a lecture, "All people have a light, but when they look at it they do not see it, so it is obscure. What is everyone's light?" No one replied, so the master himself said in their behalf, "The communal hall, the Buddha shrine, the kitchen pantry, the mountain gate."

25   Now when the great master says that everyone has a light, he does not say it is to appear later on, nor that it existed in the past, nor that it becomes apparent to a view from the side: he is stating that everyone has a light. This is exactly what is meant in the overall sense by the light of great wisdom: it should be heard and retained, enjoyed and applied, in the skin, flesh, bones, and marrow.

26   The light is everyone: Shākyamuni and Maitreya are its servants. What is not more in Buddhas or less in ordinary beings is this spiritual light, so it is existent in all; it is the whole earth as a single mass of fire.

27   The master said, "What is everyone's light?" At that time, the assembly made no reply. Even if there had been a hundred thousand apt statements, there still would have been "no reply."

28   Yunmen answered himself in their behalf, "The communal hall, the Buddha shrine, the kitchen pantry, the mountain gate." This answering himself in their behalf is answering himself in everyone's behalf, answering himself in behalf of the light, answering himself in behalf of obscurity, answering himself in behalf of the assembly's

lack of response: it is absorption in the treasury of light awakening and bringing forth radiant light.

This being so, it does not question whether you are ordinary people   29
or Buddhas, it does not discriminate between sentient and inanimate beings: having always been shining everywhere, the light has no beginning, no location. That is why it is "obscure," it is "what," it is "traveling at night," it is "impossible to conceive of even in a billion billion million aeons."

Also, a monk asked Yunmen, "The light silently shines through-   30
out countless worlds—" Before he had even finished posing his question, Yunmen quickly asked back, "Are these not the words of a famous poet?" The monk said, "They are." Yunmen said, "You are trapped in words."

Hail to the ancient Buddha Yunmen! His eyes were fast as comets,   31
his mind swift as lightning! At this point the monk was speechless. Who would not be ashamed?

Zen master Xuefeng, instructing a group, said, "The Buddhas of all   32
times turn the great wheel of the Teaching in flames of fire." Yunmen said, "The flames of fire expound the Teaching to the Buddhas of all times; the Buddhas of all times stand there and listen."

So the light of flames of fire is the site of enlightenment of the   33
Buddhas of all times, it is the teacher of the Buddhas. For this reason, all of the Enlightened Ones are always expounding the Teaching in the midst of myriad forms even as they remain at their own site of enlightenment, which is the light of complete perfect tranquillity.

It is a matter of "valuing the ears without devaluing the eyes."   34
This mass of flames of fire is not in front, not behind: it is just total manifestation.

To go on degrading yourself and limiting yourself in spite of that,   35
producing individual subjective ideas that you are basically an ignorant ordinary being, a common person with no wisdom, is truly hellish behavior slandering the Wheel of True Teaching of the Enlightened.

The exposition of the Teaching by the flames of fire indicated by   36
Xuefeng and expressed by Yunmen is a direct approach without expedients, just expounding the unexcelled Way, bringing out the totality of the teachings of the Buddha's whole lifetime.

When Xuefeng spoke as he did, this was already being burned up   37
in the flames of fire. Do you want to escape? Reciting scriptures, per-

forming prostrations, raising and lowering each foot—everything is the manifestation of the great function of light.

38   There are those who learn to wonder whose grace this depends on, uselessly toiling to quiet thoughts without knowing this hidden essence. There are also those who doubt and dismiss the possibility, making a living in a ghost cave. There are also those who go into the ocean to count the grains of sand. There are also those who are like mosquitoes breaking through a paper window. Leaving aside for the moment getting trapped in words, what would be right?

39   Although there is no more leisure time to wash a clod of earth in the mud, students of Zen should first know what is being said when they pose a question. Once we are talking about silent illumination pervading the universe, why should these be the words of a famous poet? Why should they be the words of Buddha? Why should they be your words? After all, whose words would they be? "The communal hall, the Buddha shrine, the kitchen pantry, the mountain gate." Listen clearly, hear accurately.

40   Great Master Changsha said to a congregation, "The whole universe is the eye of a practitioner. The whole universe is the family talk of a practitioner. The whole universe is the total body of a practitioner. The whole universe is one's own light. In the whole universe there is no one who is not oneself."

41   So penetrating study of the Way of the enlightened requires diligence to learn and faith to attain. Unless you form an alliance with the family of Buddhas lifetime after lifetime, how can you grasp what you hear in a lecture like this? Make sure that you do not become further estranged and further remote from it.

42   Now the universe spoken of by Changsha is a single eye of the individual involved in Zen study. The entirety of space is the total body and mind. He does not grasp the holy or reject the ordinary; he does not say that confused people are not so while enlightened people are thus. What he does is point directly to your own light: don't defer this to Great Master Changsha.

43   This sermon is an all-inclusive talk within your nostrils, a freely adapted practical lesson within your eyes. There are those who specially bring up old model koans but never attain insight or knowledge all their lives. Every one of them is the child of a rich family but has no britches.

44   Also, hearing talk of light, ignorant people think of it as like the

light of fireflies, like the light of lamps, like the light of sun and moon or the luster of gold and jewels, groping for comparisons; trying to see shining radiance, they focus on the mind and figure inside the intellect, aiming for it as a realm of utter emptiness and total silence.

For this reason they stop movement and take refuge in stillness, or they are unable to relinquish ideas of an actual entity or false ideas of the existence of something to obtain; or their thoughts of inconceivable mystic wonder go on and on unceasingly and they think too deeply only of its rarity. Such people, rice bags sleeping with their eyes open, are the only numerous ones.   45

If it were really an inconceivably mysterious matter of such great import, why do you imagine you can reach it by thinking? This is the type of bedevilment characterized by understanding the quiet reflection of the conscious spirit as the sitting of Buddha. This is why the founder of Zen explained that there is nothing holy in openness, and it is not consciously known. To be given such an explanation is something that rarely happens.   46

Zen Master Changsha said, "The reason students of the Way do not discern the real is simply that they continue to recognize the conscious spirit. It is the root of infinite aeons of birth and death, yet deluded people call it the original human being."   47

So to cultivate realization based on ideas about your own mind and assumptions about what is to be attained is to cultivate the root of birth and death.   48

Now the reference made to the real and the original human being mean the openness of the light that is inherently there and perfectly complete. Outside of the openness of the light, what thing would you try to seek so greedily? That is why there is no holiness, and it is not consciously known; it is only a holeless iron hammerhead, a great mass of fire.

Zhaozhou asked Nanquan, "What is the Way?"   49

Nanquan said, "The normal mind is the Way."

Zhaozhou said, "How should one approach it?"

Nanquan said, "If you try to head for it, you immediately turn away from it."

Zhaozhou said, "If one doesn't make any attempt, how can one know it is the Way?"

Nanquan said, "The Way is not in the domain of knowledge, yet not in the domain of unknowing. Knowledge is false consciousness, unknowing is indifference. If you really arrive at the effortless Way without a doubt, you are as empty and open as space: how can you insist on affirmation or denial?"

50   This is why the ancients, pitying those whose approach is mistaken because it is contrived based on cultivated power, painstakingly guided them by saying, "The Way cannot be attained by the conscious mind, nor can it be attained by mindlessness; it cannot be communicated by words, nor can it be reached by silence. As soon as you get involved in deliberation, you are ten million stages away."

51   People, can there be any idea of cultivating mind, or any transmundane phenomena or principles, outside of this conscious mind or mindlessness? Since it is said to be unattainable either by the conscious mind or by mindlessness, why not immediately give up false ideas of seeking mind or relinquishing mind?

52   Ordinary people who do not believe and are lazy, and are not even up to the level of this device, cling to illusory definitions of self, rush around pompously in the dreamlike evanescent world, unaware that they are possessed by demons of worldly knowledge and intellectual acumen. Their wits always at work, they imagine that the light of which they have heard tell must be like a fiery comet shooting from between the eyebrows of Buddha. Interpreting meanings literally, they never even think of finding out the real truth of the sages. Even if they appear in the world as seasoned practitioners and adepts, they have no part in higher study, so they cannot ascertain how the light throughout the whole body, the light of the realm of reality, covers the heavens and covers the earth. They are charlatans clinging to forms, unworthy even of pity.

53   Shākyamuni Buddha said, "The light of lights is not blue, yellow, red, white, or black. It is not matter, not mind. It is not existent, not nonexistent. It is not a phenomenon resulting from causes. It is the source of all Buddhas, the basis of practicing the Way of enlightening beings, fundamental for all Buddhists."

54   So the Realized One had emerged from absorption in flowery light, empty in substance and essence, sat on the regal diamond throne of a thousand lights, and expounded the light of the discipline of unity.

55   It is clearly obvious that this light is not blue, yellow, red, white, or black. It is just "the god of fire, crimson through and through," it is "a clay ox running on the bottom of the ocean," it is "an iron ox without skin or bones." It being "neither matter nor mind," why stick

a sense of seeking in your chest and repeatedly pant over the inner mind? Furthermore, it is not a causally effected phenomenon: how could it be made by cultivating realization?

Truly this is the source of the Buddhas, fundamental for all Bud-   56
dhists. Not only that, it is the light of the discipline of unity accepted and held by Vairochana Buddha since his first inspiration. Therefore it is an element of the ground of mind, detached from all labels and appearances; this is called the light of the discipline of the mind ground.

Shākyamuni Buddha said, "If people who expound the Teaching   57
stay alone in deserted places, where there is utter silence and no sound of human voices, and read and recite this scripture, I will then manifest for them the body of pure clear light. If they forget a chapter or verse, I will expound it to them so that they may comprehend it fluently."

So when you read and recite this scripture, this is the self at that   58
time therefore manifesting pure and clear light. The body and mind of the Buddhas are light. The land of all Burning Lamps is Eternally Silent Light. Pure Lands, bodies, and minds are all light; that is why we say there are eighty-four thousand lights, up to an infinite number of lights.

Zen master Puning Yong quoted the aforementioned story about   59
the flames of fire expounding the Teaching, and recited this verse to his congregation:

> "One mass of fierce flames reddens the whole sky;
> The Buddhas of all times are right in the center.
> Having expounded the Teaching, now they are done;
> Above the eyebrows there rises a pure breeze."

In the process of finding out the inner sanctum of Buddhism, sponta-   60
neously penetrating vision of the flames of fire expounding the Teaching is thus. So one mass of fierce flames blazes through time: it comes from nowhere, has no form, has no differentiation, and so ultimately has no extinction. Because it is completely undifferenti-ated, it is the scenery of the original ground of all phenomena, all beings, and all Buddhas.

Why do students today not keep this in mind or believe in it reso-   61
lutely? Because they do not believe in it resolutely, they become

lowly ignorant fools, not escaping vicious circles. They should ask themselves where the fault is, and see all the way through.

62   Those who are wedded to worldly conventions think that illusory and ephemeral phenomena are really permanent, so they are completely preoccupied with gain and loss of mundane profit. Placing profoundly abiding trust in a life that is like a temporary lamp before the wind, which cannot be guaranteed even until tomorrow, where each outgoing breath does not ensure that another ingoing breath will follow, they rejoice and lament according to vicissitudes.

63   Even your physical elements will vanish in the funeral pyre, like evaporating dew; although there is not so much as an atom of anything that you can cling to as your own, you spend your life taking it easy, as if you were master of yourself.

64   This does not depend on the teachings of the scriptures; it is an evident truth, right before our eyes. Since it is a mass of roaring flames, therefore the Buddhas of all times are also herein, and so are all beings in all forms of life also herein. In this context, how are living beings and Buddhas different? Those who erroneously cling to the ego do not believe in the light, so they are *herein* arbitrarily making themselves bob and sink in birth and death. Those who see through to the light, in contrast, are *herein* realizing impartial unhindered universal knowledge.

65   Therefore Yongjia said, "Eternal calm is not apart from right where you are; if you seek, I know you cannot see. It cannot be grasped, cannot be rejected; within ungraspability it is attained just so. The ancient Nāgārjuna said in a eulogy of wisdom, "Transcendent wisdom is like a mass of fire; it is ungraspable on all four sides."

66   Although everyone hears and reads such great teachings, you study them as if they were only relevant to others. You do not free and ease your whole being, you do not penetrate the totality. Instead you say that you are lacking in capacity, or that you are beginners, or that you are latecomers, or that you are ordinary mortals who have not cut off a single delusion. You do not put down your former views or your self-image. Dwelling in the great treasury of light all day and all night, you turn yourself into a lowly hireling, roaming in misery, a longtime pauper.

67   This is your own conceit of inferiority, having forgotten the call of your noble origins. How sad it is to take up a nightsoil bucket and become a cesspool cleaner, thinking of the body of pure light as a

defiled body full of misery. This is the saddest of sadnesses, which nothing can surpass.

The subjectivity of the self-image should be changed right away. 68
Even if you talk about the major and minor teachings, the provisional and the true teachings, the phenomena and principles of the exoteric and esoteric teachings, and the subtle messages of the five houses and seven schools of Zen, as long as you retain your self-image, you wind up in birth and death.

This is why it is said that if you interpret reality by means of the 69
mind of birth and death, then reality will become birth and death.

The idea of the self, the idea of a person, the idea of a being, and 70
the idea of a life are self-image. The idea of the physical body, prejudiced views, false views, and fixated views are self-image. Even the countless subtle veils of ignorance between standard enlightenment and sublime enlightenment are self-image. First it is called the idea of self, or intellectual habit energy; even attachment to principle, traces of enlightenment, and the view of equanimity are all different names varying according to the degree and seriousness of self-image.

If you wonder why this is, from the very first great evil, perverted, 71
and biased views even up to the last little bit of subtle ignorance, when there is no self-image, what can be called an idea of Buddha or an idea of Dharma? Who is conscious of the veil?

For this reason Zen master Dōgen said, "First you should be done 72
with the ego. If you want to be done with the ego, you should contemplate impermanence." This is direct instruction from a heart of consummate magnanimity and perfect sincerity.

"The Teaching on Pacifying the Mind," by the Great Teacher of 73
Shaolin says, "Why do people of the world fail to attain enlightenment in spite of all their studies? They do not attain enlightenment because they are self-conscious. Fully developed people do not worry in miserable situations and do not rejoice in pleasant situations; this is because they are not self-conscious."

A verse by an ancient illuminate says, 74

"Buddhas do not see themselves; wisdom is Buddha.
If you really have wisdom, there is no other Buddha.
The wise know the emptiness of the obstructions of sin;
Equanimous, they have no fear of life and death."

Not fearing life and death is because of not seeing oneself. Not seeing oneself means not being self-conscious, not having a self-image. The light of great wisdom is thus impersonal, so the verse says that wisdom is Buddha.

75   In spite of this, you think that it is a matter of loving the transitory body, which is like dew on the grass, like a floating bubble; when it comes to the great light that is your real body, you think it is an irrelevant discussion and suppose that there must be something more grandiose. Thus you waste your time talking about political conditions and the status of pious donations, without any stable practice reflecting consideration of how this idly passing life will end up.

76   If you have any attainment of faith or practice within this treasury of light, why would it be only your own personal liberation? Requiting the four debts above, providing sustenance for those in the three realms of being below, mountains, rivers, and earth, your own body and others' bodies, are all the light of suchness, illumining everywhere endlessly.

77   Great Master Caoshan said in a verse,

"The essence of awareness, round and bright, the body without form:
Do not force distance or closeness in knowledge and opinion.
When thoughts differ, they obscure the mystic being;
When mind diverges, it is not close to the Path.
When feelings distinguish myriad things, you sink into the objects before you;
When consciousness reflects many things, you lose the original reality.
If you understand completely what is in these lines,
Clearly you are trouble-free, as you were of yore."

78   This is a direct indication, a direct explanation, within the treasury of light, which furthermore gives directions for subtle cultivation of fundamental realization. It does not matter whether you are a monk or a lay person, whether you are a beginner or experienced; it makes no difference whether you are sharp or dull, or how much learning or knowledge you have. This just points directly at the formless body of the essence of awareness, round and bright, which is utterly unique and unmatched.

79   The essence of awareness is the Buddha-nature. Round brightness

is a great light; it is the formless silent light of your present illusory body. Therefore an ancient worthy said, "The whole body has no form, the whole world does not hide it."

If you still do not understand, then let me ask you this: shattering your whole body and burning up your skin, flesh, bones, and marrow, bring me one thing. At precisely such a time, the living beings and Buddhas of past and present, the ordinary mortals and sages of the three realms, myriad forms and appearances, are all without exception the formless body.   80

Master Linji said, "The physical elements are not able to expound the Teaching or listen to the truth. Your spleen, stomach, liver, and gallbladder are not able to expound the truth or listen to the truth. Space is not able to expound the truth or listen to the truth. So what can expound the truth and listen to the truth?" This independent spiritual light listening to the truth is the formless body. The ancient temporarily gave it a name for the sake of other people, calling it the "independent wayfarer listening to the truth."   81

Having spoken of the "round and bright formless body of the essence of awareness," everything has been explained in one line. Out of kindness the master goes on to speak of subtle cultivation, saying not to force distance or closeness in knowledge and opinion. Those who are close to false teachers learn only opinions and interpretations, claiming to have attained Zen beyond the Buddhas and Patriarchs by means of empowerment through study, claiming to be beyond the knowledge and perception of all others, claiming to be closer to the Zen potential than anyone else. This is a perverse mentality, possessed by the king of all demons. It is a heretical belief in having attained what one has not really attained.   82

Next, those who imagine identity and cling to appearances slack off and fail to progress simply say they are dullards; they are not studious, they are far from being learners. This is "idly producing opinions."   83

The arising of these two kinds of view, hating and loving, judging right and wrong, turns into intellectual and emotional feelings and thoughts. Therefore Caoshan cuts in two with one sword stroke, saying, "When thoughts differ, they obscure the mystic being; when mind diverges, it is not close to the Path." Does this not mean that we should abandon false teachers and approach good companions? Through the profession of false teachers, people learn opinions and   84 interpretations, thinking of near and far; this is "idly producing opinions."

85   "This Path" and the "Mystic Being" are the Sun Face and Moon Face of the light, essence of awareness. Nevertheless, from within this light a single unaware thought arises, and the errant mind increases false imaginings. These are floating clouds blocking the round and bright moon of the mind. This is why the verse says "it is not close to the Path."

86   "When feelings distinguish myriad things, you sink into the objects before you." The Buddha already said, "Mind, Buddha, and living beings—these three have no distinction." He also said, "There is only one truth." Even though you hear and read such great teachings, for your own part you arbitrarily contrast others and self, and discriminate between the noble and the base, the ordinary and the holy. Because of the beauty or ugliness of sound and form, because of poverty and wealth, loss and gain, you are taken by the objects before you. This is brought about by your reliance on intellectual views, by pride and disbelief infecting practice and realization.

87   "When consciousness reflects many things, you lose the original reality." Buddhism originally adapted to myriad different types of potential, resulting in teachings great and small, temporary and true, half and full, partial and complete, exoteric and esoteric, meditation and doctrine, the Path of Sages and the Pure Land Way. It is not that there are not many facets to Buddhism, but if you cling to them intellectually, after all you lose the original reality.

88   "If you understand completely what is in these lines, clearly you are trouble-free, as you were of yore." The way you "were of yore" means that there is no fabricated effort to cultivate realization; it is the formless body, sitting utterly still, without doubt. If you keep any intellectual interpretation on your mind, you are not trouble-free, you are not "as you were of yore."

89   Shākyamuni Buddha said, "There is nothing I gained from Dīpankāra Buddha to realize supreme perfect enlightenment." This is an expression of a meeting with Dīpankāra Buddha; it is "one statement that transcends millions." The light of this "nothing gained" should be studied.

90   Nowadays, those who shave their heads and wear black as latter-day followers of Buddha spend the days and pass the months illumined by the light of Dīpankāra, "The Lamp," but they do not wonder

what Dīpaṇkāra Buddha, The Lamp Illuminate, really is. Therefore they are not real students; they just make use of the appearance of renunciants in order to grab donations. In reality, they are actually vagrants and roustabouts.

If you deny this, let me ask you, what are the marks and refine-   91
ments of the Lamp Buddha? You cannot say anything, yet you cannot say nothing; speak quickly, speak quickly!

How sad that you only learn of the Lamp Buddha as an illuminate   92
of the past and do not know that the Lamp Buddha shines throughout all time. How then could you believe that it is teaching and attaining nirvana in your nostrils, in your eyes?

Now there is a group of the lowest type of hearer, who repeatedly   93
weary of life and death and hurriedly seek nirvana, arousing their de-termination on the basis of the idea of something really existing and something being attained. Adding religious greed on top of selfish conceit, their seeking mind never rests until they die. Teachers with-out perception praise them as good people of faith, so they take pride in egotistical clinging and possessiveness as diligent spiritual prac-tice, eventually turning into ghouls.

To begin with, the Buddhist study of perpetual energy and the pure   94
transmission of immutable radiant concentration is not like your er-roneous concentration, which approaches cultivation and realization as two stages and seeks intellectual understanding.

Master Baizhang said, "The spiritual light shines alone, utterly free   95
of senses and objects; the essence manifests, real and eternal. It is not confined to writings. The nature of mind is undefiled, originally complete and perfect in itself. Just detach it from false objects and it awakens to suchness."

This spiritual light is unbroken from the infinite past through the   96
infinite future; this is called perpetual energy. Utterly free of senses and objects, the essence manifests, real and eternal; this is called per-manent stability of radiance. Trusting in this spiritual light, abiding peacefully, imperturbable, is called the supreme concentration of simply sitting.

So there must be different levels of depth and shallowness, of lev-   97
ity and gravity, even in saying there is something attained. If you just cling to the appearances of phenomena and cultivate formal practices, seeking Buddha externally, distinguishing the real and the false in terms of writings and words, you may practice giving while dwelling

on appearances, misconstruing this to be accumulation of merit, or cause your body and mind pain for the sake of annihilating sin and producing virtue, simply taking pride in this as diligence. This is not called attaining something.

98   Even if you put aside pen and ink, abstain from social relations, sit alone in an empty valley, live off the fruits of the trees and clothe yourself with grasses, and sit all the time without lying down, in your mind you are trying to stop movement and return it to stillness, cut off illusion completely, dwell only on absolute truth, reject samsara and grasp nirvana, despising the one and loving the other; all of this is possessiveness.

99   For this reason, the great teacher Yongjia said, "If you abandon existence and cling to emptiness, your sickness is still there. This is like plunging into fire to avoid drowning. If you reject imagination to grasp truth, the grasping and rejecting mind produces clever falsehood. Students not understanding how to apply developmental practice actually wind up recognizing a thief as their own offspring. The loss of spiritual wealth and destruction of virtues inevitably derive from this mind, intellect, and consciousness." So students should plunge body and mind into the treasury of light, free and ease the whole body in the light of Buddha, sitting, reclining, and walking around therein.

100   This is why the Buddha said, "Offspring of Buddha abide in this stage, which is the experience of Buddhahood. They are always therein, walking around, sitting, lying down." These golden words should not be forgotten for even a moment by those who aspire to be offspring of Buddha. "This stage" is the treasury of light; it is the one sole vehicle to Buddhahood. Do not let a single thought turning away from enlightenment to merge with material objects transform this experience of Buddhahood into the experience of animality or ghosthood.

101   Now tell me about the marks and refinements, about the site of the nirvana, of Dīpaṇkāra Buddha, of Shākyamuni Buddha, of the seven Buddhas and generations of Zen Masters who perpetuated the flame of the lamp: do you investigate and study them as remote in time and space, or do you learn and think of them as permanently present and eternal? Would you say they are in the jewel citadel of silent light?

102   You understand that "the true reality of Buddha is like space," but at such a level, if you do not pass through and beyond the cave of

learned judgments and comparisons, how can you be called masters of the inheritance of the light of Buddha? You are jackals howling, clinging to the body of a lion.

If you cannot investigate truth through your own eyes, even if you shave your head and dress in black, you are pitiful living beings. Even if you can interpret a thousand scriptures and ten thousand treatises, you are "counting the treasures of another house," you are "seafarers who know there's something valuable but do not know the price."   103

Tell me, right now as you defecate and urinate, dress and eat, ultimately whose experience is it? And what, moreover, of the colors of the waters, the scenery of the mountains, the coming and going of heat and cold, the spring flowers, the autumn moon, thousands of changes, myriad transformations—what brings all this about? Truly this is a "countenance most wondrous, light illumining the ten directions." It is "samsara and nirvana are like last night's dream." It is "being is nonbeing, nonbeing is being." If not thus, even if you speak of "always being there on Spiritual Mountain," it is a false teaching, it is specious discourse; even if you hear of "eternally silent light that neither comes into being nor passes away," I would say it is only talk, with no real meaning.   104

In a classic statement of the discipline of unity, Shākyamuni Buddha said, "Those who entertain the idea of self and cling to appearances cannot believe in this teaching, while those who cultivate realization that annihilates life are not fertile ground. If you want to foster the sprouts of enlightenment, so that the light illumines the world, you should calmly examine the real characteristics of phenomena: they are not born and do not perish; they are not permanent and yet are not annihilated, they are not one and yet are not different; they do not come and do not go. Do not conceive discriminatory ideas, even between learning and the state beyond learning."   105

So this classic statement of light illumining the world should be heard all the way through your bones, all the way through your marrow. It is the subtle body in which the great function of the Buddhas of all times becomes manifest. Taking it upon yourself to put it into practice, would not everyone be overjoyed?   106

However, as I see students today, being grounded on ignorance, they spend their lives polishing day and night, expecting to eventually see through to the light in this way. Then again, some try to see this radiant pure light by practicing meditation to get rid of random   107 thoughts flying around, repeatedly trying to beat out the flaming fires, hoping to see the eternally silent light thereby. If you think the total nonarising of thought to be right, then are wood, stones, and clods of earth right? All of you are the lowest kind of hearer, who drowns while trying to avoid being burned. How foolish! Clinging to the sitting of the two vehicles and the inclinations of ordinary people, you want to realize supreme universal enlightenment; there is nothing more stupid and perverse.

108   For this reason it is said, "Those on the two vehicles may be diligent but lack the spirit of enlightenment; outsiders may be intellectually brilliant, but they lack wisdom. Ignorant and stupid, petty and fearful, they think there's something real in the empty fist."

109   To cultivate the mind or seek the mind in this manner is to be obstructed by calculating and figuring, burying the inherently perfect light. Not only that, it repudiates the true teaching of the Buddha and makes for uninterrupted hell.

110   Furthermore, countless abbots of monasteries from the sixth century even up until now have been mere ignoramuses, deficient in wisdom, taking in the unseeing masses of egotistical and possessive people. Can we not pity them? Can we not feel sorry for them? Even those who from time to time emerge from that nest see spirits and ghosts, their thieving mind not yet dead.

111   Some of them may wrongly give definitive approval to a temporary surge of energy, or it may happen that through a temporary inspiration they sit for a long time without lying down, so that the mind and consciousness are thoroughly fatigued, everything becomes the same to them, activity and function stop for a while, and thoughts quiet down; then they misunderstand this state, which resembles the solitary radiance of ethereal spirituality, misconstruing it to be the state where inside and outside become one, the original ground of the fundamental state of the essential self.

112   Taking this interpretation to Zen teachers who have no true perception, they present the view. Since the teachers have no eyes to perceive people, therefore they go along with the words of those who come to them, giving them worthless approval, so that they call themselves graduate Zen monks. Countless followers of the Way with shallow consciousness and little learning fall into this poison. Truly, even as we say it is the age of dereliction of the teaching, is it not all pathetic?

I humbly say to people who are real seekers, who have the same   113
aspiration, do not cling to one device or one state, do not rely on
intellectual understanding or brilliance, do not carry around what
you learn by sitting. Plunging body and mind into the great treasury
of light without looking back, "sit grandly under the eaves" without
seeking enlightenment, without trying to get rid of illusion, without
aversion to the rising of thoughts, and yet without fondly continuing
thoughts.

If you do not continue thoughts, thoughts cannot arise by them-   114
selves. Like an empty space, like a mass of fire, letting your breathing
flow naturally out and in, sit decisively without getting involved in
anything at all.

Even if eighty-four thousand random thoughts arise and disappear,   115
as long as the individual does not get involved in them but lets go of
them, then each thought will become the light of spiritual power of
wisdom. And it is not only while sitting; every step is the walk of
light. Not engaging in subjective thinking step after step, twenty-four
hours a day, you are like someone completely dead, utterly without
self-image or subjective thoughts.

Nevertheless, outgoing breathing and incoming breathing, the es-   116
sence of hearing and the essence of feeling, without conscious knowledge or subjective discrimination, are silently shining light in which
body and mind are one suchness. Therefore when called there is an
immediate response. This is the light in which the ordinary and the
sage, the deluded and the enlightened, are one suchness. Even in the
midst of activity, it is not hindered by activity. The forests and flowers, the grasses and leaves, people and animals, great and small, long
and short, square and round, all appear at once, without depending on
the discriminations of your thoughts and attention. This is manifest
proof that the light is not obstructed by activity. It is empty luminosity spontaneously shining without exerting mental energy.

This light has never had any place of abode. Even when buddhas   117
appear in the world, it does not appear in the world. Even though they
enter nirvana, it does not enter nirvana. When you are born, the light
is not born. When you die, the light is not extinguished. It is not more
in Buddhas and not less in ordinary beings. It is not lost in confusion,
not awakened by enlightenment. It has no location, no appearance,
no name. It is the totality of everything. It cannot be grasped, cannot
be rejected, cannot be attained. While unattainable, it is in effect

throughout the entire being. From the highest heaven above to the lowest hell below, it is thus completely clear, a wondrously inconceivable spiritual light.

118   If you believe and accept this mystic message, you do not need to ask anyone else whether it is true or false; it will be like meeting your own father in the middle of town. Do not petition other teachers for a seal of approval, and do not be eager to be given a prediction and realize fruition. Unconcerned even with these things, why then concentrate on food, clothing, and shelter, or about animalistic activities based on sexual desire and emotional attachment?

119   This absorption in the treasury of light is from the very beginning the site at which all Buddhas realize the ocean of enlightenment. Therefore it is sitting as Buddha and acting as Buddha, carried on in its utter simplicity. Those who are already Buddhists should sit at rest only in the sitting of Buddha. Do not sit in the sitting of hells, the sitting of hungry ghosts, the sitting of beasts, the sitting of antigods, humans, or celestial beings; do not sit in the sitting of hearers or those awake to conditioning.

120   Simply sitting in this way, do not waste time. This is called the enlightenment site of the straightforward mind, absorption in the treasury of light of inconceivable liberation.

121   This essay should not be shown to anyone but people who are in the school and have entered the room. My only concern is that there should be no false and biased views, whether in one's own practice or in teaching others.

Man-an
An Elementary Talk on Zen

Although the Way of Buddhahood is long and far, ultimately there is 1
not an inch of ground on earth. Although it is cultivated, realized, and mastered over a period of three incalculable aeons, the true mind is not remote. Although there may be five hundred miles of dangers and difficult road, the treasure is nearby. If people who study Zen to learn the Way mistake a single step or stir a single thought, they are ten trillion lands and a billion aeons away.

You should simply see your essential nature to attain Buddhahood. 2
The scriptural teachings expounded by the Buddha over the course of his career are instructions for seeing essential nature; when it comes to seeing essential nature itself and awakening to the Way, that is communicated separately outside of doctrine and does not stand on written symbols.

In this there are no distinctions between the sharp and the dull, 3
the rich and the poor, mendicants and laypeople, Easterners or Westerners, ancients or moderns. It only depends upon whether or not the will for enlightenment is there and whether instruction and guidance are mistaken or accurate.

Even if you get directions from a thousand Buddhas and myriad 4
Zen masters, if you yourself do not continue right mindfulness with purity and singleness of faith, you can never see essential nature and awaken to the Way. This is why you realize your own essential nature by means of your own mind and understand your own life by means of your own insight. If right mindfulness is not continuous and concentration is not pure and singleminded, your efforts will be in vain.

This right mindfulness means not having any thoughts; concentra- 5
tion means not conceiving any mental images. Zen master Dōgen said, "Thinking of what does not think is the essential art of sitting meditation."

If you concentrate intensely twenty-four hours a day, the same in 6 activity as in quiet, principle and fact as one, then inward and outward bedevilments lose their ways of getting at you and you get beyond all obstruction. Good and bad, right and wrong, pain and pleasure, advantage and adversity, are shed all at once, the root compulsion by beginningless ignorance is severed, and you see the original state as it was before space and time.

7   "Before space and time" does not mean something remote in space and time; don't think of it as something ancient. It is the immediate experience of seeing essential nature right now: it is the time when you let go of your self and give up compulsion.

8   It should be understood, furthermore, that invocation of Buddha-names and recitation of scriptures are also sharp swords for severing the root of compulsion. Don't think that by accumulating effort and building up merit you will be reborn after death to see Buddha; don't seek resulting rewards of blessings and graces. You should be unattached to the marvelous.

9   As the past, present, and future mind cannot be grasped, right mindfulness appears spontaneously. Whatever you are doing, concentrate wholeheartedly on questioning the inner master that perceives, cognizes, and emotes.

10   If your effort is weak, real wondering will not occur and false imagining will be hard to expel. If you want to achieve early fulfillment, brandish the precious sword given by the mind king and march right ahead: if you meet Buddhas, kill the Buddhas; if you meet Zen masters, kill Zen masters; if you meet your parents, kill your parents; if you meet the masses of living beings, kill the masses of living beings. Totally massacre everything animate and inanimate, all forms and appearances, mountains, rivers, and earth, all times and all places, good and bad, right and wrong, plus anything else that appears and disappears, coming and going through the doors of the six senses and the alleys of the seven consciousnesses. Having killed it all completely, when you turn a flip and appear in the realm of cosmic space, you can be called a real hero. When you get to this point, you will not doubt that Buddhas and sentient beings, enlightenment and affliction, samsara and nirvana, heaven and hell, are all illusions.

11   In Zen study, you should not slack off for an instant. Alerting your vital spirit as you breathe out and in, watching your step as you walk forth and back, be as if you were galloping on a single horse into an opposing army of a million troops, armed with a single sword.

As long as our concentration is not purely singleminded in both 12
activity and stillness, it will be hard to attain even a little accord.
Concentration of right mindfulness should be cultivated most especially in the midst of activity. You need not necessarily prefer stillness.

There is a tendency to think that Zen practice will be quicker 13
under conditions of stillness and quiet and that activity is distracting,
but the power attained by cultivation in stillness is uncertain when
you deal with active situations; it has a cowardly and weakly function. In that case, what do you call empowerment?

Concentration of right mindfulness is a state of absorption that is 14
in oneself twenty-four hours a day, but one does not even know it
consciously. Even though you work all day, you do not get tired out,
and even if you sit alone or stand silently for a long time, you do not
get bored. To search out enlightenment with principle and fact unified is called genuine study.

If you want to quickly attain mastery of all truths and be indepen- 15
dent in all events, there is nothing better than concentration in activity. That is why it is said that students of mysticism working on the
Way should sit in the midst of the material world.

The Third Patriarch of Zen said, "If you want to head for the Way 16
of Unity, do not be averse to the objects of the six senses." This does
not mean that you should indulge in the objects of the six senses; it
means that you should keep right mindfulness continuous, neither
grasping nor rejecting the objects of the six senses in the course of
everyday life, like a duck going into the water without its feathers
getting wet.

If, in contrast, you despise the objects of the six senses and try to 17
avoid them, you fall into escapist tendencies and never fulfill the Way
of Buddhahood. If you clearly see the essence, then the objects of the
six senses are themselves meditation, sensual desires are themselves
the Way of Unity, and all things are manifestations of Reality. Entering into the great Zen stability undivided by movement and stillness,
body and mind are both freed and eased.

As for people who set out to cultivate spiritual practice with aver- 18
sion to the objects and desires of the senses, even if their minds and
thoughts are empty and still and their contemplative visualization
is perfectly clear, still when they leave quietude and get into active

situations, they are like fish out of water, like monkeys out of the trees.

19   Even people who go deep into mountain forests, cut off relations with the world forever, and eat from the fruits of the trees as ascetics cannot easily attain pure singleness of concentration. Needless to say, it is even more difficult for those who are mendicants in name only, or shallow householders, who are so busy making a living.

20   In truth, unless you have definite certitude of overwhelming faith, or are filled with overwhelming doubt or wonder, or are inspired with overwhelming commitment, or are overtaken by overwhelming death, it is hard to attain concentration that is pure and undivided in principle and fact, in action and stillness.

21   If you are wholeheartedly careful of how you spend your time, aware of the evanescence of life, concentrating singlemindedly on Zen work even in the midst of objects of desire, if you proceed right straight ahead, the iron walls will open up. You will experience the immense joy of walking over the Polar Mountain and become the Master within the objects of sense. You will be like a lotus blooming in fire, becoming all the more colorful and more fragrant in contact with the energy of fire.

22   Do not say that it is harder for lay people living in the world of senses and desires to sit and meditate, or that it is hard to concentrate with so many worldly duties, or that one with an official or professional career cannot practice Zen, or that the poor and the sickly do not have the power to work on the Way. These excuses are all due to impotence of faith and superficiality of the thought of enlightenment.

23   If you observe that the matter of life and death is serious, and that the world is really impermanent, the will for enlightenment will grow, the thieving heart of egoism, selfishness, pride, and covetousness will gradually die out, and you will come to work on the Way by sitting meditation in which principle and fact are one.

24   Suppose you were to lose your only child in a crowd or drop an invaluable gem: do you think you would let the child or the jewel go at that, just because of the bustle and the mob? Would you not look for them even if you had a lot of work to do or were poor or sickly? Even if you had to plunge into an immense crowd of people and had to continue searching into the night, you would not be easy in mind until you had found and retrieved your child or your jewel.

25   To have been born human and heard true teaching is a very rare

opportunity; so to neglect meditation because of your career is to treat the life of wisdom of the body of truths of the Buddhas less seriously than worldly chattels. But if you search for wisdom single-mindedly like someone who has lost a child or dropped a gem, one day you will undoubtedly encounter it, whereupon you will light up with joy.

People in all walks of life have all sorts of things to attend to; how   26
could they have the leisure to sit silently all day in quiet contemplation? Here there are Zen teachers who have not managed to cultivate this sitting meditation concentration; they teach deliberate seclusion and quietude, avoiding population centers, stating that "intensive meditation concentration cannot be attained in the midst of professional work, business, and labor," thus causing students to apply their minds mistakenly.

People who listen to this kind of talk consequently think of Zen   27
as something that is hard to do and hard to practice, so they give up the inspiration to cultivate Zen, abandon the source and try to escape, time and again becoming like lowly migrant workers. This is truly lamentable. Even if they have a deep aspiration due to some cause in the past, they get to where they neglect their jobs and lose their social virtues for the sake of the Way.

As an ancient said, if people today were as eager for enlightenment   28
as they are to embrace their lovers, then no matter how busy their professional lives might be and no matter how luxurious their dwellings may be, they would not fail to attain continuous concentration leading to appearance of the Great Wonder.

Many people of both ancient and modern times have awakened to   29
the Way and seen essential nature in the midst of activity. All beings in all times and places are manifestations of one mind: when the mind is aroused, all sorts of things arise; when the mind is quiet, all things are quiet. "When the one mind is unborn, all things are blameless." For this reason, even if you stay in quiet and serene places deep in the mountains and sit silently in quiet contemplation, as long as the road of the mind-monkey's horse of conceptualization is not cut off, you will only be wasting time.

The Third Patriarch of Zen said, "If you try to stop movement and   30
resort to stillness, that stopping will cause even more movement." If you try to seek true suchness by erasing random thoughts, you will belabor your vital spirit, diminish your mental energy, and get sick.

Not only that, you will become oblivious or distracted and fall into a pit of bewilderment.

31   You should use the two methods of cessation and observation to perfect discipline, concentration, and insight. Cessation is Zen concentration, observation is insight. In cessation the mind, intellect, and consciousness are inactive, preventing all misconduct, cutting off the root of unconscious compulsion; there is no transgression of precepts, major or minor. In observation there is no attachment to appearances of conduct, all ideas of self and things are emptied, obstructions caused by beginningless habitual actions are annihilated, and the spiritual light of the essential self shines through everywhere, inside and outside.

32   There is no cessation without observation and no observation without cessation. Combining the two truths of emptiness and conditional existence, the ultimate truth of the Middle Way is established.

33   Models for practice of sitting meditation and ways of applying the mind in concentration have come down through tradition from the Buddhas and Zen masters. You should know too that there are also types of sitting meditation typically practiced by seekers of individual liberation, seekers of heavenly states, humanitarians, and assorted cultists. Those who aspire to unsurpassed enlightenment should practice the sitting meditation of Buddhas and Zen masters.

34   Buddhas and Zen masters conceive great compassion from the outset, never forgetting the great mass of living beings. Sitting in the lotus posture, keeping the body upright, maintaining correct mindfulness, cessation and observation, and tuning the breathing are essential arts of sitting meditation.

35   In a clean and uncluttered room or under a tree or atop a rock, spread a thick sitting mat. Then loosen your belt and sit. First bend the right leg and put the right foot on the left thigh. Then place the left foot on the right thigh. Now put the right hand on the left leg, palm up; place the left hand palm up on top of the right palm, and let the two thumbs brace each other.

36   Sit straight, neither leaning backward nor forward, aligning the ears with the shoulders and the nose with the navel. With the eyes open as normal, keep watch over the tip of your nose. Do not close your eyes, for that will beckon oblivion and drowsiness. Rest your mind in the palm of your left hand, and have your energy fill your lower abdomen, waist and pelvic region, and legs.

Expanding the ocean of energy in the umbilical sphere, take one 37
deep breath and expel it completely through the mouth. Then close
the lips and let fresh air enter through the nose in continuous subtle
respiration, neither hurried nor sluggish. Being aware of the exit and
entry of the breath, think of what is not thinking. If you concentrate
intently, basic energy will naturally fill you and solidify you. Your
lower abdomen will become like a gourd or a ball.

The rule for pacing meditation is to walk slowly, calmly, and care- 38
fully, half a step with each breath, following a straight course around
a square perimeter. When you want to get up from stillness to pace
around, massage and move your body, rising calmly and carefully.
Walk slowly, along a straight path.

Move the right foot first, then the left. Each time you take a step, 39
let it be half the length of your foot, and move each foot in the interval of one breath. Watch the ground about seven feet in front of you,
and stand up straight as you walk. When you want to turn, turn to
the right. Walking forward, walking back, if your concentration is
pure and single, truth will become manifest and there will be no subjectivity in your standpoint.

As for the method of tuning the breathing, after having settled in 40
your seat, nurture your mental energy in the ocean of energy and field
of elixir, not letting it push upward from the umbilical sphere.
Breathe through the nose, neither too rapidly nor too slowly, neither
panting nor puffing.

When you breathe out, know you are breathing out; when you 41
breathe in, know you are breathing in. Focus your consciousness on
your breathing, not letting consciousness go up or down or out or
in, not thinking discursively, not making intellectual or emotional
interpretations, not trying to figure anything out, simply being aware
of outgoing and incoming breathing, not missing a single breath.

When this concentration becomes continuous, the physical ele- 42
ments of the body become well tuned, the internal organs are purified, the upper parts are clear and cool, while the lower parts are
warm. Body and mind will spontaneously produce great joyfulness.

When you maintain an open, silent, radiant awareness whether 43
you are active, stationary, sitting, or reclining, vehemently arouse the
intensest determination. At this time, if you have the slightest conscious discrimination, any thought of peace, bliss, or seeing essence,

you will never be able to get out of birth and death, even in a hundred aeons and a thousand lifetimes.

44   If you have faith profoundly settled and galvanize the concentration to bring on the Great Death, suddenly you will find "the bottom fall out of the bucket" and "kick over the alchemical furnace," passing beyond myriad aeons in a single instant, crushing the universe underfoot with a step. What is there to doubt or wonder about the saying of the Indian Zen master Prajñātāra, "Breathing out, I do not get involved in objects; breathing in, I do not dwell on mental or material elements"?

45   As a beginning, when inexperienced, if your breathing becomes congested, constricted, and irregular, then rock your body forward and backward and left and right to refresh your mind. Expel the turbid energy from below the navel, in one to three breaths, with the breath passing through the nose, making it go from rough to fine, then having it go out and in very subtly.

46   If you become drowsy or distracted, then count your breaths from one to ten, stopping at ten and repeating again from one to ten. In this manner, counting up to ten over and over again, you should mentally watch your exhalations with accurate mindfulness. Techniques such as visualization of the dissolution of the material elements, visualization of bones and flesh returning to their origins, and other such traditional exercises are also effective.

47   The secret of inner gazing and nurturing life and the Immortalists' wondrous art of refining elixir are also based on the methods of tuning the breathing taught in Buddhism. When you apply your mind to it wholeheartedly, sitting meditation is really a way to present and future peace and bliss.

48   In a textbook of Immortalism it says, "What is most essential to nurturing life is refining the body. The subtle aspect of refining the body is in congealing the spirit. When the spirit congeals, energy accumulates; when energy accumulates, the elixir develops. When the elixir develops, the body is stabilized; when the body is stable, the spirit is whole."

49   Obviously the Elixir of Immortality is not a material thing after all. The spot one and a half inches below the navel is called the ocean of energy; this is the place where the basic energy is stored and nurtured. Below that is called the field of elixir; this is the site where vitality and spirit are melded. When spiritual energy always fills here,

you remain free from sickness, robustly healthy, and live for a long time without aging. For this reason, realized human beings do not belabor their vitality and do not cramp their spirit.

The art of nurturing life is like maintaining a nation. Spirit is like the ruler, vitality is like the administration, energy is like the people. To care for the people is the way to keep the nation at peace; to be sparing of your energy is the way to keep your body sound. When energy is used up, the body dies; when the people are displaced, a country perishes.

50

An enlightened leader focuses concern on those below; an ignorant ruler acts whimsically toward those below. When rulers act whimsically, then cabinet members flaunt their authority, counting on the ruler's favor and indulgence, paying no attention to the desperate straits of the people below. Greedy ministers plunder rapaciously, callous officials steal by deceit, the faithful and moral go into hiding, and the common people are embittered.

51

When concern is focused on those below, then taxes and levies are modest and honest, rewards and punishments are not arbitrary, laws and measures are just, plenty and parsimony correspond to the season, the soil is fertile, the country is strong, production is abundant, and crops are fruitful. There is no wasteland, and no starvation among the people.

52

The human body is the same way. When vitality and energy always fill the elixir field, then internal troubles do not act up and external evils cannot invade. The six bandits flee, the four demons hide. The sinews and bones are firm, there is good circulation of the blood, the heart is peaceful, and the spirit is robust.

53

If you lose concentration of accurate mindfulness, having it snatched away by a distracting object or lured away by random associations, then bedevilments arise in profusion and consequences of past actions collect on your mind and bother you. Immorality, indulgence, false opinions, and conceit increase, even to the point of destroying the seed of Buddhahood.

54

It is pitiful how human beings are all imbued with wisdom and virtue, and fully endowed with the wish-fulfilling jewel, yet they degrade themselves and impoverish themselves. Many of them say they have minimal potential, or they are sickly, or they are obstructed by their past history, or they are entangled by circumstances, or there

55

are no teachers, or the teaching is degenerate, or they have professional jobs, or they are householders.

56   People also say by way of excuse that they have parents and children, they have dependents, they have family business, they have social responsibilities, they are impure, they have troubles, there is tomorrow, there is next year, there is the next life. Creating their own laziness and boredom, lax and passive, they do not arouse the determination to practice Zen, they do not question and concentrate, they do not investigate Zen and study the Way.

57   Regarding the three poisons and five desires to be inherent nature, seeking repute and profit by flattery and deviousness as a daily occurrence, not only do they waste this irreplaceable life, they also add on to evil habits from beginningless past and suffer all sorts of problems and pains into the endless future.

58   This is most pitiful, most frightful. Having happened to be born human and had the fortune to encounter the teaching of enlightenment, they do not understand the fluctuations of their minds and do not know where their bodies will end up. Abandoning their innate wealth and nobility, burying their inherent light, they do not even know that Buddha-nature exists.

59   It is a pity that the true teaching has deteriorated and people's knowledge is inferior. People who attain the Way are few, and genuine teachers are rare. The inspirations of students today are incorrect from the start; in the course of their studies, many go on false paths.

60   Even people who are supposed to have superior faculties and great determination, to say nothing of those with mediocre or lesser potential, not infrequently take fame and profit for their inspiration and make pride their willpower. Without distinguishing whether teachers and colleagues are right or wrong, they insist on seeking enlightenment and marvels. Without letting go of fixations on their own bodies and minds, they seek only prominence and fame.

61   Even though some such people may occasionally seem to be exerting intense energy, when they deal with concrete events they backslide and slack off. Facing objective circumstances, they interrupt their concentration, so it does not continue and the Great Wonder does not appear.

62   What a waste! They wind up dying in a ghost cave in a mountain of blackness, developing nihilistic views; or else they remain fixated in the radiant light of spiritual awareness, conceiving views of Bud-

dha, Dharma, and eternity. Some recognize spiritual radiance, alert yet silent, and compare it to suchness, the essence of things.

Even if people like this meet teachers with clear eyes, they do not 63 relinquish their own opinions to learn the Way. Even if they study the koans of the ancestral teachers of Zen, they do not bring them to mind with focused concentration. Coming to impenetrable and inscrutable Zen devices, they interpret arbitrarily by rationalization and intellectual discrimination, calling that penetration through to freedom.

Even those who are supposedly Zen teachers have not cut off their 64 mental routines and have not arrived at the intent and expression of Zen. Making their living on hallucinations and altered states, they violate the rules of conduct without fear of the consequences. Neglecting the unified work on the Way that includes reading scriptures, performing prostrations before Buddhas, and simply sitting, they reject the refinement and development process that includes sweeping, drawing water, gathering firewood, and preparing meals. The Zen monasteries are like general stores at the crossroads, dealing in poetry and song, prose and verse, calligraphy and painting, calculating, stamps, tea, incenses, medicine, divination, and all sorts of other arts. They engage in trade and commerce whenever the opportunity or demand arises. Can you call this means of dealing with the masses for the sake of the people? It can hardly be called the will for Zen study.

Even if you are intelligent, psychic, eloquent, and learned, have 65 examined all principles, mastered all doctrines, and clarified all teachings, even if you can radiate spiritual light and transform the atmosphere, can tame ghosts and wild animals, and can die while sitting or standing, even if you are virtuous enough to be the teacher of kings and lords, and are even called an incarnate Buddha, unless you disregard wealth, sensuality, reputation, and profit, you can hardly be called someone with continuity of true mindfulness.

The sad fact is that both the clergy and the laity are superficial in 66 their attention to the Way. Those who abandon name and profit are really rare. Therefore the teaching centers make talks on Zen and lectures on classics their style, consider large crowds and plenty of donations to be a flourishing condition, think learning and talent are wisdom, and call fame and power virtues.

On the borderline of life and death, on the very last day, of what 67 use will any of this be? One day when you suffer illness, false thoughts will increase all the more, the fire in your heart will back up, and you will agonize in pain. After your breath stops, as the great king of the netherworld glares at you with angry eyes and questions you with an iron rod in hand, it will surely be a terrible scene.

68   When we observe the world closely, we find that more people are killed by false thoughts than by physical diseases. False thoughts are more to be feared even than poisonous vipers.

69   When you detach from false thoughts, illness is actually a teacher. Since ancient times a great number of people have attained power and seen essential nature while struggling with the agonies of serious illness.

70   If you become very sick, do not fear death or look back on life. Don the armor of patience, bundle the bow and arrows of faithfulness and justice, mount the horse of valiant power, grasp the whip of diligence, set up the standard of the Way of Unity, make selflessness and having few desires your troops, make continuous concentration of true mindfulness your general, fortify the castle of the mind king in the ocean of energy and field of elixir, store the provender of the elixir of five energies, set in motion the strategy of freedom from thought and imagining.

71   Do all this, and even if four hundred and four battle lines of sickness arise all at once, backed up by eighty-four thousand troops of bewilderment, and attack through every facet of consciousness and every feeling and emotion, still you will not be dismayed. When they ultimately surrender to the kindness and compassion of the mind king, submit to the power of the general, are cowed by the bravery of the troops, put down their weapons and give up, then you will have no opponents in the ten directions, no misery in your whole body. With right and wrong one suchness, all within the four seas will sing of great peace, and you will attain comfort and happiness in this world and the next.

72   A Chinese Zen master of the past once suffered from dysentery. When he was on the brink of death, he fought with the pain and misery to sit in meditation. After a while his abdomen growled loudly and convulsed, whereupon the dysentery remitted and he attained a great awakening.

73   A certain monk of my acquaintance once suffered from influenza so severe that he couldn't eat for eight days, running a fever so high that his tongue turned black. He suffered continuously day and night.

At this point he was scolded by his teacher. Regretting that he was still unenlightened, realizing he had been in error, he suddenly made a solemn vow. With do-or-die determination, he rolled up his sleeping mat and bravely sat on it to concentrate in Zen meditation. When he did this, the misery and the fever of the sickness suddenly dispersed. Clear and cool inside and out, body and mind in a state of sublime joy, he realized fundamental ungraspability.

I also had a similar experience. When I was twenty-eight years old 74 there was some trouble stemming from an argument, and I was poisoned. My whole body burned with pain, and for a while my arms and legs and torso turned purplish black. It would be hard to express the intensity of my pain and suffering.

At that point I conceived profound repentance. Here I had first 75 been inspired at the age of seventeen, had looked for true teachers and entered Zen communities, studied Zen and worked on the Way, even standing in water and sitting in the snow, not lying down to rest, never forgetting the quest day or night, for over ten years. Then I spent a winter retreat at a certain monastery, where I received the guidance of a teacher and thought I had passed through life and death and shed my self. Now that I was being tortured by this poison, I realized how my mind was not free. So I put forth an enormous effort to sit up, fighting the intense pain.

At this point, the first watch of the night had not yet been sounded. 76 Tuning my breathing with true mindfulness, I went into the vision of the physical elements disintegrating. All of a sudden my breathing disappeared and real vision appeared. Essence and forms both forgotten, true mindfulness continued.

Then there came the sound of a bell, echoing in space. As I ob- 77 served my own body and the appearances of others, it was all like an unbroken expanse of empty space. Then I intimately understood the preaching of the original body.

When I stirred my body and stretched my limbs, they felt most 78 extraordinarily supple and purified. The pains I had been suffering hitherto were like last night's dream, and my color also returned to normal. Physically and mentally exhilarated, I calmly rose from my seat and went outside. Looking to the east, I saw that it was already dawn.

After a little while, vomiting and diarrhea occurred all at once. It 79 was as if my guts had been used up, and I was only flesh and bones.

Meeting death while alive, finding life in death, it was as if the poison had changed into a medicinal elixir. For the first time, I detached from the dualistic views of hatred and love and attained realization of the equality of enemy and friend.

80   There were also similar cases in ancient times, such as the bodhisattva named Courageous Giving, who violated a precept, made a great vow in the midst of his consequent torment, and suddenly realized acceptance of beginninglessness. There have been those who were attacked by thousands of mosquitoes and attained enlightenment while battling with the sickening itch. There were also those who attained awakening while battling with the agony of being dismembered or having their skin and flesh burned and pierced.

81   Great Master Yunmen attained a major awakening on having his leg broken. Ninagawa Shinuemon realized awakening during an argument. The Shogun Takauji attained peace of mind on the battlefront.

82   In this context, to "fight" means not to fear and not to get involved but just to establish concentration of true mindfulness. If you plunge right ahead, both the pain and errant thoughts will turn into a mass of spirit and become unified work on the Way.

83   If you lose concentration of right mindfulness, not only will you be physically and mentally tormented by false thoughts and perverse moods in this life, you will also continue eternal birth and death, suffering great pain. This has happened to countless people past and present, both clergy and lay folk.

84   Now then, if rulers lack concentration of true mindfulness, they cannot bring peace and security to the populace. If administrators lack concentration of true mindfulness, they cannot fulfill loyalty and justice. If ordinary people lack concentration of true mindfulness, they cannot fulfill their social obligations.

85   For this reason I keep repeating that you should make your attitude of faith certain and stable, turn everything you do into a single koan, and continue concentration of right mindfulness without interruption.

86   Intensive Zen requires strength of spirit and intensity of concentration. Do not degrade yourself, do not let yourself be weakly, and do not debase yourself. The Buddhas and the Zen Masters were thus, and we are also thus. Who were the ancient kings, and who are we? Sages have horizontal eyes and vertical noses; we too have horizontal eyes and vertical noses. Breathing out and in, we do not borrow the

nostrils of anyone else; stepping forward, stepping back, we do not use another's legs. Always keeping up this determination to transcend the Buddhas and Masters, searching into the root core of one's own mind, is called a robust will.

Here it is not a question of whether you are a mendicant or a lay-person. It does not matter whether you are a man or a woman. It makes no difference whether you are keen or dull, more or less intelligent. It does not matter whether you have a lot of work to do or are at leisure. Those who make the great promise and undertake the great commitment, who are full of great faith and arouse the Great Wonder, do not fail to perceive essential nature, awaken to the Way, and attain the skin and flesh of the Buddhas and Zen Masters. 87

There have been many women with willpower surpassing that of great men, women who cultivated Zen practice and passed through the barriers of potential set up by the Buddhas and Zen Masters. Hundreds, even thousands, of enlightened rulers, wise ministers, laymen, and laywomen in India, China, and Japan have seen essential nature and realized truth. 88

If you do not liberate yourself in this lifetime, what lifetime will you wait for? Once this day has passed, that much of your life is gone too. With each passing thought, observe the impermanence of the appearances of the world and give up thinking there will be a tomorrow. With each step tread the Great Way of the mind source, and do not turn to another road. 89

You should let go your hand- and footholds, as if plunging off a precipitous cliff. When body and mind have died away at once, it is like standing right in the middle of cosmic space, like sitting in the center of a crystal vase. All of a sudden there will emerge the great state that is not ordinary, not holy, not Buddha, not mind, not a thing; you will attain penetrating realization that mind, Buddha, and living beings are one. This is the reality-body of all Buddhas, the inherent essence of all people. By realizing this, one becomes a Buddha or a Zen master; by missing this, one becomes an ordinary mortal. 90

Although people's faculties may be keen or dull, and practice and realization may be gradual or sudden, the secret I have been revealing here is the teaching of attaining Buddhahood by sudden enlightenment. It is a standard rule in which higher, middling, and lesser faculties are one whole. It is far from the gradual practice and learning of the two vehicles of individual liberation. 91

92   To think Buddha-nature is the state where mind is empty and objects are silent, where there is radiant awareness without arousing a single thought, is to consider the conscious spirit to be the original human being. It is like taking a thief to be your son, like taking a brick for a mirror, like taking brass for real gold. This is the fundamental ignorance underlying birth and death. It is like being a corpse that is still breathing. You cannot release your own radiant light, illumine the self within and shine through the mountains, rivers, and earth.

93   Even if great awakening is realized and the body of reality is clearly comprehended, if you are polluted by practice and attainment, the Buddha Way does not become manifest. You should know that there is that which is beyond even the beyond.

94   As for the Zen of the living exemplars, even if a clear mirror is placed on a stand, they break through it right away. Even if a precious pearl is in their palm, they smash it at once. A mortar flies through space, the eastern mountains walk on the water. Having the fortune to know that all living beings have Buddha-nature and that there is already a matter of utmost importance right where you stand, investigate continuously, twenty-four hours a day, in principle and in fact: what is it that is walking, what is it that is sitting, what is it that acts, what is the mind?

95   If you forge bravely and powerfully ahead, wholeheartedly questioning and wondering for three to five years without flagging, the Great Wonder will inevitably occur and you will not fail to awaken.

96   Yet even though you may attain a thoroughgoing great awakening, know that the vast ocean of Buddhism grows deeper the further you enter. If you think there is no enlightenment to attain and no community of living beings to be liberated, if you think the scriptures of the canon are toilet paper and the seventeen hundred koans are worthless, after all you are not really free and at ease; your perception is not liberated, you have not yet passed through the Zen barrier, and the thieving mind has not died. In this condition, if you do not throw away pride and conceit and quickly realize your error, you will fall into the deep pit of the two vehicles and cut off the life of wisdom of the Buddhas and Zen founders.

97   Nurturing the embryo of sagehood, cultivating practice in the aftermath of awakening, is really not easy. An ancient said, "If your potential does not leave a fixed position, it falls into an ocean of poi-

son." It is imperative to know that there is cultivation on top of realization and to preserve the Way of living Zen with hidden practice and secret application.

Do not make the mistake of maintaining the idea of having gained something, lest you become a hungry ghost forever keeping watch over a treasure, or a starveling with a hoard of wealth. Even if you see a Buddha-land manifest and perceive the realm of Buddha, you see only once, not twice. 98

I hope you will concentrate and let go as you breathe out and in, remove all leakage from the stream of mindfulness, perpetuate the bones and marrow of the Buddhas and Zen founders, dispense the pure teaching, like sweet elixir, for the benefit and salvation of all living beings, gratefully requiting the deep and far-reaching blessings you have received. 99

Notes

Treatise on the Supreme Vehicle

2. *The Ten Stages Scripture* is one of the core texts of the Ekayana ("One Vehicle," or Unitary) school of Buddhism, containing the seeds of all Buddhist teachings. The teaching of the ten stages is referred to as the Alphabet of Buddhism. See *The Flower Ornament Scripture* (Boston: Shambhala Publications, 1984–87), book 26.

4. *The Scripture Spoken by Vimalakīrti* is an important and popular text of the introductory phase of the universalist teachings of Buddhism, of which the aforementioned Unitary school is both the source and culmination. According to the scripture, Vimalakīrti was a householding Buddha who lived in the "time" of Shākyamuni Gautama Buddha.

   True thusness refers to the real character of things, apart from our subjective descriptions and interpretations of what we perceive.

5. *birthlessness* This term refers to the ungraspability of ultimate origins, experiential realization of which spontaneously eliminates mental fixation on appearances. This passage gives a way to actualize the subjective counterpart of objective reality.

6. *The Diamond Cutter Scripture* is one of the most popular Buddhist texts. It is of the *Prajñāpāramitā* or Transcendent Insight corpus of scriptures, which emphasize meaningful action without attachment to appearances.

10. *"Even if . . . virtuous deeds"* This passage refers to the *Ekayana* teaching of *The Lotus of Truth Scripture*, which says that all of those who have done the slightest good deed, even so much as absentmindedly drawing a picture of Buddha, have all attained Buddhahood. Although it may appear superficial to some, this is a surface of one of the broadest and deepest of Buddhist teachings, that of universal Buddha-nature inherent in all sentient beings.

11. *The Nirvana Scripture* is a vast collection of teachings represented as having been recited and recapitulated while Shākyamuni Gautama

Buddha was passing away into *mahāparinirvāna*, the ultimate extinction.

"*The Buddha does not preach anything*" means that Buddhist teachings are expedient techniques, not fixed dogma: they are products of enlightenment designed to lead to awakening; they are not themselves enlightenment or awakening. This distinction is critical in the actual practical application of Buddhism.

14. These symbols in *The Lotus of Truth Scripture* represent the universal Buddha-nature inherent in all beings, by virtue of which fundamental enlightenment is accessible to all conscious creatures who become aware of this subtle nature.

16. "*How wonderful*" that "*we ordinary mortals*" have such potential; "*how miserable*" that we ordinarily do not use it.

17. *The Scripture on Visualization of Infinite Life* is one of the three core texts of Chinese Pure Land Buddhism. This scripture contains an elaborate series of visualizations and meditations for mastery of mind, but the key point of the scripture is that "when you see Buddha, you are seeing mind; for mind is Buddha, mind makes Buddha."

20. *eighty-four thousand doctrines* Buddhist teachings are so many and diverse as to be conventionally described as numbering eighty-four thousand, or even more, up to an infinite number. These numbers are also symbolic of the multitude of psychological afflictions, complications, and confusions that Buddhism is designed to cure.

   three vehicles These are different levels of Buddhist principles and practices, encompassing both individual liberation and collective salvation.

   eightfold path One of the basic formulations of Buddhist practice: right perception, thought, speech, action, livelihood, effort, recollection, and concentration.

27. Ignorant activism may be well-intentioned, but it is inherently limited.

32. Chapter 5 of *The Nirvana Scripture* on the indestructible body says, "The body of the one who has realized thusness is permanently stable and indestructible. It is not a human or divine body, not an insecure body, not a body fed by material food." The text goes on to negate all sorts of conceivable descriptions of attributes of the body of realization.

   Chapter 12 of *The Scripture Spoken by Vimalakīrti*, on seeing the Immovable Buddha (Akshobhya), says, "See the Buddha as you see the real character of your own being. I see the Buddha does not come from the past or go to the future or dwell in the present." This text also goes on to refute all sorts of possible imaginations or conceptions about Buddha, so as to lead to the independent perception of the mind-Buddha, or Buddha-mind.

33. *The Four Reliances* are classical principles for the understanding of Buddhist scriptures, enunciated in *The Nirvana Scripture:*

  1. Rely on principle, not personality.
  2. Rely on the meaning, not the letter.
  3. Rely on objective knowledge, not subjective consciousness.
  4. Rely on a complete teaching, not an incomplete teaching.

34. The great Chan master Linji said that people who formally become monks or nuns but have emotional attachments to their state have merely "left one home to enter another."

Models for Sitting Meditation

1. It is critical to note that "letting go" of everything is to be done only after establishing the basic orientation of universal compassion and selfless dedication. Many people who fail to attain higher results of meditation are unsuccessful because they inwardly regard this orientation as doctrine and not practice, thus treating the act of vowing as a ritual behavior or a conventional routine. This kind of vow has no power to summon higher awareness.

2. *Then and only then* The author uses an expression that specifies the aforementioned attitude and vow as a necessary precondition for "letting go."

   body and mind are one suchness Body and mind are experienced as a single continuity, which is beyond conceptualization and therefore can only be described as "such" or "as is."

   there is no gap between movement and stillness The ultimate focus of attention remains the same regardless of internal or external movement or stillness.

3. To deliberately deprive oneself of food or sleep, thinking these to be ascetic exercise, may only serve to strengthen attachment to self-importance, besides injuring the physical organism for no good reason. There are Taoist practices of fasting and sleeplessness, but they are dangerous and never done by sensible or directed people without adequate mental and physical preparation.

4. *a quiet, uncluttered place* A place that is both psychologically and physically "quiet," not a circus of imaginations in a hall of ostentation.

5. It is dangerous to force this posture. Western models of athletic training and competition are out of place here. The ancients did not use the lotus posture to cause themselves discomfort. The critical alignments are noted in number 7. Sitting straight in a chair, standing still, walk-

ing, and lying on the right side are also commonly used meditation postures.

6. The arc of the thumbs and fingers form a loop; this particular symbol is called the sign of the cosmos.

7. Rocking back and forth and right and left is for the purpose of helping the body sense a central balance.

   A stupa is a Buddhist tomb or reliquary structure. Stupas were originally hemispherical mounds, but in the Far East they were also built as multistoried towers. Here it is the image of a multistoried tower, each story evenly supporting the ones above, to which the author refers. Beginners who still retain a complete sense of physical solidity may even use this image of being a reliquary tower as a visualization to help attain abstraction.

   One of the most famous images in Mahāyāna (Great Vehicle, or Universalist) Buddhism is that of a stupa emerging from the ground and opening up to reveal an ancient, extinct Buddha within, miraculously still alive. The emerging of the stupa from the earth is the emerging of potential based on groundwork practices, such as the vowing already mentioned. The opening of the stupa is the electrification of the spiritual spine and brain, the opening of the derelict potential left unused, even trapped, untapped by conventional education and training.

8. *Fayun Yuantong* was one of the most eminent Chan masters of Song dynasty China.

   ghost cave in a mountain of darkness A metaphor for oblivion or absorption in nothingness; often used as a term of scorn for repressive concentration and false "emptiness."

9. *Eventually you forget mental objects and spontaneously become unified.* "Eventually" means that it does not help to rush; "you forget mental objects and spontaneously become unified" means that what fragments the mind is the habit of dwelling on objects, which includes thoughts and feelings.

10. *many people do it in a pathological manner* This is why meditation practice and experience cannot really be evaluated in such terms as clock and calendar time; if the inspiration, orientation, or method is off balance, the more meditation is practiced the further it exaggerates such flaws.

11. *using the wind to blow on the fire* Authentically practiced, this kind of meditation amounts to using a natural capacity in order to foster an inherent potential.

12. *when the way is lofty, demons abound* Complacency and conceit make the mind especially vulnerable to obsession; evident attainment makes the individual a target of envy and jealousy. See also next note.

13. *The* Shurangama-sutra *(Heroic March Scripture)* This is a special text closely studied by Chinese Chan Buddhists of the post-classical era, from the Song dynasty onward. In this scripture, Buddha says, "You should know that the subtle illumination in all creatures in the contaminated world, the substance of mind completely aware, is not separate and not apart from that of the Buddhas of the ten directions.

"Because of the mistakes of your false ideas missing the truth, folly and infatuation arise. Because they produce total illusion, there is a false reality. By unceasing transmutation of illusion, the worlds of being are born. Thus all the worlds in the ten directions that are not uncontaminated, numerous as atoms, are defined by deluded, ignorant, false ideas.

"You should know that space itself arises within your mind, like a fleck of cloud dotting a clear sky, to say nothing of the worlds in space! When one individual discovers reality and returns to the source, the entirety of space, in all ten directions, completely vanishes; how could the worlds in space not be shaken apart!

"When you practice meditation and cultivate concentration, the enlightening beings in the ten directions, as well as the great uncontaminated saints, all commune, and there is profound peace right on the spot. All the demon kings, ghosts, spirits, and mundane celestials see their palaces crumble for no apparent reason; their ground quakes and splits, every creature in their water and on their land flies and bounds, all of them startled and frightened.

"Ordinary people, in the dark, do not notice any change. Those others, however, all have five kinds of psychic power, lacking only the power of freedom from all contamination. Being fondly attached to these experiences and passions of theirs, how could they let you smash their abodes? For this reason, spirits, ghosts, celestial demons, devils, and sprites will all come to disturb you in your concentration.

"However, even though the demons may have tremendous wrath in their passions, in your subtle awareness it is like wind blowing on light, like a sword slicing through water; they do not touch each other. You are like boiling water, they are like solid ice; as warmth gradually gets nearer, before long ice melts."

Tiantai manuals of "stopping and seeing" There are four Tiantai Buddhist meditation classics under this rubric, known as the *Small,* the *Great,* the *Gradual,* and *Unfixed Stopping and Seeing.* As used in a general way in Far Eastern Buddhism, based on the classics of Tiantai Buddhism, *stopping* means stopping confusion; *seeing* means observing realities. In the Tiantai manuals of stopping and seeing, there appear very concrete descriptions of demonic hallucinations.

Guifeng's Guidelines Guifeng Zongmi, who died in the mid-ninth century, was a prolific writer on the original teachings and original practices of Chan Buddhism. He is also considered a patriarch of the Chinese Flower Ornament school of Buddhism. Most of his work is lost.

Those whose preparation is insufficient One of the functions of literature on meditation is to prepare the mind for the experiences—authentic and delusive—that await consciousness beyond the boundaries of ordinary awareness.

17. *to die sitting or pass away standing* Many ancient meditation masters are reported to have died sitting or to have passed away standing, without illness, as a deliberate act to represent the transcendence of both the allure of life and the crushing power of death. In Sanskrit, nirvana is also called *amrta*, which means "the state where there is no death."

18. *What will you use to counteract karma?* Karma means "action"; in usages like this, it specifically refers to the actions of past and present that create the conditions of bondage in the present and future.

19. The final passage is reconnected to the first passage, forming a circle. The closing of this circle is symbolic of the completion of the cycle of instruction and the beginning of the cycle of application.

Guidelines for Sitting Meditation

1. *If something comes to mind, do your best to cast it away.* There are many different techniques for overcoming the influence of conditioned thoughts, but they may be classified generally into two broad categories corresponding to the Taoist terms *doing* and *nondoing.* The preceding essay presented a method characterized more by "nondoing" than by "doing," whereas this essay has more "doing" to it, even though the deliberate "doing" of overcoming the mesmerism of conditioned thought is practiced for the purpose of attaining spontaneous "nondoing" of compulsive thinking, whereby delusion does not arise even though no deliberate attempt is made to suppress it.

2. This paragraph outlines the practice of cultivating awareness of the essence of consciousness underlying the functions of consciousness.

3. It is quite possible to be dependent on conceptions without being consciously aware of it, even while in what subjectively seems to be a state of concentration without thought. This is why radical direct introspection and analytic introspection are both employed in Buddhist meditation, supplying a standpoint outside the ordinary subjectivity of the

individual as an outlook or observatory from which to view reality at large.

4. *the uncreate* This word expresses the beginningless continuity of infinity, as well as the state of mind under acquiescence to infinity, not creating self-deluding attachments to illusory thoughts.

5. *Joy* at the intimation of Buddhahood within is the first stage of enlightenment according to the comprehensive scheme of the ten stages. See *The Flower Ornament Scripture*, book 26, first part.

6. *The source of realization of enlightenment is the identity of mind, Buddha, and living beings.* This expression of the triplex identity of mind, Buddha, and all beings is a key phrase of *The Flower Ornament Scripture* in the teachings of Chan Buddhism.

7. To *turn things around* means to use things consciously for purposes of enlightenment rather than be deluded and manipulated by them. *The Flower Ornament Scripture* says, "Beings teach, lands teach, all things in all times teach, constantly, without interruption."

   Vimalakīrti is the main teacher in *The Scripture Spoken by Vimalakīrti*, a very important text that teaches the integration of nirvana and samsara in the realm of inconceivable enlightenment.

8. *Otherwise, you will be going around in circles forever.* The meditation taught here is for breaking the chain of routine perception, thought, and behavior.

A Generally Recommended Mode of Sitting Meditation

1. *Cultivation and realization* are ways to bring the human being into harmony with the Way, or objective reality; they are ways to the Way.

2. Again, the need for effort is not because the source of enlightening is not available but because our own subjective conditions make it impossible for us to avail ourselves of the enlightenment of the source.

3. The "wiping clean" process of purification of the mind itself, not attempted removal of objects.

4. *The Scripture of Complete Enlightenment* says, "Complete awareness is my sanctuary." The question of "why" is multifaceted; not only does it suggest practice of meditation wherever we are, it also suggests careful examination of the inner and outer reasons or rationales for emphasizing a particular venue.

5. Here the main answer to all the above questions is given; the answer is in the questions itself, in the subjective condition of the individual; for it is the subjective condition that filters and construes the truths set forth by the author as the setting of each conundrum in this series of

questions. For this reason, the questions should not be taken as merely rhetorical.

6. This paragraph warns about what is supposed to happen in the initial stage of realization in the exercise being taught in this treatise. This procedure follows an established pattern of preparing meditators before they plunge into intensive work.

What this passage is referring to is what Japanese Zennists call *kenshō*, "seeing essence," direct conscious experience of the essential nature of mind itself. This brings a feeling of freedom that, compared with the stickiness of mind fascinated by its own functions and productions, is utterly amazing and seems absolute to the inexperienced beginner. A good deal of Dōgen's work is devoted to helping seekers overcome this major obstacle in Zen study, the affliction caused by "light shining right in your eyes," causing a dazzling effect.

Getting beyond this stage, having *a living road of emancipation*, means bringing abstract enlightenment to life in daily activities.

7. *Transmission of the mind seal at Shaolin* refers to Bodhidharma, reputed founder of Chan (Zen) Buddhism in China, who is said to have "faced a wall for nine years." This is an expression referring to cultivation of imperturbability of mind. This immovable mind is described as being like a wall or a sheer cliff.

8. *pursuing words and chasing sayings* In Dōgen's time, academic study of Buddhism was prevalent among Japanese priests, who often pursued it without corresponding meditation or life practice.

stepping back This means disengagement from involvement in thought and its objects.

turning the light around and looking back This means inwardly looking into the source of consciousness rather than outwardly pursuing the products of consciousness.

Body and mind will naturally be shed Ordinary self-awareness is molted.

the original countenance This refers to the pristine essence of mind, and what it directly witnesses.

9. *Do not aim to become a Buddha* Subjective wishes, fantasies, imaginations, conceptions, and ambitions, no matter how seemingly sublime, can all interfere with the process.

how could it be limited to sitting or reclining? The essential technique is mental and does not involve attachment to the body in any way.

10. Again it should be pointed out that forcing the lotus or half-lotus posture does more harm than good, increasing physical egohood rather than decreasing it, expending energy rather than husbanding it.

14–15. This is the exercise of "turning the light around and looking back" mentioned in number 8. For a fuller discussion, see the Introduction to *Shōbōgenzō: Zen Essays by Dōgen* in Volume Two of this series (Boston: Shambhala Publications, 2001).

16. not practice of dhyāna This means that the meditation exercise taught here is not a system of rigidly defined stages and states; it is a direct approach to the essential nature of mind and consciousness and the immediate perception of reality.

18. When rising from intense concentration, it is important to release the mind as well as the body from the intensity of its focus before getting up.

20. The allusions are to old Zen stories of people Buddhistically awakened on seeing or hearing an object, gesture, or utterance in states of pinpoint concentration.

21. This meditation is for awakening a kind of knowledge that is not filtered and formulated by conventional intelligence. The distribution of this knowledge, therefore, does not conform to patterns ordinarily established for other kinds of abstract knowledge.

22. the process . . . is being normal. In Zen terms, "normalcy" means the mind as it is in its pristine innocence, without the exaggeration of acquired mental habits.

23. West and East The experience of Buddhist enlightenment is not obstructed by cultural differences, because it only takes place after the habit of clinging to views is relinquished.

24. Just work on sitting This can be understood both literally and figuratively. People may try all sorts of things as "spiritual exercises," when really they are secretly trying to distract, amuse, or otherwise occupy themselves. This was as rampant in Dōgen's time, relatively speaking, as it is today. The general recommendation here is not to chase after this fad and that but rather to quiet down and look right into the source of everything you are.

25. When you see into the source, you can see what is at hand without illusion or prejudice.

27. Contemplation of impermanence is commonly considered a good way to arouse the aspiration and will for enlightenment.

28. feel an elephant by hand This alludes to the ancient story of the blind men and the elephant, referring to the fragmentary nature of studies lacking direct perception of the whole.

29. Having long been thus, we should be thus. Buddha-nature is the original mind; having always had the potential for awakening, why not use it?

Secrets of Cultivating the Mind

1. *The triple world* This means the conditioned world, comprising three realms: the realm of desire, the realm of form, and the realm of formless abstraction. Buddhist enlightenment involves transcending even the formless realm in order to attain complete freedom.

3. This paragraph refers to a contemplative exercise, not to a metaphysical doctrine or belief.

4. *Dharma* means principle, truth, teaching, or reality.

5. Ascetic practices without essential insight tend to increase egoism and self-absorption rather than diminish it.

6. *The World Honored One* is an epithet of Buddha.

12. *Linji* was a great Chan Buddhist master of ninth-century China. One of the greatest Chan classics consists of a collection of this master's sayings.

14. Faith in the immanent Buddha-nature is not an inculcated belief. It may be deduced, as in this story, but is only real-ized as a direct experience.

15. Master Guizong was one of the greatest of the early classical Chan masters in Tang dynasty China. He lived in the latter eighth and early ninth centuries.

17. Many people miss opportunities to learn by expecting on-demand displays of what they personally consider to be spiritual and miraculous powers.

18. Rather than making grandiose promises, the author places the emphasis on the need for understanding and preparation.

21. *Guifeng* See note 13 of *Models For Sitting Meditation*.

22. Buddhist sages do not employ extraordinary powers for personal ends; only in pursuit of universal vows.

23. The need for understanding and preparation is exceptionally keen when dealing with attractive ideas like supranormal powers.

24. Many people who think they want enlightenment secretly want thrills. When they are no longer thrilled, they lose interest, not even realizing any enlightenment from this very sequence of events.

27–28. See note number 6 of *A Generally Recommended Mode of Sitting Meditation*.

30. See Cleary, *Shōbōgenzō: Zen Essays by Dōgen*, p. 10.

33. *you are able to use ten thousand ounces of gold in a day.* This means you can live in the world and deal intimately with the things of the world without being afflicted.

38. *Spiritual powers and subtle functions—drawing water and hauling*

wood. All actions are productions from an ultimately inconceivable source. The "water and wood," or material being (self and world), as ordinarily conceived are not the spiritual and subtle. The spiritual and subtle are the livingness that "draws" and "hauls."

39–43. The Sound Seer is a supernal bodhisattva (enlightening being) manifesting pure compassion, envisioned as watching the cries of the world. The Sound Seer's gateway into principle, or noumenon, is to focus the attention on the ineffable essence in the faculty of hearing.

47. This series of negatives is also a meditation exercise, to be worked through mindfully and contemplatively, step by step.

49. *six courses* This term is a traditional general representation of habit-ridden ways of life. The six courses are hungry ghosts, representing greed and craving; titans or antigods, representing conceit, jealousy, resentment, and hatred; animals, representing ignorance and folly; hells, representing a combination of all the above; humanity, representing social conscience and morality; celestial realms, representing higher morality and elevated psychic states. Buddhahood is beyond even the most sublime of the celestial realms.

52. *real faith* Here it is made plain that faith is not fundamentally a conceptual item or habit of thought but a manifestation of connection, however remotely sensed, with the very essence of awareness and being.

55. *five courses of existence* This term means the same thing as the six courses (note 49 above), minus the celestial course. Thus "five courses" is a general way of describing typical routines of habit, compulsion, and bondage.

57. *Master Gao* was the great Chinese Chan master Dahui Zong-gao, one of the major workers behind the Song dynasty revival of Chan. See my translations *Zen Lessons: The Art of Leadership* and *Zen Essence: The Science of Freedom,* both in this volume, for extensive reports and statements of this master.

58. *ox-herding practice* The mind is likened to an ox; the task of taming the unruly mind is likened to ox herding.

61. *followers* This term refers to followers of Buddhism, specifically those who try to annihilate passion to attain nirvana.

62. This is the morality of nondoing; do not dwell on the impulse or elaborate the thought and the act will not be forthcoming. See "Do Not Do Any Evil" in my *Rational Zen: The Mind of Dōgen Zenji* in Volume Three of this series (Boston: Shambhala Publications, 2001).

63. *six sense fields* The power of mind to organize elementary sense data is also considered a sense, the sixth sense.

68. *Caoqi* (Ts'ao-ch'i) This refers to the illustrious Sixth Patriarch of Chan Buddhism, who died in the early eighth century.

91. *eight winds* Eight influences that ordinarily affect people: gain and loss, praise and blame, honor and censure, pleasure and pain.
    three kinds of sensation Pleasant, painful, neutral.

93. *stones placed on grass* This is a metaphor for practicing repression of thought; it temporarily inhibits growth but is not permanent.

98. *The Secret of Mind Alone* This is a short work by the great Buddhist author Yanshou (ninth to tenth century). Master of the four major schools of Chinese Buddhism, patriarch of both Chan and Pure Land schools, Yanshou's work was very influential in Korea.

99. *good friends* Buddha said, "When you travel, go with those who are better than you, or at least equal. If there are none, go alone; do not travel in the company of fools." Finding good friends is a matter of how you look for them.

100. *blind tortoise/minute seed* These expressions are traditional metaphors: the rarity of meeting a true teaching is as that of the chances of a blind tortoise in the middle of the ocean coming upon a piece of driftwood; the difficulty of meeting your true teacher is said to be as that of a tiny seed dropped from the highest sky landing on the tip of a needle on the face of the earth. The implication here is that if you pay no attention to this treatise, when do you imagine you will find such an opportunity?

104. *the four realizations* These are the consummations of four stages of individual liberation: having entered the stream (of Buddhist awareness), returning once (to the mundane world before release), never returning, and entering nirvana.

107. *"I cannot do anything for those who do not ask themselves what to do."* This is a famous quotation from Confucius.

112. *skin bag* This term refers to the physical body.

Absorption in the Treasury of Light

1. *Shōbōgenzō* is a large collection of essays by Dōgen Zenji, the Zen teacher of the author of the present treatise.

2. *unobstructive application of inconspicuous practice* This is a technical expression referring to practice that is purely mental in essence and has no outwardly perceptible form. Its influence on others is also ethereal, not nonexistent in spite of being unexpressed on ordinary cognitive terms.

3. *three bodies* This is a technical term for three facets of Buddhahood: the reality body, corresponding to essence; the enjoyment body, corre-

sponding to knowledge; and the emanation body, corresponding to action.

four knowledges This term refers to four facets of the consciousness of Buddhas: the mirrorlike knowledge, seeing things as "such," impartially, like a mirror reflecting whatever is before it; the knowledge of equality, which sees things in terms of their universal essential nature; the analytic observing knowledge, which sees things in terms of their individual functions, characteristics, and appearances; and practical knowledge, which sees things in terms of composition and effect.

states of absorption numerous as atoms in every aspect of reality This expression refers to any and all possible knowledge, consciousness, perception, and awareness.

The Flower Ornament Scripture All of the chapters of this scripture in which Buddha has gone to visit a heavenly realm are especially important in Zen study.

4. *Lamplike Illuminate* The Buddha Dīpaṇkāra, an ancient Buddha whose name means "lamp," often translated into Chinese as Burning Lamp for effect. Dīpaṇkāra is very important in Buddhist symbolic mythology as the Buddha in whose presence Shākyamuni, or Gautama Buddha, the historical Buddha, was originally inspired to seek unexcelled complete perfect enlightenment.

5. *"Thus once I heard"* This refers to the traditional opening of Buddhist scriptures, and represents perceiving things just as they are, without subjective distortion of reception.

8–11. *Vairochana* "The Illuminator," or "the Great Sun Buddha," is the name of the primordial reality-body Buddha in esoteric Buddhism; in Flower Ornament Buddhism, Vairochana is the transcendent personality of the historical Buddha and also a representation of the eternal enlightenment of Buddhahood.

13. *Awakening by Light* See *The Flower Ornament Scripture*, book 9. Mañjushri represents wisdom and knowledge.

16. *Maitreya* The Buddha of the Future.

20–22. See *The Blue Cliff Record* in Volume Five of this series (Boston: Shambhala Publications, 2001), chapter 1.

24–28. See *The Blue Cliff Record*, chapter 86.

26. See *No Barrier: Unlocking the Zen Koan* in Volume Four of this series (Boston: Shambhala Publications, 2001), chapter 45.

30. See *No Barrier*, chapter 39.

38. *ghost cave* This technical term ordinarily refers to blanking the mind.

count the grains of sand This expression refers to intellectualistic literalism without the spirit of the teaching.

mosquitoes breaking through a paper window Reciting ("buzzing") without understanding.

39. *wash a clod of earth in the mud* This expression means to try to resolve delusive thoughts by conceptual elaboration.

40. *Changsha* was one of the greatest masters of the classical era of Chan.

43. *child of a rich family but has no britches.* All people have the fundamental intelligence known as Buddha-nature but are ordinarily unable to avail themselves of it.

45. Some of these delusions can be extremely subtle, so they are pointed out forcefully to call attention to them.

48. *holeless iron hammerhead* A traditional metaphor, in this case meaning that there is no way to grasp it, yet it is effective.

49. See *No Barrier*, chapter 19.

59. *Puning Yong* was a Song dynasty Chan master of the Linji school.

65. *Yongjia* was a Tiantai Buddhist meditation master also recognized as a spiritual heir of the Sixth Patriarch of Chan. In the Zen schools he is called the Overnight Enlightened Guest because he was so aware that he needed only one day with the Patriarch to complete his awakening.
    Nāgārjuna An Indian Buddhist master who lived from around 100 B.C.E. to about 100 C.E.. He is considered the fourteenth Indian ancestor of Chan Buddhism and is especially famous for his work on emptiness and transcendent wisdom. See Keizan's *Transmission of Light* in Volume Four of this series (Boston: Shambhala Publications, 2001), chapter 15.

66–67. *lowly hireling/pauper/cesspool cleaner* These are all images from *The Lotus Scripture* (another major scripture ordinarily studied by Chan and Zen Buddhists) representing those alienated from inherent Buddha-nature, thus enslaved to externals.

73. *Shaolin* is the name of a temple; here it refers to Bodhidharma, the founder of Chan in China, who lived at Shaolin temple for a time.

76. *four debts* These are the debts one owes to one's parents, to all living beings, to society, and to the Three Treasures (the Buddha, the Teaching, and the Harmonious Community).

77. *Caoshan (Ts'ao-shan)* A ninth-century Chan master, one of the great teachers of the classical era of Chan. See *Timeless Spring: A Sōtō Zen Anthology* in Volume Four of this series (Boston: Shambhala Publications, 2001).

95. *Baizhang (Pai-chang)* A great master of the classical era of Chan, said to have drafted the original rules for Chan communes, Baizhang died in the early ninth century. See *Sayings and Doings of Pai-Chang, Ch'an Master of Great Wisdom*, translated by Thomas Cleary (Los Angeles: Center Publications, 1978).

98. *samsara* Commonly translated into Chinese as "birth and death," "turning in circles," this term means routine existence.

101. seven Buddhas This refers to a lineage of seven ancient Buddhas, the seventh being Shākyamuni (Gautama) Buddha, the historical Buddha. This lineage represents the ancient and timeless roots of the teaching, the Buddhist Dharma.

107. the sitting of the two vehicles The two vehicles (known as "hearers" and "those awake to conditioning") are courses of individual liberation. Their "sitting" refers to one-sided inclination to nirvana as quiescence. See number 119.

108. the empty fist Buddhist teachings are likened to an empty fist holding an imaginary gift to pacify a crying child; that is, the teachings are only expedient means of bringing about a calculated effect, not absolute dogma to be worshipped as sacred in themselves.

110–112. This is why Chan masters in China traditionally warned people to cultivate their own perception before trying to look for a "teacher" to guide them spiritually.

118. The careerist model does not apply to enlightenment.

An Elementary Talk on Zen

1. Compare this passage with numbers 1 through 4 of *A Generally Recommended Mode of Sitting Meditation.*

8. Don't think/don't seek Meditation practice involves total absorption in the recitation itself, without anticipating results.

10. kill In Zen parlance, this means to transcend, or detach from something.

  seven consciousnesses This term refers to the consciousnesses of the six senses, plus a faculty for judgement and evaluation.

21. iron walls This refers to constrictions of consciousness.

  Polar Mountain This stands for the gravitational center of the surface plane of a mundane world. To walk over the Polar Mountain means "to overcome the world," to become free from the magnetic pull of worldliness.

22. and 26. Many people profess to believe that familial and social responsibilities conflict with meditation.

23. Again the powerful exercise of contemplating impermanence is recommended for developing the will for enlightenment.

32. two truths The two truths, absolute and relative, are that phenomena are empty of absolute identity yet exist in a temporary and conditional way.

  The Middle Way This refers to central balance between extremes, such as of emptiness and existence, rejection and attachment.

40. *ocean of energy/field of elixir* These terms refer to two sensitive points in the body below the navel, commonly used as points of focus in Taoist energetics. It is not good to focus too intently on a precise point, except for special curative purposes; filling the entire lower body with energy is the general idea here. For special instructions concerning female practitioners, see my *Immortal Sisters: Secrets of Taoist Women* in Volume Three of The Taoist Classics series (Boston: Shambhala Publications, 1999).

44. *"the bottom falls out of the bucket"* This expression means that the sense of "me" as a solid entity vanishes, the limiting encasement of the ego dissolves, and the mind is freed.

   "kick over the alchemical furnace" At this stage "the furnace" stands for the body; to kick it over means to transcend the feeling of physical selfhood clinging to the body.

   passing beyond myriad aeons in a single instant This expression refers to consciousness disentangled from the temporally conditioned worldview, which includes views of time and space. When consciousness is no longer bound to the parameters of views, it is free.

   Prajñātāra This figure is represented as the twenty-seventh Indian ancestor of Zen. See *The Book of Serenity*, chapter 3.

46. See my translation of Dōgen's *Record of Things Heard* in Volume Four of the series (Boston: Shambhala Publications, 2001).

47. See *Immortal Sisters* and my translation of Chang Po-tuan's *The Inner Teachings of Taoism* in Volume Two of The Taoist Classics series (Boston: Shambhala Publications, 1999).

48. See the chapter on Chang San-feng in my *Vitality Energy Spirit: A Taoist Sourcebook* in Volume Three of The Taoist Classics series (Boston: Shambhala Publications, 1999).

53. *six bandits* This term refers to the objects of the six senses, spoken of in reference to their capacity to "steal" attention and "rob" people of energy.

   four demons This term refers to four types of "demons" or "devils" that can "kill the life of wisdom." The four demons are the demon of the body-mind clusters (form, feeling, perception, conditioning, consciousness); the demon of afflictions (such as greed, hatred, folly, vanity, opinionated views); the demon of death; and the "heavenly devil," or the capacity for endless self-deception.

57. *three poisons* Greed, hatred, and folly.

   five desires Desires for the objects of the five basic senses.

59–66. Zen teachers of all times left many indications by which interested seekers might discern authenticity or otherwise in reputed or supposed manifestations of Zen practice or teaching.

70. *elixir of five energies* This is a Taoist term for the concentration, congealment, and crystallization of energy. The number *five* refers to five basic elements or forces; to concentrate and crystallize them together means to recollect and pool the total energy available to the body and mind.

81. *Yunmen* One of the most distinguished classical Chinese Chan masters.

   Ninagawa Shinzaemon A friend and disciple of the famous Japanese Zen master Ikkyu.

   The Shogun Takauji Fourteenth-century founder of the second military government in Japan, a noted student and patron of Zen.

94. *A mortar flies through space, the eastern mountains walk on the water.* These expressions refer to the realm of experience in which everything is inconceivable yet evident.

96. *the deep pit of the two vehicles* This expression refers to attachment to detachment.

INSTANT ZEN
Waking Up in the Present

INTRODUCTION

"While we persistently look forward for tomorrow's technologies to solve our problems," writes Robert V. Adams, CEO, Xerox Technology Ventures, and president, World Business Academy, "we often find ourselves simultaneously looking backward, reexamining ancient wisdom on how to understand and enjoy ourselves and others in the process."

As the practical relevance of ancient wisdom to modern problems becomes increasingly apparent, there is an ever greater need to retrieve these essential insights from ages of cultural overlay, embellishment, and historical decline. Whether we are simply interested in developing the cosmopolitan outlook proper to citizens of the world, or whether we are also interested in higher philosophy and free thought, today it is no longer plausible to regard world wisdom traditions as the domain of esoteric cultists and fringe intellectuals.

The effort to extract useful knowledge and pragmatic procedures from ancient lore is a hallmark of the original science of mind known as Zen. While many sects and cults eventually grew up around the traces of original Zen, as a rule these spin-offs returned to the very same sort of sentimental religiosity and dogmatic authoritarianism that original Zen eschewed, making them useless, even counterproductive, in the way of Zen mind liberation.

The essence of original Zen is self-understanding and self-realization. In classical Zen terminology this development is called attainment of maximum potential and maximum function. This is envisioned as a kind of liberation, and a kind of awakening, which the many techniques of Zen mind art are designed to provoke and develop.

The Zen understanding of the human condition is that we habitually get ourselves into all sorts of binds on account of our vulnerability to the influences of external and internal changes. The crux of the problem seems to be a lack of fluidity, a sort of rigidity in the way we view the world and think about it.

In a famous Zen simile, we are like someone in a boat who thinks the bank of the river is moving. Closer observation reveals it is the boat that is moving, resulting in a changing perspective. Similarly, through Zen understanding we can observe the changes in our bodies and minds that cause our view of the world and feelings for other people to fluctuate from time to time, altering our reactions and behavior. In this way we can gain an extra perspective on ourselves and our lives, a more objective point of view, less distorted by unexamined biases and undetected inner currents, and thus master our own potential.

What is the true self that Zen seeks to understand and to realize? "To say it is like something," replied one ancient master, "would be to miss the mark." A description, after all, is not the self itself; Zen seeks direct knowledge that must be experienced oneself. The use of Zen theory and concentration formulas is to arouse this latent faculty while making it possible to monitor its performance both rationally and intuitively.

Many famous Zen sayings illustrate the seeming paradox of the self, so near at hand and yet so subtle and inscrutable to the self itself: "Though it has long been in use, when questioned, no one knows what it is." What is this? "Everyone uses it every day, without being aware of it." How to become aware of it, and how to use this awareness as a foundation for mastering its use, is the task of Zen realization.

It could be said that the object of Zen, therefore, is to awaken the self and to develop it to a degree of maturity that is not dictated merely by physical or social needs. This involves inward discovery and empowerment of an autonomous core of subtly conscious, intelligent awareness, which oversees and harmonizes the instinctual, emotional, social, and intellectual facets of one's being.

In Zen terminology, this faculty is sometimes referred to as the "director" by way of allusion to the function of the mature self. Referred to in Zen lore as the "work," the development of the "director" is summed up with characteristic precision and beauty in a Buddhist scripture often quoted in Zen literature: "It is better to master the mind than be mastered by mind."

Thus self-knowledge is an aim, but it is also a means. Self-knowledge is a means of deeper self-understanding, and ultimately of self-realization. In other words, self-knowledge in the Zen process is not pursued by means of theoretical study but by means of itself. How this is accomplished is the content of Zen study; when this is done, everything turns into Zen learning.

There are many statements in Zen technical literature designed to orient the learner toward understanding, then experiencing, the real self, or the self apart from socially conditioned views; from which vantage point one then understands the real world through the real self.

"You do not need to seek," said one of the great masters, "but you must save yourself; no one can do it for you." The original Zen teachings fostered the utmost in supreme independence and supreme responsibility for oneself. In order to overcome the potential for self-deception inherent in this posture, Zen masters insisted on experiential insight into the most fundamental nature of being itself; this was called seeing nature, or seeing essence.

Seeing essence is also called "gaining entry," signifying the initiatory nature of this experience. Zen teachings and practices do not deal only with the process of awakening insight into essence, but also with the aftermath of awakening, the process of maturing and applying Zen consciousness.

Religious and Secular Zen

Zen arose in China several hundred years after the introduction of Buddhism there, and operated in both religious and secular contexts.

In religious contexts—first Buddhism, then Taoism, and later Confucianism—Zen taught people to study the "living word" of personal experience, rather than the "dead word" of doctrinaire dogmatism.

Religious Zen was both patronized and suppressed by despotic secular authorities, resulting in numerous distortions and deteriorations well documented in critical Zen lore. According to the accounts of the masters, by the 1100s religious Zen had largely degenerated into stagnant sects and cults.

Secular Zen is somewhat harder to trace than religious Zen. Records indicate its existence from the beginnings of Zen in China. Nearly half of the Second Patriarch's enlightened disciples were secular people, and many other lay people of both upper and lower classes are on official record through the ages as being known to have mastered Zen.

There were also many female Zen masters, again from the very beginnings of Zen. One of the greatest of these women on record was only thirteen years old when she was recognized by the most distinguished master in China. Another famous adept was barely sixteen when she was enlightened; and she was also the daughter of an enlightened woman.

One of the characteristics of degenerated religious cults, in contrast, is the spiritual suppression of women and secular people. Since the inner degeneration of religion into cults tended to coincide with the deepening of affiliation with, or captivation by, political authorities, such cults are mostly what survived as religious Zen, with official recognition and support under extremely rigid conditions. In late feudal Japan, for example, lay Zen masters were legally forbidden to lecture on Zen classics, and journeyman Buddhist priests commonly taught that females could not attain enlightenment. Zen was under arrest.

The unfortunate aberrations of misogyny and personal powermongering witnessed in modern Zen cults are, like pseudo-religious sectarianism, the heritage of such circumstances, not characteristics of original Zen itself, or of real Zen in any age. This distinction needs to be made in order to actually experience the freedom and enlightenment of original Zen, avoiding the webs of suggestion and emotional conditioning used by religious systems that have become power structures affording people means and opportunities for dominating and manipulating others.

The usurpation and alienation of Zen at the hands of ambitious careerists turning it into a cult is described by many of the masters of the eleventh and twelfth centuries. Dahui, one of the greatest of all time, wrote,

> Students in recent times often abandon the fundamental and pursue trivia; turning their backs on truth, they plunge into falsehood. They only consider learning in terms of career and reputation. All they have as their definitive doctrine is to take riches and status and expand their schools. Therefore their mental art is not correct, and they are affected by things.

Mi-an, another distinguished master of the Song dynasty, vigorously repudiated cultism and upheld secular Zen in no uncertain terms:

> Those who have not learned are in confusion; not relying on the source, they abandon their families, quit their jobs, and wander around in misery, running north and south looking for "Zen" and "Tao" and seeking "Buddha" and "Dharma" on the tongues of old monks all over the land, intentionally waiting for their "transmission," unaware they have missed the point long ago.

Zen and Culture

In the statement of its own masters, the message of Zen is "not of the East or West, North or South." It is inherent to Zen, to say nothing of common sense, that people need not adopt an Eastern culture in order to understand and actualize Zen in one's own life. The so-called "director" in Zen psychology is so called precisely because it refers to a faculty or capacity of consciousness that is not itself controlled or intrinsically modified by the processes of social and cultural conditioning.

One way to recognize a cult as a cult, in fact, is its superficial Orientalism. Changes in mood caused by environmental redecoration may occur, especially when combined with other forms of suggestion, but these are not actually Zen effects. Western Zen cults with an Oriental veneer neither reproduce Eastern cultures nor enhance Western cultures. Authentic Zen is not a sideshow; the teaching is to harmonize with the environment, as illustrated in the famous proverb, "A good craftsman leaves no traces."

There is, nevertheless, a way to describe the overall cultural context of Zen in a more specific manner. Zen master Foyan refers people to the Fifth Stage of Enlightenment according to the teaching of the Ten Stages in the comprehensive *Flower Ornament Scripture*, a favorite book of many classical masters and source of many of their teachings and techniques.

In this fifth stage, while focus is on perfection of meditation, at the same time, "The practitioners, thus engaged in developing people, with minds continually following enlightened knowledge, engaged in unregressing goodness, intent on the search for supreme truth, practice *whatever in the world* would benefit living beings." The text goes on to name occupations like writing, teaching, mathematics, science, medicine, song and dance, drama, music, storytelling, entertainment, city planning, agriculture, horticulture, and so on. The relevance of this approach to Zen, so different from that of self-centered cults, need hardly be further argued. The seventeenth-century Japanese Zen master Manan also wrote, "If you want to quickly attain mastery of all truths and be independent in all events, there is nothing better than concentration in activity."

In the world of the modern West, where democracy and individual human rights are legally recognized but not as yet fully realized, no issues could be more timely than self-understanding and self-mastery, or liberating the individual from confusing and deluding influences of all kinds so as to empower freedom of choice as an authentic individual capacity and not just an abstract constitutional right or social ideal. The bafflement and mystification of exotic cults have no place in real Zen today, East or West.

Zen Meditation

While it is common knowledge that Zen Buddhists used meditation of various sorts in their arts of mind cultivation, original Zen and imitation Zen cultism may also be distinguished in a parallel manner by comparison of specific attitudes toward meditation. Zen that is exaggerated into a meditation cult, in which meditation assumes the status of a value in itself, or attention is fixated on a given posture or procedure presented as inherently sacrosanct, is a characteristic deterioration. This is more of the nature of fetishism than enlightenment, as is particularly evident in cases where meditation is done ritualistically in random groups according to fixed schedules, even under pressure; such activity results in obsession, not liberation. This was not the procedure of the masters, and it is not recommended in classical Zen meditation texts. The great master Dahui said,

> Nowadays they sound a signal to sit and meditate. If you want a solemn scene, there you have it, but I don't believe you can sit to the point where you attain stability. People who hear this kind of talk often think I do not teach people to sit and meditate,

but this is a misperception; they do not understand expedient technique. I just want you to be in Zen meditation whether you are working or sitting, to be essentially at peace whether you are speaking, silent, active, or still.

The roots of the deterioration of meditation from a living means into a dead end were already observed in the classical era of Zen. The renowned Tang dynasty master Linji said, "There are blind baldies who, after they hve eaten their fill, sit in meditation and arrest thoughts leaking out, to prevent them from arising, shunning clamor and seeking quietude. This is a deviated form of Zen." A generation later, the redoubtable master Xuansha went even further in contrasting living Zen with pietistic quietist cults:

> This business cannot be pinned down; the road of mind and thought ends. It does not depend on embellishment; it is original true peace. In movement and action, talking and laughing, it is everywhere clear; there is nothing lacking.
>
> People these days, not realizing this truth, arbitrarily get involved in things, in material objects, influenced by all that is around them, fixated and bound up everywhere.
>
> Even if they understand, they find the material world a profusion of confusion, with labels and characteristics not corresponding to realities, so they try to freeze their minds and curtail their thoughts, returning things to voidness, shutting their eyes, clearing away thoughts over and over again whenever they arise, suppressing even subtle ideas as soon as they occur.
>
> Such an understanding is that of an outsider who has fallen into empty nothingness, a corpse whose soul has not yet dissolved. Void of awareness, void of cognition, plunged into indefinite darkness, people who plug up their ears to steal bells only fool themselves.

In the secular, busy Western world, in the crowded present day, quietism is even more out of place than it was eleven hundred years ago in China when these words were spoken. The original methods of doing the Zen work under all circumstances, the hallmark of secular Zen, seems to be best suited to contemporary conditions for the majority of individuals today.

Zen Koans

One of the main tools for Zen in action is a highly concentrated form of Zen literature commonly known in the West by the Japanese name *koan*. These Zen sayings and stories were a means used even by classical Zen masters to help people avoid the extremes of exaggerations of deviated Zen, so eloquently analyzed in their talks yet so easy to forget in the course of daily life.

These stories and sayings contain patterns, like blueprints, for various inner exercises in attention, mental posture, and higher perception, summarized in extremely brief vignettes enabling the individual to hold entire universes of Zen thought in mind all at once, without running through doctrinal discourses or disrupting ordinary consciousness of everyday affairs.

One of the original uses of Zen stories was to enable people to focus their minds in action, so as not to be dependent on external or internal quietude for meditation. This is documented in both classical and post-classical Zen lore. Like other meditation procedures, however, the interpretation and usage of Zen stories underwent peculiar metamorphoses in the imitation cults that proliferated after the golden age of Zen.

These deteriorations are, fortunately, also diagnosed by distinguished masters of the Song dynasty, so that seekers may be alert enough to avoid blind alleys in dealing with a literature that can often be difficult to understand, especially for beginners, and thus can provide a fertile field for charlatans and poseurs. Master Mi-an said,

> The reason this path has not been flourishing in recent years is nothing else but the fact that those who are acting as teachers of others do not have their eyes and brains straight and true.
>
> They have no perception of their own, but just keep fame and fortune and gain and loss in their hearts. Deeply afraid that others will say they have no stories, they mistakenly memorize stories from old books, letting them ferment in the back of their minds so they won't lack for something to say if seekers ask them questions.
>
> They are like goats crapping: the minute their tails go up, innumerable dung balls plop to the ground! Since students do not have clear perception, how are they supposed to distinguish

clearly? Students believe deeply, with all their hearts; so unseeing individuals lead unseeing crowds into a pit of fire.

In the West, where neither the Chinese language nor Buddhist thought are generally known, it is even more critical to make sure that we understand the true structure of Zen stories, and know how their structure guides constructive concentration before trying to employ them. Considering what became of Zen koans even in the land of their origin, if we are to derive any real living enlightenment from contemplation of Zen stories we must beware of naively mistaking bafflement or mystification for authentic Zen effects.

Zen Enlightenment

One of the peculiarities of Zen Buddhism is the idea that awakening can take place instantaneously. Zen training, from this point of view, does not mean learning doctrines, rituals, and postures, but preparing the mind to accept this awakening and integrate it constructively with daily life in the world.

Several deteriorations in Zen are associated with instant awakening. One is the premature induction of experience, resulting in failure to attain an integrated personality. Another is inability to sustain and develop the newly awakened consciousness, again resulting in failure to achieve complete integration. In this connection it should be noted that enlightenment in Zen generally refers to the initiatory awakening, not the full development known in classical Buddhism as complete perfect enlightenment.

A rather more common deterioration of the instant awakening of Zen is mistaking an ecstatic experience or altered state of consciousness for this Zen awakening. There are many records of this in Zen lore, where it is sometimes described as mistaking a fish eye for a pearl. Since enlightenment may often be accompanied by a release of tension, furthermore, there are cases where people mistake emotional catharsis for awakening, or even deliberately induce excessive tension in an effort to produce an ecstatic feeling of release. Attempts to mimic the Zen effect in this way can be observed in both Eastern and Western Zen cults, especially in recent generations.

A more radical deviation in the sudden enlightenment teaching was the doctrine that there is actually no such thing. This became fashionable among cultists in both China and Japan, many centuries ago. Master Dahui (1089–1163) observed,

> In the monastic Zen communities of recent times, there is a kind of false Zen that clings to disease as if it were medicine. Never having had any experiential enlightenment themselves, they consider enlightenment to be a construct, a word used as an inducement, a fall into the secondary, a subordinate issue. Those who have never had experience of enlightenment themselves, and who do not believe anyone else has had experience of enlightenment, uniformly consider empty, inert blankness to be the primordial. Eating two meals daily, they do no work but just sit, calling this "inner peace."

Those who adopted this posture in feudal Japan also spoke of "just sitting," but surrounded it with elaborate rituals, considering obedience to the regulations and observances of their cult to be all that was needed in the way of enlightenment. Back in China, master Mi-an also pointed out a more subtle fallacy of this "no enlightenment" Zen: "Just because of never having personally realized awakening, people temporarily halt sensing of objects, then take the bit of light that appears before their eyes to be the ultimate. This illness is most miserable." The construction of fancy rituals and titles to celebrate and enshrine these experiences as absolutes made the situation extremely critical in the context of religious Zen. It might be said that this is another advantage of secular Zen, wherein realization must actually be effective in all experiences and is not sacramentalized.

Historical records show the spiritual failure of the Zen-without-enlightenment movement, but they also show the attraction of this doctrine for authorities who wanted a static and ineffectual state-approved religion to absorb excess energies of the populace in a way that the authorities could control without military action against their own subjects. As the classical masters themselves already pointed out in China long ago, authoritarian cultism with its magisterial potentates, courts, regalia, and sacred mysteries, is actually a historical relic of politico-religious affairs, not the authentic heritage of enlightened living Zen.

Shortcuts to Zen

This book contains translations of general lectures on Zen by Foyan (1067–1120), who is universally recognized as one of the greatest masters of the Song dynasty Zen revival. Going back to the original and classical Zen masters, Foyan presents many simple exercises in attention and thought designated to lead to the awakening of Zen insight into the real nature of the self.

After the passing of the classical masters, very few Zen teachers equaled Foyan in the degree to which he fostered independence and autonomy and freedom in his hearers from the very outset. He was completely free of any desire for fame or followers, and made no attempt to recruit disciples. All he wanted was for people to open their own eyes and stand on their own two feet, to see directly without delusion and act on truth without confusion. It is said that dozens of his hearers attained enlightenment; at least fifteen of them are known to have become Zen masters and teachers in their own right.

Zen Lectures

Freedom and Independence

One who is not a companion of myriad things has departed the toils of materialism. The mind does not recognize the mind, the eye does not see the eye; since there is no opposition, when you see forms there are no forms there to be seen, and when you hear sounds there are no sounds there to be heard. Is this not departing the toils of materialism?

There is no particular pathway into it, no gap through which to see it: Buddhism has no East or West, South or North; one does not say, "You are the disciple, I am the teacher." If your own self is clear and everything is It, when you visit a teacher you do not see that there is a teacher; when you inquire of yourself, you do not see that you have a self. When you read scripture, you do not see that there is scripture there. When you eat, you do not see that there is a meal there. When you sit and meditate, you do not see that there is any sitting. You do not slip up in your everyday tasks, yet you cannot lay hold of anything at all.

When you see in this way, are you not independent and free?

Zen Sicknesses

The spiritual body has three kinds of sickness and two kinds of light; when you have passed through each one, only then are you able to sit in peace. In the *Heroic Progress Discourse,* furthermore, Buddha explained fifty kinds of meditation sickness. Now I tell you that you need to be free from sickness to attain realization.

In my school, there are only two kinds of sickness. One is to go looking for a donkey riding on the donkey. The other is to be unwilling to dismount once having mounted the donkey.

You say it is certainly a tremendous sickness to mount a donkey and then go looking for the donkey. I tell you that one need not find a spiritually sharp person to recognize this right away and get rid of the sickness of seeking, so the mad mind stops.

Once you have recognized the donkey, to mount it and be unwilling to dismount is the sickness that is most difficult to treat. I tell you that you need not mount the donkey; you *are* the donkey! The whole world is the donkey; how can you mount it? If you mount it, you can be sure the sickness will not leave! If you don't mount it, the whole universe is wide open!

When the two sicknesses are gone, and there is nothing on your mind, then you are called a wayfarer. What else is there? This is why when Zhaozhou asked Nanquan, "What is the path?"

Nanquan replied, "The normal mind is the path." Now Zhaozhou suddenly stopped his hasty search, recognized the sickness of "Zen Masters" and the sickness of "Buddhas," and passed through it all. After that, he traveled all over, and had no peer anywhere, because of his recognition of sicknesses.

One day Zhaozhou went to visit Zhuyou, where he paced back and forth brandishing his staff from east to west and west to east. Zhuyou asked, "What are you doing?" Zhaozhou replied, "Testing the water." Zhuyou retorted, "I haven't even one drop here; what will you test?" Zhaozhou left, leaning on his staff. See how he revealed a bit of an example, really quite able to stand out.

Zen followers these days all take sickness for truth. Best not let your mind get sick.

FACING IT DIRECTLY

If you don't ask, you won't get it; but if you ask, in effect you've slighted yourself. If you don't ask, how can you know? But you still have to know *how* to ask before you can succeed.

I have stuck you right on the top of the head for you to discern the feeling, like lifting up the scab on your moxacautery burn. Spiritually sharp people know immediately; then for the first time they attain the ability to avoid cheating themselves in any way.

I'm not fooling you. Remember the story of the ancient worthy who was asked, "What was the intention of the Zen Founder in coming from India?" Amazed, the ancient said, "You ask about the intention of another in coming from India. Why not ask about your own intention?"

Then the questioner asked, "What is one's own intention?"
The ancient replied, "Observe it in hidden actions."
The questioner asked, "What are its hidden actions?"
The ancient opened and closed his eyes to give an indication.

The ancients often took the trouble to talk quite a bit, but their descendants were not like that; they would shout at people the moment they entered the door, with no further whats or hows or maybes.

If you don't understand, there is something that is just so; why not perceive it? In other places they like to have people look at model case stories, but here we have the model case story of what is presently coming into being; you should look at it, but no one can make you see all the way through such an immense affair.

People spend all their time on thoughts that are nothing but idle imagination and materialistic toil, so wisdom cannot emerge. All conventions come from conceptual thought; what use do you want to make of them?

Wisdom is like the sun rising, whereupon everything is illuminated. This is called the manifestation of nondiscriminatory knowledge. You should attain this once, and from then on there will be something to work with, and we will have something to talk about. If you indulge in idle imagination and toil over objects, then you have nothing for me to work with.

What a laugh! When I talk about the east, you go into the west, and when I talk about the west, you go into the east; I can do nothing for you! If you could turn your heads around, when your insight opened up you'd be able to say, "After all it turns out that the teacher *has* told me, and I have told the teacher," and when the head was shaken the tail would whip around, everything falling into place. You brag about having studied Zen for five or ten years, but when have you ever done this kind of work? You just pursue fast talk.

When you have come to me and I see it as soon as you try to focus on anything, that means your inner work has not yet reached the point of flavorlessness. If you stay here five or ten years and manage to perfect your inner work, then you will awaken.

Whenever I teach people to do inner work, what I tell them is all in accord with the ancients, not a word off; understand, and you will know of the ancients. But don't say, "An ancient spoke thus, and I have understood it thus," for then it becomes incorrect.

How about the ancient saying, "It is not the wind moving, not the flag moving, but your mind moving"—how many words here are right or wrong in your own situation? It is also said, "I am you, you are me"—nothing is beyond this.

Also, someone asked Yunmen, "What is the student's self?" Yunmen replied, "Mountains, rivers, the whole earth." This is quite good; are these there or not? If the mountains, rivers, and earth are there, how can you see the self? If not, how can you say that the presently existing mountains, rivers, and earth are not there? The ancients have explained for you, but you do not understand and do not know.

I always tell you that what is inherent in you is presently active and presently functioning, and need not be sought after, need not be put in order, need not be practiced or proven. All that is required is to trust it once and for all. This saves a lot of energy.

It is hard to find people like this. When my teacher was with his teacher, his teacher used to say, "This path is a natural sublety attained by oneself," generally focusing on the existence of innate knowledge. When I saw my teacher, I was unable to express this for ten years; just because I wondered deeply, I later attained penetrating understanding and now do not waste any energy at all.

It is not that it is there when you think of it but not so when you don't; Buddhism is not like this. Don't let the matter under the vestment bury me away. If you do not reflect and examine, your whole life will be buried away. Is there in fact anything going on here?

Nowadays there are many public teachers whose guiding eye is not clear. This is very wrong! How dare they mount a pulpit to try to help others? Showing a symbol of authority, they rant and rave at people without any qualms, simply pursuing the immediate and not worrying about the future. How miserable! If you have connections, you should not let yourself be set up as a teacher as long as you are not enlightened, because that is disaster! If there is something real in you, "musk is naturally fragrant." See how many phony "Zen masters" there are, degenerating daily over a long, long time. They are like human dung carved into sandalwood icons; ultimately there is just the smell of crap.

Wishing to get out of birth and death, wishing to attain release, you try to become unified; but one does not attain unification after becoming homogenized. If you try to make yourself unified, you will certainly not attain unification.

Once a seeker called on a Wayfarer and asked, as they roamed the mountains, "An ancient teacher said he sought unification for thirty years without being able to attain it; what does this mean?" The Wayfarer replied, "I too am thus." Then he asked the seeker, "Understand?" He also gave the seeker a poem:

> The ancient teacher attains unification
> and I too am thus;
> before the end of this month,
> I will settle it for you again.

At the end of the month, the Wayfarer passed away. Tell me about unification; is it good or bad? The ancient teacher attained unification, and I too am thus. I announce to Zen seekers: facing it directly, don't stumble past. Each of you, go on your way.

SEEING AND DOING

Many are those who have seen but can do nothing about it. Once you have seen, why can't you do anything about it? Just because of not discerning; that is why you are helpless. If you see and discern, then you can do something about it.

Nevertheless, if you expect to understand as soon as you are inspired to study Zen, well, who wouldn't like that? It's just that you have no way in, and you cannot force understanding. Failing to mesh with it in every situation, missing the connection at every point, you cannot get it by exertion of force.

Whatever you are doing, twenty-four hours a day, in all your various activities, there is something that transcends the Buddhas and Zen Masters; but as soon as you want to understand it, it's not there. It's not really there; as soon as you try to gather your attention on it, you have already turned away from it. That is why I say you see but cannot do anything about it.

Does this mean that you will realize it if you do not aim the mind and do not develop intellectual understanding? Far from it—you will fail even more seriously to realize it. Even understanding does not get it, much less not understanding!

If you are spiritually sharp, you can open your eyes and see as soon as you hear me tell you about this. Have not people of immeasurable greatness said this truth is not comprehensible by thought, and that it is where knowledge does not reach? Were it not like this, how could it be called an enlightened truth? Nowadays, however, people just present interpretations and views, making up rationalizations; they have never learned to be thus, and have never reached this state.

If people with potential for enlightenment are willing to see in this way, they must investigate most deeply and examine most closely; all of a sudden they will gain mastery of it and have no further doubt. The reason you do not understand is just because you are taken away by random thoughts twenty-four hours a day. Since you want to learn business, you fall in love with things you see and fondly pursue things you read; over time, you get continuously involved? How can you manage to work on enlightenment then?

Generally speaking, there are appropriate times for those who study business. Over the age of thirty, it's better not to study, because it will be hard to learn even if you do, and it will also be of dubious value. If you have taken care of your own business, on the other hand—that is, the business of the self—then you will still be able to learn through study, because you have been transformed. But if you have done with your own business, why would you study? If you are twenty years of age or thereabouts, you can still study, but if you are spiritually sharp and intent on the matter of life and death, you won't study anything else.

Whenever you seek Zen, furthermore, your mind ground must be even and straight, and your mind and speech must be in accord. Since your mind and speech are straightforward, your states are thus consistent from start to finish, without any petty details.

Do not say, "I understand! I have attained mastery!" If you have attained mastery, then why are you going around asking other people questions? As soon as you say you understand Zen, people watch whatever you do and whatever you say, wondering why you said this or that. If you claim to understand Zen, moreover, this is actually a contention of ignorance. What about the saying that one should "silently shine, hiding one's enlightenment?" What about "concealing one's name and covering one's tracks"? What about "the path is not different from the human mind"?

Each of you should individually reduce entanglements and not talk about judgments of right and wrong. All of your activities everywhere transcend Buddhas and Masters, the water buffalo at the foot of the mountain is imbued with Buddhism; but as soon as you try to search, it's not there. Why do you not discern this?

THE MARROW OF THE SAGES

My livelihood is the marrow of all the sages; there is not a moment when I am not explaining it to you, but you are unwilling to take it up. So it turns out, on the contrary, to be my deception. But look here—where is it that I am not explaining for you?

Professional Zennists say I do not teach people to think, I do not teach people to understand, I do not teach people to discuss stories, I do not cite past and present examples; they suppose we are idling away the time here, and think that if they had spent the time elsewhere they would have understood a few model case stories and heard some writings. If you want to discuss stories, cite past and present, then please go somewhere else; here I have only one-flavor Zen, which I therefore call the marrow of all sages.

Now let me ask you something. Why do you pay respects to an icon of wisdom? Does the icon acknowledge you when you pay respects? Does it agree with you?

If you say it acknowledges you, it is a clay icon—how can it give any acknowledgment? If you say it agrees, can you agree? Since you are incapable of acknowledgment or agreement, why do you pay respects? Is it social convention? Is it producing goodness from seeing a representation?

If you say it is social duty, how can there be social convention among renunciants? How can they produce good by seeing representations?

Do you pay respects as a consequence of going along with the crowd? If so, what is the logic in that?

Here you must understand each point clearly. Have you not read how the great teacher Changsha one day turned around and saw the icon of wisdom, whereupon he suddenly realized the ultimate and said, "Turning around, I suddenly see the original body. The original body is not a perception or a reality; if you consider the original being to be the same as the real being, you will suffer hardship forever." Do you understand the logic of this?

NOT KNOWING

Sometimes when I question students, they all say they do not know or understand; they just say they eat when hungry and sleep when tired. What redemption is there in such talk? You even say you are not cognizant of whether the month is long or short, and do not care whether it is a leap year; who understands this affair of yours?

Now I ask you, how do you explain the logic of not knowing? You hear others say this, so you say it yourselves; but have you ever understood that principle of not knowing?

An ancient said, "Not knowing means nothing is not known, nowhere not reached." This is called unknowing so that you people today may reach that unknown state. This is the realm of the sages—how could it be like the blindness and nonunderstanding that people today call not knowing?

If you go on like this always declaring you don't know and are not concerned, how will you communicate if someone questions you? There might be no one to continue on the road of Zen! It won't do to be like this. Make your choice carefully!

EMANCIPATION

In ancient times a Zen worthy asked an old adept, "What is essential for emancipation?" The old adept said, "Fog is rising from your feet, reverend!" At these words, the Zen worthy suddenly got the message.

Do you know about emancipation? If you formulate the idea that you can understand, then you are blocked off from it.

Later, another adept said, "I dare not turn my back on you, master; for fog is rising from *your* feet!"

Then there is the story of when Beiyuan Tong left Dongshan. Dongshan said, "Where are you going?" Tong replied, "Into the mountains." Dongshan said, "Flying Monkey Ridge is steep—a fine sight!" Tong hesitated. Dongshan said, "Reverend Tong!" Tong responded, "Yes?" Dongshan said, "Why don't you go into the mountains?" At these words, Tong suddenly got the message.

The ancients were quite direct in their ways of helping others. Whenever people came to them, they would show them. In this case, he said he was going into the mountains; what does this mean?

People today do not realize clearly, inevitably making an understanding. By a bit of understanding, they have blocked themselves off. One can only investigate comprehensively through experience; one cannot understand just by intellectual interpretation. Once you have comprehended thoroughly with unified comprehension, you will no longer doubt.

Nevertheless, this is not easy to maintain. If you have entered into it correctly, you will not backslide. Thus, even if you have clarified what can be understood, that is not comparable to seeing what cannot be understood and also having the ability to maintain it. Then you will always be aware and always be alert.

This is why an ancient said, "The normal mind is the path; can one aim for it?" "If you try to head for it, you are turning away from it." Seeing as how you are not allowed to head for it, then how do you maintain it? It's not easy!

Is this not emancipation? If you seek a state of emancipation, this is what is called a cramp! Xuansha said, "The whole earth is an eon of hell; if you do not clarify yourself, this is a serious cramp." It will not do to idle away the time.

STOP OPINIONS

The Third Patriarch of Zen said, "Don't seek reality, just put a stop to opinions." He also said, "As soon as there are judgments of right and wrong, the mind is lost in a flurry." These sayings teach you people of today what to work on.

When you read his saying, "Don't seek reality," you say there is no further need to seek—this means you are still entertaining opinions and are in a flurry of judgments; after all you have not reached a state of mind where there is no seeking, and are just making up an opinionated interpretation.

People who study Zen nowadays are all like this; reading a transformative saying and reaching an insight into the words, then they try to apply it to all sayings, thinking they are all the same. Keeping this in their hearts, they think of it as their own attainment; far from realizing they have lost their minds by entertaining an opinionated understanding, they cling to it and will not let go. What ignoramuses!

Would you like to attain a state of mind where you seek nothing? Just do not conceive all sorts of opinions and views. This nonseeking does not mean blanking out and ignoring everything. In everyday life, twenty-four hours a day, when there is unclarity in the immediate situation it is generally because the opinionated mind is grasping and rejecting. How can you get to know the nondiscriminatory mind then?

Thus when an ancient sage was asked if the created and the uncreated are different, he said they are not. Sky and earth, rivers and seas, wind and clouds, grasses and trees, birds and beasts, people and things living and dying, changing right before our eyes, are all called created forms. The uncreated way is silent and unmoving; the indescribable and unnameable is called uncreated. How can there be no difference?

Grand Master Yongjia said, "The true nature of ignorance is the very nature of enlightenment; the empty body of illusions and projections is the very body of realities." These two are each distinct; how do you understand the logic of identity? You have to experience the mind without seeking; when they will integrate and you will get to be trouble-free.

In the ten stages of enlightenment, the fifth is the stage Difficult to Conquer, which means that it is extremely difficult to attain equality of real knowledge and conventional knowledge; when you enter this stage, the two are equal, so it is called the stage that is difficult to conquer. Students of the path should take them in and make them equal twenty-four hours a day.

And do you know they are drawn up by your nondiscriminatory mind? Like an artist drawing all sorts of pictures, both pretty and ugly, the mind depicts forms, feelings, perceptions, abstract patterns, and consciousness; it depicts human societies and paradises. When it is drawing these pictures, it does not borrow the power of another; there is no discrimination between the artist and the artwork. It is because of not realizing this that you conceive various opinions, having views of yourself and views of other people, creating your own fair and foul.

So it is said, "An artist draws a picture of hell, with countless sorts of hideous forms. On setting aside the brush to look it over, it's bone-chilling, really hair-raising." But if you know it's a drawing, what is there to fear?

In olden times, when people had clearly realized this, it became evident in all situations. Once when the great teacher Xuansha was cutting down a tree, a tiger bounded out of the woods. The teacher's companion said, "It's a tiger!" The teacher scolded him and said, "It's a tiger for you."

Another time, when he saw a seeker performing prostrations, Xuansha said, "It is because of the self that one can bow to the other." These expedients are in profound accord with the intent of Buddha.

The great teacher Fayan once pointed to a dog right in front of him and said, "An engraving." When you look at this, do not look to the dog itself for clarification; you must see it in your own experience before you can get it. Only then will you understand that saying, "As soon as there are judgments of right and wrong, you lose your mind in a flurry." I hope you get the point!

THE DIRECTOR

Even if you trust directly in the rightness of reality this very moment, already you are called a dullard; how much the more if you cannot trust directly—what are you good for then?

If you directly trust the rightness of reality, why are you called a dullard? When have you been coming and going all this time? You should know you've lost one part; then you see that what you had hitherto not comprehended turns out to be a view that has no relevance to you.

As I observe the ancients since time immemorial, there were those who attained enlightenment from confusion; all of their statements are teachings on attaining enlightenment from confusion. Then there were those who came to understand confusion after becoming enlightened; all of their statements are teachings on understanding confusion after becoming enlightened. Then again, were those for whom there is neither confusion nor enlightenment; all of their statements are teachings on freedom from both confusion and enlightenment. Next, those who attained enlightenment outside of confusion were also very numerous, so they are not worth talking about. How much less worthwhile are those who neither know enlightenment nor understand confusion! These latter are, properly speaking, merely ordinary mortals.

In ancient times, only a few people such as Nanquan and Guizong could be referred to as having vision free of both confusion and enlightenment. Students nowadays run off at the mouth talking about freedom from both confusion and enlightenment, but when have they ever actually arrived at it? Don't say things like that too easily!

Since you still have doubts, now I will ask you something. When you were first conceived in your mother's womb, what did you bring with you? You had nothing whatsoever when you came, just mental consciousness, with no shape or form. Then when you die and give up the burden of the physical body, again you will have nothing at all but mental consciousness. At present, in your travels and community life, this is the director.

Now let me ask you something. We receive portions of energy from our father and mother through their sperm and egg; clinging to what we receive, we call it our body. From the time of birth, as it gradually grows and matures, this body always belongs to the self. But tell me, does it belong to you or not? If you say it belongs to you, when first conceived you had nothing with you; when did the sperm and egg of your father and mother ever belong to you? Life can last a hundred years at most, furthermore, before the corpse is abandoned; when did it ever belong to you?

And yet, if you say it doesn't belong to you, right now there is no possibility of taking anything away. When it is reviled you anger, when it is pained you suffer; how could it not belong to you? Try to determine whether you have anything there or not, and you will find you cannot determine, because your root of doubt is not cut through. If you say you have something there, while during the process of growth from birth up to the age of twenty, there is no change in this certainty, but when you get to be forty or fifty the body changes and deteriorates from moment to moment, so you cannot say it is definitively there. But if you say there is nothing there, nevertheless you can perform all sorts of actions, so you cannot say there is nothing.

Once upon a time, a man lost his way on a journey, so he lodged in a vacant cottage. That night a ghost came, carrying a corpse. Then another ghost came and said, "That's my body!" The first ghost said, "I got it over yonder." Then the second ghost snatched it away by force. The first ghost said, "There's a traveler here who can stand witness!" So the two ghosts approached the man and said, "Who brought this corpse?"

The traveler reflected, "Both of the ghosts are evil; at least one of them is sure to hurt me. I've heard that if one avoids telling a falsehood when facing death, one will be born in heaven." So he pointed to the first ghost and said, "This ghost brought it."

Enraged, the second ghost tore out the traveler's arms and legs. Now the first ghost, repentant and grateful, said, "Your word of testimony for me has crippled you." So the first ghost used the corpse to patch the man up. The parts were again taken by the second ghost, and the first ghost repaired the man once again. Finally both ghosts wound up on the ground trying to eat the man's flesh as fast as they could, each one trying to get more than the other. When all of the man's flesh had been consumed, the ghosts left.

Now the traveler saw his parents' bodies right in front of his eyes, already devoured by the ghosts. Then he gazed upon his own changed body and wondered what it was. "Is it me? Is it not me? Is it something? Is it nothing?" He went crazing thinking about these things, and bolted off into the night.

Eventually he came to a cloister. There he saw a mendicant, to whom he related the foregoing events. The mendicant saw that he would be easy to teach and to liberate, because he already knew that his body was not his possession. So the mendicant gave the traveler a summary of the teaching, and he actually attained enlightenment after that.

You people just talk about studying Zen by bringing up stories as if that were Buddhism. What I am talking about now is the marrow of Zen; why do you not wonder, find out, and understand in this way? Your body is not there, yet not nothing. Its presence is the presence of the body in the mind; so it has never been there. Its nothingness is the absence of the body in the mind; so it has never been nothing.

Do you understand? If you go on to talk of mind, it too is neither something nor nothing; ultimately it is not you. The idea of something originally there now being absent, and the idea of something originally not there now being present, are views of nihilism and eternalism.

SAVING ENERGY

Generally speaking, practical application of Zen requires detachment from thoughts. This method of Zen saves the most energy. It just requires you to detach from emotional thoughts, and understand that there is nothing concrete in the realms of desire, form, and formlessness; only then can you apply Zen practically. If you try to practice it otherwise, it will seem bitterly painful by comparison.

Once there was a disciplinarian monk who had kept the precepts all his life. As he was walking one night, he stepped on something that squished, which he imagined to be a frog, a mother frog laden with eggs. Mortified at the thought of having killed a pregnant frog, when the monk when to sleep that night he dreamed that hundreds of frogs came to him demanding his life. He was utterly terrified.

Come morning, the monk went to look for the frog he had squashed, and found that it had only been an overripe eggplant. At that moment, the monk's perplexities abruptly ceased; realizing there is nothing concrete in the world, for the first time he was really able to apply it practically in life.

Now I ask you, when he stepped on it by night, was it a frog or an eggplant? If it was a frog, yet when he looked at dawn it was an eggplant; if it was an eggplant, yet there were frogs demanding his life the night before. Can you decide? I'll try to decide for you:

> Feelings of frogs may be shed,
> but the idea of eggplant remains.
> If you would be free
> of the idea of eggplant,
> strike the evening chime at noon.

THE MOST DIRECT APPROACH

Why don't you understand the essence that has always been there? There is not much to Buddhism; it only requires you to see the way clearly. It does not tell you to extinguish random thoughts and suppress body and mind, shutting your eyes and saying "This is It!" The matter is not like this.

You must observe the present state. What is its logic? What is its guiding pattern? Why are you confused? This is the most direct approach.

How about when I have not spoken to you, and you have no heard me; is there any point in coming and going? At such a time, do not make up forced rationalizations.

From the Buddhas above to the totality of beings below, all is *thus*. In this sense, sages and ordinary people are equal, wrong and right are equal, samsara and nirvana are equal. Now I ask you, whose business are the ancient Buddhas, and the generations of past, present and future? Whose business are the contaminated lands of the ten directions?

I say, if you understand all this thirty years from now, you will realize that I did tell you. Just don't say, "This is It!" If you do, that is called the view of an outsider.

ASLEEP

Right now if you are questioned and cannot speak, where is the fault? It is generally because of seeing forms where there is no form, hearing a voice where there is nothing said, forcing rationalizations where there is no reason, asserting control where there is no control.

If you cannot get rid of this, that is referred to as "diseased eyes still there, flowers in the sky fall in confusion." Why? Just because mind is still there; so you cannot speak.

There is not much to Buddhism; it only requires you to make a statement plainly and simply, that is all. But what is a plain and simple statement? If someone asked me, I'd say, "It's already become two statements." Understand?

An ancient said, "The Buddhas and Zen masters have given a clear and detailed explanation of what is beyond words, but most of those who get here are confused, muddled, and uncomprehending."

If you don't see this, you are asleep on your feet. You are always in the light, and yet do not know it, even with your eyes open. How do you expect me to do anything for you?

NO SEEING

When I bring up one thing and another for you as I do, you think I am explaining Zen; but the minute you go into action you make it into worldly convention.

Only if you keep your attention on it will you be able to make a discovery; but as I see, most of you just remain in eyes and ears, seeing and hearing, sensing and feeling—you've already missed the point. You must find the nondiscriminatory mind without departing from the discriminating mind; find that which has no seeing or hearing without departing from seeing and hearing.

This does not mean that "no seeing" is a matter of sitting on a bench with your eyes closed. You must have nonseeing right in seeing. This is why it is said, "Live in the realm of seeing and hearing, yet unreached by seeing and hearing; live in the land of thought, yet untouched by thought."

INDEPENDENCE

What do you people come to me for? Each individual should lead life autonomously—don't listen to what other people say. An ancient declared, "I knew how to lead life by the time I was eighteen." You people must learn to live independently.

You say, "Lead what life?" Just do not seek elsewhere. Most people today are compulsively active; this is already not knowing how to lead life. This is called abandoning home, scattering the family, and becoming a drifter. Clearly this is not understanding. Just searching and seeking, studying a bit of intellectual knowledge, memorizing a few sayings, is called "hauling manure inside."

When you get here, your actions have to be truly accurate; eventually it will sink in thoroughly, and then you will understand. An ancient said, "Everywhere is you. Go east, and it's you; go west, and it's you. Who are you?" If you say, "Me," this is emotional and intellectual consciousness, which you must pass through before you attain realization.

In ancient times Vasubandhu asked Asanga, "Elder brother, when you went to the inner palace, what teaching did Maitreya expound to you?" Asanga replied, "He expounded *this* teaching." Now tell me, what teaching is *this?* You must be able to discern it before you can realize it.

Don't fix recognition on *this.* Many people have been fooled by the term *this.* That is why they speak of illness as if it were medicine. Therefore we say they are pitiful.

IN TUNE

Don't say what is speaking right now is It; that's not quite right. As soon as there is an affirmation, then there is a denial. That is the reason why it is said, that no verbal expressions correspond to this reality.

What you must do is live in harmony with it. This matter is not in another; but are you in tune with it? And if you are in tune, in tune with whom?

If you say you are in tune with the ancients, the ancients are gone. If you say you are in tune with a teacher, a teacher has no connection with you.

This is why the sages compassionately told us to tune into the source of our own minds. Now tell me, what is the source of mind, to which one tunes in on one's own?

If you mindfully try to tune into mind, you will definitely be unable to tune in. You have to tune in with mindless mind.

LEARNING ZEN

You must be attuned twenty-four hours a day before you attain realization. Have you not read how Lingyun suddenly tuned in to this reality on seeing peach blossoms, how Xiangyan set his mind at rest on hearing the sound of bamboo being hit?

An ancient said, "If you are not in tune with this reality, then the whole earth deceives you, the environment fools you." The reason for all the mundane conditions abundantly present is just that this reality has not been clarified. I urge you for now to first detach from gross mental objects. Twenty-four hours a day you think about clothing, think about food, think all sorts of various thoughts, like the flame of a candle burning unceasingly.

Just detach from gross mental objects, and whatever subtle ones there are will naturally clear out, and eventually you will come to understand spontaneously; you don't need to ask. This is called putting conceptualization to rest and forgetting mental objects, not being a partner to the dusts.

This is why the ineffable message of Zen is to be understood on one's own. I have no Zen for you to study, no Doctrine for you to discuss. I just want you to tune in on your own.

The only essential thing in learning Zen is to forget mental objects and stop rumination. This is the message of Zen since time immemorial. Did not one of the Patriarchs say, "Freedom from thoughts is the source, freedom for appearances is the substance"? If you just shout and clap, when will you ever be done?

THE BASIS OF AWARENESS

Expand enlightenment, and the mind is always calm; go along with things, and consciousness runs at a gallop. I only wish to be rich in enlightenment though personally poor, generous with virtue though emotionally aloof.

Here, I am thus every day, thus all the time. But tell me, what is "thus"? Try to express it outside of discriminatory consciousness, intellectual assessments, and verbal formulations.

This reality is not susceptible to your intellectual understanding. Now those who think, attend, and reflect all have some intellectual understanding; but then when they turn back to examine their own eyes and think of the mind that thinks, at this point why do people unknowingly say, "It has never been blue, yellow, red, or white; it has no appearance, no form"? I tell you, this is what I call talk; it is not your original mind.

How can you think of your original mind? How can you see your own eye? When you are looking inward, furthermore, there is no seeing subject. Some people swallow this in one gulp, so their eye of insight opens wide and they immediately arrive at their homeland.

How can people nowadays reach the point where there is no seeing and no hearing? Everything is always there; you see people, houses, and all sorts of forms, like boiling water bubbling.

When you were infants, you also heard sounds and saw forms, but you didn't know how to discriminate. Once you came to the age of reason, then you listened to discriminatory thinking, and from that time on have suffered a split between the primal and the temporal.

At this point, it is inevitably hard for people to restore natural order even if they want to. Those who attain enlightenment do not see walking when they walk, and do not see sitting when they sit. That is why the Buddha said, "The eyes seeing forms is equivalent to blindness; the ears hearing sounds is equivalent to deafness."

How can we say we are as if blind and deaf? When we hear sound, there is no sound to be heard; when we see form, there is no form to be seen. What we see and hear is all equivalent to an echo. It is like seeing all sorts of things in a dream—is there all that when you wake up?

If you say yes, yet there's only the blanket and pillow on the bed; if you say no, yet all those things are clearly registered in your mind, and you can tell what they were. The same is true of what you see and hear now in broad daylight.

So it is said, what can be seen by the eye or heard by the ear can be studied in the scriptures and treatises; but what about the basis of awareness itself—how do you study that?

JUST BEING THERE

> Where is Shakyamuni, the Buddha?
> What? What?
> Where is Bodhidharma, Founder of Zen?
> Just there.

How do you explain the logic of just being there? It's unavoidably hard to clarify. If you can clarify this, you will finally know that true reality is always there.

Many Zen specialists say, "The mention itself is It." Then what about when you're dying, or too sick to speak? It is necessary to penetrate this experientially before you'll get it.

Have you not read how a seeker asked Deshan, "Where have the ancient sages gone?" Deshan said, "What? What?" Does that mean that "what" is itself the sages?

You people either interpret literally or else fall into conventional echoes of what is said. If you don't fall into echolike expressions, then you fall into wordlessness and speechlessness.

This reality you actually cannot figure out by conceptual interpretations; if you keep any of that on your mind, it turns into an inclination, alienating you from your self. Even if you try to attain harmony by means of mystic devices and wonderous doctrines, you will certainly be unable to do so. If you do not think at all, though, that won't work either. You must personally experience it before you will attain clear vision with no doubt.

TWO SICKNESSES

When people today studying Zen learn it wrongly, it is because of no more than two sicknesses.

One sickness is speechless, formless motionlessness in the haunt of the mind-body complex, where you say, "Even if the Buddhas and

Zen Patriarchs came forth, I would still just be thus." This is one sickness.

Next is to give recognition to that which speaks, hears, works, acts, walks, stands, sits, and reclines. This is also a sickness. Do you know that activity is the root of suffering, sustained by the power of wind?

If people can get away from these two sicknesses and can engage in total investigation, someday they should wake up. Otherwise, there is no cleaning things up.

There are also two kinds of benefactors who speak bitterly as an expedient for two kinds of students.

Students of one type make up rationales on their own and express things on their own, advancing and withdrawing, raising their fists and joining their palms, thinking this to be the way of Zen. Benefactors, seeing them this way, speak bitterly to them, saying, "You have misunderstood. Why is your attention so fixated when there is really no problem?" This is one kind of benefactor.

Another type of student says, "I do not understand, I do not know. Why? Because I am not tuned in at all." Therefore benefactors, seeing people thus, tell them, "There is nothing the matter with you; why do you seek to understand and tune in?" This is another kind of benefactor.

If both the former and latter types of students hear benefactors speaking like this, and are able to turn their attention around and study through experience, they will inevitably attain clarification. If they just stay they don't understand, they are creating their own stagnation; even after a thousand years they would just be the same.

Fortunately, you are in its very midst; if you go on saying you do not understand and seek to tune in to it, when will you ever be done?

Do you want to understand? You must not set up limited measurements; you must apprehend it directly before you can get it.

MIND ITSELF

Let me give you an illustration. People have eyes, by which they can see all sorts of forms, like long and short, square and round, and so on; then why do they not see themselves? Just perceiving forms, you cannot see your eyes even if you want to. Your mind is also like this;

its light shines perceptively throughout the ten directions, encompassing all things, so why does it not know itself?

Do you want to understand? Just discern the things perceived; you cannot see the mind itself.

An ancient said, "The knife does not cut itself, the finger does not touch itself, the mind does not know itself, the eyes does not see itself." This is true reality.

SEEING THROUGH

You people have been standing here for quite a while; have you seen a single real teacher yet? Don't keep on standing there for nothing.

I am only what I call a provisional elder. An ancient sage said, apropos of this, "Just using provisional terminology to guide people, Buddha was an old Indian mendicant, who did not trouble you to discriminate appearances and grasp forms."

What is Shakyamuni the Buddha? Who is Bodhidharma, the founder of Zen? Was there any Buddhism before the founder came here? How can you say there was none? If you say there was none, that is just self-deception. When Bodhidharma was facing a wall for nine years, were there so many verbal teachings and public cases? To see through in this way is a very economical shortcut.

When you had not come here, I had not seen you and you had not seen me. If you do not see me and I do not see you, how can there be discernment and clarification? If you can attain clarification, what else is the matter?

Before Buddha appeared in the world, it was thus; after Buddha appeared in the world it was also thus, and after Buddha passed away it was still thus. If you arrive at this state of thusness, there is really nothing the matter at all.

As you people go about your daily activities and take care of your needs as they arise, how can you say there is nothing the matter? Only those who have actually seen it can know it is so.

In ancient times, when Kasyapa the Elder paid respects to the Buddha at the assembly on Spiritual Peak, on seeing the vast crowd in a state of dignified composure, he had an insight and said, "This immense crowd here now is as if it had never been." You tell me, what does this mean?

A while ago you people were in your own places, where you didn't see so many people. Now that you're here, clearly you see a considerable number of people. How can you say they are as if they had never been?

In olden times, a certain old adept asked a seeker, "Where have you just come from?" The seeker replied, "The city." The adept said, "Where are you now?" The seeker said, "The mountains." The adept said, "I have a question to ask you. If you can answer, you may stay. If not, then leave. Now then, when you left the city, the city was lacking you; when you came to the mountains, the mountains had you extra. If you are absent in the city, the reality of mind is not universally omnipresent; if you are an extra in the mountains, then there is something outside of mind." The seeker had nothing to say.

If you can comprehend this, as it is said, you will not fall into nihilism or eternalism; your six sense faculties will be peaceful, and you will be tranquil and quiet whether active or still. One mind unborn, myriad entanglements cease.

Otherwise, if you are not like this, you fall into nihilism or eternalism, depending on being or nonbeing. This is like running away from home.

At this point, I really do not tell you to expend the slightest bit of effort; you will then get an understanding in this way. If you want to harmonize with this reality, making it so there is no gap, then you have already split away from it.

When I contemplated this matter in the past, I used to think it would take two or three lifetimes to attain enlightenment. Later, on hearing that someone had an awakening, or someone had an insight, I realized that people today can also become enlightened. At times when it is possible to minimize involvements, study your self clearly; this is very important.

SPEAKING EFFECTIVELY

If someone should question you, how would you speak? Can you speak effectively? If you can only speak after thinking and concentrating, what use is your statement?

At midnight, how do you speak? Getting up at dawn, how do you speak? In the hallway, in the washroom, how do you speak?

Can you speak effectively? Your eyes must be clear before you can.

NAKED REALIZATION

Just now an assistant came and announced that the rain isn't stopping, and people may not be able to hear if a meeting is held in the rain. Supposed the rain stopped right now—then would you hear?

I say it's best when the rain doesn't stop. Why? Because you are not deliberately trying to listen.

How about when they say the sound of the rain has given you a sermon? Is that correct? I do not agree; the sound of the rain *is* you giving a sermon. But do you understand? Clarify it directly; then what else is there?

People who go journeying to study Zen today should bring a statement to harmonize with the teacher. Why do you pain yourself and cramp yourself as you do?

Let me also ask you, what teacher would you harmonize with? If you want to harmonize with a teacher, just get to know your own mind.

Now let me ask you, what is your mind? And how do you know it?

Here you cannot force an understanding; you must actually look inward and discover it.

The ancients had no choice but to make provisional explanations where there is no explanation, skillfully employing expedient means where there are no expedients. One day when Xuansha went into the mountains, he encountered a tiger. His assistant told him there was a tiger there, but Xuansha just said, "It's your tiger." Now with mountains and rivers crisscrossing the land, domains of existence everywhere, discriminating thoughts branching off in a thousand ways and diverging in a million ways, how can you explain this logic of "it's yours"?

If you don't understand this, you will be fatally obstructed everywhere. It's just because you have been following material senses and been influenced by things since time immemorial. You try to point out—what are things, and what are you?

This is why a seeker asked Xuansha, "I have just entered the community; please show me a way of access." Xuansha said, "Do you hear the sound of the valley stream?" The seeker said, "Yes." Xuansha said, "Gain access form here."

Nowadays people do not clearly understand this story, simply saying, "The essence of mind is omnipresent; who else hears?" What relevance has this sort of discourse? You must be completely naked before you will attain realization.

For now I ask you, have you dressed?

You can be so shameless!

SEEING MIND

As soon as you rationalize, it's hard to understand; you must refrain from rationalization before you can attain realization.

Hearing such talk, some people immediately declare, "I have nothing to say at all, and no reason either." They do not realize this is in fact a rationalization!

I will settle something for you right now: the ultimate rule is to see your own mind clearly. That is what Buddhism is, as far as I am concerned.

An ancient said, "The mind does not know itself, the mind does not see itself." So how can you see it clearly?

Even though it's your own mind, it's hard to see. All the sages since time immemorial have been people who clearly saw their own minds. My late teacher was someone who saw his own mind, but among those here who were also associated with him in the past, there are very few who clearly see their own minds.

Mind does not see mind; to get it, you must not see it as mind. This is a realm apart from thoughts.

Now if I say this to people, they think I am criticizing everyone else, but if I do not talk about it, it will be hard to elucidate. Zen teachers of a certain type say to people, "Fools! Why don't you understand this thing?" First they make a cliche of "your own mind," then try to use the mind to "realize" it. This is called driving a spike into a stump and then running round and round the stump. They pass it on this way, and it is taken up this way, knocking on their chairs and holding up their whisks. This is called trying to use the mind by means of the mind.

There is another type of Zen teacher who tells people not to make logical assessments, that they lose contact the minute they speak, and should recognize the primordial. This kind of "teacher" has no explanation at all. This is like sitting on a balloon—where is there any comfort in it? It is also like the croaking of a bullfrog. If you entertain such a view, it is like being trapped in a black fog.

I am exhorting you in utter seriousness; I am not lying, I am not making up rationalizations to trap people, I will not allow people to oppress the free. I have no such reasons. If you recognize this, that is up to you. If you say you also see this way, that is up to you. If you say that everything is all right according to your perception, that is up to you. If you say your mind is still uneasy, that is up to you. You can only attain realization if you don't deceive yourself.

There are quite a few Zen teachers in the world, talking about Zen, talking about Tao. Do you think they are self-deceived, or not self-deceived? Do you think they are deceiving others, or not deceiving others? It is imperative to discern minutely.

In the old days, when I was in the school of my late teacher, I once accepted an invitation to go somewhere. On the way I ran into a downpour and slipped in the mud. Feeling annoyed, I said to myself, "I am on the journey but have been unable to attain Zen. I haven't eaten all day, and now have to endure this misery too!" Then I happened to hear two people ranting at each other, "You're still annoying yourself!" When I heard this, I suddenly felt overjoyed. Then I realized I couldn't find the state where there is no annoyance. That was because I couldn't break through my feelings of doubt. It took me four or five years after that to attain this knowledge.

Now you should exercise your attention in this way. I have brought up the saying that inanimate things teach, but many are those who misunderstand. When you see inanimate things, you say they're inanimate, and when you see animate beings you consider them animate.

If you who study Zen do not understand the teaching of the inanimate, how can you understand the task of the journey? If those who act as teachers do not understand the teaching of the inanimate, how can they deal with people in beneficial ways?

I urge you to examine closely enough to effect an awakening. If you do not yet have an awakened perspective, then approach it in a relaxed manner; do not rush.

DISCOVERY

My teacher used to tell a metaphysical story. Suppose two people from a foreign country come to a great nation to investigate things.

When they first enter the territory, the two have a discussion and decide to part ways; one will go east, the other west. From state to state they go, county to county, traveling over hill and dale, until they arrive at the eastern capital. The two suddenly run into each other at the gate of the capital city. As they look at each other, without saying a word, the things they had discussed in their own country are clear. Now they go in, side by side, unknown to anyone.

Strange! Tell me, how is it when they run into each other? It is like Zen practitioners working: today they realize a little bit, tomorrow they find out a little bit, and they keep on investigating until one day it becomes evident to them. This is like that encounter at the gate of the capital city. This is called awakening, or breakthrough, or discovery. You must attain this at least once; only then can it be said that the task of the journey is done.

It is also like meeting your father in a big city many years after having left your home town. You do not need to ask anyone whether or not it is your father.

Just keep focused in this way. Do not take it for idleness; time does not wait for anyone. An early teacher said, "Don't waste time!" Each of you should work on your own.

SHOW THE TRUTH

An ancient said, "There is no drum sound in a bell, and no bell sound in a drum." How can students today manage to reach this state? Sometimes when I give personal interviews, you make a statement, and then when I press you further you merely insist you have already replied, and there could be nothing else. Quite clearly, if you work in this way you have not got a grip on the matter at all.

Idiots! Haven't you read the saying of ancient sages, "Show the truth in every word, refer to the source in every statement." You do not yet understand; you just adopt positions at random. Don't be like this any more when you come for interviews. While it can be said you do not understand, you can be straightened out.

REAL ZEN

Those who claim to be Zennists must trust in what people who know say before they will attain it. If you do not believe, you make all talk useless. If you just listen without believing to the talks of people who know, how can you be called Zennists?

Real Zennists understand it all when the grass bends in the breeze, when dust rises in the wind; they discern immediately before any signals have occurred, before falling into trains of thought, before anything stirs. Only then can one be called a Zennist.

Why? This thing is used against birth and death, so you have to be someone who's not far off in order to get it.

Haven't you read how Yunyan studied with Baizhang for twenty years without clarifying this matter? His elder brother Daowu bit his finger to the quick out of concern for him. See how that man of old still did not worry even though he hadn't clarified this matter, saying he did not understand. His will never gave out, and he didn't go chasing after verbal expressions either.

And how about master Xuefeng, who went to Touzi's three times and Dongshan nine times! When he was at Touzi's school, one day he rolled up the screen and entered the hermitage. When Touzi saw him coming, he got off his bench and stood.

Xuefeng hesitated, searching for something to say; Touzi pushed him out. Xuefeng could only cry. Later, when he went to Dongshan, he was still unable to understand. Then, when he went to Deshan, he asked, "Has the student a part in the enlightenment of the sages of time immemorial?" Deshan hit him and exclaimed, "What are you saying!" At that, Xuefeng's mind opened up, like a bucket with the bottom fallen out. When he got to Tortoise Mountain, however, he said he still had some doubt. See how that man of old would not rest until his mass of doubt had been broken up. So it is said, "The task done, the mind rests; this actuality, after all, is everywhere you find it."

Nowadays most Zen students create interpretations based on words, arbitrarily assuming mastery, or else they take stories of the ancients' awakenings and look at them, calling this "gazing at sayings." What relevance is there? When Xuefeng went to Touzi three times and Dongshan nine times, do you suppose he did it for the sake of words?

You should simply step back and study through total experience. How do you step back? I am not telling you to sit on a bench with your eyes closed, rigidly suppressing body and mind, like earth or wood. That will never have any usefulness, even in a million years.

When you want to step back, if there are any sayings or stories you don't understand, place them in front of you, step back and see for yourself why you don't understand.

Professional monks say, "Thinking will not do; not thinking will not do either." Then how do they teach people to contemplate? I tell you, just step back and look.

Phew! Sure gives people trouble! Sure is hard to understand! But look here—what is it that troubles people? Who is it that troubles anyone? Step back and look in this way; gradually you will wake up, with each passing day illumination will expand and enlarge.

And yet, you should not fanatically recognize this alone and immediately claim perfect attainment, for then you are dependent and fixated. Then it will be ineffective. You must apply some wisdom in your observation.

The ancients allowed you to focus on a route: if you stop and step back in this way, I guarantee there is a reason. This is what is considered incomprehensible and not susceptible to knowledge.

There is also a type who talks wildly and speaks at random, questioning this and that. Again, just step back and look; what is it that talks wildly and speaks randomly? Just turn your attention around and reflect. Go on working like this, and eventually you will be sure to awaken. If you don't believe it, there's nothing I can do about that.

When I first called on a certain teacher, he taught me to contemplate this saying: "What is the great meaning of Buddhism? Next to the city of the King of Chu, the river flows eastward." He also taught me to contemplate the saying, "It's not the movement of the wind, nor the movement of the flag, but the movement of your mind."

Then when I left and went to call on teachers all over the land, I asked them questions. The ancients were wholly true to reality, and the old teachers explained in countless ways, but I simply could not understand.

Finally I left to travel to eastern China, but halfway there I turned around and came back. Now I was told to contemplate the story, "If you kill your parents, you repent before Buddha; if you kill Buddha, where do you repent?" Yunmen said, 'Exposed.' " This case study is like a hot iron ball in the mind, and I suffered all kinds of trouble for seven years. Those of you who have studied Zen for a long time will know what I mean.

Let me tell you another story. When Huaitang started to study Zen, he first saw Yunfeng Yue. For three years, he could not understand what Yunfeng was talking about. He also studied with Zen master Nan, and after two years still did not understand. Then he went to spend a summer retreat in a cloister. In *Transmission of the Lamp*, he read the story where someone asked Duofu, "What is the bamboo grove of Duofu?" He replied, "One cane, two canes slanted." At this, Huaitang finally opened up and awakened.

Nowadays people just call these dialogues. This is because of lack of precision in applying effort, failing to understand the expedient devices of the ancients. I urge each of you, since you are already in a society, to study the path independently, not spending any time uselessly, taking enlightenment as your rule.

Wonder

Association with good companions is a serious recommendation of the ancient sages. Students today should follow the words of the Buddhas and Patriarchs by finding a teacher to attain discernment. Otherwise, how can you call yourselves students?

If you want to clarify this matter, you must arouse wonder and look into it. If you wonder deeply about this matter, transcendental knowledge will become manifest. Why? The task of the journey just requires the sense of doubt to cease. If you do not actively wonder, how can the sense of doubt cease?

My teacher was thirty-five years old before he became a monk. He stayed in the city of Chengdu to listen to lectures on *The Hundred Phenomena as Only Representation*. There he heard a saying of how when a Buddhist enters the path of insight, knowledge and principle merge, environment and mind join, and there is no distinction between that which realizes and that which is realized. A Hindu challenged the Buddhists, "If there is no distinction between what realizes and what is realized, what is used as proof?" No one could answer this challenge, so the Buddhists were declared the losers in debate. Later the Buddhist canonical master of Tang came to the rescue of the doctrine: "When knowledge and principle merge, environment and mind unite, it is like when drinking water one spontaneously knows whether it is cool or warm."

Now my teacher thought, "It may be cool or warm, all right; but what is this business of spontaneous knowing?" He wondered and questioned very deeply. He asked the lecturer about the principle of spontaneous knowing, but the lecturer couldn't answer; instead, he said, "If you want to clarify this principle, I cannot explain it, but in the South there are adepts who have found out the source of the enlightened mind; they know about this matter. You will have to journey for it."

So my teacher went traveling. He went to the capital city, and all around the eastern riverlands, asking every Zen adept he could find about this matter. And everyone he asked gave him a reply. Some explained, some spoke in aphorisms. In any case, his feeling of doubt remained unbroken.

Later he came to Fushan. Seeing that everything Fushan said in lectures and interviews was relevant to what was in his mind, he wound up staying for a year. Fushan had him contemplate the phrase, "Buddha had a secret saying, Kasyapa didn't conceal it?"

One day Fushan said to him, "Why didn't you come earlier? You should go call on Baiyun Duan." So my teacher went to Baiyun. One day when he went into the teaching auditorium, all of a sudden he realized great enlightenment. "Buddha has a secret saying, Kasyapa didn't conceal it'—of course! Of course! When knowledge and principle merge, environment and mind unite, it is like when one drinks water one spontaneously knows whether it's warm or cool. How true these words are!" Then he composed a verse on his attainment:

> At an idle patch of field before the mountain
> Politely I question an aged grandfather.
> How many times have I sold and bought myself?
> Charmingly, the pine and bamboo draw a clear breeze.

When Baiyun read this, he nodded. Is this not a case of doubting and wondering profoundly, approaching people who know, and only then succeeding in clarification?

What about the travels of my late teacher calling on teachers—why did he later say he questioned an aged grandfather? What about selling and buying oneself—what is that? You should realize there is no excess; what the man of old said is all you.

He also said, "I have never had a single statement to reach you. If I had a statement to reach you, what use would it be?" Do you want your feeling of doubt broken? You too must be like my late teacher once before you can accomplish it.

JUST THIS

Consider the case of Grand Maestro Ma: seeing a monk going downstairs, the Maestro called to him, "O Worthy!" When the monk turned his head, the Maestro said, "From birth to death, it's just this person; why turn your head and revolve your brains?" That monk understood the essential message at these words.

What is the logic of this? "From birth to death, it's just this person." Tell me, what person is it? As soon as you arouse the intention to see "this person," then you do not see this person.

"This person" is hard to see. Very, very hard. People today simply say, "This is 'this person'—who else is there? There couldn't be any other." Ninety-nine out of a hundred understand in this way; what grasp have they? If you interpret in this way, how can you understand the matter of "from birth to death," and how can you immediately see it as "just this person"?

If you do not see "this person," you have no idea how your mortal being will end up.

What about this lecturing and listening right now—is there actually lecturing and listening, or is there no lecturing and listening? If you say you are standing there while I am sitting here, I am lecturing and you are listening, any villager can say such things—how can you call yourselves Zennists? If you say there is no lecturing and no listening, still he made the statement "from birth to death, it's just this person."

Therefore, when you get to this point, you need to find a realized individual to discern precisely.

Before I had understood, I was totally helpless, so I asked of my teacher. As soon as I'd ask a question, my teacher would just say, "I don't understand. I don't know. I'm not as good as you." I also asked if Zen is ultimately easy to learn or hard to learn. He just told me, "You're alright; why are you asking about difficulty and ease? Learning Zen is called a gold and dung phenomenon. Before you understand it, it's like gold; when understood, it's like dung." I didn't accept this at the time, but now that I've thought it over, although the words are coarse the message in them is not shallow.

These are examples of how perfectly realized people never utter a single word or half a phrase without purpose. Whenever they try to help others, they never give random instructions, and they do not approve people arbitrarily. Nowadays there are teachers all over who sometimes speak correctly and sometimes speak without a grasp. Why? Because they have not yet attained perfect realization. Sometimes they approve people and say they are right, but then sometimes they say they are not right; how is it possible to clarify "from birth to death, it's just this person" in such a manner?

When you look closely, you see that people of the present are none other than people of yore, and the functions of the present are none other than the functions of the past; even going through a thousand changes and myriad transformations, here it is just necessary for you to recognize it first hand before you can attain it.

The reason people today cannot attain it is just because they do not know how to distinguish it with certitude. How is it that they cannot distinguish it with certainty? They just make up interpretations of ancient sayings, boring into them subjectively. If you just do this, you will never understand. Why? I tell you, if you "turn your head and revolve your brains," you're already wrong. The most economical way here is to save energy, not asking about this and that but clearly apprehending it in the most direct manner.

You people first came forth with rationalizations, using ancient sayings to wrap and bind yourself. It's like scattering a handful of dirt on a clean surface.

I have told you that you should not come here now as you were before. You must attain an understanding before this is possible. Some say, "I was just so before, and I am just so now." Right away you run into emotional consciousness.

How can I blame you? The ancients were so compassionate as to tell you, "Walking is Buddha walking, sitting is Buddha sitting, all things are Buddha teaching, all sounds are Buddha's voice." You have misunderstood, supposing that all sounds are actually the voice of Buddha and all forms are really forms of Buddha. Since it is not admissible to understand in this way, then what would be right?

I tell you, the instant you touch upon signals, you're already alienated; when you want to manifest it by means of the light of knowledge, you've already obscured it. Now, don't hold onto my talk; each of you do your own work independently. You may contemplate the stories of ancients, you may sit quietly, or you may watch attentively everywhere; all of these are ways of doing the work. Everywhere is the place for you to attain realization, but concentrate on one point for days and months on end, and you will surely break through.

When Guling returned from his journey, his mentor asked him, "You left me to go traveling; what did you attain?" Guling said, "I saw Baizhang and attained peace and bliss." Then he quoted a verse by Baizhang:

> The spiritual light, shining independently,
> transcends the senses and objects;
> the essence is revealed, real and internal,
> not confined to written words.
> The nature of mind has no stain;
> it is basically complete of itself.
> Just detach from false mental objects
> and be enlightened to being-as-is.

On hearing these words, the old mentor realized enlightenment.

Also, master Xuefeng, on seeing a breeze stirring taro leaves, pointed them out to a student. The student said, "I am quite frightened." Xuefeng clucked his tongue and said, "It's an event in your own house; why are you afraid?" That student then had an awakening too.

Since the whole time is an event in your own house, why don't you understand? Because you wander off everywhere, you are not at home all the time. But now that you're facing a teacher, don't let yourself forget. This is called acting according to reason, knowing the ultimate within oneself.

From birth to old age, it's just this person; why turn your head and revolve your brains? Each of you look into this on your own.

KEEP EVOLVING

If you have just now understood, where is that which you couldn't understand before? If you can't understand now, when will you understand?

Just examine over and over in this way, and you should come to understand. That is why it is said, "What you misunderstood before is what you now understand; what you now understand is what you misunderstood before."

It is also said, "When light comes, darkness vanishes; when knowledge comes into play, confusion is forgotten." But can it actually be so? How can it be so? That would mean there is darkness to be destroyed and there is confusion to be removed. Have you not read the ancient saying, "Don't change the former person, just change the former behavior."

You Zen followers say, "What is the difficulty? Misunderstanding is just 'this person,' and understanding is just 'this person.' There can be no other." But then when asked what "this person" is, you are helpless; or else you talk at random. This is because of not having attained truly accurate realization. This is a disease that has entered your bones and marrow.

People in error attach recognition to a lifetime of cessation. Indeed, they "stop" not only for one lifetime, but for a thousand lifetimes, myriad lifetimes. As for the spiritually sharp, they should know how to experientially investigate who "this person" is, directly seeking an insight.

Whew! Buddhism today is lackluster; even in large groups it's hard to find suitable people. As long as you people are here studying the path in this school, you should not waste the twenty-four hours of the day; focus on attaining insight.

You people are still not far off; have you not read how master Linji said, "There is a true person of no rank in the naked mass of flesh, always going out and coming in the doors of your senses; those who haven't witnessed it, look!" At that time, a student came forward and asked, "What is the true person of no rank?" Linji got out of his chair, grabbed the student, and said, "Speak! Speak!" The student hesitated, trying to think of something, so Linji pushed him away.

Linji also said, "Your eyes radiate a light that shines through the mountains and rivers." The ancients were so compassionate, yet people today don't take it to heart, so they need to look for someone to find certainty.

Have you not read how Yantou, Xuefeng, and Jinshan went to see Linji, then met Elder Ding on the way? Yantou asked, "Where are you coming from?" Ding said, "From Linji." Yantou inquired, "Is the teacher well?" Ding said, "The teacher has passed away." Yantou said, "We came especially to pay respects to the teacher Linji, but now we hear he has passed away, and we do not know what he said. Please quote an example or two of his sayings." Ding then cited the foregoing story about Linji's saying, "There is a true person of no rank in the mass of naked flesh, always going out and coming in through the doors of your senses; those who have not yet witnessed it, look!" When a student came forward and asked what the true person of no rank is, Linji got out of his chair, grabbed the student, and said, "Speak! Speak!" When the student hesitated, trying to think up something to say, Linji pushed him away and said, "What a dry turd the true person of no rank is!" Then Linji went back to his quarters.

Hearing this recital, Yantou was stunned. Jinshan remarked, "Why didn't he say, 'In the mass of naked flesh is not a true person of no rank'?" Ding grabbed him and said, "Tell me, how far apart are a true person of no rank and not a true person of no rank? Speak quickly!" Jinshan's face paled, then clouded. Yantou and Xuefeng both said, "Please forgive this novice for insulting you, Elder." Ding remarked, "If it hadn't been for you two old guys, I'd have punched this little bed-wetter out!"

Look: when Jinshan said, "Not a true person of no rank," why did Ding not agree? How can students today reach such a state? They just recognize the mortal body and forcibly act as if they were in charge, unable to let go of it. Now I will cite some stories for you to consider.

Xuefeng called on Touzi and asked, "Is there anyone to call on here?" Touzi threw down his hoe. Xeufeng said, "Then I'll dig right where I am." Touzi said, "Dullard!" Even though he said he would dig right where he was, he was still called a dullard.

When Great Elder Nanji met Xuefeng, their conversation was in complete accord. Xuefeng sent him to see Xuansha. Xuansha asked, "An ancient said, 'Only I can know this.' How do you understand?" Nanji said, "You should realize there is someone who does not seek to know." Xuansha said, "You are a Great Elder—why go to so much trouble?" What is the logic of this?

When my late teacher was in the school of Master Baiduan, the master cited an ancient saying, "It is like a mirror casting images; when an image is formed, where has the shine of the mirror gone?" At the time, there were a number of students in the group who offered replies, but the master did not accept any of them. In those days, my teacher was working as a fundraiser; when he came back, Baiduan cited the foregoing saying and asked him about it. My teacher approached, offered greetings, and said, "Still not far off." Baiduan clapped and laughed. Everyone thought Baiduan was pressing to make him chief fundraiser; what kind of talk is that?

Here I only require you to study the path. Your first priority, twenty-fours hours a day, should be to get rid of unenlightened egotism toward others. Why? Egotism toward others is the business of mediocrities.

My late teacher never had any egotism toward others. As his assistant I saw quite a lot, but I never saw him have a single thought of annoyance. Once when he was at Haihui, there was a certain senior monk serving as superintendent of hospitality. When my late teacher sent a great elder to lead the community at Sihai, he had the superintendent of hospitality escort him. The senior spat in my teacher's face and said, "Who are you to tell me to escort him?" He kept on with this vile talk, so my teacher finally gave up. No one knew about this. Later, when my teacher came to Taiping, he nominated that individual to be keeper of the treasury, and also made him assembly leader. My teacher himself asked to be made superintendent of the institution, and even nominated the other for the abbacy there at Taiping. The governor did not approve of this appointment, and the superintendent reviled my teacher, saying he did not support him strongly enough. Now my teacher finally spoke out; "This fellow," he said, "has hollered at me twice!" By this we can see he had no egotism toward others.

People now want to understand theoretically at once, as soon as anything is said. How can you learn the way in this fashion? Sometimes I see beginners come to interviews helpless to do anything about the fact that I have already seen through them. They are like villagers armed with carrying poles trying to do battle with a general. Here I am fully equipped; in my hand is the hundred-pound sword of a legendary warrior, while they have nothing but a carrying pole. They strike a blow, and, seeing the man not move, they strike several more times and leave. It's not that I fear them; it's because they are no match for me. Ha, ha!

I urge you not to be crude minded. In your conduct, day and night, keep evolving higher; then even if you do not attain enlightenment, you will still be a highly refined individual. Be sure to be attentive.

APPROVAL

As soon as you accept and approve anything, recognizing it as your own, you are immediately bound hand and foot and cannot move. So even if there are a thousand possibilities, nothing is right once you have recognized, accepted, and approved it as your own.

It is like making a boat and outfitting it for a long journey to a land of treasures, then as soon as you get started you drive a stake in the ground and tie the boat down, then row with all your might. You may row till the end of time, but you will still be at the shore. You see the boat moving from side to side, and think you are on the move; but actually you haven't gotten anywhere.

It is also like someone turning a millstone, going round and round in circles from morning till night. What a laugh! If someone whose eyes are unclear saw you fixated on recognition and told you it was right, he'd been seen through by someone with clear eyes; on examination, there would be quite a few loose ends.

These days quite a few just employ this path of "right now," totally unable to get out of the immediate present. Nailed down in this way, they try to study Zen without getting the essential point. Once they have taken it up, they have already misunderstood; acting as if they were in charge, they do not realize Buddhism is not understood in this way.

Have you not read how Magu met Zhangjing, staff in hand? Magu shook the staff once and stood there serenely. Zhangjing said, "Yes!" He also met Nanquan the same way, and Nanquan said, "No!" Magu said, "Zhangjing said yes; how can you say no?" Nanquan said, "Zhangjin is right, but you are wrong. This is vulnerable to outside influences, and ultimately disintegrates." Only then did Magu see his error.

Look, people: if you are about to misunderstand your whole life, how can you not go to someone to find certainty?

When I first went on my journey, I read verses by my teacher and immediately believed this man spoke like the ancient sages and must have genuine realization. So I studied with him for ten years. One of those verses said,

> To learn the way, first you must find out
> the ultimate point;
> hearing sound and seeing form
> are inconceivable.
> If you discuss high and low
> based on words,
> it's just like before you were enlightened.

Another verse said,

> There is a road to emptiness;
> everyone arrives.
> Those who arrive then realize
> the excellence of the aim.
> The mind ground does not grow
> useless plants and trees;
> naturally the body spontaneously
> radiates clear light.

When I was young, even though I had not attained the way, in my heart I knew these were extraordinary lines. But how about hearing sound and seeing form? They are both conceivable; how can they be inconceivable? Then when he talks about realization, he turns around and says, "It's just like before you were enlightened." Everything before enlightenment is conceivable; how can you see a realization? This man attained nonattainment; only when you reach the ultimate stage can you be like this. Only after ten years did I actually understand him.

Generally speaking, when you go journeying to learn the path to enlightenment, you seek. Do not sit ignorantly, but go to someone to find out the truth with certainty. When this truth is hard to realize, that is called unfinished business. Have you not heard it said that once you realize, then there's a difference? Yesterday one had breakfast and dinner, today one has breakfast and dinner—is it the same person as before? There's a difference; it's not the same. Zhaozhou said to someone, "Have you had breakfast yet?" He said, "Yes." Zhaozhou said, "Go wash the dishes." This is different.

Do you suppose I am an ordinary man? You tell me where the difference is.

SELF-KNOWLEDGE

I tell people to get to know the self, but seekers who hear this equate it with what beginners see, and think there is nothing hard to understand about it. You should take it more slowly for a while, and be more careful. What do you call the self?

How about the sayings of ancient worthies on the self? "Roaming the mountains, enjoying the rivers"—you say, "I understand—who else is it?" Another saying goes, "It is your self"—you say, "I understand this too; it is myself." But how about the reply, "Mountains, rivers, the whole earth"? It is also said, "When you eat, the meal is your self"—how do you understand that? You still can't get to it. An ancient worthy said, "The whole earth is your self"—so how can you clear your mind?

Whenever I see that people have misunderstood, I quote ancient stories to question them. For example, Jingqing asked Xuansha, "I have just entered the school; please point out a way in." Xuansha said, "Do you hear the sound of the valley stream?" Jingqing replied, "Yes." Xuansha said, "Enter from here." Jingqing got the message from this. I ask you, when he heard, what did he hear? Everyone says he heard the sound of the water, but what use is such an interpretation? According to their view, the hearing clearly takes in everything at once, so there is no sound to be found apart from this hearing; everything being a manifestation from one's subjectivity, it is representation of active consciousness. Some answer that it was not the sound of water he heard, but his self. To this I say, how can the self hear the self? This is what is called recognizing mind, recognizing nature.

Buddhism is an easily understood, energy-saving teaching; people strain themselves. Seeing them helpless, the ancients told people to try meditating quietly for a moment. These are good words, but later people did not understand the meaning of the ancients; they went off and sat like lumps with knitted brows and closed eyes, suppressing body and mind, waiting for enlightenment. How stupid! How foolish!

STEP BACK AND SEE

An early teacher said, "Is it the wind ringing, or is it the chimes ringing?" He should have stopped right there, but he went on to vex others by saying, "It is not the wind or the chimes ringing, but only your mind ringing." What further opportunity to study to you seek?

When Zen came to China, an early teacher said, "It is not the wind or the flag moving; it is your minds moving." The ancient teacher gave this testimony; why don't you understand? Just because of subject and object. That is why it is said, "The objective is defined based on the subjective; since the objective is arbitrarily defined, it produces your arbitrary subjectivity, producing difference where there was neither sameness nor difference."

People nowadays talk about certain discernment, but how do you discern with certainty? It is not a matter of declaring, "This is an initiatory saying, this is a saying for beginners, that is a saying for old-timers." It's not like this at all. As a matter of fact, letting go all at once is precisely how to discern with certainty—there will be no different focus at any time.

You get up in the morning, dress, wash your face, and so on; you call these miscellaneous thoughts, but all that is necessary is that there be no perceiver or perceived when you perceive—no hearer or heard when you hear, no thinker or thought when you think. Buddhism is very easy and very economical; it spares effort, but you yourself waste energy and make your own hardships.

If you do not see the ease, then sit for a while and examine the principle. Since you have come here to study Zen, don't come here with imagination and figuring like you find in other places; just step back and look, and you will surely understand.

However, there are those who accept attunement and those who do not; there are the foolish and the wise, there are those who can be saved and those who cannot be saved.

Those who do not accept attunement insist on using fluctuating habit-ridden consciousness and energy from food. When questioned, they make their eyes bulge, walk back and forth, hold up their regalia, accepting and approving perceptions and emotions in the dimness of their skulls and bodies. This is irremediable. Just let go, then step back and look; only then will you understand.

There are senior students of a certain type who say, "I do not reason, I make no calculations; I am not attached to sound and form, I do not rely on either the impure or the pure. The sage and the ordinary mortal, delusion and enlightenment, are all completely empty; there are no such things in the Great Light."

They are shrouded by the light of knowledge, attached to an extreme of knowledge. This is also irremediable.

Of these two illnesses, the former is slighter than the latter. If those who have illness are willing to set it aside, step back and look, they too will naturally understand.

This task spares energy to the utmost. The way of the ancients is very economical and most quintessential.

Why do you waste energy? Sometimes I observe seekers come here expending a lot of energy and going to great pains. What do they want? They seek a few sayings to put in a skin bag; what relevance is there?

Nevertheless, there is a genuine expedient that is very good, though only experienced seekers will be able to focus doubt on it. It is like when Xuansha was going to give a talk on the teaching one day, but didn't speak a single word, no matter how long the assembly stood there. Finally they began to leave in twos and threes. Xuansha remarked, "Look! Today I have really helped them, but not a single one gets it. If I start flapping my lips, though, they immediately crowd around!" You come here seeking expedient techniques, seeking doctrines, seeking peace and happiness. I have no expedient techniques to give people, no doctrine, no method of peace and happiness. Why? If there is any "expedient technique," it has the contrary effect of burying you and trapping you.

Zhaozhou said, "Just sit looking into the principle; if you do not understand in twenty or thirty years, cut off my head." This too was to get you to become singleminded.

Have you not read how the Second Patriarch of Zen used to expound the teaching wherever he was, and everyone who heard him attained true mindfulness? He did not set up written formulations and did not discuss practice and realization or cause and effect.

At that time, a certain meditation teacher heard about the Zen patriarch and sent a senior disciple to spy on his lectures. When the disciple didn't come back, the meditation teacher was enraged. When they met at a major convocation, the teacher personally said to his former disciple, "I expended so much effort to plant you; how could you turn your back on me this way?" The former disciple replied, "My vision was originally right, but was distorted by teachers." This is what Zen study is like.

Later, someone asked Xuefeng, "How is it when one's vision is originally correct but distorted by teachers?" Xuefeng said, "Confused encounter with the founder of Zen." The seeker asked, "Where is one's own vision?" Xuefeng said, "It is not gotten from a teacher." This is the way you have to be before you attain realization.

Of old it was said, "Enlightenment is always with people, but people subjectively pursue things." In scripture it says, "If you can turn things around, they are the same as realization of suchness."

But how can things be turned around? It is also said, "All appearances are unreal; if you see appearances are not inherent characteristics, the you see realization of suchness."

Just step back, stop mental machinations, and look closely. When suddenly you see, nothing can stop you.

ALL THE WAY THROUGH

"No delusion, no enlightenment"—only when you have arrived at such a state are you comfortable and saving energy to the maximum degree. But this is simply being someone without delusion or enlightenment; what is there deluding you twenty-four hours a day? You must apply this to yourself and determine on your own.

All realms of existence are there because of the deluded mind; right now, how could they not be there? Once you realize they are not there, they cannot delude your feelings and certainly cannot do anything to you. It is necessary to attain the reality where there is no delusion and no enlightenment before you can become free and unfettered.

People on the journey call this the reality under the vest; if this reality is not fully realized, it is a disaster.

The patriarch Ashvaghosha explained three subtle and six coarse aspects of mentation; stir, and there is suffering. How to not stir? Uttering a few sayings does not amount to talking of mysteries and marvels, or explaining meanings and principles; sitting meditation and concentration do not amount to inner freedom.

Think about it independently. Other people do not know what you are doing all the time; you reflect on your own—are you in harmony with truth or not? Here you cannot be mistaken; investigate all the way through.

When my late teacher appeared in the world to teach, he said, "I rise from this jewel flower throne and sit upon it every day along with all of you; it is just that you avoid what is right before you." This is a good saying. He also remarked, "In over ten years at one place, I couldn't find a worthy opponent; only when I went elsewhere did I actually see such a person as would live up to my sense of indignation." Good words; few people can talk like this.

I spent over thirty years journeying; you people were not even born when I found the way. If younger folk believe what I am talking about, you will step back each day, look into yourselves, and see all the way through.

COMPREHENDING EVERYTHING

The Zen school is called the school of Kasyapa's great absorption in quiescence. Without stirring a thread, all is understood; without stirring a hair, all is realized.

It is not just a matter of not stirring and letting it go at that. Do not rouse the mind or stir thoughts throughout the twenty-four hours of the day, and you should be able to comprehend everything. This is called being a member of Kasyapa's school. Only then can you enter great absorption in quiescence.

Now what is there that acts as a mental object and an obstruction? Although people can investigate, people can study, they cannot understand by arousing the mind and stirring thoughts. When you encounter a situation or hear a saying, if your thoughts stir, your mind gets excited, and you make up an interpretation, in any case you are in a scattered state.

When Elder Ming has accomplished "not thinking good or bad," only then did he manage to see; thereupon he said, "Although I was in the school of the Fifth Patriarch of Zen, I really did not know what the Buddha meant by saying, 'Not this shore, not the further shore, not the current in between.' " Nanquan said, "It is not Buddha, it is not a thing." This is precisely what you are focusing on now. Simply study in this way.

Just as a scholar has the attitude of an official once he's passed the civil service examination, you must come to the realization that you are Buddha; only then will you be free from doubt. Each of you must take responsibility for this yourself; don't pass the time pursuing the hubbub.

SEEK WITHOUT SEEKING

There is something in each of you that you will only be able to perceive when you turn around. So how does one turn around? By non-seeking seeking, seeking without seeking. This is precisely what people find hard to deal with or get into. How can you seek if you are not seeking? How can you not seek if you are seeking? If you only seek, how is that different from pursuing sounds and chasing forms? If you do not seek at all, how are you different from inert matter?

You must seek, and yet without seeking; not seek, yet still seek. If you can manage to penetrate this, you will then manage to harmonize seeking and nonseeking. So it is said, "Nonseeking nonseeking—the body of reality is perfectly quiescent. Seeking seeking—responsive function does not miss. Seeking without seeking, nonseeking seeking—objects and cognition merge, substance and function are one." Therefore you find the three bodies, four knowledges, five yes, and six spiritual powers all come to light from this. Students must be able to turn around and search all the way through in this way before they can attain realization.

A seeker asked Yangshan, "What special pathway do you have? Please point it out to me."

Yangshan said, "If I said there is anything in particular or nothing in particular, I would confuse you even more. Where are you from?"

The seeker said he was from such and such a place. Yangshan asked, "Do you still think of that place?"

The seeker replied, "I think of it all the time."

Yangshan said, "What you think of are the buildings, towers, and habitations, of which there are a variety. Now think back to what thinks—is there a variety of things there?"

The seeker replied, "There is no variety of things there."

Yangshan said, "Based on your perception, you have only attained one mystery. You have a seat and are wearing clothes, hereafter see for yourself."

This seeker said that the object of thought is varied, while the thinker is not varied. This view is biased; this is what prompted Yangshan to say he had only attained one mystery—his perception of the path was not accurate.

If you ask me, the object of thought, with a variety of buildings and houses, is in fact not various, while the unvaried thinking subject is in fact various. This can be demonstrated. Right now there is a variety before your eyes; there are not so many of these. There are, similarly, many types of the unvaried.

When the seer Bhishmottaranirghosha took the seeker Sudhana by the hand, Sudhana saw Buddhas as numerous as atoms in infinite worlds. When the seer let go of Sudhana's hand, everything was as it had been before. Now how do you understand this reversion to normal on release of the hand? You'd better understand!

ORIGINAL REALITY

An ancient sage said, "Every phenomenon is the original reality." Fine. Yunmen held up his cane and said, "This is not the original reality." After a pause, he said, "If so, then the three poisons, four perversions, five clusters, six senses, twelve media, eighteen elements, and twenty-five realms of being are not the original reality." Why not understand in this way—you'd save quite a bit of effort.

Buddhism is a most economical affair, conserving the most energy—it has always been present, but you do not understand.

I tell you, moreover, that there is nothing that is true and nothing that is not true. How can there be truth and untruth in one thing? Just because of seeking unceasingly, everywhere is seeking; pondering principles is seeking, contemplating the model cases of the ancients is also seeking, reading Zen books is also seeking; even if you sit quietly, continuously from moment to moment, this too is seeking.

Do you want to understand? Then that seeking of yours is actually not seeking. This is extremely difficult to believe and to penetrate, hard to work on. Those of you who are not comfortable are that way, generally speaking, because you are either oblivious or excited. That is why you say you do not understand.

Right now, how can you avoid being oblivious or excited? When that very thought of yours arises, it is the flowing whirl of birth and death: do you consider it habit-activated consciousness, or do you consider it immutable? Contemplate in this way over and over again, and you will have a bit of guiding principle.

SAME REALITY, DIFFERENT DREAMS

People may sleep on the same bed, under the same covers, yet their individual dreams are not the same. An ancient sage said, "We share the same one reality, yet do not realize it." For example, within the single reality of life and death, there are those who can enter into life and death without being bound by life and death, and there are those who are bound by life and death in the midst of life and death. In the midst of the same common reality, one person is bound while another is freed; is this not the individual differences in the dreams?

You usually make birth and death into one extreme, and absence of birth and death into another extreme; you make thinking into one extreme and nonthinking into another extreme; you make speech into one extreme and nonspeech into another extreme. Here I have neither the business of Zen monks, nor anything transcendental; I just talk about getting out of birth and death. This is not a matter of simply saying this and letting the matter rest at that; you must see that which has no birth or death right in the midst of birth and death.

The great master Yongjia visited the Sixth Patriarch of Zen and said, "The matter of birth and death is serious; transitoriness is swift." The Sixth Patriarch said, "Why not comprehend the birthless and realize what has no speed?" Yongjia said, "Comprehension itself is birthless; realization of the fundamental has no speed."

When Caoshan took leave of Dongshan, Dongshan asked, "Where are you going?" Caoshan replied, "To an unchanging place." Dongshan retorted, "If it is an unchanging place, how could there be any going?" Caoshan replied, "The going is also unchanging."

Were these not realized people? You make thought one extreme and nonthinking another extreme; you make the unspoken outside of the spoken—even if you understand the unspoken clearly, as soon as words are spoken they block you.

Why not study Zen in this way—walk, stand, sit, and recline all day long without ever walking, standing, sitting, or reclining.

Sometimes seekers come here, utter a phrase, and clap their hands; how does this amount to an understanding beyond dualistic extremes?

You should think in this way: "Clearly I am in the midst of birth and death; how can I get free of birth and death?" Don't say this itself is It, that you basically have no birth or death. It is not realized by your uttering this statement.

There are those who hear someone say there is no birth and death, and immediately say, "Right! There is originally no birth or death!" If you make your interpretation in this way, it will be impossible to understand.

Since it does not admit of rationalization and contrived understanding, and does not admit of being explained away, how can you work on it? An ancient said, "I only use what you bring me to point out an entryway to you." Take care.

WATCH YOURSELF

As I see members of present-day Zen communities, it is as if none of them are talking about this reality. Now wherever you go there are Zen communities and teachers preaching Zen and Tao, holding interviews and lectures, all talking about this matter—why do I say they haven't been talking about it at all? They are talking, to be sure, but they cannot actually speak of it. Not only can they not speak of it, they are unable to see it. Not knowing how to work on it as it is, they simply say, "When the true imperative is brought up in its entirety, the ten directions are cut off: any Buddha that shows up will get a beating, and any demon that shows up will get a beating." They fanatically talk Zen, but never touch upon what is most urgent.

What I talk of here is something that others neglect. I casually pick it up from a trash heap and ask people about it, but they cannot say anything. Right now, when people who have already entered the room, inquired into the way, and attained understanding see the incense stand, is it an incense stand or not? If they sat it is an incense stand, this is the same as ordinary people. If it is not an incense stand, to whom was the incense stand given away? Lightly question them, and they go to pieces. This is because they have always been working in idleness.

Now let me ask you a question. Never mind about since you've been here; before you went journeying, before you entered this community, when you saw an incense stand, what did you call it? You called it an incense stand. Everyone calls it an incense stand; why do you not think why you call it an incense stand? Zen should be studied in this way; you must understand what has been in you since beginningless time. Master Siushan said, "If you don't see the original reality, obstacles will follow you all along; if people have obstacles, they go wrong countless thousands of times."

My teacher said, "Suppose a bit of filth is stuck on the tip of the nose of a sleeping man, totally unknown to him. When he wakes up, he notices a foul smell; sniffing his shirt, he thinks his shirt stinks, and so he takes it off. But then whatever he picks up stinks; he doesn't realize the odor is on his nose. If someone who knows tells him it has nothing to do with the things themselves, he stubbornly refuses to believe it. The knowing one tells him to simply wipe his nose with his hand, but he won't. Were he willing to wipe his nose, only then could he know he was already getting somewhere; finally he would wash it off with water, and there would be no foul odor at all. Whatever he smelled, that foul odor wouldn't be there from the start. Studying Zen is also like this; those who will not stop and watch themselves on their own instead pursue intellectual interpretation, but that pursuit of intellectual interpretation, seeking rationales and making comparative judgments, is all completely off. If you would turn your attention around and watch yourself, you would understand everything. As it is said, 'When one faculty returns to the source, the six functions are all in abeyance." Just see in this way, and you will have some enlightened understanding.

UNDERSTAND IMMEDIATELY

Ha, ha, ha! You still don't understand on your own. I tell you this—if you still don't understand on your own, then how will you understand if you go somewhere else?

At other places, they either put you through changes, or abruptly fixate you. Here, I neither put you through changes nor abruptly fixate you. This saves energy and is easy to comprehend; so why don't you understand? Because of your millions of rationalizations; these make it hard for you to understand.

Buddhahood is an easily comprehended state, comfortable, and pleasant. But even though it is easily understood, nevertheless it is hard to enter into and hard to work on. At other places, if they abruptly fixate you, then you have something to work on; if they put you through changes, then you have something to chew on.

People come here and declare that they do not dare to say they are right. So why don't you dare say you are right? Then how should you be? Why not look at it in this way?

I'm just afraid you will misunderstand here and get the wrong idea. I just want to have you understand immediately, without stirring a single thought.

Then again, there are those who say, "According to my view, everything is all right." They are like scorched sprouts, like rotten seed, which will never grow. When you have declared you're right, then how can you be helped out any more? This is why it is said that ordinary people may still evolve.

There are also those who, having understood, still cannot express it in speech. Even if they talk of it, they do not make any sense. Don't be careless and crude; examine carefully.

I am a fellow seeker with you; if I comprehend, you must comprehend too. If you don't comprehend, I don't comprehend either.

Have you not read how Xuansha pointed to a white spot on the ground in front of him and asked a student, "See?" The student said, "Yes." Xuansha said, "I see, and so do you. Why don't you understand?"

One of my fellow students, one Elder Li, saw my late teacher for a year and a half; every time he went in for a personal interview, the teacher would just say to him, "Elder, have you distinguished black and white at all?" Every time he went, this is what happened. How do you interpret talk like this? How do you work?

Nowadays there are no adepts like this helping people. There are no elders who seek like this either. Anyone else would have gotten upset. One day he heard the teacher say in a lecture, "Going in and out the same door—hereditary enemies," and suddenly his previous understanding turned out to be like flowers in the sky, and he now saw the truth.

You should work in this way and realize enlightenment in this way. Zen should be studied this way. As none of you have had an awakening, you should look straight into your vital spirit. If no one told you and no one instructed you, it would be hard to work. Now that you have met someone, you should work. You must distinguish black and white before you can do it.

INSTANT ENLIGHTENMENT

Those who are now on the journey should believe that there is such a thing as instant enlightenment. In other places they also should say that there is such a thing as instant enlightenment; if they have no instant enlightenment, how can they be called Zen communities?

It's just because what they have inherited and transmit is only the practice of looking at the model cases of the ancients. They may contemplate one or two examples and get a rough bit of knowledge, a bit of interpretation. If there is any point they cannot understand, they seek a gap to bore into, seeking understanding. Once they have understood, they say the matter is only like this, and then they immediately go on to circulate it in the Zen communities. None of them have ever spoken of what instant enlightenment is. If there is no such thing as instant enlightenment, how can you free your mind of the twenty-five states of being in the three realms? How can you free your mind of the sensation of uncertainty?

Now there have already been professional priests coming here saying, "Perception is unobscured," totally accepting perception and claiming that is right. That means they do not see what is not obscured. When I ask them about other worlds, they do not know; and when I question them about the senses and objects, it turns out they have not broken through. How can they imagine that the feelings and perceptions of ordinary people are exactly the same as instant enlightenment?

Today I say to everyone, just trust that there is such a thing as instant enlightenment. It is like a farmer finding an alchemical pill as he plows the fields; after taking it, the whole family goes to heaven. It is also like a commoner being appointed prime minister.

In the Teachings it says that those ordinary feelings and perceptions of yours are like unbaked clay, which is useless before it has been fired. You have to bake it in a hot fire before it is useful; that is like an instant enlightenment.

When I came out of Szechwan, I only called on one person. I know this person's talk was the same as the ancients. I once asked my teacher, "I've heard it said that there is enlightenment in Zen; is that so?" My teacher said, "If there were no enlightenment, how could it be attained? Just investigate in an easygoing way." So I studied in a relaxed frame of mind. There was a certain Elder Fu, whose insight was so luminously clear that I used to go to him with questions. But he just used to tell me, "You must make a living on your own; don't come questioning me."

One day he recited a story to me: Zhaozhou showed some fire to a student and said, "Don't call it fire. What is it?" I wondered deeply at this: obviously it is fire—why not call it fire? I contemplated this for three years, always reflecting, "How dare I use the feelings and perceptions of an ordinary man to ask about the realization of sages?"

I have also heard what it says in the *Lotus Scripture*, "This truth cannot be understood by the discriminations of discursive thought," and have always kept this in mind. Today when you say you are right just as you are, that is because you have produced an interpretative understanding, and so do not understand.

Once my teacher went to the residence of Judge Li, who invited him into the library. After lighting some incense, the judge picked up a copy of *Transmission of the Lamp* and said to the teacher, "Although I am a man of the world, I have always taken an interest in this path. Whenever I read this book I find many points I do not understand." My teacher said, "This matter is not understood in that way. You need to have realization of enlightenment first. If you have enlightenment, you naturally need not ask others about whatever you do not understand. If you have no enlightenment, even what understanding you do have is not yet right either." The judge remarked, "My teacher, you have spoken rightly."

As for me, since I was the superintendent of guests, I attained understanding at the fireside; after that, there was nothing I did not understand. You must see the reality of instant enlightenment yourself before you can attain it. No one in the Zen communes of the present time tells of it.

ZEN MASTERY

There is nothing in my experience that is not true. If there were anything at all untrue, how could I presume to tell others, how could I presume to guide others? When I affirm my truth, there is no affirming mind and no affirmed objects; that is why I dare tell people.

As for you, obviously there is something not true; that is why you come to someone to find certainty. If you had found truth already, then when would you go off questioning another?

However, here I just point out where you're right. If you're not right, I'll never tell you that you are. When you *are* right and true, then I'll agree with you. Only bet on what's right and true.

I see through everyone. If I've seen people, I know whether or not they have any enlightenment or any understanding, just as an expert physician recognizes ailments at a glance, discerning the nature of the illness and whether or not it can be remedied. One who knows all this only after a detailed inquiry into symptoms is a mediocre physician.

This is like a story I have quoted on another occasion. Fayan pointed to a hanging screen, whereupon two students went and rolled it up. Fayan said, "One gain, one loss." People like you, in your state, must not say, "What gain or loss is there?" Some say, "One went to roll up the screen with understanding—this is gain. One went to roll up the screen without understanding—this is loss." If this were so, how could a remedy be possible?

Now if you have not managed to understand clearly, it is because your enlightenment is not true; like someone ignorant of medicine claiming to be a doctor, you cannot discern when people understand, and you cannot tell when they do not understand—you cannot discern at all whether or not they have any insight. Then how can you help people? How can you teach people? You must examine reality through and through before you can.

If you are willing to examine reality through and through, you will not fail to understand. Have you not read how an ancient said, "Just sit there investigating the truth for twenty or thirty years; if you do not attain understanding, cut off my head and make a piss pail out of it." Seekers sometimes say this is right, but when it comes to investigating reality through and through, they change unstably. It is like watching a horse ridden past a window; in a flash it's gone.

One must be like thirty tons of iron, which cannot be pulled forward or pushed back—only then do you know it's the real thing. People like you stir the minute you're shaken by someone; one more push, and you tumble.

You should be so perfectly clear that you see your three hundred and sixty joints and eighty-four thousand pores open up all at once; inside your body and outside in the physical world, every phenomenon is the original reality—nothing is not It. Only then will you get it.

But professional priests nowadays can only speak after dawdling; if I proceed all at once, they have nothing to cling to and think they have wasted their time. You people had better not waste this time! Since you are already involved, stabilize and awaken your vital spirit in the effort to find out the truth.

EQUALITY

If you talk about equality, nothing surpasses Buddhism. Buddhism alone is most egalitarian. If one says, "I understand, you do not," this is not Buddhism. If one says, "You understand, I do not," This is not Buddhism either. In the Teachings it says, "This truth is universally equal, without high or low—this is called unexcelled enlightenment." My perception is equal to yours, and your perception is equal to mine.

And yet, an ancient also said, "I know everything others know, but others do not know what I know." Why don't they know? Because they harbor "high and low" in their minds, and do not rely on enlightened insight; thus they see this world full of all kinds of crap.

What the Sage taught is an egalitarian teaching; he said, "I get all types of beings to enter nirvana without remainder, whereby I liberate them. I have liberated countless sentient beings in this way, yet there are really no beings who attain liberation." Is this not an egalitarian teaching?

An ancient said, "Nirvana is called universal liberation; it takes all in uniformly, without remainder; no matter what type of being, empty or existent, sinking or floating. The supernal being can descend to live on earth; the way of enlightenment is inherently omnipresent. If suddenly the slightest thing is there, one lingers forever on this shore." If there is the slightest leftover, that is "this shore," the mundane. It is also said, "In an instant one flows into ideation, which constitutes the root of birth and death." How can you have random realizations and arbitrarily produce intellectual interpretations?

In ancient times, there was an adept who told people, "Each of you has your inspiration; when you first determined to go journeying, you must have made this determination on account of life and death. Some may have aroused the determination to avoid misery, or because of the pressure of circumstances; in any case it is called inspiration. Why? To get people to look at their initial inspiration." That is, if your original thought of inspiration has not changed, turning back to it is most powerful.

This is the Zen for you to study; if you actually attain it, it is simply clear purity of mind. When you seek out teachers along the way and contemplate day and night, you are simply nurturing this mind. Then when you have awakened and realized it, you will then see that it had not been lost even before you were inspired. The saint Ashvaghosha said of this, "Initial enlightenment is itself fundamental enlightenment; fundamental enlightenment itself is unconscious.

The nonduality of the initial experience and the fundamental reality is called ultimate enlightenment."

It is also said, "At the time of initial inspiration one attains true enlightenment," meaning first realize the fruit, and the six perfections and myriad deeds of Buddhas are a matter of ripening. This is why I have you just investigate the initially inspired mind. And my perception is one with yours; why not understand in this way?

CLEAR EYES

People with clear eyes do not settle complacently into fixed ways. The reason you haven't attained this in everyday life is simply that your eyes are not clear. If your eyes were clear, you'd have attained it. That is why it is said that people with clear eyes are hard to find. As soon as you say "This is thus and so," that is a complacent fixation; people with clear eyes are not like this.

Have you not read how Deshan said, to an assembly, "Tonight I will not answer questions. Anyone who asks a question gets a thrashing." How could anyone without clear eyes comprehend this? Fail in the slightest to comprehend this, and you fall into conceptual thought, which constructs signals. That is why Deshan's normal experience of life was comprehended by only one person, Yantou. Therefore I say you have to have clear eyes before you can attain this.

FINDING CERTAINTY

The original Zen masters are real true friends. Ha, ha, ha! One can only say this much; if you understand, you can have the experience yourself. Then you will have something to act on. If you get involved in rationalizations, comparisons, and verbalizations, then you do not understand, and you cannot experience it yourself.

When you are going about and doing your chores, do you see that the original Zen masters are real true friends? Since you don't see, when asked about it you get flustered.

Where is the problem? The problem lies in the fact that you are always coming from the midst of conceptual comparisons, and do not personally attain experience. All of you go sit on benches, close your eyes, and demolish you thinking all the way from the Milky Way above to Hades below before you can make a statement or two. But when you get to a quiet place, you still don't get the ultimate point. Before your eyes is nothing but things that obstruct people. Lightly questioned, you cannot reach the aim.

Right now, let's base the discussion on realities; we mustn't talk at random. For the moment, let me ask you this: when you haven't eaten anything at all for three days, can you be active? Certainly you cannot be active. Only after eating something can you be active. If so, it is all food energy. But when you get here, if you want to find suitable people, first it is necessary to see that which is not food energy. Zen should be studied in this way; this alone is called finding certainty.

Once you have eaten, that should sustain you as you take this matter up and look into it. But you are totally ignorant of this matter; instead you try to apply it in idleness, discussing right and wrong, focusing on useless things, either thinking about them or trying to demolish them. What a pity! It's all misapplication.

You do not realize that as soon as you aim your mind you're already a generation too late! In an instant, you have flowed into ideation, which forms the root of birth and death.

Furthermore, if you don't know even while physically alive, where will you seek after your material body dissolves?

In recent days there are those who just sit there as they are. At first they are alert, but after a while they doze. Nine out of ten sit there snoozing. How miserable! If you do not know how to do the inner work, how can you expect to understand by sitting rigidly? This is not the way it is. How can you see?

When Danxia held up a whisk, Layman Pang held up a hammer. When Danxia tossed his whisk down, Layman Pang put his hammer down. The next day, Layman Pang said, "How do you interpret yesterday's case?" Danxia relaxed and reclined. Layman Pang left. Are these not real knowers? How could this admit of your arbitrary explanations, or permit you to add explanatory footnotes?

Also, Yantou said, "These who cultivate purification must let it come forth from their own hearts in each individual situation, covering the entire universe." How can this be quiet sitting and meditating?

My teacher said, "When you sleep, study Zen as you sleep; at meals, study Zen as you eat." An ancient also said, "When you sit, there is the logic of when you sit; when you stand, there is the logic of when you stand."

Have you not read how Touzi asked Cuiwei, "Can I hear the secret message of Zen?" Cuiwei stood and looked around. Touzi said, "I don't understand the hidden statement; please give me another indication." Cuiwei said, "You want to get soused with a second ladle of foul water?" Touzi was thereupon enlightened.

You people have not attained the experience, so you miss quite a few good things in the course of a day. That is why I say the original Zen masters are real true friends. The path of the original Zen masters is like the bright sun in the blue sky—why are there people losing the way?

GET AN UNDERSTANDING

When you cannot understand, where is your mistake? You do not understand at all; fundamentally not understanding, you then seek understanding. An ancient said, "Don't abandon this world and cling to the beyond; for if you do so, it will be even harder to understand." I told you that you fundamentally do not understand; why not look at it as when Fayan was journeying and Dizang asked him where he was going; when Fayan replied that he was journeying, Dizang asked, "And do you understand what the journey is for?" Fayan answered, "No." Dizang said, "If you want to know what the journey is for, the one who does not understand is it." Fayan realized enlightenment from this. I ask you, since he did not understand, then how did he attain? You must find a way to penetrate before you will know.

This is not a matter of forced understanding, or all sorts of contrived understanding. Since you basically do not understand, what are you capable of doing? You need to examine attentively; look to see where the not understanding comes from.

Do you want to know? This nonunderstanding of yours basically comes from nowhere. Since it comes from nowhere, how could this not understanding be? And when you understand, the nonunderstanding goes nowhere. When you look at it in this way, you may be sure of attaining clarification.

As long as you do not know how to be people in the midst of enlightening realities, you only exercise your minds in the mundane world. If you have never taken a moment to look into this matter, how could you actually understand right away? When someone asks you a question, you talk randomly; but this is not a matter that can be handled in this way.

In the old days I once heard an old mendicant relate that Master Xianglin saw a seeker coming and said, "I do not deny that you can talk about it, but by the time you've gone two or three steps down the stairs, you're already no longer thus. Better not talk wildly!" See how the ancients examined from the root how people are to go about things. In Buddhism, no waste is reasonable; get an understanding of it!

PRINCIPLE AND PHENOMENA

Grand Master Yunmen said, "If you really have not yet attained, for now follow principle to gain discernment." Students of Zen should also proceed in accord with principle, not being so presumptuous as to hope for something transcendental.

In general, students nowadays make phenomena into one extreme and principle into another extreme. This causes them to be physically and mentally uneasy. Why not have phenomena always conform to principle?

Without even talking about the phenomena of beginningless time, just consider the instant of conception, when there is a sudden change of the physical body and the material world; from that point on, all is phenomena. Every diverse element in the conditional body is a phenomenon. Right now, how can you clear your mind of these phenomena so as to conform to principle?

Phenomena have discrete forms, while principle is formless. Once the ancients realized the principle, they adapted to phenomena in accord with principle. Have you not read how someone once clapped his hands and laughed on hearing a signal sounded, saying, "I understand! I understand!" Is this not following principle to learn? Why not observe in this way twenty-four hours a day, doing inner work like this? Eventually it will ripen, and you will naturally harmonize with the principle.

One of the original Zen masters said, "If you want to attain harmonization quickly, just speak of nonduality." It is not a matter of just saying it and thereupon understanding; you must actually attain harmonization before you can realize this. Guishan said, "Phenomena and principle are not two; the real Buddha is suchness as is."

I have seen many who cannot follow principle; when they take it up, they turn it upside down at once. They make useless theoretical interpretations of the sayings and model cases of the ancients, their different challenges, records of seasonal addresses, and the modalities of their individual schools, considering this to be Zen study. How miserable! Study of the path is not like this.

People of the later generations are even more ignorant; spending ten or fifteen years on vain conceit, they attain nothing at all. You have unconsciously acquired habits of thinking about yourself and others, and hardly even give a thought to the matter of independence. How will you be in the future?

Don't keep standing here—each of you find out on your own.

Keys of Zen Mind

You should not set up limitations in the boundless void, but if you set up limitlessness as the boundless void, you encompass your own downfall. Therefore, those who understand voidness have no concept of voidness.

If people use words to describe mind, they never apprehend mind; if people do not describe mind in words, they still do not apprehend mind. Speech is fundamentally mind; you do not apprehend it because of describing it. Speechlessness is fundamentally mind; you do not apprehend it because of not describing it. Whatever sorts of understanding you use to approximate it, none tally with your own mind itself.

A high master said, "It is only tacit harmony." Because it is like this, if you haven't attained the path yet, just do not entertain any false thoughts. If people recognize false thoughts and deliberately try to stop them, it's because you see there are false thoughts. If you know you're having false thoughts and deliberately practice contemplation to effect perception of truth, this is also seeing that there are false thoughts. If you know that falsehood is fundamentally the path, then there is no falsehood in it. Therefore those who master the path have no attainment. If the path were sought by deliberate intention, the path would be something attained. Just do not seek elsewhere, and realize there is no confusion or falsehood; this is called seeing the path.

In recent times, everyone says, "Nothing is not the path." They are like people sitting by a food basket talking about eating; they can never be filled, because they do not themselves partake. Realization obliterates the subject-object split; it's not that there's some mysterious principle besides. In your daily activities, when you see forms, this is an instance of realization; when you hear sounds, this is an instance of realization; when you eat and drink, this is an instance of realization. Each particular is without subject or object.

This is not a matter of longtime practice; it does not depend on cultivation. That is because it is something that is already there. Worldly people, who do not recognize it, call it roaming aimlessly. That is why it is said, "Only by experiential realization do you know it is unfathomable."

People who study the path clearly know there is such a thing; why do they fail to get the message, and go on doubting? It is because their faith is not complete enough and their doubt is not deep enough. Only with depth and completeness, be it faith or doubt, is it really Zen; if you are incapable of introspection like this, you will eventually get lost in confusion and lose the thread, wearing out and stumbling halfway along the road. But if you can look into yourself, there is no one else.

Once we say "this matter," how can we know it any more than that? "Knowledge" may be arbitrary thought, but this matter itself isn't lost. The path is not revealed only after explanation and direction; it is inherently always out in the open. Explanation and direction are expedient methods, used to get you to realize enlightenment; they are also temporary byroads. Some attain realization through explanation, some enter through direction, some attain by spontaneous awakening; ultimately there is nothing different, no separate attainment. It is simply a matter of reaching the source of mind.

People say that to practice cultivation only after realizing enlightenment is in the province of curative methodology, but Zen also admits of using true knowledge and vision as a curative. In terms of a particular individual, however, this may not be necessary.

"The path of Buddhahood is eternal; only after long endurance of hard work can it then be realized." It is continuous throughout past, present, and future; the ordinary and the holy are one suchness—this is why it is said that "the path of Buddhahood is eternal." If you do not produce differing views, you never leave it—this is the point of "long endurance of hard work." Ultimately there is no separate reality—thus it is said that it "can then be realized."

This is a matter for strong people. People who do not discern what is being asked give replies depending on what comes up. They do not know it is something you ask yourself—to whom would you answer? When people do not understand an answer, they produce views based on words. They do not know it is something you answer for yourself—what truth have you found, and where does it lead? Therefore it is said, "It's all you." Look! Look!

Some people say, "The verbal teachings given out by the enlightened ones since ancient times circulate throughout the world, each distinctly clear. Why is all this oneself? That is profound ingratitude toward the kindness of the ancient sages." I now reply that I am actually following the source message of the enlightened ones; you yourselves turn your backs on it, not I. If you say they have some doctrine, you are thereby slandering the enlightened.

Do not be someone who finally cuts off the seed of enlightenment; if you do not discern the ultimate within yourself, whatever you do will be artificial. No matter how much you memorize, or how many words you understand, it will be of no benefit to you. Thus it is said, "You want to listen attentively to Buddha; why doesn't Buddha listen to himself? If you seek a formal Buddha outside the listening, it will not resemble you."

An adept said, "For me to make a statement in reply to you is not particularly hard; now if you could gain understanding at a single saying, that would amount to something." If you do not understand, then I have gone wrong.

Students nowadays all consider question and answer to be essential to Zen, not realizing that this is a grasping and rejecting conceptual attitude. Terms such as study "in reference to principle" and "in reference to phenomena" are recently coined expressions. Even if you have a little perception, you still shouldn't stop; haven't you heard it said that the path of nirvana aims at absolute liberation?

You have to be able to monitor yourself. When people proceed on the path because they are confused and do not know their own minds, they come to mountain forests to see teachers, imagining that there is a special "way" that can make people comfortable, not realizing that the best exercise is to look back and study your previous confusion. If you do not get this far, even to go into the mountain forests forever will be a useless act.

Confusion is extremely accessible, yet hard to penetrate. That is why ancient worthies said, "It is hard to believe, hard to understand."

This is an explanation of the path characteristic of the instant school. Looking back into what has been going on is already an expression of change; but what about if you do not do so! Later generations eventually took this statement to refer to plain ordinariness, but this is just failure of understanding and absorption on the part of later students.

Since time immemorial, there have been two kinds of method: there is true method, which is what is called the exposition that has no interruption; then there is expedient method, which is what is referred to as subtle response to all potentials. If you gain entry by way of true method, you understand spiritually in a natural and spontaneous manner without needing to make use of contemplation, never to regress, with countless wondrous capacities. If you gain entry by way of expedient method, you must "take the seat, wear the clothing, and hereafter see for yourself" before you can attain. This can not yet be considered ultimate. These two kinds of method are one reality, and cannot be lost for an instant; students should think about this.

Xuefeng said to people, "Don't have me make a statement that refers to you; if there is a statement that refers to you, what use is it?" It is simply that the ancient had no choice and could not avoid speaking in these terms; later people who did not understand the ancient's intention thought it means that there is nothing to say about one's self; thus they misunderstood.

People nowadays mostly take the immediate mirroring awareness to be the ultimate principle. This is why Xuansha said to people, "Tell me, does it still exist in remote uninhabited places deep in the mountains?"

Enlightenment of mind and seeing its essence should be like Xuefeng and Xuansha; genuine application to reality should be like Nanquan and Zhaozhou. Students nowadays just take the methods of the ancients to be the way of Zen; they are unable to study from the same source as the ancients themselves did.

It is like a strong man carrying a heavy load over a log bridge without losing his balance. What supports him like this? Just his single-minded attention. Working on the path is also like this; as it says in scripture, a lion has all of its power whether it is catching an elephant or a rabbit. If you ask what power we should have all of, it is the power of nondeception. If you see anything in the slightest different from mind, you forfeit your own life. Thus for those who attain the path, there is nothing that is not it.

This power is very great; it is only that the function of the power is made deficient by infections of unlimited misapperception. Without all these different states, different conditions, different entanglements, and different thoughts, you can transform freely, however you wish, without any obstacle.

You shouldn't strain to seek the path; if you seek it, you will lose the path. You need not strain to make things fluid; if you try to make them fluid, things remain as they are. If you neither seek nor try to produce fluidity, the path will merge with things; then what things is not the path?

Suppose a man with clear eyes goes into a jewel mine but does not know how to go about it; in other words, suppose he thinks he can go in without a torch to light the way. Then when he bumps his head and hurts himself, he thinks it to be a dangerous cave, not a jewel mine. An intelligent person going in there would take a lamp to light up the mine to view; then all kinds of jewels could be selected at will and taken out. Similarly, you should be using the light of insight and wisdom twenty-four hours a day, not letting the six fields of sense objects hurt you.

In the old days, Assembly Leader Yong took leave of Fenyang along with Ciming, but Yong had not yet completely realized the marvel; though he had followed Ciming for twenty years, after all he was not free and untrammeled. One night they sat around the brazier until very late; Ciming picked up the fire tongs, hit the embers, and said, "Assembly Leader Yong, Assembly Leader Yong!" Yong clucked his tongue and said with disapproval, "Foxy devil!" Ciming pointed at Yong and said, "This tired old guy still goes on like this!" In this way Yong finally realized the ultimate end. Nevertheless, he continued to follow Ciming to the end of his life. Whenever Ciming would pose complex stimulating questions that the students could not answer, Yong alone hit the mark, and Ciming would nod approval.

This is called medicine without disease. Few of those who study it attain the essential; needless to say, mere intellectuals of later times have no way to comprehend this matter. Your attainment of it should be like Yong, your activation of the medicine should be like Ciming; then, hopefully, you will be all right.

When you find peace and quiet in the midst of busyness and clamor, then towns and cities become mountain forests; afflictions are enlightenment, sentient beings realize true awakening. These sayings can be uttered and understood by all beginners, who construe it as uniform equanimity; but then when they let their minds go, the ordinary and the spiritual are divided as before, quietude and activity operate separately. So obviously this was only an intellectual understanding.

You have to actually experience stable peacefulness before you attain oneness; you cannot force understanding.

In recent generations, many have come to regard question-and-answer dialogues as the style of the Zen school. They do not understand what the ancients were all about; they only pursue trivia, and do not come back to the essential. How strange! How strange!

People in olden times asked questions on account of confusion, so they were seeking actual realization through their questioning; when they got a single saying or half a phrase, they would take it seriously and examine it until they penetrated it. They were not like people nowadays who pose questions at random and answer with whatever comes out of their mouths, making laughingstocks of themselves.

People who attain study the path twenty-four hours a day, never abandoning it for a moment. Even if these people do not gain access to it, every moment of thought is already cultivating practical application. Usually it is said that cultivated practice does not go beyond purification of mind, speech, action, and the six senses, but the Zen way is not necessarily like this. Why? Because Zen concentration is equal to transcendent insight in every moment of thought; wherever you are, there are naturally no ills. Eventually one day the ground of mind becomes thoroughly clear and you attain complete fulfillment. This is called absorption in one practice.

Nowadays people only work on concentration power and do not open the eye of insight. For them, stories and sayings just become argumentation, unstable mental activity.

Zen study is not a small matter. You do not yet need to transcend

the Buddhas and surpass the adepts; but once you have attained it, it
will not be hard to transcend and surpass them if you wish.

SITTING MEDITATION

The light of mind is reflected in emptiness;
its substance is void of relative or absolute.
Golden waves all around,
Zen is constant, in action or stillness.
Thoughts arise, thoughts disappear;
don't try to shut them off.
Let them flow spontaneously—
what has ever arisen and vanished?
When arising and vanishing quiet down,
there appears the great Zen master;
sitting, reclining, walking around,
there's never an interruption.
When meditating, why not sit?
When sitting, why not meditate?
Only when you have understood this way
is it called sitting meditation.
Who is it that sits? What is meditation?
To try to seat it
is using Buddha to look for Buddha.
Buddha need not be sought;
seeking takes you further away.
In sitting, you do not look at yourself;
meditation is not an external art.
At first, the mind is noisy and unruly;
there is still no choice but to shift it back.
That is why there are many methods
to teach it quiet observation.
When you sit up and gather your spirit,
at first it scatters helter-skelter;
over a period of time, eventually it calms down,
opening and freeing the six senses.
When the six senses rest a bit,
discrimination occurs therein.
As soon as discrimination occurs,

it seems to produce arising and vanishing.
The transformations of arising and vanishing
come from manifestations of one's own mind.
Put your own mind to use to look back once:
once you're returned, no need to do it again;
you wear a halo of light on your head.
The spiritual flames leap and shine,
unobstructed in any state of mind,
all-inclusive, all-pervasive;
birth and death forever cease.
A single grain of restorative elixir
turns gold into liquid;
acquired pollution of body and mind
have no way to get through.
Confusion and enlightenment are temporarily explained;
stop discussing opposition and accord.
When I think carefully of olden days
when I sat coolly seeking,
though it's nothing different,
it was quite a mess.
You can turn from ordinary mortal to sage
in an instant, but no one believes.
All over the earth is unclarity;
best be very careful.
If it happens you do not know,
then sit up straight and think;
one day you'll bump into it.
This I humbly hope.

Notes

Zen Sicknesses

The three kinds of sickness of the spiritual body are descriptively termed "leaving before arriving," "attachment after arriving," and "penetration with no reliable basis." The meanings can be deduced from these names.

The two kinds of light of the spiritual body refer to the gross and subtle semblance of something actually being there. These semblances are called "light not penetrating freely." This does not mean that free penetration results in total absence of appearances, but that appearances are not made into objects of gross or subtle fixation. This can only be understood by experiencing it.

The *Heroic Progress Discourse* is a Buddhist text commonly used by Chinese Zen practitioners for self-monitoring during the declining centuries of Zen Buddhism in China, from the Song dynasty onward. See *Dream Conversations* for a more accessible discussion of Zen sicknesses.

Zhaozhou (pronounced Jow-joe) (778–897) and Nanquan (pronounced Nan-chwen) (747–834) were two of the very greatest adepts of classical Zen. The vastness and clarity of Nanquan's mind can be glimpsed in such sayings as these: "The true principle is one suchness: unobtrusive practice of inner application, unknown to anyone, is called nonleaking knowledge. Nonleaking, inconceivable, is equivalent to the immutability of space, not the current of birth and death. The Way is the Highway, unimpeded nirvana full of wondrous capacities. Only thus do you attain freedom in all activities. This is what is meant by the expression 'Acting without fixation in all activities,' and the expression 'absorption in universal activity, manifesting the physical body everywhere.' Because nobody knows, one's operations are traceless and imperceptible; the truth is spontaneously effective, the subtle function intrinsically adequate. The universal Way has no form, Truth has no opposite; so they are not in the realm of perception or cognition. There are neither coarse nor fine conceptions in it." Nanquan also defined Zen practice in this way: "Right now, just understand the principle of suchness, being-as-is, and act on it directly. Why not ask how to act on it? Just understand the essence that has been thus for infinite eons does not fluctuate or change—this in itself is practical application."

Like other classical masters, Nanquan denounced cultism: "Nowadays there are too many 'Zen Masters'! I'm looking for an innocent, but can't find one! I don't say there are none at all, only that they are rare." He also said, "Just embody practical application in touch with reality; do not say 'I am a Zen Master'!" Asked about practical application, he said, "If you need to act, act; don't just follow behind another!" To explain the nonconventional nature of the special Zen consciousness, Nanquan said, "The basis of understanding does not come about from perception and cognition. Perception and cognition are conditioned, only existing in relation to objects. The spiritual wonder is impossible to conceive, not relative to anything. That is why it is said that wondrous capacities are spontaneously effective and do not depend on other things."

Zhaozhou, who attained enlightenment at a word from Nanquan, also spoke of a fundamental awareness underlying Zen consciousness: "This essence existed before the world existed; this essence will not dissolve when the world disintegrates." Statements like this, it must be realized, are not philosophical arguments, but exercises in attention. This is made clear in Zhaozhou's manner of addressing the usage and inner meanings of symbolic language in Zen: "A gold Buddha cannot get through a furnace, a wooden Buddha cannot get through a fire, a clay Buddha cannot get through water. The real Buddha sits within; 'enlightenment,' 'nirvana,' 'suchness,' and 'buddha-nature' and all clothing sticking to the body."

See also *No Barrier*, chapters 1, 7, 11, 14, 19, 27, 30, 33, 34, and 37.

Facing It Directly

Yunmen (d. 949), was one of the latest and greatest masters of the classical era, known for exceptional brilliance. He said, "Why do you traipse around with your luggage through a thousand towns, over ten thousand miles? What are you missing? You are fine; who has no lot? If you can't even manage to take responsibility for yourself on your own, you shouldn't accept deception from others, or take people's judgments. As soon as you see old monks open their mouths, you should shut them right up; and yet you act like flies on manure, struggling to feed off it, gathering in threes and fives for discussion." He also said, "Ordinary phonies consume the piss and spit of other people, memorizing a pile of junk, a load of rubbish, running off at the mouth wherever they go, bragging about how they can pose five or ten questions. Even if you pose questions and answers from morning to night until the end of time, would you ever see? Where is the empowerment?"

Yunmen was one of the first Zen masters known to have given overt instructions for contemplating Zen stories and sayings as an expedient method of cultivating Zen consciousness: "The ancients had a lot of complications to help you, such as Xuefeng's saying, 'The whole earth is you,' Jiashan's saying, 'Pick out the teacher in the hundred grasses; recognize the emperor in a bustling market place,' and Luopu's saying, 'As soon as a particle of dust arises, the entire earth is contained therein; the whole body of a lion is on the tip of a single hair.' Take these up and think about them over and over again; eventually, over time, you will naturally find a way to penetrate. No one can substitute for you in this task; it rests with each individual, without exception." This is quite different from the highly artificial standardized and pressurized "koan study" as practiced in many present-day Japanese and American Zen cults, most of which does not follow the teachings of the original Zen masters, but actually dates only from the nineteenth and twentieth centuries. Yunmen was outspoken about the futility of cubic attitudes of emotional enthusiasts; he said, "You rush here pointlessly; what are you looking for? All I know how to do is eat, drink, piss, and shit; why do you make a special interpretation? You travel around to various places studying Zen, inquiring about the path, but let me ask you a question: what have you learned at all those places? Try to bring it out." He also insisted on common sense in Zen practice: when someone asked, "What is the road beyond?" Yunmen replied, "$9 \times 9 = 81$." Asked about Zen in these terms, "How does one apply it on the road?" Yunmen replied, "$7 \times 9 = 63$." These are not silly nonsequiturs, like so much nonsense seen in cults; and they are not just numerological symbolic statements either. Nine times nine does equal eighty-one, in the daily world we face when we wake up in the morning; a variety of "Zen" that does not help you is obviously not too useful, and has to retreat into the bosom of a cult, a tribe of supposedly "like-minded" people who agree to agree. See *The Blue Cliff Record*, chapters 6, 8, 14, 15, 22, 27, and 34; and *No Barrier*, chapters 21, 39, and 48.

Seeing and Doing

The statements about learning business may require some clarification. One of the main ideas is that it is better to learn professional skills when young so that you may have more freedom for other interests later on. Another idea is that too much interest in business can inhibit this freedom. Yet another is that after enlightenment things can often be mastered without having to be learned. People in the East often studied Zen to improve their skills in arts, crafts, writing, government, soldiering, and other businesses, even to the extent that secondary purposes crowded out the original essence of Zen.

The Marrow of the Sages

Changsha lived in the ninth century. A wandering teacher with no fixed abode and no fixed doctrine, Changsha was one of the greatest classical masters. He said, "The entire universe is your own light; the entire universe is within your own light; there is no one in the whole universe that is not you. I always tell you that the realms of desire, form, and formless abstraction, the enlightened ones, the universe, and the totality of all beings, are the light of universal perfect wisdom. When the light has not yet shone forth, where can you turn to become intimately acquainted with it? Before the light shines forth, there is no news of Buddhas or sentient beings; where do we get the mountains, rivers, and earth?" See also *No Barrier,* chapter 46.

The icon of wisdom is a statute of Manjushri, a personification of wisdom, commonly used in Zen meditation halls as a reminder that "there is no meditation without insight," in the word of Buddha himself as written in the ancient *Dhammapada.* For more on Manjushri, see *No Barrier,* chapter 42, and *The Flower Ornament Scripture,* chapters 8, 9, 10, and 39.

Not Knowing

There are still Zen cultists who stick to their "not knowing" in the blind and ignorant manner described here; they even have their Western imitators.

Emancipation

Dongshan (pronounced Doong-shan) (806–869) was one of the great classical masters, particularly noted for the didactic scheme known as the Five Ranks, which Dongshan and his distinguished student Caoshan used to analyze the structures of Zen sayings and stories to define and describe stages of practice and realization.

Stop Opinions

In Buddhist psychology, opinions are considered one of the major afflictions, psychological conditions or disturbances that inhibit the evolution of consciousness. Because people become narrow-minded and bigoted by fixation on their own ideas and opinions, subjective views are considered afflictions.

The Third Patriarch of Zen died in 609. The sayings quoted are from his *Poem on Trust in the Heart*, one of the earliest Zen classics. Because of the importance of this text in understanding the theory and practice of instant Zen enlightenment, I have included a complete translation in an appendix to this book that begins on page 589.

Grand Master Yongjia (d. 712) was a master of the Tiantai school of Buddhism; he visited the illustrious Sixth Patriarch of Zen and was instantly recognized as an illuminate. Because of this, in Zen tradition Yongjia is also referred to as the Enlightened Overnight Guest. He is here quoted from his *Song on Realization of Enlightenment*, another early Zen classic.

"Difficult to Conquer" is the fifth of the Ten Stages of Enlightenment as expounded in *The Flower Ornament Scripture* (book 26). Containing the prototypes of all Buddhist teachings and practices, the Ten Stages are called the Alphabet of Buddhism. The fifth stage is one in which perfection of meditation is cultivated in harmony with useful worldly occupations, integrating transmundane and conventional realities.

Xuansha (pronounced Shwen-shah) lived in the ninth century. Originally a fisherman, he later became one of the greatest Zen masters of all time. According to tradition, he attained instant enlightenment spontaneously one day when he stubbed his toe as he started out on a journey. Xuansha placed great emphasis on independent investigation into the source of confusion and understanding. He said, "The substance of phenomena is inherently uncreated and inherently indestructible. Everything is just so, now and forever; so how is it possible to not understand? If you don't understand, it's just you; if you do understand, it's still just so. So what is the difference between understanding and not understanding? The substance of enlightenment may emerge or disappear, becoming passive or active freely, with countless ineffable functions. Even right here and now there are thousands of uncanny functions taking place, all just so; myriad transformations and developments are also just so. Why? Because they are inherently there, inherently complete, their essence and characteristics always there; this is the 'Buddha' of immutable knowledge. This is why it is possible to 'not know' and 'not understand,' just as someone who is full of benevolence is not aware of it. Simply because that which is permanent and unchanging is there, you therefore say you don't recognize or sense it. You may know it and sense it, but don't try to quantify it!" See *The Blue Cliff Record*, chapters 22 and 88 and the supplemental biography of Grand Master Tsung I.

Fayan (pronounced Fah-yen) (885–958) was one of the last grand masters of the classical era of Zen. His school consisted mostly of advanced students, and on the whole is generally notable for erudition in Buddhist psychology and philosophy as well as subtle enlightenment. Four of his many disciples were teachers of kings in China and Korea. Something of the subtle simplicity of his manner of teaching can be seen from his lectures: "Zhaozhou said, 'Don't waste energy.' This is a very good saying; why not go on as ever. Things of the world have ways of access; how could Buddhism have none? It just seems that way if you don't go on as ever. Therefore all the Buddhas and all the Zen Masters simply attain within going on as ever." See also *The Blue Cliff Record*, chapter 7, and *No Barrier*, chapter 26.

The Director

Guizong (pronounced Gway-dzoong) lived in the eighth century. He is sometimes referred to as one of the very greatest Zen masters of all time, but relatively little is known of his teaching. He said, "The ancient worthies since time immemorial were not without knowledge and understanding; those lofty people were not the same as the common run. Now you cannot mature yourselves and stand on your own, so you pass the time uselessly. Don't misapply your minds; no one can take your place, but there's nothing for you to worry about either. Don't seek from others. All along you have been depending on interpretations from others, so you get bogged down whatever you say, and your light does not penetrate freely simply because there is something in front of your eyes."

Independence

Vasubandhu and Asanga were Indian Buddhist writers who promulgated the Vijnanavada, or Explanation of Consciousness, one of the main streams of Buddhist thought, which Asanga is said to have learned from a teacher named Maitreya. In Chinese Zen, Vasubandhu was considered the twenty-first Indian Zen Patriarch. "This" means "suchness," (Sanskrit *tathata*), also referred to as "thusness," (*bhutatathata*) or "being-as-is" (*yathabhuta*). See also *Transmission of Light*, chapter 22, and *Buddhist Yoga*, which outlines the theory and practice of Vijnanavada Buddhism, one of the Indian antecedents of Zen.

Learning Zen

Lingyun and Xiangyan (pronounced Shyang-yen) both studied Zen for a long time without success, eventually to attain instantaneous enlightenment through unexpected impacts. Lingyun woke up one day when he happened to see peach trees in blossom, while Xiangyan finally awoke one day on hearing the sound of bamboo being hit by some pebbles he swept off the pathway.

"If you just shout and clap, when will you ever be done?" This passage refers to imitators who literally "shout and clap" in the pretended show of "nonconceptual" realization or "transcendental" enlightenment. People like this still exist, and even have their imitators in the supposedly rational West. These are among those who have mistaken Zen "mindlessness" for ordinary witlessness.

Seeing Through

In the Far East, Kasyapa the Elder was traditionally considered the First Patriarch of Zen in India. See *No Barrier*, chapter 6, and *Transmission of Light*, chapter 2.

For more on Bodhidharma, the Founder of Zen in China, see *No Barrier*, chapter 46, and *Transmission of Light*, chapter 29.

Real Zen

Yunyan, Baizhang, Daowu, Xuefeng, Touzi, Dongshan, and Deshan were all classical Zen masters; many stories about them can be found in *The Blue Cliff Record*. See *No Barrier*, chapter 13 for Deshan and Xuefeng, chapter 2 for Baizhang. The record of Xuefeng's (822–908) sayings also provides some of the clearest indications of the theory and practice of classical Zen: "You must see your essence before you attain enlightenment. What is seeing essence? It means seeing your own fundamental nature. What is its form? When you see your own fundamental nature, there is no concrete object to see. This is hard to believe in, but all Buddhas attain it." He also explained how many terms are used to achieve the same focus of attention: "Names of the unified mind are buddha-nature, true suchness, the hidden essence, the pure spiritual body, the pedestal of awareness, the true soul, the innocent, universal round mirrorlike knowledge, the open source, the ultimate truth, and pure consciousness. The enlightened ones of past, present, and future, and all of their discourses, are all in your fundamental nature, inherently complete. You do not need to seek, but you must save yourself; no one can do it for you."

Yunfeng Yue, Huaitang, and Zen Master Nan were exceptional Zen masters of the early Song dynasty.

Wonder

The Hundred Phenomena as Only Representation is a classic treatise on the Buddhist Explanation of Consciousness, Vijnanavada, which deals with the relationship between mind and objects.

Fushan and Baiyun Duan were among the greatest early Song dynasty masters. See *Zen Lessons*, pages 17–21 and 27–30.

Just This

Grand Master Ma, also known as Mazu or Ancestor Ma (709–788) was one of the most brilliant of the early classical masters, said to have had from eighty-four to 139 enlightened disciples. He said, "The Way does not need cultivation; just don't pollute it. What is pollution? As long as you have a fluctuating mind creating artificialities and pursuing inclinations, all is pollution. If you want to understand the Way directly, the normal mind is the Way. What is the normal mind? It has no artificial contrivance, no right or wrong, no grasping or rejection, no nihilism or eternalism, no ordinariness and no sanctity." See also *No Barrier*, chapter 30.

Keep Evolving

Linji (d. 866) was one of the greatest classical masters, famed for his blasting directness. He said, "What I teach people just requires you not to take on the confusion of others. Act when necessary, without further hesitation or doubt. When students today do not attain this, wherein lies their sickness? The sickness is in not trusting yourself. If your inner trust is insufficient, then you will frantically go along with changes in situations, and will be influenced and affected by myriad objects, unable to be independent. If you can stop the mentality of constant frantic seeking, then you are no different from Zen masters and Buddhas." See also *Zen Essence* in this volume, pages 136–140. Elder Ding was one of Linji's spiritual heirs; his story is told in *The Blue Cliff Record*, chapter 32.

Approval

Magu, Zhangjing, and Nanquan were all students of Great Master Ma. See *The Blue Cliff Record*, chapter 31, for further comments on this story.

Step Back and See

The Second Patriach of Zen was a monk for a time, then was laicized during the persecution of Buddhist orders in northern China in the middle of the sixth century. He is said to have then spent thirty years as a day laborer in a big city. When asked why he did not return to religious orders but instead worked at menial jobs, the Second Patriarch replied, "I am turning my mind by myself; what business is it of yours?" It is recorded that he used to give informal talks outside the gates of large Buddhist monasteries, drawing such crowds that the formal clerics were furious. He lived to be more than a hundred years old, but eventually he was put to death by people opposed to spiritual freedom. One traditional version of his story is found in *Transmissions of Light*, chapter 30. The story of his enlightenment given in *No Barrier*, chapter 41, is a diagram of a key method of Zen meditation called "turning the light around and looking back."

All the Way Through

Ashvaghosha, an Indian Buddhist writer, was the reputed author of *Awakening of Faith in the Great Vehicle*, a treatise highly esteemed in China. Ashvaghosha was one of the principle expounders of Vijnanavada, and in Chinese tradition is considered the Twelfth Patriarch of Zen in India. See *Transmission of Light*, chapter 13.

The three subtle and six coarse aspects of mentation refer to an analytic scheme used in Buddhist yoga for self-observation. The three subtle aspects are: 1) inherited predispositions and habits; 2) entertaining of subjective assumptions; and 3) subjective perception of objects. The six coarse aspects follow on these: 1) cognition; 2) continuity; 3) clinging; 4) defining and labeling; 5) developing habitual compulsive behavior; and 6) suffering bondage to habitual compulsive behavior.

Comprehending Everything

Kasyapa's place in Zen tradition is epitomized in *No Barrier*, chapters 6 and 22; and *Transmissions of Light*, chapter 2. For the story of Elder Ming, see *No Barrier*, chapter 23, and *Transmissions of Light*, chapter 34.

Seek without Seeking

The three bodies, four knowledges, five eyes, and six spiritual powers refer to attributes of a Buddha, or fully enlightened individual.

The three bodies are the reality body, or pure spiritual body of essence; the enjoyment body, or the differentiated spiritual body of knowledge; and the emanation body, or the energetic body of physical manifestation.

The four knowledges are the mirrorlike knowledge, which simply reflects being as is; the knowledge of equality, which penetrates appearances; observational knowledge, which distinquishes phenomena; and practical knowledge, which employs the body.

The five eyes are: the physical eye, the clairvoyant eye, the eye of wisdom, the eye of objectivity, and the eye of complete awareness.

The six spiritual powers are: psychic travel, clairvoyance, clairaudience, mind reading, direct knowledge of life histories, and ending of contamination and indulgence.

Yangshan (813–890) was one of the great classical masters. For an analysis of the story of Yangshan cited here as a guide to meditation, see *Shobogenzo: Zen Essays by Dogen*, Introduction. For more on Yangshan, see also *Zen Essence*, pages 141–142; and *No Barrier*, chapter 25.

Bhishmottaranirghosha and Sudhana are figures in the book "Entry into the Realm of Reality" in *The Flower Ornament Scripture*.

Same Reality, Different Dreams

The Sixth Patriarch Huineng (638–713) is one of the most important figures in the tradition of instant Zen. He was an illiterate woodcutter, yet had the "teachless knowledge" esteemed by Zen Buddhists. For his story, see *No Barrier*, chapters 23 and 29; and *Transmissions of Light*, chapter 34. A Song dynasty painting of the Sixth Patriarch is featured on the cover of this book.

Caoshan (pronounced Tsow-shan) (840–901) was a great classical master particularly noted for his work on structural analysis of symbolism with the Five Ranks scheme. See *No Barrier*, chapter 10.

Birth and death (Sanskrist *samsara*) refers to the continual varying and shifting of mental states, moods, and thoughts in the ordinary mind. Getting out of birth and death means stabilizing the autonomous function of the "directorate" faculty of the essential mind, which is not emotionally influenced by the wavering of moods or the rise and fall of thoughts and ideas.

Understand Immediately

For more on the methods of Foyan's teacher, the redoubtable Wuzu, see *No Barrier*, chapters 35, 36, and 38; *Zen Lessons*, chapters 18–28; and *Zen Essence*, "Zen Master Wuzu" chapter.

Instant Enlightenment

Several ideas from the Buddhist *Lotus Scripture* are commonly cited in Zen talks. One is the inconceivability of ultimate truth; another is the compatibility of all productive work with reality.

"Twenty-five states of being in the three realms" refers to the spectrum of conditioned mental states in the instinctual, emotional, and intellectual domains.

"Other worlds" refers to worlds of experiences other than one's own personal subjectivity; here the teacher is talking about sensitivity and perceptivity, not other planets.

"Breaking through senses and objects" refers to penetrating the distinction between the primordial and the conditioned, with the result that one is no longer deluded into thinking that the way one perceives the world is intrinsically definitive.

Transmission of the Lamp is one of the early compendia of Zen lore, a source of countless stories, sayings, and poems.

Zen Mastery

For an explanation of the two monks rolling up the screen, see *No Barrier*, chapter 26.

Clear Eyes

Deshan (pronounced Duh-shan) (781–867) was one of the great classical masters: once a Buddhist scholar, he originally set out to refute the Zen claim of instant enlightenment. His own understanding refuted by an enlightened Zen nun, Deshan was sent on to her teacher and attained instant enlightenment himself. Deshan lived on a mountain for a long time and refused to become a public teacher until he was put under arrest by a government official who was interested in Zen and wanted Deshan to teach. Deshan's arrest, recorded as historical fact, is also a useful metaphor for what actually happened to Zen Buddhism after the golden age; it was put under arrest by the authorities. See *No Barrier*, chapters 28 and 13.

Yantou (827–887) was another great classical master, one of the freest and most outstanding of all time. He said, "Just let go and be natural and naked: you do not need to keep thinking fixedly. In the dark, the moment you prize anything, it has turned into a nest, a dodge. The ancients called this clothing sticking to the body, a disease most difficult to cure. When I was journeying in the past, I called on teachers in one or two places; they just taught day and night concentration, sitting until your buttocks grow calluses, and all the while your mouth is drooling. From the start they sit in the utter darkness in the belly of the primordial Buddha and ignorantly say they are sitting in meditation conserving this attainment. At such times, there is still desire there! Have you not read the saying, 'When independent and unimpassioned, you yourself are Buddha'! An ancient remarked, 'If you poison the milk, even clarified butter is deadly.' This is not something you attain by hearing, not something you reach or abide in, not something in your forms; don't misperceive what is merely a gate or a door, for that will cheat you on the last day of your life, leaving you in utter chaos, of no help to you at all. What you should do is avoid artificialities and concocted eccentricities: just take care of your physical needs, passing the time according to your place in life. Do not disturb social order, pretentiously identifying yourself as one who follows the Path."

Finding Certainty

Danxia (pronounced Dan-syah) (738–824) and Layman Pang (n.d.) were both students of Great Master Ma. On Danxia, see *The Blue Cliff Record*, chapter 76. On Layman Pang, see *The Blue Cliff Record*, chapter 42. On the great master Cuiwei (pronounced Tsway-way) (ninth century), see *The Blue Cliff Record*, chapter 20. On Touzi (pronounced Toe-dz) (845–914), see *The Blue Cliff Record*, chapters 41, 79, 80, 91, and the supplemental biography of Ta T'ung.

Get an Understanding

Xianglin (tenth century) was a student of the great master Yunmen.

Keys of Zen Mind

Fenyang (947–1024) was one of the very greatest masters of the early Song dynasty; he studied with more than seventy teachers and collected and commented on a great deal of Zen lore, attempting to harmonize all the various traditions of Zen. Ciming (pronounced Tse-ming) was one of his most eminent spiritual heirs. For more of the work of Fenyang, see *Zen Essence*, pages 146–147, and *The Blue Cliff Record*, "Traditional Teaching Devices."

Sitting Meditation

Foyan's teachings on meditation, much like those of the ancient masters, are quite different from the obsessive compulsive attitudes inherited by Western Zen cultists from Japanese sectarians automatically following late feudal and neo-imperial models of Zen organization and discipline. Foyan's teachings were evidently different from those of obsessive cultists of his own time too. Xutang (pronounced Syw-tahng), whose student Jomyo imported Zen to Japan in the thirteenth century, is on record as teaching, "It is essential not to become attached to the form of sitting; when you sit, you should do so in a suitably convenient manner. If you lack inner direction, you will uselessly weary your spirit." Under the military authoritarian regimes that actually controlled most of the Zen establishments in feudal Japan, this original flexibility tended to give way to extreme disciplinarian rigidity. For more on authentic methods of Zen meditation, see *Minding the Mind*. For more on Buddhist theory and practice of meditation in general, see *Buddhist Yoga*.

Appendix
Song of Trusting the Heart
Sengcan, the Third Patriarch of Zen

The Ultimate Way is without difficulty; it's only averse to discrimination;
Just do not hate or love, and it will be thoroughly clear.
A hairsbreadth's miss is as the distance between sky and earth.
If you want to have it appear before you, don't keep conforming and opposing.
Opposition and conformity struggling becomes a sickness in the mind.
If you don't know the hidden truth, you work in vain at quieting thought.
It is complete as space itself, without lack or excess.
It is indeed because of grasping and rejecting that you are therefore not thus.
Do not pursue existing objects, do not dwell in forbearance of voidness:
In a uniformly equanimous heart these quietly disappear of themselves.
Stop movement to return to stillness, and stopping makes even more movement:
As long as you remain in dual extremes, how can you know they're of one kind?
If you don't know they're of one kind, you will lose efficacy in both realms.
Trying to get rid of existence in obscuring being;
Trying to follow emptiness is turning away from emptiness.
Much talk and much cogitation estranges you from it even more:
Stop talking and cogitating, and you penetrate everywhere.

Return to the root and you get the essence;
Follow perceptions and you lose the source.
The instant you turn awareness around, you transcend the
    emptiness before the eon.
Changes in the emptiness before us all come from arbitrary
    views:
It is not necessary to seek reality, all that is needed is ending the
    views.
Dualistic views do not abide; be careful not to pursue them.
As soon as there is affirmation and denial, you lose your mind
    in confusion.
Two exist because of one; do not even keep the one.
When the one mind is unborn, myriad things have no fault.
No fault, no things; unborn, unminding.
When the subject disappears from objects, objects submerge
    along with the subject.
Objects are objects because of the subject, the subject is the
    subject because of objects.
If you want to know them both, they are basically one void.
One voidness the same in both equally contains myriad images.
If you do not see fine and coarse, how could there be preference?
The Great Way is broad, without ease or difficulty.
Small views and foxy doubts slow you up the more you hurry.
If you cling to it, you lose measure, and will inevitably enter a
    false path.
Let it be as it naturally is; its substance neither goes nor stays.
Let your nature merge with the Way, and you will roam free of
    vexation.
Tying down thoughts goes against the real; oblivion is not good.
It is not good to belabor the spirit; why estrange the familiar?
If you want to gain the way of oneness, don't be averse to the
    six sense fields.
The six sense fields are not bad; after all they're the same as true
    awakening.
The wise do not contrive; fools bind themselves.
Things are not different in themselves; you arbitrarily get
    attached yourself.
If you take the mind to use the mind, is this not a big mistake?

When deluded, you create peace and chaos, when enlightened, there is no good or bad.

All dualistic extremes come from subjective considerations.

Dreams, illusions, flowers in the air; why bother to grasp them?

Gain, loss, right, wrong; let them go all at once.

If the eyes do not sleep, dreams disappear of themselves.

If the mind does not differ, all things are one suchness.

One suchness embodies the mystery, utterly still and unconditioned.

To see all things equally, is to return again to the natural state.

Without any reason therefore, you cannot judge or compare.

Stopping is movement without motion, movement is still without stopping:

Since both are not established, how can one be such?

When you find out the ultimate consummation, you do not keep rules and models.

When the mind in harmony is equanimous, all doings come to rest.

When doubts are thoroughly cleared, true belief is directly in tune.

Nothing at all stays; there's nothing to fix in mind.

When open and clear, spontaneously aware, you aren't wasting mental effort.

The realm that is not an object of thought cannot be assessed by conscious feelings.

The reality realm of true suchness has no other or self.

If you want to tune in right away, just speak of nonduality.

Nonduality is all the same; there's nothing it doesn't contain.

The wise ones of the ten directions all enter this source.

The source is neither expansive nor contracted; one instant is ten thousand years.

There is nowhere that it is not; the ten directions are right before the eyes.

The small is the same as the large; you forget all about the bounds of objects.

The largest is the same as the small; you do not see beyond it.

Being is none other than nonbeing, nonbeing is none other than being;

Anything that is not like this definitely should not be kept.

One is all, all are one;
If you can just be like this,
What ruminations will not end?
The true mind is nondual, nonduality makes the mind true.
There's no more way to talk of it; it is not past, or future, or
   present.

Printed in the United States
by Baker & Taylor Publisher Services